The Global Financial Crisis and Asia

The Global Financial Crisis and Asia

Implications and Challenges

Edited by
Masahiro Kawai, Mario B. Lamberte,
and Yung Chul Park

OXFORD
UNIVERSITY PRESS

OXFORD
UNIVERSITY PRESS

Great Clarendon Street, Oxford, OX2 6DP,
United Kingdom

Oxford University Press is a department of the University of Oxford.
It furthers the University's objective of excellence in research, scholarship,
and education by publishing worldwide. Oxford is a registered trade mark of
Oxford University Press in the UK and in certain other countries

First Edition published in 2012

Impression: 2

British Library Cataloguing in Publication Data

Data available

ISBN 978–0–19–966095–7

Printed in Great Britain by
MPG Books Group, Bodmin and King's Lynn

Preface

Most Asian economies managed to dodge the worst of the 2007–09 global financial crisis, but they were battered by a drop in exports that hurt growth. The good news is that Asia is rebounding from the most serious slump since the Great Depression. Yet questions remain. Is the recovery sustainable, and what risks lie over the horizon?

The aim of this book, written by prominent experts in Asian economies, is to analyze the impact of the global financial crisis on Asia, to assess policy responses to the crisis, to identify lessons on avoiding future crises, and to outline policy recommendations that can help guide Asian governments and policymakers to accelerate development.

The worst is behind us, but big challenges lie ahead. One is that Europe and the US are unlikely to be engines of global growth, so Asian economies need to create their own economic drivers. In the post-crisis period, Asia should not follow the old course that relied heavily on a few export-oriented polluting industries. Asian economies need to adapt and rebalance expansion toward domestic and regional demand with a focus on social inclusion and environmental sustainability. A stronger and more resilient Asian economy could provide benefits to the global economy and be a source of global leadership.

The fact that Asian economies were able to take aggressive steps to mitigate the impact of the global recession underscored the dramatic improvement since the 1997–98 Asian financial crisis. Nonetheless, more work remains to be done, such as the need to maintain open trade and investment regimes, reduce excessive dependence on exports to advanced economies, lessen risks associated with volatile capital flows, and strengthen regional cooperation and integration.

This book is part of the Asian Development Bank Institute's ongoing analysis of emerging markets in Asia. I am confident that policymakers, academics, and economists will find within these thoroughly researched pages valuable information and policy proposals that will help advance development and improve the well-being of the people of Asia.

Masahiro Kawai
Dean and CEO
Asian Development Bank Institute

Contents

List of Figures

List of Tables

List of Abbreviations

ABCP	asset-backed commercial paper
ACU	Asian Currency Unit
ADB	Asian Development Bank
AFSB	Asian Financial Stability Board
AMRO	ASEAN+3 Macroeconomic Research Office
ASEAN	Association of Southeast Asian Nations
BEA	Bureau of Economic Analysis
BOP	balance of payments
CBO	Congressional budget office
CDOs	collateralized debt obligations
CDS	credit default swaps
CGE	computable general equilibrium
CGIF	Credit Guarantee and Investment Facility
CMI	Chiang Mai Initiative
CMIM	Chiang Mai Initiative Multilateralization
CPFF	commercial paper funding facility
CPI	consumer price index
CRAP	capital risk weighted assets ratio
E&E	environment and energy
ECB	European Central Bank
ECBs	external commercial borrowings
ECFA	Economic Cooperation Framework Agreement
EMs	emerging markets
EONIA	Euro OverNight Index Average
EPF	Employers' Provident Fund
EU	European Union
Euribor	Euro Interbank Offered Rate
FDI	foreign direct investment

FDIC	Federal Deposit Insurance Corporation
FED	US Federal Reserve
FII	foreign institutional investment
FTA	free trade agreement
FTAs	free trade areas
FTSE	The Financial Times and Stock Exchange
GDP	gross domestic product
GFC	global financial crisis
GLCs	government-linked companies
GSEs	government-sponsored enterprises
ICT	information and communication technology
IFI	international financial institutions
IIFCL	India Infrastructure Finance Company Limited
IMF	International Monetary Fund
IPO	initial public offerings
IR	international reserves
IT	information technology
KDI	Korea Development Institute
LATAM	emerging Latin America markets
LCPI	life cycle permanent income
LGFPs	Local Government Financing Platforms
LGIVs	Local Government Investment Vehicles
Libor	London Interbank Offered Rate
MBS	mortgage-backed securities
MPC	Monetary Policy Committee
MSCI	Morgan Stanley Capital International
NAFTA	North American Free Trade Agreement
NBFC	non-banking financial companies
NEM	New Economic Model
NIEs	newly industrialized economies
NKEAs	national key economic areas
NREGP	National Rural Employment Guarantee Program
OECD	Organization for Economic Co-operation and Development
PBC	The People's Bank of China
PPIP	Public–Private Investment Program
PMI	purchasing managers' index

PRC	The People's Republic of China
PTA	preferential trade agreement
R&D	research and development
RBI	Reserve Bank of India
ROO	rules of origin
SDR	special drawing rights
SIVs	structured investment vehicles
SLR	statutory liquidity ratio
SMEs	small and medium enterprises
SOEs	state-owned enterprises
SPV	special purpose vehicle
SRIs	strategic reform initiatives
TAF	term auction facility
TALF	term asset-backed securities loan facility
TARP	troubled asset relief plan
TEPCO	Tokyo Electric Power Company
TFP	total factor productivity
UK	United Kingdom
US	United States
VAR	vector autoregression
WPI	wholesale price index
WTO	World Trade Organisation

List of Contributors

Joshua Aizenman, Program Director, Social Sciences Division, Economics Department, University of California, Santa Cruz, USA

Prema-Chandra Athukorala, Professor of Economics, Research School of Pacific and Asian Studies, Australian National University, Canberra, Australia

Barry Bosworth, Senior Fellow, Economic Studies, and the Global Economy and Development programs, International Economics Department, Brookings Institution, Washington DC, USA

Dongchul Cho, Professor, Korea Development Institute (KDI), School of Public Policy and Management, Seoul, Republic of Korea

Barry Eichengreen, Professor of Economics and Professor of Political Science, University of California, Berkeley, USA

Aaron Flaaen, Senior Research Assistant, Brookings Institution, Washington DC, USA

Souvik Gupta, Staff Member, Regional Studies Division, Asia and Pacific Department, International Monetary Fund, Washington DC, USA

Somchai Jitsuchon, Research Director for Macroeconomic Development and Income Distribution, Thailand Development Research Institute, Bangkok, Thailand

Masahiro Kawai, Dean and CEO, Asian Development Bank Institute, Tokyo, Japan

Archanun Kohpaiboon, Assistant Professor, Faculty of Economics, Thammasat University, Bangkok, Thailand

Rajiv Kumar, Secretary General, Federation of Indian Chambers of Commerce and Industry, New Delhi, India

Mario B. Lamberte, Former Director of Research, Asian Development Bank Institute, Tokyo, Japan

Jacques Miniane, Staff Member, the Regional Studies Unit, Asia and Pacific Department, International Monetary Fund, Washington DC, USA

Shankaran Nambiar, Professor, School of Business, Manipal International University, Petaling Jaya, Malaysia

Yung Chul Park, Distinguished Professor, Division of International Studies, Korea University, Seoul, Republic of Korea

Eswar S. Prasad, Tolani Senior Professor of Trade Policy, Cornell University, and Senior Fellow, the Brookings Institution, Washington DC, USA

Chalongphob Sussangkarn, Distinguished Fellow, Thailand Development Research Institute, Bangkok, Thailand

Pankaj Vashisht, Research Associate, Indian Council for Research on International Economic Relations (ICRIER), New Delhi, India

Charles Wyplosz, Professor of International Economics and Director of the International Centre for Money and Banking Studies, Graduate Institute, Geneva, Switzerland

Yongding Yu, Academician, Chinese Academy of Social Sciences, and former Director-General of Institute of World Economics and Politics, Beijing, the People's Republic of China

Bin Zhang, Research Fellow, Research Center of International Finance, Institute of World Economics and Politics, Chinese Academy of Social Sciences, Beijing, the People's Republic of China

Part I
Overview

1

Introduction and Overview

Masahiro Kawai, Mario B. Lamberte, and Yung Chul Park

1.1 Purpose of the book

The global financial crisis of 2007–09 did not originate in Asia, and Asian economies were mostly spared the direct losses from holdings of toxic assets or from the seizing up of the financial system. Nevertheless, Asian economies were hit hard by the downturn in export demand, and, in some cases, by turbulence in foreign exchange and capital markets resulting from a sudden stop in the inward flow, and/or the withdrawal, of capital. Although the economic recovery has already begun (Figures 1.1a and 1.1b), there remain some questions regarding its sustainability. At the time of the writing of this book, the United States (US) still lacks a credible medium-term plan for debt reduction and the sovereign debt problems in the Eurozone have not yet been resolved decisively. In its newly released Global Economic Prospects (January 2012), the World Bank has lowered its economic forecasts for 2012 and 2013 and advised developing countries to prepare for further downside risks, as Eurozone debt problems and weakening in several big emerging economies are dimming global growth prospects. For Asia, the longer-term implications of the global financial crisis are perhaps even greater than the short-term ones. That is, the export-led growth model, which was so spectacularly successful in driving Asian growth in earlier decades, seems to have hit significant limits.

For a variety of reasons, growth in the developed economies will likely fall compared with earlier decades, so developed economies are likely to provide less of a source of growth of demand for Asian exports than they did previously. Also, the period of rapid Asian export growth was accompanied by a sharp worsening of global payments imbalances. This appears to have contributed to the economic instability that culminated in the global financial crisis. Asia's future growth path needs to avoid such a large and unsustainable imbalance. In order to address the widening economic and social division

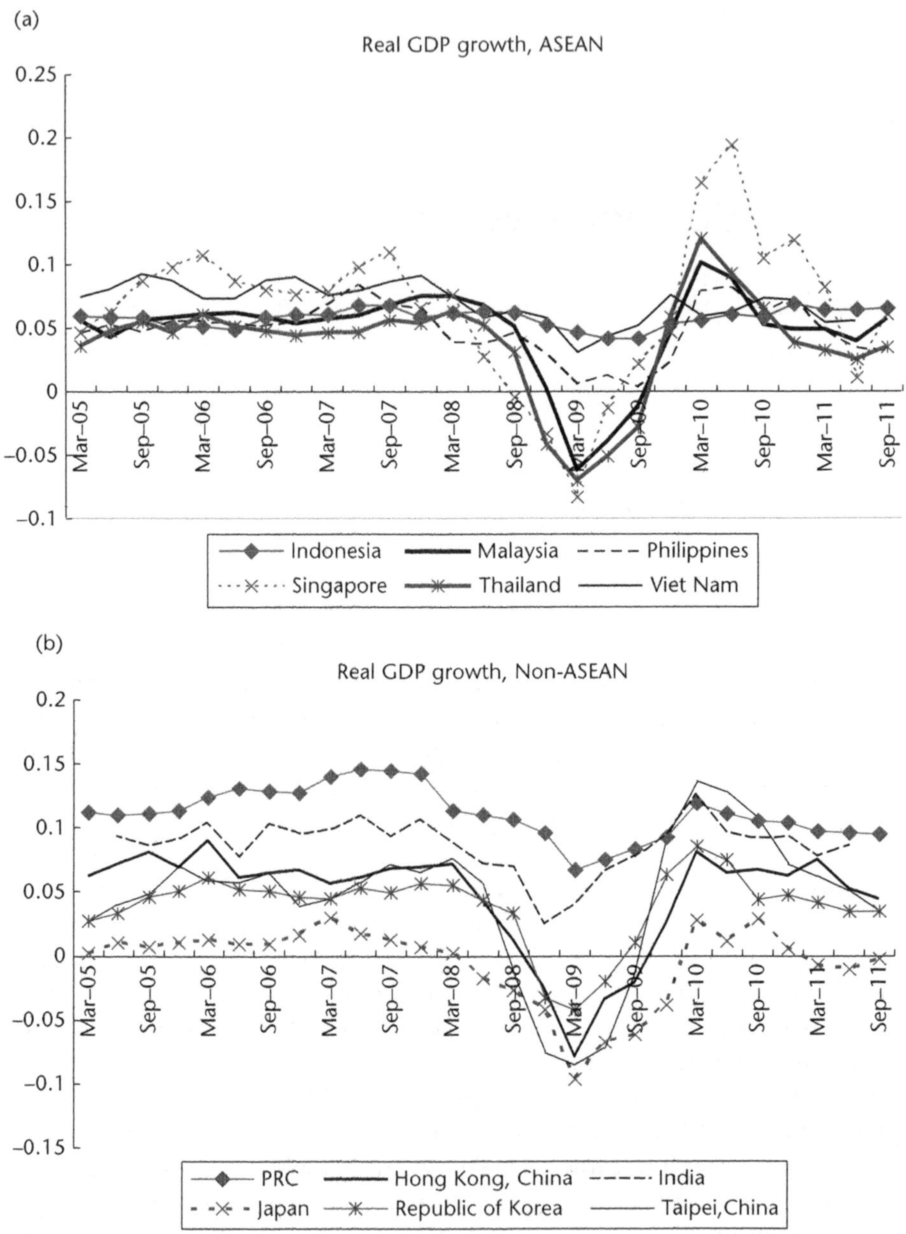

Figure 1.1 Real GDP growth of selected Asian countries March 2005–September 2011
Source: The CEIC database, accessed on January 18, 2012

and increasing environmental degradation that commonly accompany rapid economic growth, developing Asian economies must tackle the challenge of making growth more inclusive and sustainable.

Asian economies need to adapt to this difficult environment and to rebalance growth toward a greater reliance on domestic and regional demand and with a greater emphasis on social and environmental stability. By balanced growth, we mean not only growth that is consistent with smaller global imbalances and less dependent on exports, but also growth that is inclusive and environmentally sustainable. This new development paradigm for Asia could enable the region to become not only a more important source of global demand but also an inclusive and green region. This change would require a series of domestic structural reforms in Asia and intensive regional policy coordination. We argue that the present situation presents an excellent opportunity to make the needed structural changes.

The aim of this book is to identify and analyze the impact of the global financial crisis of 2007–09 on Asian economies, to assess the short-term and longer-term policy responses to the crisis in terms of their effectiveness and sustainability, and to draw lessons about how best to avoid and/or mitigate future crises and to identify structural policy recommendations that can help guide Asian policymakers to expand the growth potential of domestic and regional demand in coming years, and thereby create a basis for sustainable and inclusive long-term growth. These issues and policies span a variety of dimensions, including macroeconomic policy (monetary, fiscal, and foreign currency management), real sector issues (trade and industrial structure), infrastructure, labor market and social policy, financial sector reform and regulation, and regional cooperation and financial architecture.

Section 1.2 reviews the background of the crisis, including its sources in the US and Europe and the possible contribution to it of the global imbalance. Section 1.3 analyzes the impacts of the crisis on Asian economies, tracing out the financial, trade, and exchange rate channels, and identifying the factors that determined the variation of impacts across those economies. Section 1.4 reviews the fiscal, monetary policy and other responses of both advanced economies and emerging Asian economies to the crisis, including examining their effectiveness and sustainability. Section 1.5 summarizes the lessons from the global financial crisis, focusing on the need for Asian economies to reduce both their vulnerability to financial crises and their reliance on exports to developed economies, and to rebalance growth toward domestic and regional demand, while at the same time ensuring that such growth is inclusive and environmentally sustainable. Section 1.6 suggests some policy measures that can help achieve this end. While Asia was recovering from the global financial crisis, Japan, the second largest economy in Asia, was hit by devastating disasters. Section 1.7 discusses the regional and global impacts of Japan's triple disasters. Section 1.8 concludes.

1.2 The background of the crisis

1.2.1 *Roots in the US*

The global financial crisis had its roots in the development of a bubble in the US housing market, especially in the so-called subprime market. Four major contributing causes of the crisis have been identified: excessively easy monetary policy; regulatory failures, both at the microprudential and macroprudential levels; the buildup of global balance of payments imbalances; and weaknesses in the international financial architecture. However, there is still relatively little consensus among analysts about the relative contributions of these factors. The first factor featured in the debate between John Taylor (Taylor 2009) and US Federal Reserve (Fed) Chairman Ben Bernanke (Bernanke 2010) about the appropriateness of the monetary stance in the period 2002–06. In any case, it is clear that the Fed was inclined not to lean against emerging asset bubbles, as it believed that such bubbles were difficult to identify, and that it could move swiftly to clean up the damage afterward.

The second factor includes numerous regulatory lapses, including the sharp deterioration of the quality of mortgage loans in the previous decade, the lack of oversight over "shadow banking" activities (including off-balance-sheet structured investment vehicles of banks), the proliferation of credit default swaps (CDS), the procyclical bias and scope for moral hazard of the Basel II capital requirements for banks, the lack of oversight of and special resolution arrangements for nonbank financial institutions, overly fragmented regulatory structure, regulatory gaps, a lack of attention given to financial derivatives, excessive regulatory reliance on credit ratings, and the problem of "too-big-to-fail" and "too-interconnected-to-fail" institutions, especially those with large international operations. The third factor refers to the large and persistent current account deficits in the US and equally large and persistent current account surpluses in East Asian and oil-producing countries. See, for example, IMF (2009b). The global imbalance issue is described in more detail below.

Bosworth and Flaaen (Chapter 2) tend to give most weight to the second factor, concluding that "[t]he enormous growth of the subprime mortgage market, and the lack of regulation and prudent lending procedures that characterized this market, appear to be the most decisive factors. The complexity of the subsequent mortgage-backed securities led to the general failure of both regulators and purchasers to adequately assess the risks associated with these assets."

The dislocations of the financial sector spilled over dramatically into the real economy in September 2008, following three major events identified by Bosworth and Flaaen (Chapter 2)—the government takeover of Fannie Mae and Freddie Mac on September 8, the Lehman bankruptcy on September 15, and the Federal Reserve's bailout of AIG on September 16. The severity of the economic downturn in the US reflected numerous channels, including large losses of wealth by the household sector and sharply reduced bank lending due to capital losses from non-performing loans and toxic asset holdings, funding difficulties, and increased concerns about risk.

1.2.2 *Transmission to Europe*

Wyplosz (Chapter 3) describes the transmission of the crisis to Europe, together with the contribution of home-grown factors, notably the development of major housing bubbles in a number of countries, including Denmark, Ireland, the Netherlands, Spain, and the United Kingdom (UK). In Europe, financial institutions not only invested heavily in toxic financial assets, but also had exposure to inflated domestic real estate and volatile Eastern European economies (a closer parallel to the Asian financial crisis of 1997–98). They financed these risky investments largely by wholesale funding through international and domestic capital markets. In the Eurozone, (those countries officially adopting the euro as their currency) a single monetary policy allowed for divergences among countries in real interest rates and real effective exchange rates due to different inflation rates. As a result, countries with higher inflation rates faced lower real interest rates, thereby fueling active housing markets, property development, and foreign lending. These activities contributed to a buildup of macroeconomic financial risks in Eurozone countries such as Ireland, Spain, and Greece, while even more extreme risks developed in peripheral countries such as Iceland, Hungary, and the Baltic States, where European banks had large exposures.

1.2.3 *Role of global imbalance*

Although Asia played little role in the first two contributing causes, it featured heavily, along with the oil-producing nations, in the third contributing factor—the global imbalance. Figure 1.2 shows the trend of major current account imbalances. The US current account deficit tended to mirror Japan's current account surplus during the 1980s and 1990s. However, more recently, Japan's surplus was somewhat eclipsed by the rise of that of the People's Republic of China (PRC). Asia excluding Japan and the PRC recorded a consistently large and positive surplus after the Asian financial crisis in 1997–98, although again it was overshadowed by that of the PRC from 2005 on. The surplus of oil-producing countries also contributed significantly to the overall balance during periods of high oil prices.

The global imbalance partly reflected a large excess of savings over investment in Asia. The view is widespread, although controversial, that the global

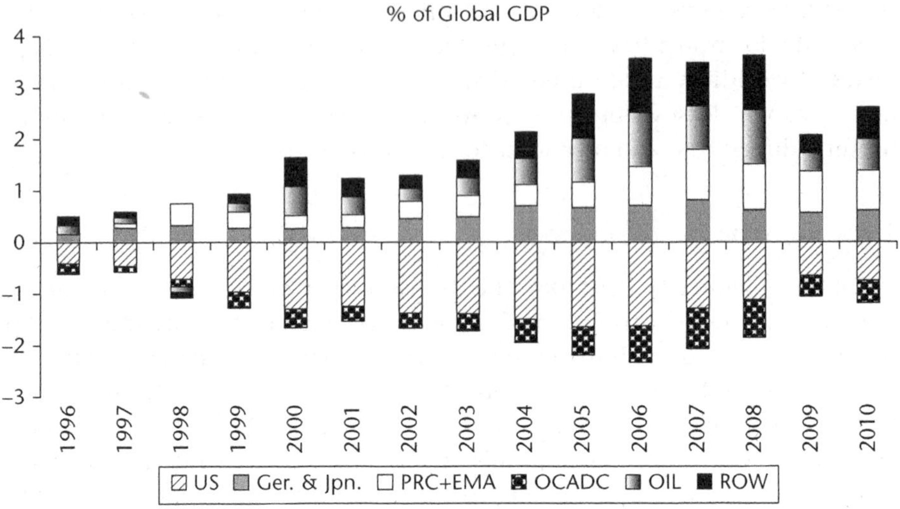

Figure 1.2 Path of major current account imbalances

Source: IMF WEO database, accessed in September 2011

Note: Ger.&Jpn. = Germany and Japan; the PRC + EMA = the People's Republic of China + Emerging Markets of Asia; OCADC = Other Current Account Deficit Countries; OIL = Oil exporting countries; ROW = Rest of the World

payments imbalance contributed to the global financial crisis by fostering international capital flows from the surplus to deficit countries, which depressed global long-term interest rates, and thereby led to the development of asset price bubbles around the world, most notably in the US housing market. This capital movement fueled the "global savings glut" identified in Bernanke (2005) as the possible answer to the "conundrum" described by his predecessor Alan Greenspan (Greenspan 2005).[1]

We are somewhat skeptical about this view. To be sure, the accumulation of large-scale foreign exchange reserves by several Asian and other economies may have contributed to low long-term interest rates in the US and elsewhere. However, we believe that the main responsibility for the development of housing price bubbles and excessive financial risk-taking rests with the relevant domestic monetary and financial sector authorities. Bosworth and Flaaen (Chapter 2) also conclude that the global imbalances were a contributory factor, but not the main one. One persuasive piece of evidence is that Canada—which faced long-term interest rates very similar to those of the US during the past decade and bigger increases in housing prices—managed to avoid a financial crisis, mainly as a result of much more prudent financial sector regulation that limited the buildup of leverage. Bosworth and Flaaen

[1] This refers to the apparent decoupling of short-term and long-term US interest rates during the period 2002–05.

also note that the real effective US dollar exchange rate tended to depreciate during the period from mid-2002 to 2008, which is not consistent with the idea of capital inflows being a major driving force.

Prasad (Chapter 13) finds that the PRC's national savings and current account surpluses dominate the region's saving–investment balances. The PRC accounts for just under half of GDP in Asia ex-Japan, but accounts for 60 percent of total gross national savings and nearly 90 percent of the current account surplus of the region. Its growth pattern has been very striking, with investment accounting for half of GDP growth, while the share of private consumption in overall GDP dropped to about one-third (the lowest in the sample of Asian countries) and private savings rates rose sharply, both for households and corporations. For households, Prasad finds that the increasing private burden of education and health expenditures seem among the strongest candidates for explaining the increase in saving rates, at least during a transition period. Regarding the high rate of corporate savings, Prasad suggests a number of factors, including financial repression with subsidized credit to state-owned enterprises (SOEs), subsidies on land and energy costs, monopoly power of some SOEs, and the inadequacy of financing for the private sector.

1.2.4 *Weakness in international financial architecture*

Another contributing factor in the development of the crisis was a weak international financial architecture that was unable to cope with the pace and complexity of financial globalization and rapid innovation. The International Monetary Fund (IMF) failed to discern the depth and severity of the macroeconomic and financial risks, and was not able to compel either the US or Europe to take the necessary policy steps to reduce such risks. Moreover, there was no international framework capable of regulating, monitoring, and supervising the cross-border activities of systemically important financial institutions, their products, and, more generally, global financial markets. The existing delegation of responsibilities between home- and host-country regulators proved woefully inadequate.

1.3 Impacts of the global financial crisis on Asia

The global financial crisis hit Asian economies via three main channels—direct financial impacts, exports, and foreign exchange rate movements. This section describes the impacts from each channel.

1.3.1 *Financial channel*

Asian economies were for the most part innocent bystanders caught up in the global financial crisis. Their economic and financial fundamentals had improved substantially since the time of the Asian financial crisis. Their financial systems were still relatively "backward" in terms of the amount of reliance on sophisticated derivative products such as asset-backed securities, while their financial regulators were much less bewitched by notions of self-regulating markets, and hence much more willing to impose prudential norms on lending behavior.[2] Asian economies' exposure to foreign currency debt was much reduced, and they had built up substantial foreign exchange reserves. Asia held relatively little toxic financial assets, so total financial losses resulting from them accounted for only about 6 percent of global losses, according to IMF estimates (Table 1.1).

A proactive approach to financial regulation in Asia paid dividends in terms of limiting the direct financial impacts of the crisis. Zhang and Yu (Chapter 7) point out that the PRC's financial institutions were not seriously affected by the global financial crisis because of their limited involvement in overseas financial markets. Kumar and Vashisht (Chapter 8) note that the imposition by the Reserve Bank of India (RBI) of a higher provisioning requirement on commercial bank lending to the real estate sector helped to curb the growth of

Table 1.1 Total estimated financial sector losses as of October 2009 (US$billions)

	Total assets	Losses	Losse as % of total assets	Losses as % of global losses
Asia				
Total loans	6,150	97	1.6	5.1
Total securities	1,728	69	4.0	7.5
Total loans and securities	7,879	166	2.1	5.9
Europe				
Total loans	25,979	1,142	4.4	60.3
Total securities	9,261	476	5.1	52.0
Total loans and securities	35,240	1,618	4.6	57.6
United States				
Total loans	8,059	654	8.1	34.5
Total securities	4,502	371	8.2	40.5
Total loans and securities	12,561	1,025	8.2	36.5
Total				
Total loans	40,188	1,893	4.7	100.0
Total securities	15,491	916	5.9	100.0
Total loans and securities	55,680	2,809	5.0	100.0

Source: IMF (2009a)

[2] Kawai (2011), for instance, points out that "some Asian countries have strengthened lending regulations for highly volatile sector, specifically the real estate sector" (p. 124).

a real estate price bubble. This was one of the few global examples of a countercyclical capital provisioning requirement by any central bank. A ban on complex structures like synthetic securitization coupled with a close monitoring of appropriate lending norms by RBI also ensured a better quality of banking assets. Cho (Chapter 9) points to the improved financial position of both Korean banks and corporations and better financial regulation as positive factors. Jitsuchon and Sussangkarn (Chapter 10) cite the conservatism of the Thai financial sector following the experience of the Asian crisis as one reason for the lack of an appetite for exotic financial products.

However, Asian economies suffered sharp capital outflows—as developed country financial institutions withdrew capital from the periphery to bolster the reserves in their home countries—which developed into a US dollar liquidity shortage in some countries, especially the Republic of Korea (hereafter, Korea), India, and Indonesia. Korea faced a sharp capital outflow even though it thought it had adequate foreign exchange reserves of well over $200 billion. In India, interbank rates spiked to 20 percent after the Lehman shock. The region was affected in other ways, too. Loss of investor confidence resulted in large sell-offs in equity markets and widening credit spreads for emerging Asian borrowers. As a result, new equity and bond issuance was either postponed or reduced (Lee and Park 2009). Indonesia and Malaysia also faced large capital outflows. In addition, Athukorala and Khopaiboon (Chapter 5) and Jitsuchon and Sussangkarn (Chapter 10) cite the drying up of trade finance as a factor contributing to export weakness during the crisis.

1.3.2 *Export channel*

While exports were the main savior of Asian economies during the Asian financial crisis, they proved to be their chief source of vulnerability during the global crisis, due to the collapse of demand in the developed economies. In fact, Jitsuchon and Sussangkarn (Chapter 10) suggest that Thailand became more dependent on exports as a result of its adjustments following the Asian financial crisis. With the failure of Lehman Brothers in September 2008, the crisis in the US and Europe moved quickly from the financial sector to the real economy. Real GDP contracted sharply in the US, Europe, Japan, and other economies affected by sudden stops—or even reversals—of capital flows and sharp declines in exports. Exports plunged across the world, delivering a major shock to even those economies that were little affected by the initial financial shock.

Asian economies were hit hard by the downturn in export demand, and, in some cases, by turbulence in foreign exchange and capital markets as a result of a sudden stop in the inward flow, and/or the withdrawal, of capital. During the fourth quarter of 2008, GDP contracted in the more open Asian economies: by 7.5 percent in Taipei,China by 4.1 percent in Thailand; by 3.3 percent in Korea; and by 2.7 percent in Hong Kong, China. Exports virtually collapsed, industrial production declined sharply, and real GDP contracted steeply in Japan; in the newly industrialized economies of Hong Kong, China; Korea; Singapore; and Taipei,China and in export-dependent middle-income Association of Southeast Asian Nations (ASEAN) countries like Malaysia and Thailand. Real GDP did not contract in the PRC, India, or Indonesia but their growth rates slowed.

This outcome is consistent with the findings of Gupta and Miniane (Chapter 4) that export shocks have substantially larger effects on growth in economies with high export exposure, mainly because investment in such economies also tends to be highly correlated with exports. In terms of magnitude, they find that a 15 percentage point decline in year-on-year growth of real exports—a decline of a similar magnitude to that experienced in Asia during the crisis—leads in the estimated model to a 6 percentage point decline in real investment growth in high export exposure economies, versus a 2 percentage point decline in low export exposure economies. Cho (Chapter 9) suggests that the sharp decline in imports by the PRC further contributed to the very large drop in Korea's exports, possibly reflecting overheating of the PRC economy.

The large size of the impacts was surprising to many who favored the theory that Asian economies had managed to "decouple" from the growth of the advanced economies, due to the increasing share of intra-regional trade in total Asian trade. Athukorala and Kohpaiboon (Chapter 5) show that, for East Asia, intra-regional trade hit 45 percent of exports and 63 percent of imports by 2006–07. Nonetheless, they argue that decoupling never happened, because the rise of intra-regional trade simply reflected the development of trade in intermediate goods as the result of increased segmentation of production chain networks that were still ultimately linked to export markets for final goods in advanced economies. Nambiar (Chapter 11) also notes that claims that Malaysia has decoupled from the US do not seem valid.

Park (Chapter 6) takes issues with this view. Reviewing recent changes in intra-regional trade and financial linkages with global financial markets together with the episode of the 2008 crisis, he shows that the available evidence does not confirm either decoupling or re-coupling. On a longer-term perspective, however, he argues that the three free trade areas (FTAs) of the PRC, Japan, and Korea with ASEAN (which have entered into force) and a proposal for creating an FTA among Japan, Korea, and the PRC, which is no longer idle speculation, will spur intra-regional trade.[3] With increases in

[3] ASEAN member countries are: Brunei Darussalam, Cambodia, Indonesia, Lao PDR, Malaysia, Myanmar, the Philippines, Singapore, Thailand, and Viet Nam.

income throughout the region, East Asia will witness a continuing expansion in intra-regional trade, much of which will consist of intra-industry trade that is more horizontal than before. At the same time, if East Asia succeeds in instituting an efficient capital control regime and in strengthening the Chiang Mai Initiative Multilateralization (CMIM), which will be part of a global liquidity safety net, it will be able to better cope with the volatility of capital flows to the region. Together these developments will then help speed up economic integration among ASEAN, Japan, Korea, and the PRC to build a region that is more self-contained than before, as it will be less affected by the cyclical movements of the industrialized countries in North America and Europe.

Athukorala and Kohpaiboon (Chapter 5) also find the degree of export contraction (on average about 20 percent) was remarkably synchronous among the countries, regardless of the differences among these countries in the degree of export orientation, or degree of dependence on the US and other developed country markets. Moreover, the drying up of trade credit and traders' overreaction to a possible collapse in demand probably played a role in the total decline in trade.

Nonetheless, a key difference from the Asian financial crisis is that domestic demand held up reasonably well in many economies despite the plunge in exports. This was because the shock was essentially external, rather than developing from a domestic financial crisis. For example, Cho (Chapter 9) argues that this contributed to the relatively small impact of the crisis on employment in Korea.

1.3.3 *Exchange rate channel*

Large-scale capital outflows during the global financial crisis tended to depress foreign exchange rates of Asian economies, and also led to large reductions of international reserves (IR) in most cases. From its peak in July 2007 to the trough in March 2009, the Korean won fell the most of any Asian currency, down 58 percent, followed by the Indonesian rupiah and the Indian rupee. Cho (Chapter 9) argues plausibly that the large fall of the won reflected the relatively high exposure of the Korean economy to external short-term debt. However, unlike the Asian crisis, currency mismatches were much lower during the global financial crisis, and this also limited the financial impacts of the crisis on Asian economies.

Aizenman (Chapter 14) examines factors that affected the apparent willingness of currency authorities to tolerate large losses of foreign exchange reserves during a crisis situation. He finds that trade related factors are more significant in accounting for the pre-crisis IR level of countries that experienced a sizable depletion of their IR in the first phase of the crisis, in line with the buffer stock interpretation of the demand for IR. On the other hand, countries whose pre-crisis demand for IR was more sensitive to financial factors refrained from using IR altogether, preferring to adjust through larger depreciations. He concludes tentatively that the adjustment of emerging markets during the global liquidity crisis was constrained more by their fear of losing IR than by their fear of floating.

1.4 Policy responses

1.4.1 *Advanced economies*

The severity and synchronous nature of the global downturn soon led to the realization that it had the potential to become a global depression, potentially the worst since the Great Depression. The IMF and other global organizations called for large-scale and coordinated global responses to provide support for both the global economy and financial sector (Freedman et al. 2009). The Group of 20 (G20) summit, first held in Washington (November 2008) and then in London (April 2009), Pittsburgh (September 2009), Seoul (November 2010), and Cannes (November 2011) became the premier forum for international policy coordination efforts to enable the global economy to recover from the crisis and put economic activity back on track to sustainable growth.

Industrialized economies injected massive liquidity into their financial markets to avert a systemic collapse of their banks and financial institutions. At the same time, central banks reduced policy rates to historic lows. New measures were also introduced to ensure the availability of funds to keep financial markets functioning. In addition, massive fiscal stimulus packages were implemented to prevent a sharp contraction in the economies of the US, Europe, and Japan. These measures are described in detail in Bosworth and Flaaen (Chapter 2) for the US and in Wyplosz (Chapter 3) for Europe. Overall, the combination of these measures staved off a meltdown that had threatened the industrial world (ADB 2009b).

1.4.2 *Asian economies*

Similar to the US and Europe, many Asian economies responded with aggressive measures to ease monetary and fiscal policy and to support national financial systems. Although it is difficult to estimate the actual impact of these packages, The Asian Development Bank (ADB) estimated that fiscal stimulus measures taken by the PRC, Malaysia, Singapore, and Viet Nam exceeded 5 percent of GDP, while those of Hong Kong, China; India; Japan; Korea; the Philippines; Taipei,China; and Thailand amounted to between

2 percent and 5 percent of GDP (ADB 2009a). Zhang and Yu (Chapter 7) provide details on the PRC's massive stimulus package, which was directed at boosting domestic demand and an improvement of economic structure, and was estimated to total CNY4 trillion. Only one-quarter of the package was financed by the central government, leaving the rest to local government financing, including bank loans, and the private sector. They also note the rapid growth of bank lending in the PRC as a result of monetary easing.

Kumar and Vashisht (Chapter 8) conclude that the monetary authorities in India acted aggressively once it was clear that inflationary pressures had subsided and growth was beginning to slacken. Unfortunately, because of the government's large borrowing requirement and the stickiness in deposit rates that keep the cost of funds high for the banks, the policy rate cuts did not filter into the retail credit market.

Jitsuchon and Sussangkarn (Chapter 10) provide interesting information on the role of income transfers in the Thai government's fiscal stimulus program. They emphasize that the transfers must be made to the right target groups, and any leakage to ineligible recipients, such as high-income people, must be kept to a minimum. However, this does not seem to have been the case in Thailand, where transfers likely reached the urban poor, but not the poorest segments in the rural areas.

Nambiar (Chapter 11) notes that when it became clear that the Malaysian economy would be affected by the global financial crisis, the government reacted by launching stimulus packages in November 2008 and March 2009, accompanied by an interest cut made by the Bank Negara Malaysia.

As a result of these large-scale measures, combined with their fundamental financial and economic resilience, Asian emerging economies led the global growth recovery, having averaged 10 percent annualized growth on a simple average basis from April through September 2009, a very impressive performance. Growth was especially strong in the PRC; India; Korea; Malaysia; the Philippines; Singapore; Taipei,China; and Viet Nam. In view of its size, the PRC made by far the largest contribution to regional growth, and perhaps the largest to global growth.

The fact that Asian economies were able to take aggressive policy measures underscored the dramatic improvement that had taken place in their macroeconomic and financial sector fundamentals since the Asian financial crisis. A number of regional central banks had achieved low inflation, as a result of adopting inflation-targeting regimes, while many governments had substantially reduced fiscal deficits and contained levels of public debt. Private sector banks and nonfinancial corporations had also achieved stronger balance sheets—including lower non-performing loan ratios and higher capital adequacy ratios—and less exposure to adverse currency movements.

Nevertheless, the large stimulus measures did not come without potential costs. Even if the countercyclical effects are strong, fiscal stimulus could be counterproductive in the long run as it could raise the real interest rate, mask structural weakness, and postpone much needed structural reforms. Furthermore, Asian policymakers are well aware that, for their export-oriented economies, there is a limit to the extent to which expansionary monetary and fiscal policy can fill the void created by the decline in external demand. Zhang and Yu (Chapter 7) detail three major concerns about the PRC package: (1) the efficiency of such large-scale infrastructure investment and the potential future rise of non-performing loans and corruption; (2) the lack of necessary adjustments in the real sector in terms of reallocating capital to higher-productivity areas in manufacturing and services; and (3) impairment of market competition and private investment resulting from the government's excessive involvement in the industrial sector. Jitsuchon and Sussangkarn (Chapter 10) also express concerns about fiscal sustainability if the crisis is long-lived, although that did not prove to be the case. Nambiar (Chapter 11) points out that some of the measures included in the stimulus packages are ill-conceived in that they treat the economic problem as one that will be short lived. For instance, the heavy emphasis placed on providing loans through the government-linked companies will do little to bolster the private sector's participation in the economy throughout the crisis and after.

Some Asian economies, notably Korea, India, and Indonesia, faced significant stresses on their financial systems due to drains on foreign exchange reserves. They had to resort to swap lines from other central banks, including the US Federal Reserve, the Bank of Japan, and the People's Bank of China to procure adequate sources of hard currency. Aizenman (Chapter 14) finds that the exposure of US banks to emerging markets was the most important selection criterion for swap lines from the US Federal Reserve.

1.5 Lessons from the global financial crisis

Lessons from the global financial crisis fall into three broad areas: those related to the prevention, mitigation, and management of financial crises and other external shocks; those related to the achievement of "growth rebalancing" toward a pattern of growth less dependent on exports to the advanced economies and more reliant on domestic and regional demand; and those related to promoting more open trade. Rebalancing measures can be taken at the national level, as well as at the regional level, including measures to encourage trade and other forms of regional cooperation.

1.5.1 *Preventing/mitigating and managing financial crises and other shocks*

The global financial crisis highlighted numerous weaknesses in the financial systems of advanced economies and in the global financial architecture. Lessons of the crisis for the advanced economies and the global financial architecture highlighted the following requirements to[4]:

- expand the regulatory perimeter, close regulatory gaps, and prevent regulatory shopping;
- strengthen capital requirements, especially for systemically important institutions;
- set liquidity standards and strengthen liquidity provision;
- set maximum standards for leverage;
- establish mechanisms for resolution of all systemically important institutions;
- revise monetary policy frameworks to adopt financial stability as an explicit responsibility and to take asset prices into account;
- establish a macroprudential framework that identifies risks building up in the system as a whole, and possesses the prudential tools and the authority to take steps to ameliorate those risks;
- reduce the procyclicality of regulations and accounting rules;
- develop a robust framework for clearing and monitoring trades of derivative products;
- expand the monetary policy framework to take financial stability and asset prices into account;
- increase coordination of global surveillance;
- reform the relation of home- and host-country regulators for international financial institutions; and
- develop a framework for the resolution of international systemically important financial institutions.

Wyplosz (Chapter 3) argues that one key lesson from the Eurozone experience was the benefits from a common currency, which meant that Eurozone member policymakers did not have to worry about sudden and wide shifts in relative competitiveness or high levels of currency mismatches. On other hand, recent developments show that the challenges of coordinating fiscal

[4] See IMF 2009b, de Larosière (2009), FSA (2009), and the Group of 30 (2009), among others.

policies and government debt management under a single currency in the Eurozone have proved daunting.

As noted above, Asian economies suffered relatively little direct financial impacts during the global financial crisis, as a result of improved financial performance after the Asian financial crisis, better financial regulation, a massive build-up of foreign exchange reserves, more flexible currency regimes, and small holdings of toxic assets. Nonetheless, the crisis highlighted unfinished work for Asian economies left over from the Asian financial crisis, and some new work as well.

In particular, the continued vulnerability of Asian economies to volatile capital flows presents a major challenge. The high costs associated with accumulating international reserves and their contribution to global imbalances point to the need for other approaches. Asian economies need to complete work on a regional facility for the provision of hard currency liquidity, including a surveillance unit. Aizenman (Chapter 14) outlines the case of supplementing hoarding of international reserves with a Pigovian tax-cum-subsidy scheme on external borrowing. The logic of the scheme follows from the negative fire-sale externalities associated with large inflows of capital. Specifically, studies showed that external debt associated with maturity and currency mismatches increases the downside risk of costly sudden stops crises, so incentives should be offered to discourage such debt issuance. Deepening domestic financial markets, especially bond markets, can also enhance their function as a "spare tire" in the case of sudden stops resulting in capital outflows.

Eichengreen (Chapter 12) notes that the crisis serves as a reminder of the risks of excessive dependence on foreign finance. Countries with large current account deficits and external financing requirements were disproportionately hit by the crisis as foreign investors deleveraged and capital flows dried up. Strengthening domestic financial systems, surveillance, regulation, and monetary policy frameworks, as well as enhancing regional economic and financial cooperation, could also contribute to reducing vulnerability to external shocks and reducing the likelihood of internal shocks developing.

The crisis also shows the need to maintain strong economic and financial fundamentals and adequate fiscal and monetary policy space to respond to shocks, as noted by Gupta and Miniane (Chapter 4), Cho (Chapter 9), and Eichengreen (Chapter 12). One of the key findings of Gupta and Miniane is that recessions characterized by financial stress tend to be deeper and more lasting, chiefly because of the impact of such stress on the credit channel. More flexible use of monetary policy has been facilitated by the shift from exchange rate targeting to inflation targeting.

1.5.2 *Emphasizing growth rebalancing*

Having achieved the goal of short-term economic recovery, Asian policy-makers now need to focus on measures to restore sustainable medium- to long-term economic growth. This means that Asian economies should not simply go back to a pattern of export-led growth as followed prior to the global financial crisis, but rather should rebalance demand toward domestic and regional demand. The current situation calls for measures to reduce internal and external imbalances and lessen excessive dependence on export growth targeted at the US and European markets. Moreover, the new growth pattern needs to be more inclusive and environmentally sustainable, in order to offset some of the excesses that developed during the period of export-led growth.

Rebalancing is defined as the process of removing the bias against the nontradable sector. Countries adhering to an export-led growth strategy are likely to maintain internal terms of trade that are in favor of tradables. In such economies, the relative prices of tradables are kept at artificially higher levels so as to induce the allocation of resources to export-oriented industries. Rebalancing growth will require the elimination of this structural bias so as to facilitate the allocation of more resources to the non-tradable sector. To this end, it is necessary to wind down the incentive schemes for export promotion that often include tax breaks, preferential lending, and other explicit and implicit subsidies to exporters.

In embracing a rebalancing strategy, distinctions should be made between an export-led growth strategy and export-led growth. The former is a strategy in which the underlying incentive structure is biased in favor of exports; this is not the case for export-led growth. Because of comparative advantage and other structural characteristics, some market-oriented open economies may rely more on external demand for growth than others, even though their incentive schemes are neutral, and they may run either deficits or surpluses on their current accounts. With the exception of the PRC, most East Asian export-oriented economies have phased out the subsidization of exports, including keeping the currency undervalued, and as such they may be classified as export-led growth countries with relatively neutral incentive schemes (Blanchard and Giavazzi 2006). There are four main reasons for the need for rebalancing.

Reduce the dependence of growth on exports to the advanced economies. Asian economies benefited tremendously from export-led growth centered on US and European markets during the years leading up to the global financial and economic crisis. However, US consumer spending will likely remain sluggish over many years to come, as US households repay debt and rebuild wealth. In addition, the size of US and European potential GDP may have shrunk and their potential growth rates are likely to be lower over the medium-term.

Gupta and Miniane (Chapter 4) find that economic recoveries in Asia have typically relied mainly on exports, and hence have tended to be weaker than those in other regions. Therefore, weak demand growth in the advanced economies would further attenuate the potential for an export-led recovery in Asia. Zhang and Yu (Chapter 7) point to the huge buildup of capacity in the tradable sector in the PRC, while Jitsuchon and Sussangkarn (Chapter 10) cite the heavy dependence on export growth that developed in Thailand after the Asian crisis. Nambiar (Chapter 11) argues that Malaysia is still following an export-led growth strategy that is now less viable. He alludes to the problem of the "middle-income trap" facing Malaysia, that is, it cannot compete for FDI as it could ten years ago, since it neither has the unskilled labor advantage, nor an abundant supply of skilled, knowledge-intensive labor.

Reduce risks associated with unsustainable global imbalances. The global payments imbalance was a reflection of US overspending and East Asia's (and oil producers') underspending relative to their respective outputs. To the extent that such imbalances contributed to the global financial crisis, a more balanced pattern of growth in Asia is likely to contribute to more stable growth, both in the region and globally. Of course, Asia cannot achieve this alone, as imbalances need to be addressed by both surplus and deficit countries.

Reduce vulnerability to external shocks. The size of the shock experienced by Asian economies during the global financial crisis was roughly proportional to the share of exports in GDP, especially exports directed at final demand in the developed economies. Until now, export volatility may have been seen as a necessary price to achieve high growth. Now that the potential growth of developed economy export markets has slowed, the volatility entailed by such export-dependence becomes less tolerable. Relying more on domestic and regional demand should lessen the degree of correlation with global cycles, thereby potentially reducing the volatility of output.

Eichengreen (Chapter 12) points out that a strategy of export-led growth entails greater risks than appreciated previously. Not only is global demand volatile; but trade appears to be more elastic with respect to the cycle and more vulnerable in downturns than previously thought. The destabilizing macroeconomic impact is even greater to the extent that a growing share of investment in emerging markets is export linked. Eichengreen also notes that, in the longer run, this episode of heightened currency volatility will undoubtedly encourage more discussion of collective currency pegs, common currency baskets, and regional monetary unions.

Reduce distortions to economic structure that hinder growth and reduce welfare. The path of export-led growth led many Asian countries to ignore or suppress measures that could raise the growth potential from domestic and regional demand. These include exchange rate adjustments, deregulation, dismantling of export subsidy arrangements, financial development, regional trade and investment agreements, measures for income redistribution, and improvements in social safety nets. Gupta and Miniane (Chapter 4) emphasize the need for structural reforms such as an expansion of social safety nets and a deepening of domestic financial markets if Asian economies are to diversify their sources of growth more durably. Zhang and Yu (Chapter 7) highlight the limited progress of market reforms in service nontradable sectors, such as education, medical health, environment, finance, communication, and transportation.

Exchange rate adjustments are a key aspect of growth rebalancing. The appreciation of Asian currencies against the US dollar is likely to be a necessary and important ingredient for global rebalancing. Until now, pressure from exporters favored undervalued exchange rates that benefited them but discouraged investment in services and other nontradables. Low exchange rates also tended to depress real incomes and purchasing power, which discouraged consumer spending.

Productivity growth in service sectors has often been hindered by excessive regulation and barriers to entry that stifle competition. Deregulation of service sectors, including financial services, and development of regional investment and FTAs were often not given sufficient priority. Financial "repression" was used as a tool to guide domestic savings toward favored sectors, especially exporters, while denying consumers the ability to achieve higher asset returns or borrow against future income. Credit provision to small and medium enterprises (SMEs) was frequently given short shrift as well.

Exporting sectors were often viewed as the primary vehicle for absorbing excess labor from the agricultural sector. However, in many cases, they proved to be not very effective in this role, mainly because the high capital intensiveness of export industries limited the degree of labor absorption. Studies show that labor absorption of exporting sectors over the past decade was in many cases much lower than in earlier periods. As a result, dual labor market structures persisted. The current situation provides a good opportunity to review labor market policy with an eye toward making labor markets more inclusive and overcoming dualistic labor markets. Income distribution policies also need to be reviewed. For example, Jitsuchon and Sussangkarn (Chapter 10) call for a deepening of the export sector, that is, reducing imports and increasing local value-added, as one response to this. They also favor measures to improve income inequality, including fiscal measures, micro credit policies, and equitable enforcement of laws.

The expansion of manufacturing production was often encouraged regardless of the cost in terms of degradation of public health and the environment, and excessive consumption of fuels whose use generates greenhouse gases. Such a development path is no longer sustainable. Moreover, innovations related to energy conservation and greenhouse gas reduction may prove to be dynamic new sources of growth.

1.5.3 *Maintaining open trade and avoiding protectionism*

The need to avoid protectionism and maintain open trade is a key lesson from this and earlier crises. Athukorala and Kohpaiboon (Chapter 5) warn that increased export competition resulting from weak final demand markets may well encourage a wave of "new protectionism" or beggar-thy-neighbor policies. These include export subsidies, anti-dumping complaints, and a stringent implementation of technical, sanitary, and phytosanitary standards, as well as massive financial support extended to automobile manufacturers in the US and some other countries. They suggest the formation of a region-wide free trade agreement, encompassing ASEAN, the PRC, Japan, and Korea, and possibly India as one option. Nevertheless, FTAs can pose a host of complications in dealing with intermediate goods which may be subject to multiple tariffs at various stages of production. Athukorala and Kohpaiboon suggest that East Asian policymakers consider the example of the Information Technology Agreement and examine the possibility of extending it to cover trade in electrical goods and other new products.

1.6 Recommendations to achieve rebalancing for a stable, balanced, and sustainable development

There are many policy measures that can be adopted to encourage growth rebalancing. The concept of "rebalancing" should not be limited to the idea of correcting unsustainable current account imbalances, although that is the starting point. A closely related aspect is balanced growth, which means growth that is socially and environmentally more sustainable. Asia's growth model so far has neither adequately emphasized the importance of social inclusiveness nor the environmental consequences of growth. As a result, high economic growth has been accompanied by the social divide—such as inequalities in income distribution—and environmental degradation. Asia needs to achieve growth that is more inclusive, in that it creates employment and reduces poverty; and growth that is sustainable, in that it is consistent with the long-term stabilization of greenhouse gas emissions and other resource constraints. Policies for encouraging growth rebalancing are grouped into eight major areas: rebalancing spending; rebalancing production; enhancing social inclusion; supporting environmental improvement; improving macroeconomic stability; deepening the financial sector; promoting regional cooperation; and reform of the international financial architecture.

Rebalancing spending. Correction of the global current account imbalance needs to be addressed by both surplus and deficit countries. However, it is clear that some Asian policies have contributed to such imbalances. This includes: depressing foreign exchange rates through large-scale accumulation of foreign exchange reserves; distorting resources toward exporting sectors through various subsidy programs; maintaining an underdeveloped financial sector that limits consumption-related borrowing; and excessive regulation of service sectors that limits their expansion and productivity growth.

Adjustments on the demand side encompass shifts in the spending composition toward tradable goods and an expansion of domestic demand and regional demand for goods and services. In view of the high rates of saving and relatively neutral incentive schemes in emerging Asia, one may conclude that the bulk of Asia's current account surplus does not come from Asia's exceptional success in pushing out exports as much as it does from a high propensity to save and stagnant investment demand. Growth rebalancing should therefore be geared to removing structural impediments to consumption and investment. Such a rebalancing strategy would help improve the allocative efficiency of the economy, while making it less vulnerable to external shocks.

Rebalancing growth therefore entails policy changes and institutional reform that would eliminate structural impediments that constrain households to save more than their counterparts in advanced countries. Although there is a vast literature on saving behavior in emerging economies, variables that are closely associated with changes in the propensity to save tend to differ from country to country. In terms of the rebalancing strategy, some of the reforms that would help induce households to consume more as a proportion of their income include: (1) the establishment of an efficient system of social protection; (2) the expansion and improvement of the efficiency of public and private pension, public health care, and education systems; (3) the phasing out of restrictions on consumer credit; and (4) the creation of financial institutions specializing in household lending.

In some countries, such as the PRC, the share of household income in GDP is low, and both corporate and household savings are large relative to GDP. Substantial scope exists for these economies to reduce corporate savings and increase household consumption. For example, government policies to raise dividend revenues from state-owned enterprises and transfer such revenues to households would effectively augment household income and thus stimulate household consumption. These policies at the same time reduce corporate savings and discourage excessive and often inefficient investment by state-owned enterprises.

Structural measures to reduce precautionary savings—and thus stimulate the household propensity to consume—should be given high priority, particularly through the strengthening of social protection systems, including larger public spending for basic health care, education, and housing as well as system building for health and unemployment insurance and retirement pensions. Zhang and Yu (Chapter 7) and Prasad (Chapter 13) argue that increasing spending on the social safety net and other government insurance mechanisms could help reduce precautionary motives for saving, such as providing public pension schemes, health insurance, and unemployment insurance. Better provision and delivery of health care for older citizens will become increasingly important due to lengthening life spans, the increasing cost of health care and rising dependency ratios of older persons to working-age persons. In addition, income redistribution from the rich to the poor would also stimulate national household consumption as the poor typically have a higher propensity to consume than do the rich. Jitsuchon and Sussangkarn (Chapter 10) discuss income redistribution policy options in Thailand. Nambiar (Chapter 11) note that re-involving the government in education and training as well as in the provision of health care and low cost housing will, among other things, release savings for consumption purposes.

In contrast, a high priority should be given to encouraging in investment in a number of countries, especially those such as India, where infrastructure investment needs are high, and ASEAN countries, particularly Indonesia, Malaysia, the Philippines, and Thailand, where the ratio of investment to GDP dropped sharply after the Asian financial crisis of 1997–98. Investment can be encouraged both through targeted public investment, especially in infrastructure, and improvement of the investment climate (including supply-side environments to attract private investment). While reviving investment is critical, it will have to be managed in a way that will refocus the allocation of investment away from export-led industries and toward the nontradable sector, improving social welfare education, health care, and the pension system, and protecting the environment. For example, Zhang and Yu (Chapter 7) call for a reduction in the various subsidies that distort production in favor of tradable goods in the PRC. In this regard, the adoption of a low-carbon and green growth strategy will help protect the environment and also help boost the domestic demand for a variety of new services that a green growth strategy is expected to generate.

Rebalancing production. The second priority is to strengthen the supply side of the economy in order to promote areas with future potential for long-term growth through investment, innovation, and deregulation. Adjustments on the supply side encompass shifts in the production structure, innovations that create regional demand, and increases in productivity in services sectors through structural reforms and deregulation. These changes could result from policy changes, such as deregulation and increases in public and private investment. Target areas include human resources (education, health care, and training), knowledge activities (research and development [R&D], and information and communication technology [ICT]), physical infrastructure, services sectors, and green growth. Investment in human resources and knowledge is the key driver of competitiveness and economic growth in the current era of globalization.

The services sector is a prime target for measures such as deregulation to raise productivity. Zhang and Yu (Chapter 7) argue that more deregulation should be introduced in the PRC in service sectors such as railways, medical care, education, finance, telecommunication, energy, and express delivery. Such deregulation policies should focus on relaxing market entry restrictions for private investment and a reduction of the government's intervention in pricing. Kumar and Vashisht (Chapter 8) also call for deregulation, and increased investment in education, social, and physical infrastructure in India. Cho (Chapter 9) argues that Korea does not have a significant overall savings–investment balance, but it still can promote deregulation to encourage service sector development and productivity growth.

Fostering new "green" industries is an important initiative as it promotes economic growth that is much less dependent on extra-regional markets, while addressing Asia's environmental and climate change challenges. In the post-crisis period, Asian economies should not simply follow the same course as before, relying heavily on a few export-oriented polluting industries that use a narrow range of carbon-intensive energy sources. Green economic growth is consistent with long-term sustainability and, at the same time, could help create jobs, raise skills, and boost Asia's competitiveness. A green Asia could be a world leader in low-carbon technology, innovation, and growth.

Infrastructure investment also plays a key role in facilitating faster growth of productivity and bringing together demand and supply within the region. Infrastructure investment needs are high, which will require regional planning and financing arrangements in many cases. Asian policymakers should focus on the "soft" component—policies, regulations, rules, and procedures—in order to make the "hard" component of infrastructure work. In many cases, public–private partnerships are essential to attract private sector funding and management know-how while mitigating risks involved. Infrastructure development, particularly in transport, energy, and ICT, is essential to forge cross-border connectivity and expand trade and investment opportunities. Strong regional cooperation among Asian economies is crucial for establishing Asia-wide physical connectivity towards a "seamless Asia" (ADB and ADBI 2009). Regional infrastructure will need to be geared increasingly towards supporting Asian production networks and regional supply chains to target Asian markets and promote intra-Asian trade.

Asia has 1.1 billion people who are middle-class or wealthier, and the number is growing rapidly. Trade liberalization, especially the creation of a large region-wide FTA, can make a notable contribution to growth rebalancing. This could expand markets for Asian firms and consumers and create greater trade and investment opportunities within the region, allowing more production and spending. In addition to the liberalization of trade in goods and services, the liberalization and harmonization of cross-border investment is also critical to further expanding regional markets. Both firms and consumers in Asia would benefit from economies of scale, dynamic efficiency, and greater trade and investment opportunities within the region. Consolidating the existing Asian "noodle bowl"—an array of overlapping bilateral and plurilateral FTAs in the region—into a single agreement is thus a high priority.

Enhancing social inclusion. Sustainable growth means growth that reaches all segments of society, expands access to opportunities, and contributes decisively to reduce poverty. In some Asian countries, the perpetuation of dual labor market structures limits the extent to which economic growth benefits a substantial segment of the population. In others, such as the PRC, labor market distortions and limits on domestic labor mobility depress the overall level of household income as well as tend to increase income inequality. Governments need to examine a variety of ways in which the distribution of income can be improved, including, in some cases, targeted income transfer programs. Labor market policies emphasizing investments that maximize employment opportunities can also contribute to this.

Enhancing social protection and increasing public investment in infrastructure, health and education contribute to the sustainability and inclusivity of growth by making it easier for people to participate in economic growth. Nambiar (Chapter 11) cites the need for improved investment in public goods in Malaysia. Investment in public education is one of the biggest keys to opening up paths of economic advancement for an increasing proportion of the population. Labor market reforms to increase employment opportunites for young adults, improve the flexibility and relevance of skills training systems, and create more secure jobs with adequate social protection can reduce uncertainty in income prospects.

SMEs provide the bulk of employment in Asian economies, and effective policies are needed to promote SMEs and service industries to better align domestic production with domestic demand and trade within the region. Kumar and Vashisht (Chapter 8) argue that raising the potential growth rate in India requires another round of structural reforms that will improve the investment climate, especially for SMEs that employ the majority of the work force.

Supporting environmental improvement. Balanced and sustainable growth also means growth that is consistent with environmental constraints. The biggest long-term challenge is to develop an economic growth path consistent with the reduction of greenhouse gas emission levels to a level consistent with only a modest rise in global average temperatures. Other concerns that need to be addressed include environmental degradation, and shortages of key resources such as energy and water. This new development paradigm should focus on green growth and fostering strong regional cooperation. These efforts can also contribute to the reduction of greenhouse gases (such as carbon dioxide) emissions and, hence, mitigate climate change. Asia needs to focus on innovation and technological capacity in order to integrate the guiding principles of energy efficiency and environmental protection into all economic activity. Thus, Asia should put a high priority on supporting R&D towards eco-innovation and green services as well as investment in skills development and local capacity to supply green products. In this way, a "green Asia" can be created.

Improving macroeconomic stability. More efforts are needed to make macroeconomic policy frameworks consistent with stable and sustainable growth. First, monetary policy frameworks should take asset prices and financial stability into account. More broadly, there is a need for coordinating monetary policy and macroprudential supervisory policy to achieve the objectives of price stability and financial stability. Second, the region's fiscal authorities need to put greater emphasis on making countercyclical fiscal policy more effective, including expanding automatic stabilizers such as unemployment insurance.

Third, regarding management of capital flows, experiences show that a sudden reversal of capital inflows has been a major cause of a reserve currency liquidity crisis in emerging economies, This fear of the crisis has led to holding large amounts of reserves for self-insurance, thereby exacerbating the global imbalance. National authorities must improve their ability to prevent capital flow volatility from adversely affecting their economies. Capital controls could be considered as a viable macroprudential measure if designed properly. At the Seoul G-20 summit the leaders called attention to the need to introduce capital control—to be managed in a prudent manner to moderate large capital inflows—in particular speculative portfolio capital in emerging economies. The IMF has softened its traditional position and has proposed a set of guidelines on capital control (Ostry et al. 2011). They argue that there is no easy way of ranking control instruments in terms of welfare. This means that capital controls need to be country and risk specific and to be designed in a way that will mitigate opportunities for arbitrage arising from differences in the capital control regime in different countries.

Improving surveillance and strengthening regional financial sectors against future financial shocks can make an important contribution to supporting stable domestic demand growth. The current crisis shows the importance of implementing a framework for macroprudential financial supervision and regulation—a powerful systemic stability regulator—that possesses effective prudential tools.[5] Steps to improve microprudential regulation and reduce the procyclicality of financial regulation are also important.

Crisis management can be improved by: having a coordinated set of financial authorities that between them cover all phases of the crisis; ensuring there are credible ex ante means of handling failures in all financial institutions, particularly those that operate across borders; implementing an effective deposit insurance system; and improving resilience against shocks by substantial enhancement of regional mechanisms, among others, through an Asian Financial Stability Board (AFSB).[6]

Prasad (Chapter 13) points out that in some countries with tightly managed exchange rates, a more flexible exchange rate regime that allows the exchange rate to respond to productivity growth differentials relative to trading partner countries could generate positive wealth effects through favorable terms of trade changes. This would encourage private consumption and also reduce the reliance on foreign demand. A more flexible exchange rate, by creating space for more independent monetary policy, could also generate more macroeconomic stability, which in turn would have a more favorable effect on both output and employment growth.

Deepening the financial sector. Prasad (Chapter 13) argues that the development of a broader array of financial markets, including insurance, corporate bond markets, and derivatives markets (such as currency futures) would provide a larger set of instruments for saving and borrowing, which would allow for more efficient risk sharing and intertemporal smoothing of consumption. It would also allow for more diversification opportunities across different types of income (labor versus financial income) and also across different types of assets. Firms would also need to rely less on retained earnings for financing their investment if a broader set of financing opportunities were available. Also, a better-functioning and well-regulated financial system could increase the productive efficiency of capital by channeling funds into more productive uses, providing credit to corporations and entrepreneurs, and enabling more efficient risk sharing which would promote entrepreneurial activity. This would also help promote employment growth.

A further deepening and integration of financial markets could also help support the region's long-term growth by helping to recycle Asia's high savings for investment in worthy projects in the region, particularly when

[5] See Kawai and Pomerleano (2011) for a discussion of systemic stability regulator.

[6] This "forum would bring together all responsible authorities—including finance ministries, central banks, and financial supervisors and regulators—to discuss regional financial market vulnerabilities, regional capital flows, common issues for financial sector supervision and regulation, and efforts at regional financial integration" (p.138).

capital flows from other regions are volatile. Deeper and more integrated financial markets can also provide a "spare tire" to guard against the withdrawal of bank lending from the region during economic downturns.

Prasad also argues that a financial sector that can finance SME businesses—including trade—and consumer purchases of durable goods and residential housing is also quite important to strengthen both the supply and demand sides of the economy. A large segment of the population in poorer economies, particularly in rural areas, does not have access to the formal financial system. This has implications not just for consumption and saving patterns, but also for economic welfare more broadly. Access to a formal financial system would generate better returns on savings and reduce the incentives for households to save more in order to self-insure against health and other risks. It would also give small-scale entrepreneurs the opportunity to raise funds without having to create and use their own savings.

Strengthening regional cooperation. The global financial crisis highlighted the need for policy coordination, not only within regions, but across regions as well. Eichengreen (Chapter 12) argues that policymakers need to ensure that they have access to international liquidity in the event of a liquidity shortage and/or a currency crisis, through the IMF, central bank currency swaps, or a regional arrangement such as the CMIM. Expansion of the CMIM, including strengthening the newly established ASEAN + 3 Macroeconomic Research Office (AMRO), could contribute importantly to creating a regional institution to monitor international risks and provide hard currency liquidity when needed. The creation of an Asian Financial Stability Board can also further the cooperation of fiscal, monetary, and financial authorities in the region.

Asian policymakers need to develop an institutional framework that helps to facilitate better coordination on exchange rates, which will accommodate a general appreciation of their currencies and reduce concerns about unilateral currency appreciation, as well as greater intraregional exchange rate stability. The immediate focus of such cooperation is not necessarily the stabilization of intra-regional exchange rates (although that is helpful in itself) but on increasing the currencies' collective flexibility against the US dollar.

Further development of Asian bond markets (through the Asian Bond Markets Initiative, Asian Bond Funds, and Credit Guarantee and Investment Facility [CGIF]) could provide important support to countries seeking to increase investment for growth, whether for infrastructure or other types of private investment. Development of a market for bonds denominated in an Asian Currency Unit (ACU) could also contribute to widening the regional bond market. Other measures such as encouraging regional credit rating agencies, harmonizing tax rules and regulations on inward investment, and developing an infrastructure for currency hedging and swaps can make regional bond markets more attractive to issuers and investors. An

Asian Infrastructure Investment Fund could facilitate regional infrastructure investment.

Intra-regional trade can be enhanced by more systematically aligning regional cooperation efforts. Institutional mechanisms can be put in place that will facilitate the establishment of a single region-wide free trade agreement that will standardize rules, tariffs, and agreements. This will not only ease implementation but can encourage greater trade across the region.

Reforming the international financial architecture. Reform of the international financial architecture can play a key role in stabilizing financial systems and promoting growth. Asian policymakers should actively participate in forums such as the Group of 20 and the expanded Financial Stability Board to put their imprint on reforms of the global financial system, and support regional cooperation and integration initiatives. Asian economies need to contribute to the reform of global supervision, regulation, and resolution of cross-border financial activities of both systemically important and less important institutions. Recent events have pointed up the problems with a dollar-based reserve system. Here officials from emerging markets may have become more vocal, but they have yet to adequately specify their objectives (Eichengreen, Chapter 12).

Asian policymakers should also aggressively support reforms of both the function and the governance structure of the Bretton Woods institutions, including the IMF and the World Bank. The governance structure of these institutions needs to reflect the increased economic importance and voice of Asia, as well as its successful experience in weathering the current crisis. The effectiveness of these institutions needs to be enhanced to help support growth in emerging economies.

1.7 Japan's triple disasters

On March 11, 2011, Japan was hit by an earthquake which was the biggest recorded in Japanese history and the fourth largest in the world. The tsunami that followed devastated three prefectures in Japan, and damaged the backup electricity generating systems at the Fukushima Daiichi nuclear plant, causing Japan's worst nuclear disaster. The damaged nuclear plant reduced substantially the electric power supply capacity of the Tokyo Electric Power Company (TEPCO) to its service area, which includes industries that produce critical components of the global supply chain. Transport disruptions affected both inputs and outputs of these industries.

Figure 1.3 Real growth rates of Japan's industrial production and exports (2005 = 100)
Sources: Ministry of Economy, Trade and Industry of Japan (METI), Bank of Japan, and the CEIC database, accessed January 31, 2012.

1.7.1 *Impact on Japan's economy*

The impact of the triple disaster on Japan's production and exports became immediately evident. Industrial production plunged year-on-year in March and in subsequent months (Figure 1.3). Export growth rates which closely follow industrial growth rates also plunged.

In the first and second quarter of 2011, GDP plunged by 0.25 percent and 1.8 percent, respectively, compared to the same periods in the previous year. These declines are due partly to the disruptions of the supply chain. At the time of the writing, the Japanese government had passed three supplementary budgets amounting to 18.1 trillion yen for reconstruction purposes so that the economy can quickly recover from the triple disaster.

1.7.2 *Regional and global impacts*

The triple disasters have short-term negative impacts on growth in the rest of Asia as a result of both demand-side and supply-side effects. On the demand side, weaker consumption and investment in Japan will reduce demand for imports from the rest of Asia. On the supply side, disruptions of production supply chains will have negative impacts in some cases, while substitution to other sources of supply in the region will have offsetting positive impacts.

Demand-side impacts on the rest of the region are expected to be small. Japan only represents about 10 percent of emerging Asia's export demand. The country with the largest exposure to Japan is Indonesia (20 percent of total exports), followed by the Philippines, Thailand, and Viet Nam.

Supply-side disruptions, mainly supply chain disruptions as a result of damage to Japanese factories, transportation bottlenecks, and electric power shortages, pose a greater potential problem for other Asian producers. Despite the supply chain disruption caused by the triple disasters, activity in emerging Asia appeared on the whole robust (IMF 2011).

Major industries worldwide have been affected by the supply chain disruptions in Japan, especially in the automobile and electronics sectors. In the automobile sector, many global companies depend on a multitude of Japanese parts, including gears, LCD screens, and sensors of various kinds—even various paint colors. In the electronics sector, Japan's producers have high global market shares in a number of critical segments:

- 30 percent of global flash memory and 15 percent of D-RAM chips
- Difficult-to-replace source for mobile handset parts
- 10 percent of global technology hardware
- 30 percent of lithium-ion battery cells.

These supply chain constraints are expected to ease over time as Japanese suppliers adjust their lines, both in Japan and abroad, and foreign competitors expand production where they are able to do so. In the automobile sector, for example, the recovery of the supply chains has been much faster than expected due to cooperation between parts and components suppliers and auto assemblers (Urata 2011).

Natural disasters including the triple disasters and more recently, the widespread flooding in Thailand, and their related impacts have highlighted how vulnerable the modern manufacturing economy has become to supply chain disruptions. High levels of specialization of production, especially for high value-added products sourced in Japan, physical dispersal of factories, and lean "just-in-time" inventory systems mean that the loss of even one critical part can bring the whole production process to a halt. In the context of growth rebalancing discussed earlier, disaster risk management deserves greater attention both at the national and regional levels.

1.8 Conclusions

Asian economies have already recovered strongly from the global financial crisis, reflecting their aggressive moves to ease monetary and fiscal policy as well as the underlying fundamental strength of their economies. However, the biggest challenge lies ahead. Given that it is unlikely that the US and Europe will be engines of global growth, Asian economies should contribute to global economic adjustment by creating their own growth engines. This is the only way for Asia to be able to sustain long-term economic growth in the post-crisis era, and would also contribute to the growth of the global economy. In order to achieve this, Asia needs to transform itself into a large consumer market while maintaining its competitiveness, by rebalancing sources of growth away from excessive dependence on extra-regional demand—particularly the US and the European Union—toward domestic and regional demand. Asian firms can target the rising high-income and middle class in emerging Asia—the PRC, India, and ASEAN—which could become a major source of final consumption demand. The global crisis should be viewed as a positive opportunity to push ahead with these needed structural changes.

This growth rebalancing effort requires closer policy coordination in Asia in order to pursue structural adjustment, integration of regional markets, and socially inclusive and environmentally sustainable growth. Such cooperation would go a long way in creating the foundations for an Asian economic community. Key elements of this cooperation include measures to: deepen social protection to support social resilience; increase infrastructure investment to create a "seamless Asia"; enhance productivity in the services sector; establish a region-wide FTA to encourage intra-regional trade in goods and services and investment to benefit from economies of scale and the dynamic efficiency of a larger market; promote a shift to a low-carbon society and support green growth; and deepen and integrate the financial sector to facilitate the recycling of Asia's high savings for investment within the region. A stronger, balanced, and more resilient Asian economy, with multiple sources of growth, could provide benefits to the global economy, and be a source of global leadership.

References

ADB and Asian Development Bank Institute (ADBI) (2009). *Infrastructure for a Seamless Asia*. Manila: ADB.

Asian Development Bank (ADB) (2009a). *Asian Development Outlook*. Manila: ADB.

—— (2009b). *Asian Development Outlook 2009 Update*. Manila: ADB.

Bernanke, B. (2005). The Global Saving Glut and the U.S. Current Account Deficit. Remarks at the Homer Jones Lecture, St Louis, Missouri. March 10. Available: http://www.federalreserve.gov/boarddocs/speeches/2005/20050414/default.htm.

—— (2010). Monetary Policy and the Housing Bubble. Speech at the Annual Meeting of the American Economic Association, Atlanta, Georgia. January 3. Available: http://www.federalreserve.gov/newsevents/speech/bernanke20100103a.htm#fs4.

Blanchard, O. J. and F. Giavazzi (2006). Rebalancing Growth in China: A Three-Handed Approach. *China and World Economy* 14(4): 1–20.

de Larosière, J. (2009). *The High Level Group on the Financial Crisis: Report*. Brussels: European Commission.

Financial Services Authority (FSA) (2009). *The Turner Review: A regulatory response to the global banking crisis*. London: FSA.

Freedman, C., M. Kumhof, D. Laxton, and J. Lee (2009). The Case for Global Fiscal Stimulus. IMF Staff Position Note SPN/09/03. Washington, DC: IMF.

Greenspan, A. (2005). Testimony to the Committee on Financial Services, US House of Representatives on the Federal Reserve Board's semiannual Monetary Policy Report. July 20. Available: http://www.federalreserve.gov/boarddocs/hh/2005/july/testimony.htm.

Group of 30 (2009). Financial Reform: A Framework for Financial Stability. Working Group on Financial Reform. Washington, DC: Group of 30. Available: http://www.group30.org/pubs/recommendations.pdf.

International Monetary Fund (2009a). *Global Financial Stability Report. Responding to the Financial Challenges Ahead*. Washington, DC: IMF.

—— (2009b). *Initial Lessons of the Crisis*. Washington, DC: IMF.

—— (2011). Japan: Spillover Report for the 2011 Article IV Consultation and Selected Issues, IMF Country Report No. 11/183. IMF: Washington, DC: IMF. Available: http://www.imf.org/external/pubs/ft/scr/2011/cr11183.pdf.

Kawai, M. (2011). "G-20 Financial Reforms and Emerging Asia's Challenges." In *Asia and Policymaking for the Global Economy*, edited by K. Derviş, M. Kawai, and D. Lombardi, pp. 105–41. Washington, DC: Brookings Institution Press.

Kawai, M. and M. Pomerleano (2011). "Who Should Regulate Systemic Stability Risk? The Relevance for Asia." In *Financial Market Regulation and Reforms in Emerging Markets*, edited by M. Kawai and E. S. Prasad, pp. 171–202. Washington, DC: Brookings Institution Press.

Lee, J. W. and C. Y. Park (2009). Global Financial Turmoil: Impact and Challenges for Asia's Financial Systems. *Asian Economic Papers* 8(1): 9–40.

Ostry, J. D., A. R. Ghosh, K. Habermeier, L. Laeven, M. Chamon, M. S. Qureshi, and A. Kokenyne (2011). "Managing Capital Inflows: What Tools to Use?", IMF Staff Discussion Note SDN/11/06, Washington, DC: IMF.

Taylor, J. (2009). The Financial Crisis and the Policy Responses: An Empirical Analysis of What Went Wrong. NBER Working Paper No. 14631. Cambridge, MA: NBER.

Urata, S. (2011). Keeping Japan's Disaster-Damaged Auto Supply Chains Competitive. *East Asia Forum*. June 15. Available: http://www.eastasiaforum.org.

World Bank (2012). *Global Economic Prospects: Uncertainties and Vulnerabilities*. Washington, DC: The World Bank. January.

Part II

Crisis in the US and Transmission to Europe

2

America's Financial Crisis: The End of an Era

Barry Bosworth and Aaron Flaaen

2.1 Introduction

Over the past quarter century, American economists and policymakers have been very active in providing policy advice to other countries about how to avoid and/or manage financial crises. In many cases the essence of the advice was "you should be more like us". Suddenly, the United States (US) has been hit by its own financial crisis—one that is extraordinary in both its breadth and severity. While prior financial panics in individual countries or regions have involved output declines of equal or greater magnitude, the global dimensions of the current crisis are unprecedented. The crisis began in the US, but has now spread to the rest of the world economy. The transmission channel with Europe has been largely through a linkage of financial markets and institutions on both sides of the Atlantic that shared some of the same flaws and excesses. But for Asia and much of the developing world, the transmission has been largely through an extraordinary collapse of global trade.

This chapter summarizes some research on the origins of the crisis, traces the evolution of the credit panic that hit in late 2008, its impact on the real economy, and the extraordinary policy actions that have been taken to mitigate the economic losses. As with past financial crises, the current downturn will end and the economy will recover. However, as we argue below, the crisis will likely come to represent a major regime change, greatly altering the future shape of the US and global economies. The era of self-regulation of financial institutions is over, and the role of monetary policy has been greatly altered. The binge of consumer spending also seems to have come to an end, as households focus on rebuilding their balance sheets. If the US is to restore full employment, it must not only rebuild its financial industries but also rejuvenate its export industries and achieve a more balanced external position. This raises two challenges for the rest of the global economy. First, they must develop new drivers of demand growth; countries will not be able to rely on growing exports to the US market, and they will need to emphasize the development of domestic and regional markets. Second, frustration with the effort to develop export markets in a time of slow global growth may push politicians toward a more protectionist policy stance.

2.2 Origins

The precise causes of the financial crisis remain surprisingly controversial. Much of the recent analysis has emphasized the role of developments within the US housing and financial markets. Home prices began to rise rapidly in the late 1990s and, by the year 2000, had far exceeded the growth in either incomes or rent values (Figure 2.1). At their peak in 2006, home prices were nearly 50 percent above a norm defined by their historical relationship to household income. Most analysts point to the excesses of the subprime

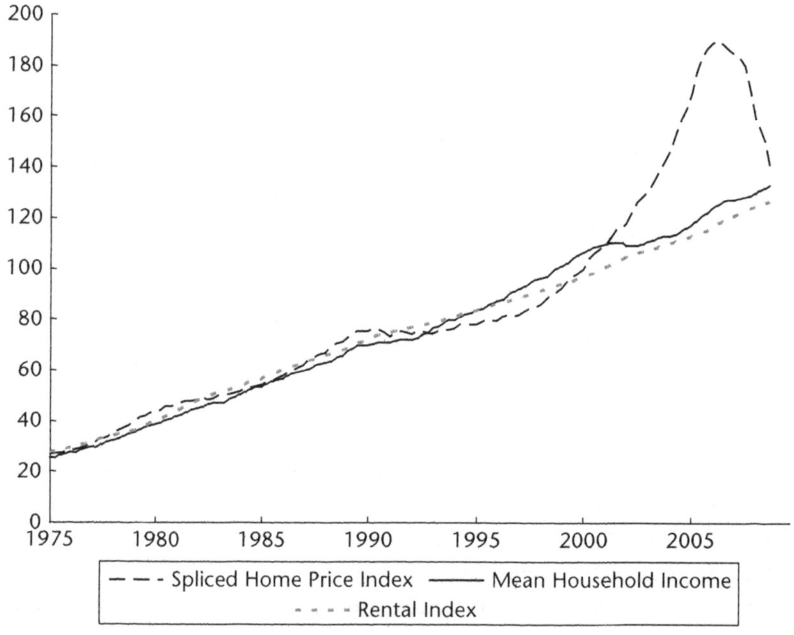

Figure 2.1 Household income, home prices and rental index 1975Q1–2008Q4 (2000Q1 = 100)

Sources: Standard and Poor's (2009), Census Bureau (2007), and Bureau of Economic Analysis (BEA) (2009).

Notes: The Spliced Home Price index extends the Case-Shiller index backwards for 1975–86 using the OFHEO home price index. Quarterly mean HH income is linearly interpolated from Census annual data and then adjusted so that the average over four quarters equals annual income exactly. The income and rental indices are adjusted so that their average over the period through 2001 equals that of the home price index. Fourth quarter 2008 income values are extrapolated.

mortgage market in the US and the subsequent transformation of those assets into exotic secondary market instruments as key factors that led to the housing price bubble. The bursting of this bubble and the subsequent collapse of the market for subprime mortgages initiated a chain-like collapse of markets for securitized assets and a crisis of confidence among financial institutions.

Some economists argue, however, that the excesses in the housing and mortgage-backed securities markets were merely proximate causes and point to what they regard as more fundamental determinants that created an environment in which the speculative excesses of the real estate and securitized asset markets could flourish. They emphasize either (1) a US monetary policy that remained stimulative for too long after the 2002 recession (Taylor 2009) or (2) excess saving outside the US that drove down global interest rates to levels that fueled the speculation. While both of these hypotheses could serve to explain the consequent bubble in US asset prices, they do not provide an immediate explanation as to why defaults in a relatively small portion of the credit markets (subprime mortgages) had such catastrophic, system-wide consequences.

The subprime market. Subprime mortgages were originally perceived as a beneficial development whereby a greater proportion of low-income, minorities, and higher-risk households could be granted access to financial markets and the opportunity to become homeowners. The marketing of the subprime, alt-A, and home equity loans relied on independent mortgage originators who were part of a financial network that developed in parallel to the issuance and securitization of conventional mortgages by the government-sponsored enterprises (GSEs).[1] The system of securitization operated by the GSEs established strict standards for conforming mortgages, requiring full documentation of the borrower's financial condition and the valuation of the property. In contrast, the subprime market operated with fewer constraints. The originators wrote the mortgage loans, provided a short-term guarantee (usually 90 days), and sold the loans to private arrangers who subsequently pooled the mortgages and issued securities that were backed by the mortgage pool. As a substitute for the GSE guarantees, mortgage-backed securities were rolled over into collateralized debt obligations (CDOs), which were sold in a series of tranches where the junior tranches absorbed the initial defaults and senior tranches were viewed as very secure and were often assigned an AAA rating.

The network of subprime operations was essentially unregulated and the originators in particular operated with less concern about reputational issues

[1] Alt-A is a designation for mortgages that are deemed riskier than prime mortgages but not as risky as subprime mortgages. Typically, alt-A mortgage borrowers are characterized as people without full documentation, higher than average loan-to-value ratios, or lower credit scores.

or loan quality. With minimal capital requirements, the costs of entry and exit from the industry were low. Subprime mortgages often incorporated low down payment requirements and a significant prepayment penalty.[2] Underwriting standards declined as loan originators focused on collecting fees on loans that they quickly resold. Due to the complexity and lack of transparency in these markets, purchasers of the mortgage-backed securities in the secondary market also failed to accurately evaluate the quality of the underlying assets and to understand the risks involved. Because regulators were largely absent, the major source of information on the risks of the mortgage-backed securities were the credit rating agencies—principally consisting of Standard & Poor's, Fitch, and Moody's. Yet these agencies also failed to provide an accurate assessment of risk. The credit rating agencies received payment for their ratings directly from the issuers of the financial products being rated, thereby creating a clear conflict of interest and a subsequent tendency for issuers to "shop around" for the agency willing to give them the highest rating. The result was a broad underestimate of the degree of risk associated with these new securities, and the sheer complexity of their design prevented many from taking a closer look.

The non-prime mortgages described above expanded from 15 percent of new originations in 2001 to 50 percent in 2006. The proportion of these mortgages that were securitized also rose sharply over the same period to reach 90 percent in 2007. By 2005, subprime mortgages represented about US$2.5 trillion out of a total residential mortgage stock of about US$11 trillion. The greater risk of the subprime mortgages is evident in the 12 percent of outstanding loans that are in foreclosure, compared to less than 2 percent for conforming mortgages. Many housing analysts assert that without the prominent role of subprime mortgages, the increase in home prices would have been choked off at a much earlier stage: potential buyers would not have been able to obtain a conforming mortgage at such elevated levels relative to their incomes.

The growth of the subprime mortgage market was accompanied by a number of other financial innovations that camouflaged risk. When subprime mortgages began to default in large numbers it became difficult to accurately trace through the implications for the valuations of the CDOs, which did not trade on organized markets. That rapid growth of these securities within off-balance sheet entities called structured investment vehicles (SIVs) also led to large increases in the size of the issuing institutions without a matching increase in capital. The lower capital requirements associated with such SIVs

[2] There are a number of papers that review the operations of the subprime market and its role in initiating the financial crisis. We found the following to be particularly useful: Gramlich (2007); Baily, Litan, and Johnson (2008); Gorton (2008); Ashcraft and Schuerman (2008), and Hatzius (2008).

allowed these financial institutions (often investment banking firms) to dramatically increase their effective leverage ratios.

Further problems arose in the means by which financial institutions financed their off-balance sheet activities. The long-term assets such as mortgage-backed securities and CDOs were financed by issuing short-term liabilities such as asset-backed commercial paper (ABCP) and overnight repurchase agreements. According to Baily, Litan, and Johnson (2008), of the enormous growth in the issuance of ABCP from around US$30 billion in February 2005 to over US$80 billion in early 2008, nearly all had a maturity of between one and four days. Because these liabilities were cheaper than long-term borrowing, they allowed financial institutions to fund their high-value mortgage-backed assets at a substantial margin. While asset prices continued to rise, rolling over these short-term commitments did not pose a serious problem. It was not until credit markets dried up and risk premiums increased sharply in 2008 that financial institutions found themselves not only with falling asset prices but also exposed to a severe maturity mismatch. As banks were forced to move the SIVs onto their balance sheet or were unable to rollover their short-term liabilities, their leverage ratios increased further.

The emphasis on subprime mortgage defaults and the consequent insolvency of major financial firms as the primary cause of the recession highlights concern about the risks of financial innovation. Past innovations were perceived as major contributors to growth and the efficiency of the US financial system and a rationale for sharply limiting regulation. Yet, the costs of this crisis will outweigh the benefits of financial market innovations for decades to come.

Fundamental factors. Asset market bubbles like that of the US housing market have been common throughout history, and the rapid price rise was not limited to the US alone. From 1997 to 2007, housing prices were rising even more rapidly in several European countries, including Spain, Ireland, and the United Kingdom. Some researchers suggest that the repetitive nature of asset price bubbles and the cross-national pattern of the housing price increases point to more fundamental underlying causal factors than innovations in US mortgage markets alone. The most obvious candidate is a low level of nominal and real interest rates in the US and in the global economy. The inflation adjustment for the United States is based on a survey of inflation expectations.[3] Lacking a measure of inflation expectations for other countries, we constructed an alternative estimate of the real bond rate using a Hodrick-

[3] The measure of the real interest rate is constructed using survey data on 10-year expected inflation from the Survey of Professional Forecasters (1990–2007), and a survey of financial market participants for 1981–89. Expected inflation for years before 1981 was constructed by the staff of the Federal Reserve. The data were obtained from Clark and Nakata (2008).

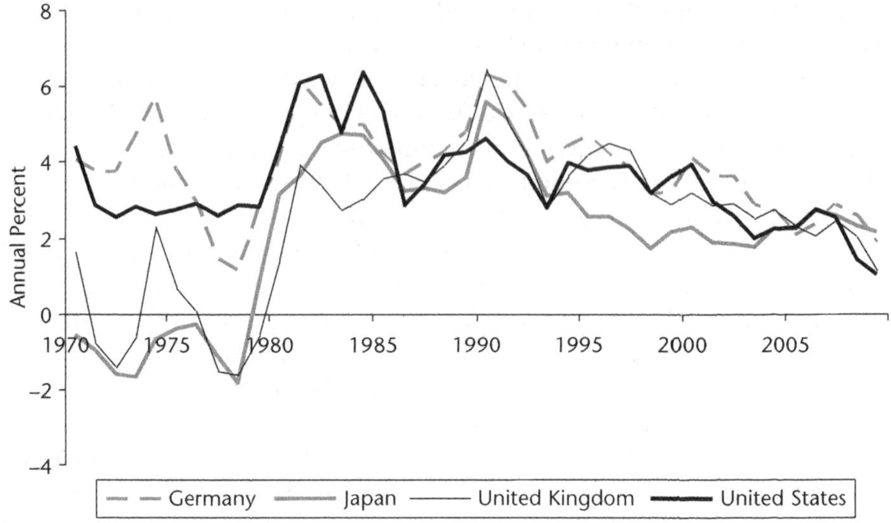

Figure 2.2 Real long-term interest rates: United States, United Kingdom, Germany, and Japan

Sources: United States: Federal Reserve Bank of New York and Bureau of Economic Research (BEA); United Kingdom, Germany, and Japan: Organization for Economic Cooperation and Development (OECD).

Note: Real rates calculated based on GDP price deflators using a Hodrick-Prescott filter. The consumer price index (CPI) is used for Germany and Japan.

Prescott filter to smooth the actual inflation rate. The results are shown in Figure 2.2 for Germany, Japan, the UK, and the US.[4] Both nominal and real interest rates have fallen to levels not seen since the 1970s and there has been a marked convergence across countries; nevertheless, the decline in real rates has been ongoing for the past quarter century, and they do not seem abnormally low by the standards of the 1970s or earlier decades.[5] Thus, it is not evident that the extent of the decline or the absolute level of real interest rates in the current decade is unprecedented. The current low level of interest rates, however, is at the center of explanations that place the blame for the financial crisis on either mistakes in US monetary policy or an excess of global saving.

Taylor (2009) offers the most prominent critique of US monetary policy in the years leading up to the crisis. He asserts that the monetary authorities, by holding short-term rates at too low a level in the aftermath of the 2002 recession, contributed in a major way to the housing price bubble of 2003–06. He conducted a counterfactual simulation showing that a monetary policy more consistent with the rules-based approach of 1980–2000 would have

[4] Quarterly data on nominal interest rates and GDP price deflators was taken from the data files of the OECD.

[5] The behavior of nominal and real rates over the past 150 years in the US was examined in Summers (1983).

raised interest rates, cut off the boom in the housing market at an earlier stage, and, by inference, prevented many of the excesses that developed in the subprime market. In their defense, the monetary authorities were seeking in 2002–03 to counter what was widely seen as a jobless recovery in the midst of low inflation. When growth accelerated in early 2004, policy did change and interest rates were steadily increased over the next two years. Thus, much of the discrepancy between Federal Reserve Board policy and Taylor's preferred path is limited to 2002–03.

Alternatively, some economists have linked the mortgage market crisis to the large external imbalances of prior years and what they perceive to have been an excess of saving outside the US. That argument gained momentum after a speech by Ben Bernanke in 2005 in which he asserted that, rather than the US saving too little, the rest of the world saves too much (Bernanke 2005). It became fashionable to focus on the saving-investment (S-I) balances of the surplus countries, rather than that of the US. In effect, the US was perceived as passively accommodating imbalances that originated in Asia after the 1997–98 financial crisis (Cooper 2008). The capital inflows in turn drove down real interest rates and enabled the excess consumption and speculative excesses in the US.[6] That perspective has gained popularity in the US, where an increasing number of economists have written about the saving surplus that emerged in the People's Republic of China (PRC) in 2005 and later years.[7] In contrast to Taylor, advocates of the surfeit of saving perspective trace the low level of interest rates to global factors outside the US. However, both explanations go on to relate the excesses of a house-price bubble and exorbitant risk-taking in the subprime market due to low interest rates.

Given the accounting identity that global saving must match global investment, it is not very meaningful to simply divide the global aggregate into two regions and assign a direction of causality, as Bernanke did. If the US has a large current account deficit, the rest of the world, by definition, must have a surplus. It is equally difficult to attribute a current account surplus either to an excess of saving or a shortfall of investment without constructing a counterfactual. In addition, a focus on *ex post* saving and investment may be a poor guide to a priori plans.

[6] One of the most developed models is presented in Caballero, Farhi, and Gourinchas (2008). The perspective of excess saving outside the US as the primary cause of low interest rates is echoed in the comments of Lawrence Summers, Bradford DeLong, and Richard Cooper at the 2008 conference where the paper of Caballero and others was presented. See also Cooper (2008).

[7] In some respects, it is reminiscent of the debate between the US and Japan on the origins of the two countries' external imbalances in the 1980s. In that period, US economists emphasized excess saving and a current account surplus in Japan as a primary cause of the external imbalances between the two countries, whereas Japanese policymakers pointed to a large public sector deficit and declining private saving in the US.

Regional saving and investment patterns are summarized in Figure 2.3. The S-I balance of the US, shown in Panel 1, shows a longstanding decline in saving that began in the early 1980s. A portion of the recent drop can be traced to the re-occurrence of sustained negative saving in the public sector, but the private saving rate has also remained at historically low levels. On the other hand, the US has continued to offer very good investment opportunities—superior to those of most other industrial countries—and the investment rate shows no secular pattern of decline comparable to that for saving. The result has been heavy reliance on foreign capital inflows, but with few strains as foreigners also perceived the US as offering attractive investment opportunities. Prior to the crisis, rates of both saving and investment have declined in advanced economies other than the US (Panel 2), but largely in a parallel fashion that led to no consistent shift in the S-I balance.

As shown in the third panel, the economies of emerging Asia have long had extraordinarily high rates of saving and investment. The high investment rate was tied to their rapid rates of overall economic growth and the need for a matching expansion of the capital stock. Similarly high rates of income growth are associated with elevated rates of saving and it may be that the saving has been augmented by a sharp reduction in the birth rate (Bosworth and Chodorow-Reich 2006). However, it is strikingly apparent that the large change in the S-I balance is on the investment side, due to its limited recovery in the aftermath of the 1997–98 financial crisis. There is also a rise in the S-I surplus in the PRC after 2004 and the emergence of a large current account surplus (Panel 4). The result of these regional patterns of saving and investment has been the current account balances shown in Table 2.1 in which the US has an extraordinarily large deficit and the other regions of the world are in net surplus. However, the change relative to the 1990s is in the growth of the US deficit and the increased surpluses of emerging Asia and the Middle East.

We construct a normative standard for evaluating saving and investment in each region by estimating a "warranted" rate of investment that is based on the trend rate of growth of output and an assumed constant capital–output ratio. That is, we estimated the rate of investment required to maintainbalanced growth along an estimated potential output path. The warranted investment rate, $\bar{I}/Y$, is defined as

$$\bar{I}/Y = (g + d) \cdot k, \tag{1}$$

where g = trend growth of output,
d = depreciation rate,
k = capital–output ratio.

Specific values for each region are shown in Table 2.2. The trend growth rate is based on the estimated annual growth of GDP over the period of 1995–2007, and the depreciation rates and capital–output ratios are averages taken from

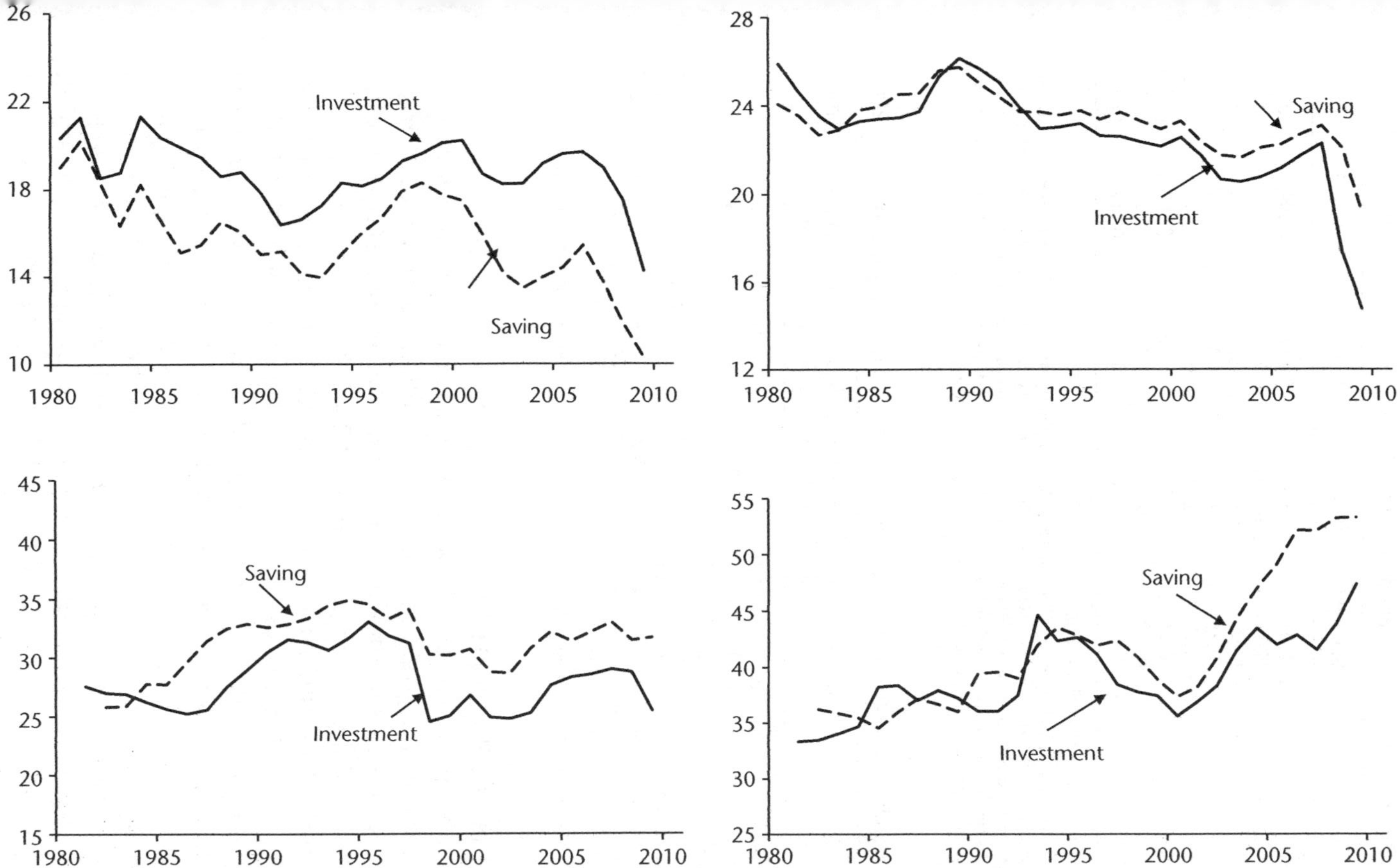

Figure 2.3 Saving and investment 1980–2009, regional averages, percent of GNI

Panel 1: United States

Panel 2: Industrial Countries (excluding US)

Panel 3: Emerging Asia (excluding the PRC)

Panel 4: The PRC

Table 2.1 Current account as a share of world GDP, selected regions and years[a] (%)

Region	1980–89	1990–99	2000–05	2006–08	2009
Emerging Asia	(0.01)	0.06	0.38	0.89	0.81
Emerging Latin America	(0.11)	(0.14)	(0.02)	0.04	(0.03)
Europe	(0.01)	0.08	0.22	0.16	0.15
Japan	0.26	0.36	0.35	0.33	0.24
Middle East	0.13	(0.03)	0.20	0.48	0.13
Other countries	(0.31)	(0.21)	(0.00)	(0.12)	(0.23)
US	(0.50)	(0.43)	(1.41)	(1.34)	(0.65)
Discrepancy	0.54	0.30	0.27	(0.44)	(0.42)

Source: IMF World Economic Outlook, April 2011.

[a] In this table, Emerging Asia = Hong Kong, China; India; Indonesia; Korea; Malaysia; Philippines; Singapore; Taipei, China; Thailand, and the PRC. First column average is for 1982–89. Emerging Latin America = Argentina, Brazil, Chile, Columbia, Ecuador, Mexico, Peru, Venezuela. Europe = Austria, Belgium, Denmark, Finland, France, Germany, Greece, Ireland, Italy, the Netherlands, Norway, Portugal, Spain, Sweden, Switzerland, and the United Kingdom. Middle East = Bahrain, Egypt, Iran, Jordan, Kuwait, Lebanon, Libya, Oman, Qatar, Saudi Arabia, Syria, UAE, and Yemen.

Table 2.2 Warranted investment vs. actual investment: select economy groups, 2002–2007

	World	United States	Advanced Economies	Developing Economies	Emerging Asia	PRC
Actual investment	22.2	19.0	20.8	27.2	27.3	41.5
Actual saving	22.4	14.2	22.2	30.3	31.4	47.5
Capital–output ratio	2.8	3.0	3.0	2.5	2.5	2.5
Depreciation	5.0	5.0	5.0	5.0	5.0	5.0
Trend output growth	3.1	3.0	2.7	5.5	7.6	9.6
Warranted investment rate	22.2	24.1	23.2	26.3	31.5	36.6

Source: International Monetary Fund, 2009.

Note: The PRC values for saving and investment are taken from World Bank: World Development Indicators (2009).

Bosworth and Collins (2003). The bottom portions of the table report the warranted investment rate and the actual saving and investment rates for the global economy, US economy, aggregate of other advanced economies, developing economies, economies of emerging markets of East Asia (excluding the PRC), and the PRC over the period of 2002–07.

The warranted investment rate for the global economy is estimated at 22 percent, which is very close to the observed average for 2002–07. Thus, judged by this standard, recent rates of global saving and investment seem quite normal. The warranted investment rate of the US is estimated to be slightly higher than the global average because of a higher capital–output ratio. However, the striking feature in the US is the extremely low level of national saving, which is sufficient to finance only 60 percent of long-run investment needs. Actual rates of investment also appear a little low in 2002–07, perhaps because the falling relative price of capital goods has reduced the nominal magnitudes.[8] In developing countries and the emerging economies of East Asia, the higher long-term output growth rates yield much higher estimates of the warranted rate of investment, but there are indications of an excess of saving in the current decade that becomes particularly large after 2004. The surplus also seems particularly large in East Asia (and the PRC in particular) where both actual saving and investment are well above the warranted rate. In addition, the measures for the developing economies included the very large surplus in the oil-producing states of the Middle East. Overall, it is hard to support the view that global saving is particularly high. Instead, it seems misallocated across regions relative to investment. It is not evident that those imbalances should translate into a particularly strong impact on the level of global interest rates.

The methodology does leave a considerable range of uncertainty, however. We used a lower capital–output ratio for the developing countries (2.5) than the advanced economies (3.0), but it might be reasonable to argue for a higher marginal rate in the former as part of a catch-up process. If we use the same marginal capital–output ratio in both regions, there is a small saving deficiency in the developing world as a whole, but still a surplus in East Asia. In both regions, the actual rate of investment falls short of that required for balanced growth. While the regional imbalances in saving and investment are sufficient to account for the regional imbalances in trade flows, it is difficult to believe that the relatively small deviations of global saving from our investment norm or from the historical average are sufficient to provide the basis for an ever-declining real interest rate and a global financial crisis. It implies an extraordinary fragility of financial markets.

The emphasis on foreign capital inflows into the US as the primary causal factor also presents some puzzles. First, the US exchange rate fell continuously from mid-2002 up to the intensification of the crisis in the fall of 2008. The JP Morgan trade-weighted real exchange rate indicates a 30 percent decline over the six years (Figure 2.4).

If the motivating force behind the global imbalances was a strong demand for dollar-denominated assets, we would have expected a currency appreciation.[9] Second, we do not see any evidence of a widening of risk spreads between BAA corporate and government bond rates within the US, as would be expected if the inflows were motivated by a foreign demand for the safest assets. Instead, risk differentials decline in the years after the 2002 recession

[8] In addition, the US has long reported a much lower level of general government investment than other countries.

[9] The exchange rate index of the Federal Reserve shows a smaller 25 percent decline. The difference is largely due to the use of the consumer price index (CPI) in the Federal Reserve measure compared to wholesale prices excluding food and fuel in the JP Morgan index. Differences in the trade weights used for aggregation also have some effect.

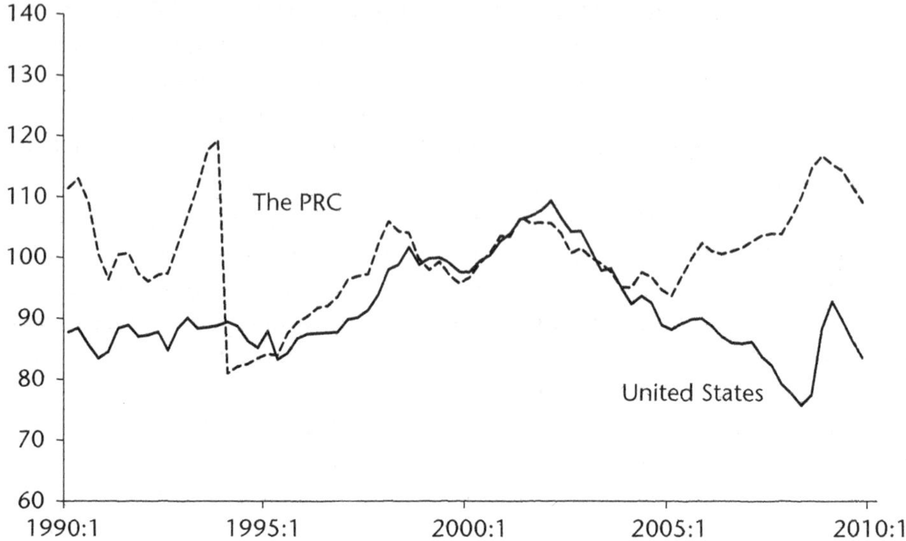

Figure 2.4 Trade-weighted exchange rate, 1990–2010
Source: JP Morgan real broad effective exchange rate indices, June 2011.

and were slightly smaller than the average of the 1990s right up to the onset of the crisis. Instead, investors seemed relatively unconcerned about risk.

Another complication with the capital flows explanation is the possibility that the wealth effect associated with rising housing prices led to a consumption boom, which in turn drove the US current account into greater deficits. Thus, the direction of causation could run from increased house prices to capital flows, rather than the other way around. Aizenman and Jinjarak (2008) formally explore the relationship between current account balances (and hence capital flows) and the relative prices of national real estate markets. While they generally identify the causation as flowing from past current account deficits to present real estate price increases in a panel of countries, a Granger causality exercise for the US alone does suggest the presence of a two-way causality between housing wealth and the current account. Another study by Bracke and Fidora (2008) uses a structural VAR analysis to distinguish between the "excess liquidity" and "saving glut" hypotheses. They interpret their results as suggesting that excess monetary liquidity is the more important factor.

In summary, it seems reasonable to argue that a low level of global interest rates contributed to the asset price boom in housing markets and the speculative excesses. However, low real rates also characterized earlier decades without leading to the speculative excesses we have recently witnessed. We believe that the main reason for the speculative excesses is that the low interest rates of recent years impinged on a substantially different financial structure, especially in the US. The evolution of financial markets in the intervening years gradually led to behavior that encouraged speculative activity and systematically made it both more difficult for financial firm executives to evaluate risk and more rewarding to tilt the emphasis toward short-term gains in making risk-reward trade-offs. The promotion of new financial innovations (the "originate and distribute" lending model, CDOs, and over-the-counter sale of derivatives) without a rigorous effort to evaluate their implications for systemic risk, a compensation system that emphasized high immediate returns, and a compliant financial regulatory structure all stand out as important direct contributors.[10] It is difficult to explain the crisis in terms of macroeconomic conditions without reference to the microeconomic distortions in the US financial system.

2.3 The financial panic of 2008

The housing price bubble burst in mid-2006 and both housing prices and housing starts began a long period of contraction (Figure 2.5). With declining home prices, borrowers were unable to refinance their loans and default rates soared (Figure 2.6). Against this backdrop, problems in the markets for

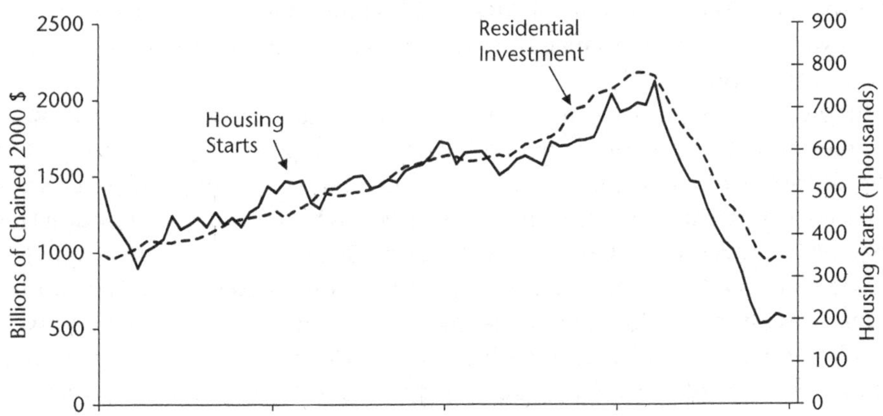

Figure 2.5 US housing starts and residential investment, 1990–2009
Sources: U.S. Census and BEA.

[10] The role of compensation schemes is discussed in Bebchuk and Fried (2003).

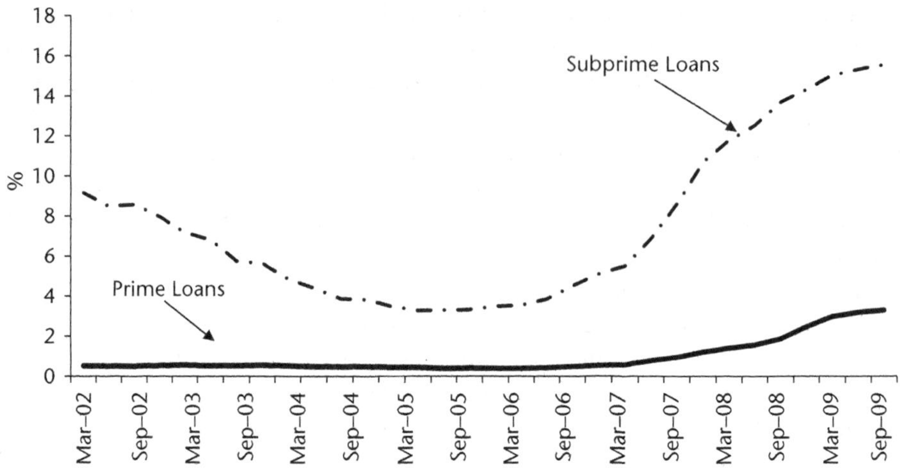

Figure 2.6 Foreclosure inventory at end of quarter, 2002–2009 by loan type
Source: Mortgage Bankers Association.

mortgages and mortgage-backed securities festered for over two years. The situation exploded into a full-blown financial panic only in September of 2008 with three major events: the government takeover of Fannie Mae and Freddie Mac on 8 September, the Lehman bankruptcy on 15 September, and the Federal Reserve's bailout of AIG on 16 September. In all three cases, the firms were unable to refinance their debt because of increasing investor/partner uncertainty.

In the case of the two mortgage firms, the basic problem seemed quite simple: they departed from their core function of providing support for the securitization of high quality mortgages and began engaging in large-scale purchases on their own account of high-risk, high-yield subprime mortgages that did not meet their own underwriting standards. They lacked the capital to support such activities, and once the government stepped in with a guarantee, private investors fled in fear of a takeover that would wipe out their equity.

Lehman was in some respects a bank, but with the critical distinction that, unlike the deposits of a commercial bank, its short-term liabilities were not insured. Thus, when rumors spread about losses on its longer-term assets—particularly mortgages—it could not sustain a refinancing requirement that amounted to about US$100 billion per month. Lehman was a major participant in the market for mortgage-backed securities (MBS) and CDOs. It became a prime example of the difficulties of valuing these financial instruments and the uncertainties surrounding the solvency of the institutions that held them. The crisis of confidence spread to the remaining investment banks that were either taken over by merger or converted to holding companies under the Federal Reserve's supervision. A large money market fund failed or "broke the buck" after writing off debt from Lehman. The result was a run on mutual funds and a disruption of the commercial paper market.

AIG had become a major provider of credit default swaps (CDS) that serve as insurance contracts against default for a wide range of financial instruments. The purchaser makes periodic payments in return for a payoff in the event of a default on a specified financial instrument. Their issuance is unregulated, however, and the purchaser need not actually own the underlying insured instrument. Thus, like other financial derivatives, the CDS can serve as a tool of either hedging or speculation. It is also sold over the counter rather than on organized exchanges. The market has grown at an explosive rate from about US$1 trillion in 2000 to over US$50 trillion by mid-2008.

Initially, AIG was effectively selling its AAA rating to debt issuers of lower quality; but once the magnitude of its activities became known and the performance of the original debt issuers deteriorated, AIG lost its high-quality rating and began to face pressures from counterparties to increase the collateral behind the insurance. That pushed the firm into a large negative cash flow position and forced it to sell assets at discounted prices.

Precipitated by the failure or government takeover of these three institutions, and amidst growing pressures for a more coordinated and systematic response, the Bush administration requested US$700 billion in funds from Congress on 19 September. The Troubled Asset Relief Plan (TARP) was initially voted down by Congress on 29 September, but later passed on 3 October. In the intervening period, the financial panic had spread to incorporate the broader equity markets. Between 19 September and 9 October, the stock market plummeted by 28 percent. In addition, a general loss of confidence and extraordinary levels of uncertainty led to a freezing of significant portions of the financial system.

Half the TARP funds were disbursed over the remainder of 2008. The stock market fell sharply again in early 2009 when the new Obama administration failed to produce a decisive plan to deal with the financial problems. Meanwhile, the Federal Reserve reduced the federal funds rate to 0–0.25 percent and created a wide range of lending facilities to supply credit directly to submarkets of the financial system.

While the difficulties of the banks have occupied most of the public's attention, it is important to remember that they account for only a portion of total credit flows in the US economy. In the years prior to the crisis, 70–80 percent of the borrowing of nonfinancial borrowers was in the form of loans from commercial banks and similar direct-lending institutions. However, large portions of that debt were subsequently securitized and reissued as marketable debt instruments. After deducting reissuance of asset-backed securities (ABS), commercial banks' share of the debt issues declined to an average of 40 percent in 2000–06, and direct-market lending grew in importance. The market for agency issues of mortgage-backed securities has continued to function, but funds raised through ABS issues, which accounted for 25 percent of the credit flow in 2000–06, turned negative in late 2007 and contracted by US$400 billion in 2008 and $740 billion in 2009. Thus, the freezing of credit flows in late 2008 extended beyond the banking sector alone.

2.4 Real sector implications

Up to September 2008, few forecasters anticipated a serious economic decline. The general expectation was that the fall in housing construction would be offset by an expansion of exports, as a declining dollar would strengthen the country's competitive position. For example, the Congressional Budget Office (CBO) published a budget update in early September that reflected its survey of a wide range of private economic forecasts. GDP growth was estimated to be slightly above 1 percent annually in 2008 and 2009, and a recovery with a 3.6 percent growth rate was projected for 2010. In the aftermath of the September financial turmoil, GDP declined by a 9 percent annual rate in the fourth quarter and continued to decline in to the middle of 2009. Unemployment rose to over 9.5 percent of the labor force. In its January 2009 assessment, the CBO reduced its projected level of GDP by 4 percent for 2009 and 6 percent for 2010 and 2011. Similar large revisions are evident in the IMF projections for the global economy. Clearly, the events of September had a very large impact on expectations of the future course of the economy.

In the fourth-quarter of 2008, production losses were very widespread. Consumption contributed 3.5 percentage points to the decline, and investment accounted for another 5.5 percentage points. In addition, international trade was severely disrupted: while the fall in exports subtracted 3 percentage points from the GDP growth, it was more than offset by an even larger drop in imports. Government spending recorded a small positive growth. The CBO's March 2009 economic forecast, published after passage of the economic stimulus program, projected a 3 percent drop in GDP in 2009, followed by a return to a 3 percent growth rate in 2010. According to the CBO, the unemployment rate would rise from 4.7 percent in 2007 to 9 percent in 2010, but decline rapidly in the following years. Both the Administration and the CBO projected rapid recovery.

The projections of the administration and the CBO seem optimistic, particularly because of the delays in establishing a program for resolving the mortgage and financial sector problems. While past recessions have tended to be V-shaped, with a sharp contraction of economic activity followed by an equally sharp expansion, recoveries from financial crises seem more gradual and are normally stretched out over several years (Reinhart and Rogoff 2008).

One major reason for anticipating a slow recovery involves the very large wealth losses experienced by households. Despite a near zero rate of saving, the wealth–income ratio within the household sector, driven by capital gains, rose dramatically over the past quarter century from an average of 4.8 in 1960–80 to a peak of 6.3 during the dot.com bubble of 2000. After the 2002 recession, it recovered to a peak of 6.5 in 2006, mainly as a reflection of rising home prices. The most straightforward explanation for the low rate of household saving during the period is this large increase in the stock of household wealth. If consumption is a function of income and wealth, the saving rate will be inversely related to the wealth–income ratio. As shown in Figure 2.7, capital gains were more than sufficient to offset the decline in saving throughout the 1990s and the current decade. But at valuations in effect at the end of 2008, the wealth–income ratio has fallen back to the historical average of 4.8 percent. Thus, it would seem that households may need to devote several years of increased saving to rebuild their financial balance sheets. If that is the case, consumption can be expected to remain 2–3 percent of GDP below the share that was prevalent prior to the crisis.

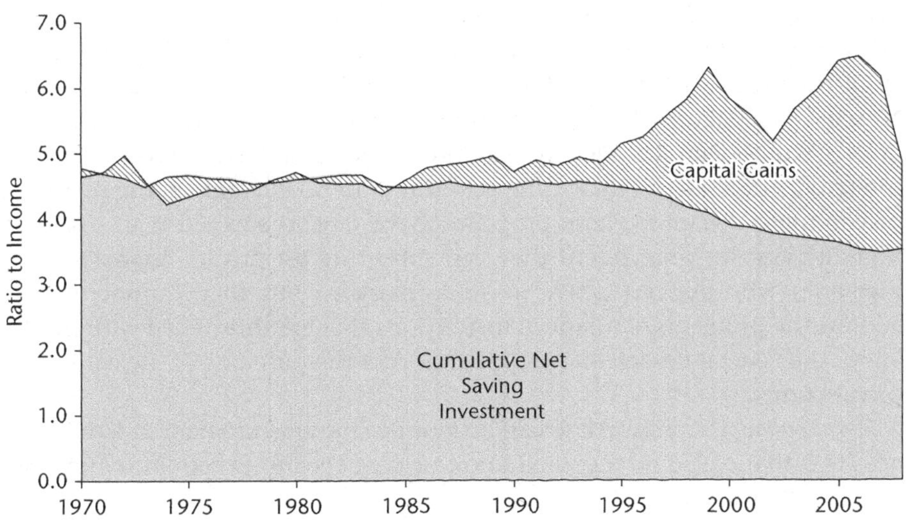

Figure 2.7 Household wealth as a ratio to income: 1970–2008

Source: Computed from tables B100 and R100 of the Flow of Funds Accounts. Cumulative Net saving flows are converted to real values, cumulated, and converted back to nominal values.

2.5 The policy response

American policy reacted to the post-September events in a very aggressive fashion. The traditional tool of monetary policy was quickly exhausted as the target for the benchmark federal funds rate was reduced to between zero and 0.25 percent. The Federal Reserve moved on to implement a radical range of new policy actions involving direct participation in markets for private securities. Congress also approved a multi-year fiscal stimulus program that amounts to 2 percent of GDP in 2009 and 2010 before tailing off in later years. However, the government has stumbled in its efforts to clean up and restore the financial system.

Monetary policy. The Federal Reserve began to ease interest rates in September 2007, and by the end of 2008, the federal funds rate had been effectively reduced to zero. However, even before the Bear-Stearns bankruptcy in March 2008, the Federal Reserve began to expand its operations into non-traditional areas that came to involve the direct supply of credit to a wide range of financial markets. Most notable are: (1) a Commercial Paper Funding Facility (CPFF), which finances the purchase of commercial paper directly from eligible issuers; (2) the Term Auction Facility (TAF), which allows banks and other financial institutions to pledge collateral in exchange for a loan; and (3) the direct purchase of mortgage-backed securities issued by the three government-sponsored enterprises. In addition, the Federal Reserve was active in restoring the operation of securitization markets through the Term Asset-Backed Securities Loan Facility (TALF).

The sum of these actions has seen the balance sheet of the Federal Reserve swell from under US$900 billion in August of 2008 to over US$2 trillion by March 2009 (Figure 2.8).[11] In addition, responding to a global shortage of dollars, the Federal Reserve engaged in currency swap arrangements with 14 foreign central banks. Finally, the government also guaranteed the new debt of commercial banks. These programs have largely succeeded in restoring liquidity and to some extent they can substitute for private financial intermediaries who are not active in some markets; but they cannot directly address the problems of financial institutions that are threatened with insolvency. The Federal Reserve has stopped short of the purchase of the equities of private firms.

Fiscal policy. Congress passed an economic stimulus program in late February 2009 that called for a combination of tax cuts and expenditure increases

[11] Some of the new policy measures were adopted prior to September, but their effect was largely limited to the composition as opposed to the size of the Fed's balance sheet. These activities are sometimes referred to as quantitative easing, but the term does not really fit. The focus is not on increasing the supply of money, but rather the intervention in specific credit markets to influence both the maturity structure and risk premiums on interest rates for different forms of private credit.

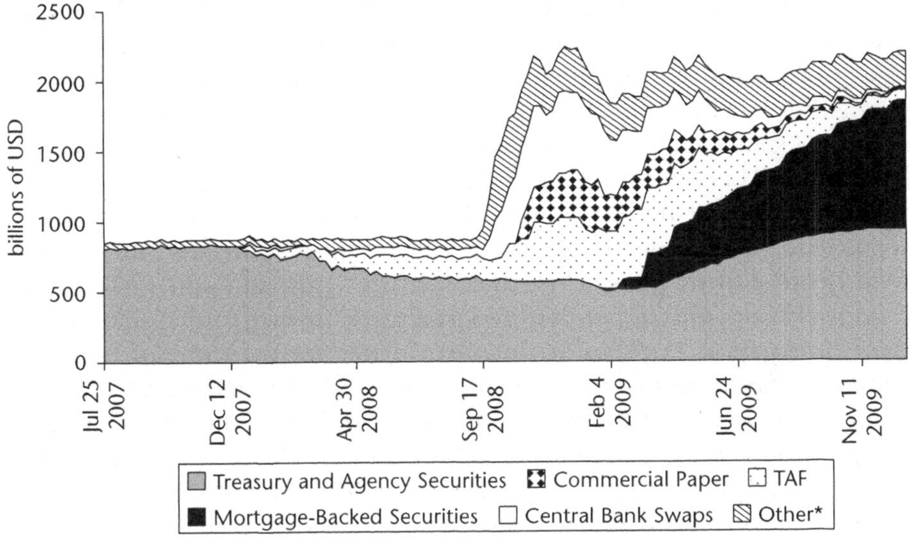

Figure 2.8 Balance sheet of the Federal Reserve: July 2007–March 2009

Source: Federal Reserve Board of Governors, H.41 Release Treasury securities include repurchase agreements.

Note: Other is composed of "other assets," "float" plus the discount window, primary dealer and other broker–dealer credit, asset-backed commercial paper money market mutual fund liquidity facility, credit extended to AIG, the Term Asset-Backed Securities Loan Facility, and equity holdings for AIG and Bear-Stearns.

Table 2.3 Schedule and composition of US fiscal stimulus 2009[a]

	2009	2010	2011	2012 & beyond	Total
Expenditure measures	184	143	84	89	500
Infrastructure and other	32	47	47	78	204
Safety nets	77	14	5	7	103
State aid and education	75	82	32	3	192
Revenue measures	99	116	37	(33)	219
Individual income	37	80	32		
Corporate income	57	32	(2)		
Other	5	4	7		
Total	283.0	259.0	121.0	56.3	719.3
(as % of GDP)	2.0	1.8	0.8	0.4	5.0

Sources: IMF staff estimates and Congressional Budget Office.

[a] Total reported amount excludes the temporary "patch" of approximately $68 billion providing taxpayer relief with respect to the Alternative Minimum Tax. This amount is included in the baseline stimulus of $787 billion reported by CBO.

equal to US$787 billion, but many evaluations exclude the extension of some existing tax measures from the computation of the stimulus and estimate the actual effect at US$720 billion (4.8 percent of GDP). As shown in Table 2.3, the measures are spread over several years, with 40 percent to be spent in 2009 and a slightly smaller amount in 2010. Roughly 90 percent of the total stimulus takes place during the first three years. The bulk of the program takes the form of expenditure increases, but they are scheduled to be temporary and the program should have only modest effects on the long-term budget situation. Both the Obama administration and the CBO projected a strong recovery in 2010 and 2011 and a return to trend growth by 2011.

Much of the debate over the fiscal stimulus has centered on its relative composition of tax reductions, transfer payments, and infrastructure projects. Infrastructure spending is believed to have the largest multiplier effects, but historically the projects are subject to long lags. Tax cuts can be enacted in a short time period, but some economists argue that the stimulus effects of temporary tax measures are particularly small.[12] This issue was taken up again in two important studies that tracked the effects of the 2002 tax stimulus (Johnson, Parker, and Souleles 2006; Agarwal, Liu, and Souleles 2007). Using micro data, both of those studies concluded that the spending of low-income and credit-constrained households responded strongly to the tax rebates. Because the US downturn is expected to last for several years, the lag in expenditure programs was a less effective argument than in the past, and the stimulus measure that emerged from Congress included a very diversified set of programs, some with short lags and others stretching several years into the future.

The federal government entered the recession with a substantial budget imbalance, and the additional fiscal measures, including the financial bailout (TARP), yield a fiscal deficit near US$2 trillion for FY2009 and US$1.5 trillion in FY2010. Absent further actions, the deficit would decline back below US $0.5 trillion in later years. However, the Obama administration also has an ambitious domestic agenda of its own, which is projected to push the long-term deficit up to about US$1 trillion per year (5–6 percent of GDP). The trends in federal outlays and revenues as shares of GDP are displayed in Figure 2.9. These ratios have been quite stable throughout the last half-century, in the range of 20 percent (except for a modest downward movement of the expenditure share in the 1990s due to the end of the cold war, and a coincident rise in the revenue share during the high-tech boom in equity markets). Expenditures are now projected to rise up to 24 percent of GDP, and revenues may decline to 18–19 percent of GDP if the tax cuts are extended.

Financial reconstruction. Creating an effective policy for restructuring the financial system is the greatest problem still facing the government. The basic framework of a program is well known as similar plans have been executed in both the US and other countries (Waxman 1998). The first step

[12] A more general discussion of the role of fiscal policy for counter-cyclical stabilization is provided by Auerbach (2005).

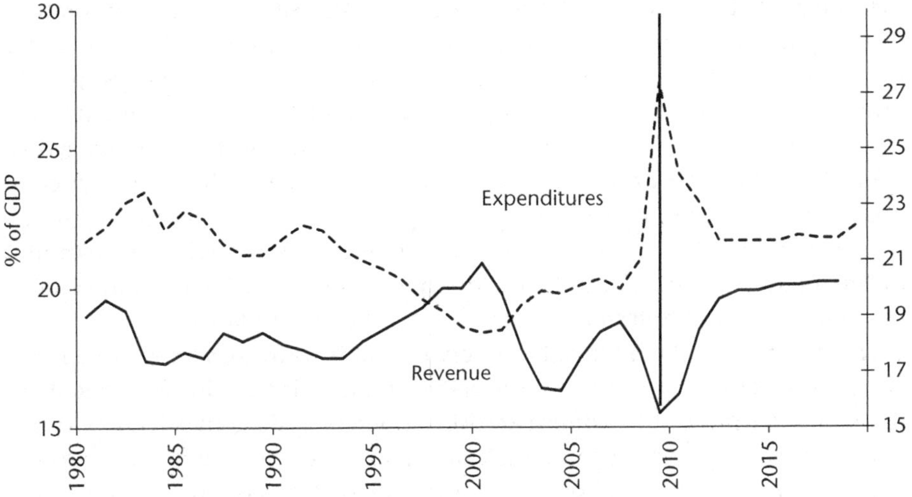

Figure 2.9 Federal Government revenues and expenditures, 1980–2019
Source: Congressional Budget Office, Preliminary Analysis of the President's Budget.

is an accurate assessment of the losses in individual financial institutions. That is followed by a process of writing off the losses against equity capital and perhaps moving the non-performing assets to a separate asset management corporation, which would subsequently sell off these assets over a sustained time-period. Third, the affected financial institutions must be either closed or recapitalized so that there is no continuing uncertainty about their financial condition. The experience of several countries would suggest the potential for a fourth component of this process, which involves restarting the lending process and restoring trust in the financial system after the banks are recapitalized. In subsequent years, those banks that are taken over by the government can be sold back to the private sector.

For the US, the major problem seems to be the magnitude of the funds that are required and the difficulty of obtaining congressional authorization. Hence, the Obama administration has not taken the conventional path. Instead, it has sought to provide guarantees and other incentives to attract private-sector partners. The Public–Private Investment Program (PPIP) will use US$75–100 billion of TARP funds to form public–private partnerships aimed at purchasing distressed loans and securities.[13] Those partnerships will be able

[13] Details are available at: http://treas.gov/press/releases/tg65.htm.

to leverage their funds further through Federal Deposit Insurance Corporation (FDIC) guarantees of their debt and by borrowing from the US Treasury. However, the risks to the partners are very asymmetric in that the private firm's losses are limited to their original investment—the government loans and guarantees are nonrecourse—while they participate fully in any gains. While the program is expected to attract some participants, it does not directly address the need for additional equity capital. The fear is that the administration will not act on a scale sufficient to provide a comfortable level of capital in the financial system, and the de-leveraging and other financial uncertainties will be allowed to fester for years, as was the case in Japan.

The debate over the financial recovery program continues to be driven by a basic disagreement over the condition of financial institutions—particularly the banks. Critics of the Administration's policies believe that large portions of the financial system are fundamentally insolvent, and thus some version of the procedure outlined above for removing bad assets and recapitalizing the system is a prerequisite for a sustained recovery. Such a program would require far more resources that those left in the TARP program. Others believe that the declines in asset values have overshot as the result of the panic, and that the passage of time will resolve many of the solvency problems. The second perspective seems to motivate the Administration's relatively modest proposals for reconstructing the banks combined with its wait-and-see approach.

Even if the current crisis can be resolved, the US is faced with the need to rebuild large portions of the financial system on a new institutional structure. Having intervened to bail out large numbers of financial firms, rampant moral hazards make a return to the old system impossible. Yet it is difficult to outline a new structure without knowing what portions of the old system will survive. The Federal Reserve in particular will have the formidable challenge of reversing its current course and returning to its former arms-length interaction with the financial system. Clearly, the new system will involve more regulatory oversight, but an effective formula for anticipating systemic risks has yet to be developed.

Many see increased regulation as a solution to the prior problems, but the history of regulation in the US is that the regulated ultimately capture the regulator and convert the process to restrict competition. This is particularly true in the financial area, where Wall Street firms and the tremendous rents they could dispense came to have a dominating influence on US government policy. Instead, greater attention should be given to reversing the concentration of economic power in the hands of large financial institutions and a return to a more competitive system with a fundamental focus on simple transparency and standardized transactions in open markets.

The future structure of monetary policy is also very problematic. The earlier emphasis on narrow policy rules, such as inflation targeting, appears to have left policymakers blind to a wider range of concerns such as asset market bubbles and excessive risk taking. Yet the broadening of the agenda necessarily implies a more powerful and discretionary role for monetary authorities, which will heighten concerns about accountability.

2.6 Global implications

An end to the consumption binge of the last decade should be good news for the US economy. A lessened focus on domestic consumption would imply a shift of resources toward the export sector and a gradual reduction in the current US account imbalance to more sustainable levels. However, export-led growth will be a difficult achievement in a depressed global economy in which many countries may see exports as a route out of the recession. In addition, the panic that hit the global financial system in late 2008 has initiated a flight to the safety of US Treasury securities and an appreciation of the US dollar that has undone about half of the prior depreciation that had been underway since mid-2002 (Figure 2.4).

The recovery is likely to be marked by a higher private saving rate, weak domestic investment, and a very large government budget deficit. That is not a sustainable domestic situation, and the economy will ultimately have to be restructured with a much greater focus on exports. Using 2000–05 as a benchmark, the US needs to shift a minimum of 3 percent of GDP from domestic consumption to the export sector. The shift of expenditures into the export market will require a substantial depreciation of the dollar exchange rate on a trade-weighted basis. Past research suggests that the price elasticities of exports and imports are both about unity. Thus, the required long-run depreciation of the dollar is 30 percent.

Surprisingly, that process was actually underway prior to the crisis: the real exchange rate was down by 30 percent from its 2002 peak, and the trade imbalance had already fallen by 1 percent of GDP from its 2005 level. At current levels of the dollar, however, it is not at all clear that the process of expenditure switching will continue. It seems more likely that pressures to engineer a quick recovery will lead to a heavy reliance on fiscal stimulus and a higher public sector deficit as an offset to increased private saving. Perhaps continued fiscal deficits will intensify foreign concerns about increased investment in dollar-denominated assets, and place downward pressure on the dollar. Such a process would promote the desired shift of resources into the tradables sector.

2.7 Conclusions

This review has summarized some of the research on the proximate and fundamental determinants of the current financial crisis. The enormous growth of the subprime mortgage market, and the lack of regulation and prudent lending procedures that characterized this market, appear to be the most decisive factors. The complexity of the subsequent mortgage-backed securities led to the general failure of both regulators and purchasers to adequately assess the risks associated with these assets. It is reasonable to suggest that a low level of global interest rates helped create an environment conducive to the bubble in housing markets. However, we believe this was a contributing rather than fundamental factor. If the US asset price bubble was a consequence of large global imbalances brought on by strong demand for dollar-denominated assets, we would have seen an appreciation of the US dollar in the years preceding the crisis. Moreover, global interest rates were low, but not at unprecedented levels, and other economies experienced similar patterns of housing prices without comparable damage to their financial institutions. The distorted incentives and flawed regulatory structures surrounding US financial institutions were a distinctly American feature that precipitated the current global financial crisis.

Looking ahead, a sustained economic recovery seems unlikely until the uncertainties surrounding the solvency of major financial institutions and excessive mortgage indebtedness of American households have been resolved. There are substantial doubts about the potential success of the government's bailout plan. The fundamental problem continues to be the political constraints on the government's ability to obtain sufficient budget funds to recapitalize the financial system, leaving it with second-best options. Finally, the crisis and the large wealth losses may trigger a long-sought rebalancing of the nation's saving and investment and a necessary reduction in the current account balance. That will create substantial challenges for other countries that have become overly dependent on exports to the US market.

References

Agarwal, S., C. Liu, and N. S. Souleles (2007). The Reaction of Consumer Spending and Debt to Tax Rebates: Evidence from Consumer Credit Data. NBER Working Paper No. 13694 (December). Available: http://www.nber.org/papers/w13694.

Aizenman, J. and Y. Jinjarak (2008). Current Account Patterns and National Real Estate Markets. NBER Working Paper No. 13921 (April). Available: http://www.nber.org/papers/w13921.

Ashcraft, A. B. and T. Schuerman (2008). *Understanding the Securitization of Subprime Mortgage Credit*. Staff Report No. 318, Federal Reserve Bank of New York (March).

Auerbach, A. (2005). The Effectiveness of Fiscal Policy as Stabilization Policy. Paper presented at the Bank of Korea International Conference on the Effectiveness of Stabilization Policies: Seoul. May.

Baily, M., R. Litan, and M. Johnson (2008). The Origins of the Financial Crisis. Fixing Finance Series #3, Initiative on Business and Public Policy at Brookings (November). Washington, DC: Brookings Institution.

Bebchuk, L. and J. Fried (2003). Executive Compensation as an Agency Problem. *Journal of Economic Perspectives* 17(3): 71–92.

Bernanke, B. (2005). The Global Savings Glut and the US Current Account Deficit. Paper presented at the Homer Jones Lecture, St Louis, Missouri, April 14.

Bosworth, B. and G. Chodorow-Reich (2006). Saving and Demographic Change: the Global Dimension. The Brookings Institution Available: http://www.brookings.edu/papers/2006/1101useconomics_bosworth.aspx.

Bosworth, B. and S. Collins (2003). The Empirics of Growth: An Update. *Brookings Papers on Economic Activity* 2003(2).

Bracke, T. and M. Fidora (2008). Global Liquidity Glut or Global Savings Glut? Working paper 911, European Central Bank.

Bureau of Economic Analysis (2009). National Income and Product Accounts. Washington, DC: BEA. Available: http://www.bea.gov/national/nipaweb/SelectTable.asp?Selected=N.

Caballero, R., E. Farhi, and P. Gourinchas (2008). Financial Crash, Commodity Prices and Global Imbalances. *Brookings Papers on Economic Activity*: Fall 2008: 1–55.

Census Bureau (2007). Income, Poverty, and Health Insurance Coverage in the United States: 2007. Current Population Reports: Consumer Income. Washington, DC. Available: http://www.census.gov/prod/2008pubs/p60-235.pdf.

—— (2009). Manufacturing and Construction Division: New Privately Owned Housing Units Started. Washington, DC. Available: http://www.census.gov/const/startssa.pdf.

Clark, T. and T. Nakata (2008). Has the Behavior of Inflation and Long-Term Inflation Expectations Changed? *Federal Reserve Bank of Kansas City Economic Review*, first quarter of 2008: 17–50.

Congressional Budget Office (2009). A Preliminary Analysis of the President's Budget and an Update of CBO's Budget and Economic Outlook. (March). Washington, DC. Available: http://www.cbo.gov/doc.cfm?index=10014.

Cooper, R. (2008). Global Imbalances: Globalization, Demography, and Sustainability. *Journal of Economic Perspectives* 22(3): 93–112.

Federal Reserve Bank of New York (2009). Statistical Release H.15: Selected Interest Rates. New York. Available at http://www.federalreserve.gov/releases/h15/data.htm.

Federal Reserve Board of Governors (2009a). Factors Affecting Reserve Balances, H.4.1 statistical release. (April 8). Washington, DC. Available: http://www.federalreserve.gov/releases/h41/.

—— (2009b). Flow of Funds Accounts, Flows and Outstandings. Z.1 statistical release. (March). Washington, DC. Available: http://www.federalreserve.gov/RELEASES/z1/Current/data.htm.

Gramlich, E. (2007). Booms and Busts: The Case of Subprime Mortgages. Paper presented at the Federal Reserve Bank of Kansas City Symposium, Jackson Hole, Wyoming, August 31–September 1.

Gorton, G. B. (2008). The Subprime Panic. NBER Working Paper No. 14398 (October). Available: http://www.nber.org/papers/w14398.

Hatzius, J. (2008). Beyond Leveraged Losses: The Balance Sheet Effects of the Home Price Downturn. *Brookings Papers on Economic Activity* 2008(2): 195–227.

International Monetary Fund (2009). The Size of the Fiscal Expansion: An Analysis for the Largest Countries. Fiscal Affairs Department. (February). Washington, DC: IMF. Available: http://www.imf.org/external/np/pp/eng/2009/020109.pdf.

Johnson, D., J. Parker, and N. S. Souleles (2006). Household Expenditure and the Income Tax Rebates of 2001. *American Economic Review* 96(5): 1589–610.

JP Morgan (2009). Estimates of Trade-Weighted Exchange Rates (Private Correspondence).

Mortgage Bankers Association (2009). National Delinquency Survey. Available: http://www.mortgagebankers.org/ResearchandForecasts/ProductsandSurveys/National-DelinquencySurvey.htm.

Office of Management and Budget (2009). Fiscal Year 2019 Budget Overview: A New Era of Responsibility. Washington, DC, February. Available: http://www.whitehouse.gov/omb/budget/Overview/.

Organisation for Economic Co-operation and Development (OECD) (2009a). Economic Outlook. Accessed April 18, 2009. Paris: OECD. Available: http://stats.oecd.org/index.aspx?r=445591.

——(2009b). Monthly Economic Indicators. Accessed April 18, 2009. Paris: OECD. Available: http://stats.oecd.org/index.aspx?r=445591.

——(2009c). National Accounts Volume II. Accessed April 18, 2009. Paris: OECD. Available: http://stats.oecd.org/index.aspx?r=445591.

Reinhart, C. and K. Rogoff (2008). Is the 2007 US Sub-Prime Financial Crisis So Different? An International Historical Comparison. Mimeo. Cambridge, MA: Harvard University.

Standard and Poor's (2009). S&P/Case-Shiller Home Price Index. Available: http://www2.standardandpoors.com/portal/site/sp/en/us/page.topic/indices_csmahp/0,0,0,0,0,0,0,0,0,1,3,0,0,0,0,0.html.

Summers, L. (1983). "The Non-adjustment of Nominal Interest Rates: A Study of the Fisher Effect," in *Symposium In Honor Of Arthur Okun*, edited by J. Tobin, Washington, DC: Brookings Institution.

Taylor, J. (2009). *Getting Off Track: How Government Actions and Interventions Caused, Prolonged and Worsened the Financial Crisis*. Stanford: Hoover Institution Press.

Waxman, M. (1998). *A Legal Framework for Systemic Bank Restructuring*. Washington, DC: World Bank (September).

World Bank (2009). World Development Indicators. Accessed April 18, 2009. Available: http://ddp-ext.worldbank.org/ext/DDPQQ/.

3

The Eurozone in the Global Financial Crisis

Charles Wyplosz

3.1 Introduction

Europe has tilted into recession a bit later than the United States (US) did, but the decline is of the same magnitude. While this is not surprising, it brings up a number of questions. First, was the crisis imported from the US or largely homemade? Indeed, house prices rose considerably in some European countries, in bubble-like fashion. The sharp decline that followed the housing price bubble burst has put a number of commercial banks under strain, at a time when these or other banks also suffered from exposure to the US mortgage market. This chapter starts by laying down the facts of what led to the current European crisis in Section 3.2 and then attempts to disentangle the causes and effects in Section 3.3, where the chapter argues that Europe never had a chance to avoid contagion from the US. Trade and financial links—some of which operate through third countries, those in East Asia in particular—are simply too powerful. At the same time, domestic conditions were often critical in a number of countries where house prices had generated unsustainable booms, even though there is no European equivalent to subprime lending.

A comparison of the economic situation across the Atlantic cannot be complete without looking at policies. Section 3.4 looks at fiscal policies and provides currently available evidence that suggests Eurozone governments have showed considerable restraint in using this instrument, something that may well be a consequence of the Stability and Growth Pact. While *de facto* suspended due to exceptional circumstances, the pact is bound to be reactivated when the situation improves. This may deter governments from undertaking active countercyclical policies. Section 3.5 examines monetary policy, showing that the European Central Bank (ECB) intervened promptly and massively to attempt to maintain liquidity in the money market. It is also argued that the ECB was more focused on (then high) inflation than on the (then largely unexpected) upcoming recession.

The last section offers some concluding remarks that may be interesting for East Asians. The quietness on the currency front—the *raison d'être* of the monetary union—is a remarkable achievement. It has not prevented markets from discriminating among countries, but this time through another channel: the markets for public bonds. Reasons why both the ECB and national governments have acted more prudently than most other developed countries are also discussed.

3.2 Facts

With some delay, the Eurozone has been hit by the financial crisis that erupted in August 2007. Figure 3.1 shows that the Eurozone's economy peaked in the first quarter of 2008 and then quickly plunged into a severe recession.[1] The

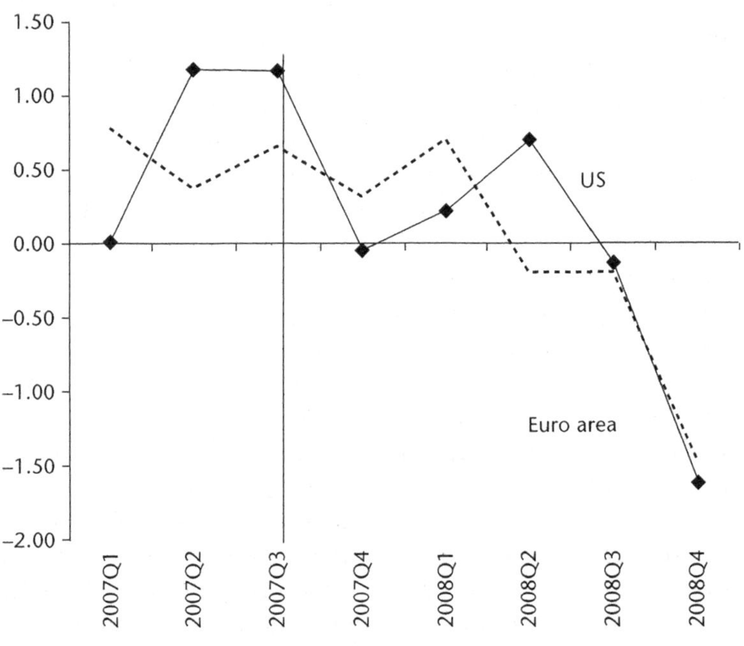

Figure 3.1 Quarterly real GDP growth rates
Source: International Financial Statistics, IMF.

[1] The Centre for Economic Policy Research's Euro Area Business Cycle Dating Committees also dates the peak to the first quarter of 2008, more precisely January 2008, see http://www.cepr.org/data/Dating/.

apparent immunity from the financial crisis led to a European version of the decoupling theory, which has proven as wrong in Europe as elsewhere around the world.

In fact, the financial crisis started at the same time in Europe as in the US. The "official" starting date, August 9, 2007, corresponds to the announcement by BNP-Paribas that it was suspending redemption of three funds because of lack of liquidity in the market. This was, in fact, the second warning shot. In early June of that year, a similar move by Bear Stearns had gone almost unnoticed. That same day, the ECB started to inject massive amounts of cash into the interbank market, followed a few days later by the US Federal Reserve Board (hereafter, the Fed).

This is also the time when both central banks started to lose control of interest rates in the unsecured sections of the interbank markets. This is illustrated in Figure 3.2, which displays the spreads between the three-month Euro Interbank Offered Rate (Euribor) and the Euro OverNight Index Average (EONIA) rates, in the case of the Eurozone, and between the three-month dollar London Interbank Offered Rate (Libor) and the Federal Funds

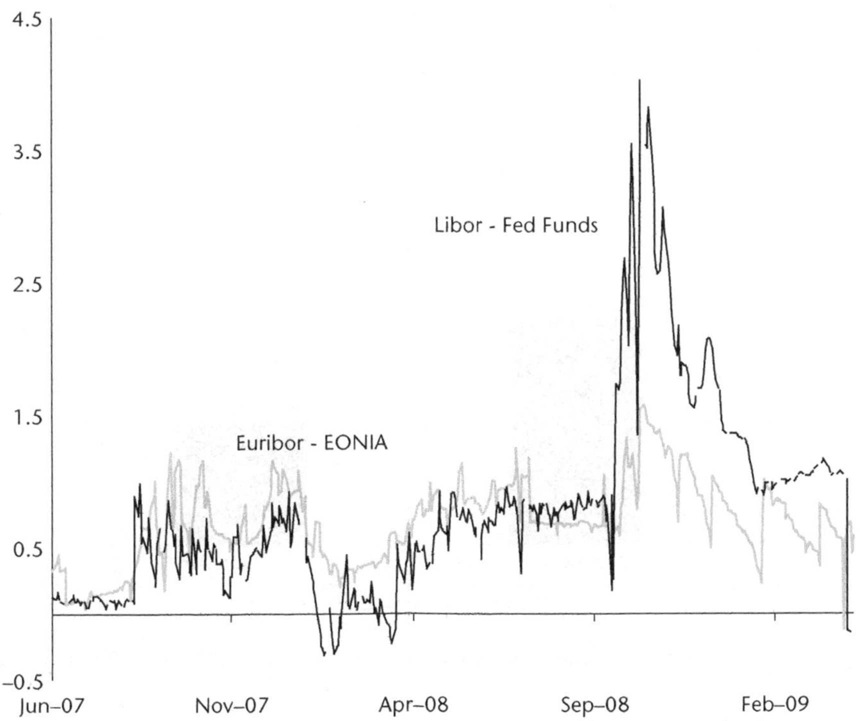

Figure 3.2 Interest rate spreads in dollars and euro

Sources: Euribor (http://www.euribor.org/), The British Bankers' Association (http://www.bba.org.uk), European Central Bank (ECB), and Fed Reserve Bank of New York.

rates in the US. In normal times, the spreads between the unsecured Euribor and Libor and the corresponding EONIA and Federal Funds rates essentially reflects the maturity difference—three months vs. overnight—and amounts to about 10 basis points. As Figure 3.2 shows, both spreads instantaneously rose and became quite volatile. Volatility reached new highs in September 2008, following the demise of Lehman Brothers Holdings, Inc. To a large degree, therefore, financial markets were impacted in broadly similar ways on both sides of the Atlantic. This is further confirmed by Figure 3.3, which reports the extent of duress suffered by banks in the form of writedowns and capital raised since the beginning of the crisis. For both measures, so far at least, Europe is found to have suffered less than the US but not by a large margin, as the difference with Asia illustrates.

Much the same can be said about house prices. Although there are large differences from one Eurozone member country to another, on average, Europe[2] was subject to a nearly identical bubble, as Figure 3.4 documents. The relative time profiles of house prices mirror those of gross domestic product (GDP): they peaked earlier in the US than in Europe and the decline is now nearly identical. This observation suggests that the much maligned

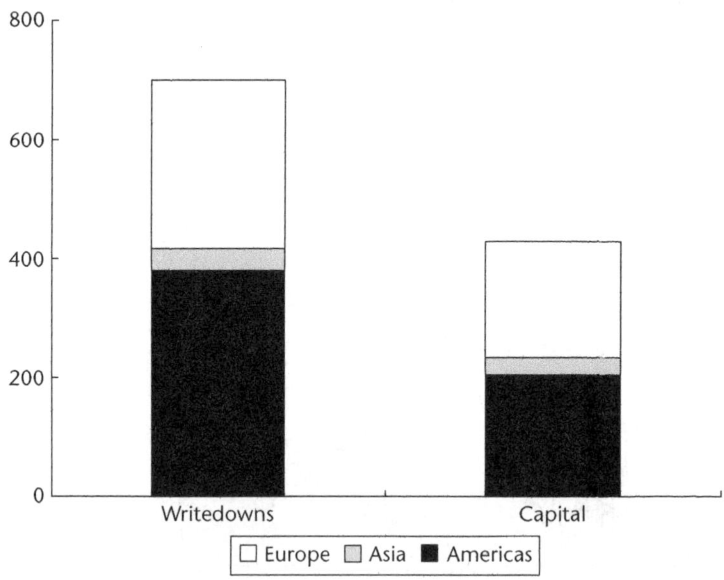

Figure 3.3 Banks under duress: writedowns and capital raised 2007 Q3–2008Q3 in US $billions

Source: Bloomberg.

[2] The data refer to the euro area.

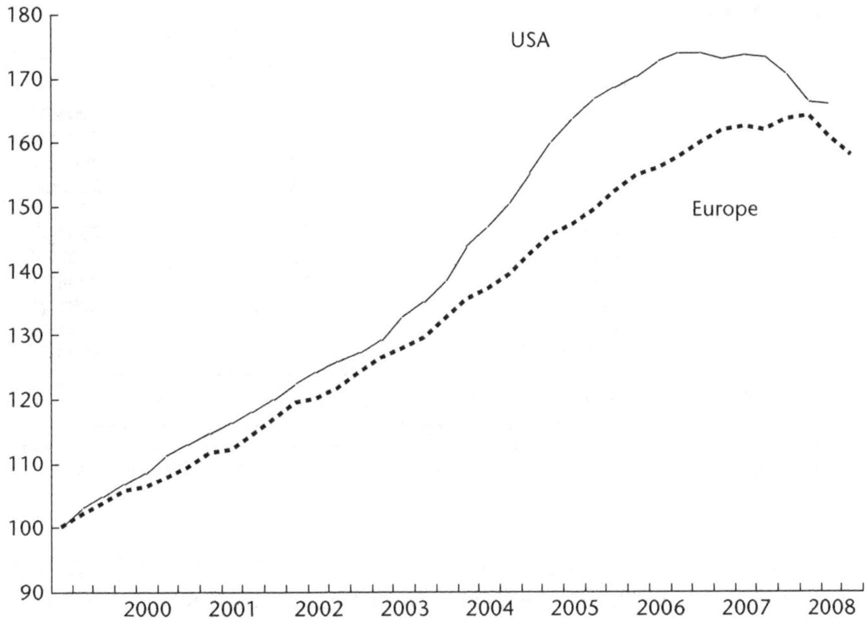

Figure 3.4 House price indexes: USA vs. Europe, January 2000–January 2009
Sources: OFHEO Data and European Central Bank Data (ECB).

subprime mortgages may have been more a consequence than a cause of the house price bubble. It does not suggest, however, that subprime mortgages were not a key factor in triggering and spreading the financial crisis once the bubble had burst.

3.3 Interpretations

A perplexing message of the facts collected in the previous section is that financial conditions have been broadly similar in the Eurozone and in the US and yet the recession hit the US faster than it did in the Eurozone. By the end of 2008, however, the impacts seen in each region were quite similar. This section examines some plausible interpretations.

3.3.1 *The pricking of the house price bubble*

A first obvious interpretation is that the crisis started where it originated, in the US, where the housing market indeed peaked nearly a year beforehand, in 2006 (Figure 3.4). This view rests on causality running from housing prices

Table 3.1 House price turnaround

House price peak	Country	Pre-peak increase (%)	Cyclical peak
2006Q3	Ireland	298	2006Q3
2006Q4	Denmark	145	2007Q3
	Spain	113	2007Q2
	US	61	2007Q4
2007Q1			
2007Q2	Italy	30	2007Q3
	Finland	96	2007Q4
2007Q3	France	92	2008Q1
	Sweden	110	2008Q1
	UK	164	2007Q3
2007Q4	Netherlands	146	2008Q2

Source: World Economic Outlook Database, IMF.

Notes: No house price peak in Germany and Portugal; missing information for Austria and Belgium. The price increase is measured in real terms and relative to the average over 1992–95, a period of relative house price stability, generally followed by continuous growth. The cyclical peak is estimated by the author on the basis of quarterly GDP growth behavior.

to economic growth, through four possible channels: (1) wealth; (2) non-performing losses and bank stress; (3) loss of collateral and reduced borrowing; and (4) contraction of the house-building industry. Causality could run in the opposite direction though probably not in the US, where housing prices peaked a year before the crisis; but, quite possibly in Europe, where the peak mostly occurred after the onset of the financial crisis.[3] The scenario would be one where large losses suffered on US mortgage-backed securities led banks to deleverage and sharply reduce the amounts of new loans. This would adversely impact the housing market and depress prices while generally restricting credit to the private sector. In short, did Europe fall victim to its own house price bubble or is Europe's crisis due to European bank exposure to US mortgages?

Looking in more detail at the timing of events does not shed much light on the question. Table 3.1 shows that in two of the countries house prices peaked before (Ireland) or at about the same time (Denmark and Spain) as in the US, but elsewhere they peaked significantly later. The table also suggests that there is no relation between the timing and the size of the bubble, when the latter is measured as the increase in real house prices over the last period of relative stability. Europe had nurtured its own bubbles and they exploded apparently randomly. In that sense, there is little evidence of causality from the US to Europe. If anything, the timing would imply that Ireland is the source of the world crisis, a rather implausible assertion.

[3] For a recent empirical study on causality between credit and house prices, and extensive references, see Goodhart and Hofmann (2008).

Yet the coincidence is troubling. Rather than a European story versus an American story, this could be a global story. House prices had risen enormously on both sides of the Atlantic, probably for the same reasons. As discussed in Bosworth and Flaaen (Chapter 2), ample liquidity provided by low interest rates and high saving rates in emerging market countries encouraged bank lending and led to unreasonably low assessment of risks. Few developed countries (Austria, Germany, and Switzerland) escaped the fad. On both sides of the Atlantic, discussions of the impending end of the bubbles were rife and investors were scrutinizing every possible signal. Once the bubbles started to deflate, banks all simultaneously faced a rising tide of non-performing loans. The main difference between the US and Europe is that securitization of mortgages was mostly developed in the US and the resulting securities were bought in the US. In that sense, contagion went from the US to Europe, and the delayed impact is understandable.[4]

3.3.2 *The banking sector*

According to Figure 3.3, European banks have been less affected than US banks, but the difference is not very large. However, writedowns and recapitalization are imperfect measures of the severity of the bank crisis. Writedowns depend upon local regulations and on their enforcement. Like recapitalization, they also depend on various measures that governments may take to alleviate the situation. Governments may buy toxic assets at favorable prices or provide guarantees for either assets or liabilities. Central banks may also provide liquidity, which may defer writedowns and recapitalization, depending on the regulatory regime.

Looking at public support thus provides an alternative gage of the deterioration of the financial sector. According to Figure 3.5, with the exception of Ireland, financial institutions from the Eurozone countries have received comparatively less support than the US has. Two non-Eurozone countries, Sweden and the United Kingdom (UK), on the other hand, appear between the US and the Eurozone countries.

An additional piece of information concerns credit to the private sector. If losses have been large, one would expect deleveraging to have led to a credit crunch. Figure 3.6 shows that credit has considerably declined, but it does not tell us why, and this is crucially important. The situation could indeed reflect a supply-side crunch, but it could equally well correspond to a sharp decline in

[4] It may be interesting to note that Spanish banks were forbidden by their central bank from buying asset-backed securities. Given the size of the Spanish bubble, however, Spanish banks and the Spanish economy ended up being hurt as much as—if not more than—other European countries.

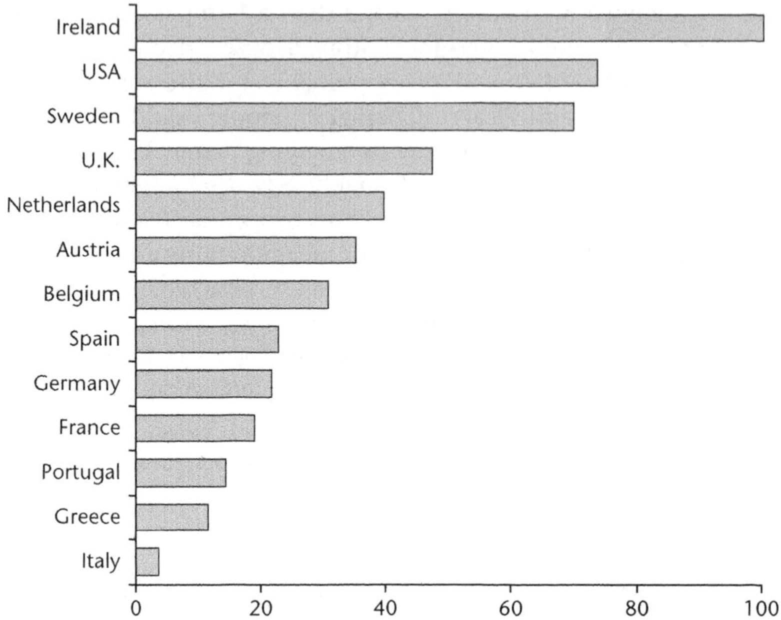

Figure 3.5 Public support to the financial sector (as of February 18, 2009, % of GDP)
Source: International Monetary Fund (2009).

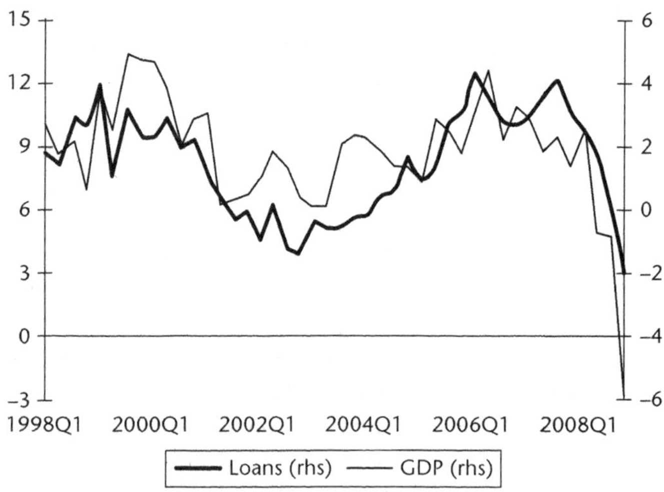

Figure 3.6 Credit in the Eurozone (% change)
Source: European Commission (2009), *Quarterly Report of the Euro Area* 8(1).

demand for loans as economic conditions worsen. One reason to doubt the credit crunch interpretation is that the figure suggests that credit has declined less than could be expected on the basis of previous experience.

At this stage, it is impossible to determine with any precision the degree of deterioration of national financial systems. The available information could suggest that the US banking system has been more affected by the crisis than has been the case in the Eurozone countries. Alternatively, it may be that the US authorities have taken more forceful action and have managed to at least compensate for the earlier damage created by the subprime mortgage crisis. This would explain the early decline in the US and the similarity of the overall effect by the beginning of 2009, but not the rebound observed in the US in 2008.

3.3.3 *The role of welfare systems*

As in Asia, some market economists and officials have put forward the decoupling theory, in which case, Europe would not be subject to contagion from the US. Their arguments were based on empirical work that did not detect any increase in comovements of key economic variables in recent years, despite evidence that trade and financial integration was deepening (Doyle and Faust 2005). A further reason why decoupling would occur in the European case, it was argued, is the existence of a large welfare system. High unemployment benefits and progressive income taxation deliver large automatic stabilizers, while universal health care and unfunded pensions—not in all countries, see below—reassure households at a time when asset values fall precipitously.

However, in actuality, decoupling did not materialize. The belief that the automatic stabilizers would be enough to offset the shock has been shown to be incorrect or, at least, overblown. By definition, the stabilizers offset less than 100 percent of shocks, so they cannot deliver decoupling, but they can reduce the impact. In fact, estimates of the stabilizers indicate that the absorbing effects are a small fraction—at most 25 percent, and usually much less—of the original shock (Fatas and Mihov 2001).

While the decoupling theory has proven to be wrong, welfare system differences may go some way to explaining why the crisis may have taken hold more slowly in the Eurozone than in the US or UK. On the other hand, these differences would predict that, overall, the impact of the crisis should be less profound in Europe. Although it is too early to draw any sharp conclusion, the evidence presented in Figure 3.1 does not provide support for this view.

3.3.4 *Limited Exposure to Markets*

European households hold fewer financial assets than do US households, especially because pensions are largely unfunded in a number of countries. With the exception of the Netherlands (149 percent of GDP in 2007), Ireland (94 percent), and Finland (78 percent), pension fund assets total less than 25 percent of GDP among Eurozone countries, and often significantly less.[5] This means that wealth destruction affected households mostly after house prices started to decline, which took place over a period of one year, as discussed in Section 3.3.1. This would help to explain the delayed onset of the recession in Europe but not its depth.

In fact the depth of the recession has come as a surprise, as evidenced by the unending revisions of forecasts since 2007, all downward. True, house price declines have been pronounced in Europe, but the expected magnitude of their impact remains unclear. Buiter (2008) argued that housing wealth has no impact on consumption, suggesting that unless house prices include a bubble component, in equilibrium housing wealth equals the present value of rental costs. The presence of a bubble does not alter the conclusion. If, however, the bubble is expected to be temporary, its present value is nil. Rational home-owners, therefore, should not have felt richer as the bubble grew and should not feel poorer now, after its collapse. Of course, rationality is not necessarily a good starting point for analysis, and other aspects—especially the use of houses as collateral—weaken the result. It remains that the influence of fluctuations of house prices on consumption may be much smaller than is often claimed.

3.3.5 *Assessment*

The Eurozone entered into recession later than the US, but then, when the area finally entered into recession, the decline was rapid and steep. In the third quarter of 2008, the Eurozone growth rate was negative and of the same order of magnitude as the US rate. Interpreting the difference turns out to be more challenging than expected on the basis of popular explanations of the crisis.

The general view is that the bursting of the US house price bubble led to nonperforming mortgage loans, which badly impaired the US banking system. Through securitization, non-US banks, chiefly European banks, were also deeply affected. As bank lending fell, a vicious cycle started to unfold, going from reduced demand (consumption and investment) to falling house and asset prices and to further bank stress. Of course, via exports, the recession was propagated and possibly expanded internationally. Because the EU and

[5] Source: Organisation for Economic Co-operation and Development Global Pension Statistics.

US are reasonably closed economies, this last effect has been ignored in previous analyses, but it is well understood and therefore does not need much more attention at this stage.

While the decoupling hypothesis was clearly wrong from the beginning, a number of factors should have mitigated the impact of the financial crisis in Europe. It can be argued that the acquisition by European banks of securities backed by US mortgages spread the impact of the US house price bubble burst to Europe, thus aggravating the impact of Europe's own house price bubble. While correct, this observation ignores the fact that some countries, chiefly Germany and Austria, never had house price bubbles and yet are sharing in the recession. The export channel may be part of the explanation, but then it should be a mitigating factor for the other countries.

Another puzzling observation is that, with few exceptions, European households are much less exposed to stock market swings than are US households. In addition, bank distress seems to have been deep in Europe, but somewhat less severe than in the US. On both counts, therefore, a less severe downturn could have been expected. In addition, the famed European welfare systems imply that the automatic stabilizers are more powerful. On these grounds, too, a muted response could have been expected.

Working in the opposite direction is that the house price bubbles may have been larger in several European countries than in the US (Table 3.1). The worst case is Ireland and this is indeed where the recession is deepest (–7 percent in 2008Q4). But other countries with very large declines in house prices—the Netherlands, Spain, and Denmark—have not fared worse than the US has, while a country like Germany is facing a deep recession.

Elucidating these issues would require a quantitative analysis that goes beyond the scope of this paper. In the next section, whether economic policy choices help to better understand the outcomes is discussed.

3.4 Policy responses

3.4.1 *Monetary policies*

The ECB reacted immediately and forcefully to disruptions on the interbank market by injecting hitherto unseen amounts of liquidity. The ECB soon developed a dichotomy principle, distinguishing between its two core functions. In order to achieve orderly conditions on the financial markets, it would provide as much liquidity as needed. Liquidity provision, however, would not interfere with interest rate setting, which would remain driven by monetary policy objectives. Rejecting any link between quantity and price could seem strange. The ECB's reasoning was based on the distinction between unsecured interbank rates and the policy rate—the former largely exceeded the latter (Figure 3.2).[6] The ECB considered that it would pursue two intermediate objectives that were temporarily disjoint: set the policy rate (i.e. the refinancing rate, or "the refi") and as well as close the gap between the interbank rate and the policy rate. The dichotomy had some logic to it, but only up to a point. Since the market rate is a key channel of monetary policy transmission, the ECB could not just set the policy rate on the basis of previous experience. It had to recognize that the market rate was at least as important for monetary policy as the refi.

This may help to explain why it took 14 months for the ECB to start lowering its policy rate, which it did for the first time in October 2008. The contrast with the Fed is striking. In September 2007, the Fed promptly lowered its policy rate, then held it steady at 2 percent until the Lehman Brothers

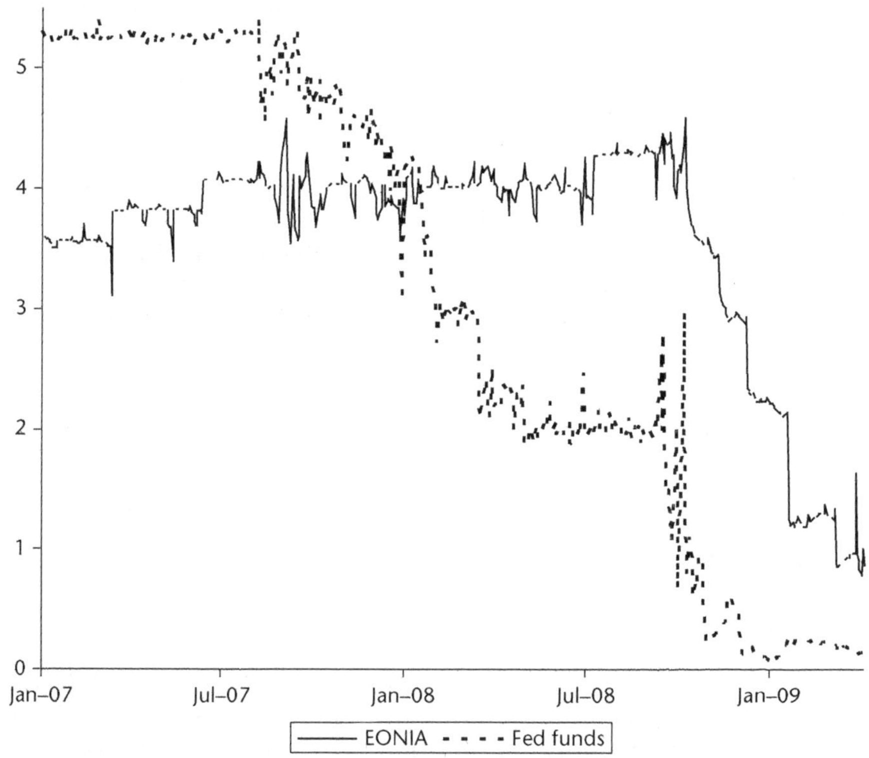

Figure 3.7 Interest rates in the Eurozone and the US (interbank rates)
Sources: European Central Bank (ECB) and Federal Reserve Bank of New York.

[6] Figure 3.2 displays the spread between unsecured (Euribor three months) and secured (EONIA) market rates, not between Euribor and the policy instrument, the main refinancing rate.

Holdings collapse, at which point it drove the interest rate down to the zero lower bound (Figure 3.7).

In contrast the ECB kept its policy rate at 4 percent, reaching its high point in July 2007, until it raised the rate by 25 basis points in July 2008. As abundantly explained in its monthly press conferences, the ECB was more concerned by inflation, which had been steadily rising since 2006 in part because oil, commodity, and food prices were skyrocketing, than about growth and unemployment. Along with most other forecasters, the ECB did not foresee that the ongoing financial crisis would eventually provoke a recession. Indeed, the Eurozone economy peaked in 2008Q1, when inflation was still rising (Figure 3.1).

The problem, of course, is that monetary policy operates with lags of at least two quarters and possibly significantly more. With hindsight, the ECB should have started to lower its policy interest rate by fall of 2007 at the latest, which is what the Fed did. Was the Fed more prescient? One important difference is that the financial crisis erupted in the US, so the risk to growth was more immediate there than in Europe. In fact, the situation promptly deteriorated in the US, which greatly simplified the usual tradeoff between growth and inflation that bedeviled the ECB. Another factor is that the US financial system was under intense pressure while, initially at least, only some European banks were in a precarious situation. It also matters that the Fed did not develop the dichotomy principle of the ECB and attempted to restore stability in financial markets through both liquidity injections and interest rate cuts. Finally, it bears recalling that the Fed has a dual mandate while the ECB's mandate is hierarchical, with inflation at the top.

At any rate, whatever the reasons, it appears *ex post* that monetary policy in the Eurozone did not address the crisis until it was under way. Previous sections sought to explain why growth declined so fast in the Eurozone, relative to the US, once the recession got under way. One element of the answer is that monetary policy was late by almost a year. It is important to note that this conclusion is easy to draw after the fact. Back then, very few, if any, foresaw the seriousness of the ensuing recession. If any mistake was made, it was in the area of economic forecasting, an assessment that is surprisingly de-emphasized in current debates.

3.4.2 *Fiscal policies*

It was noted earlier that the automatic stabilizers are larger in continental Europe than in the US or UK. It was further observed that the stabilizers only mitigate shocks but are far too weak to offset them by a wide margin. It follows that fiscal policies may have been automatically countercyclical but that does not mean that, overall, they have been used to thwart the recession. In examining this issue, note that a number of systematic studies (Galì and Perotti 2003; Wyplosz 2005; Fatas and Mihov 2009) have documented the tendency for fiscal policy to be procyclical in many European countries. What about this time?

To gage the situation, the combination of the automatic stabilizers and of discretionary actions need to be examined. Preliminary evidence is presented in Figure 3.8 for a subset of countries (the four large European countries that belong to the Group of 20 and the US). The data are estimates compiled by the International Monetary Fund (IMF) on the basis of policy announcements for the whole period 2008–10. They represent the change in budget balances as a percent of GDP, distinguishing discretionary actions and automatic stabilizers. The figure suggests that budget balances have deteriorated less in the three Eurozone countries than in the UK and US. Not surprisingly, this is also where the automatic stabilizers are larger. As a corollary, discretionary actions are more limited in the Eurozone countries, actually estimated to be nearly nonexistent in France and Italy. In addition, the time profile of the changes is backloaded for the three Eurozone countries, a reflection of the important role played by the automatic stabilizers as the economic situation deteriorates.

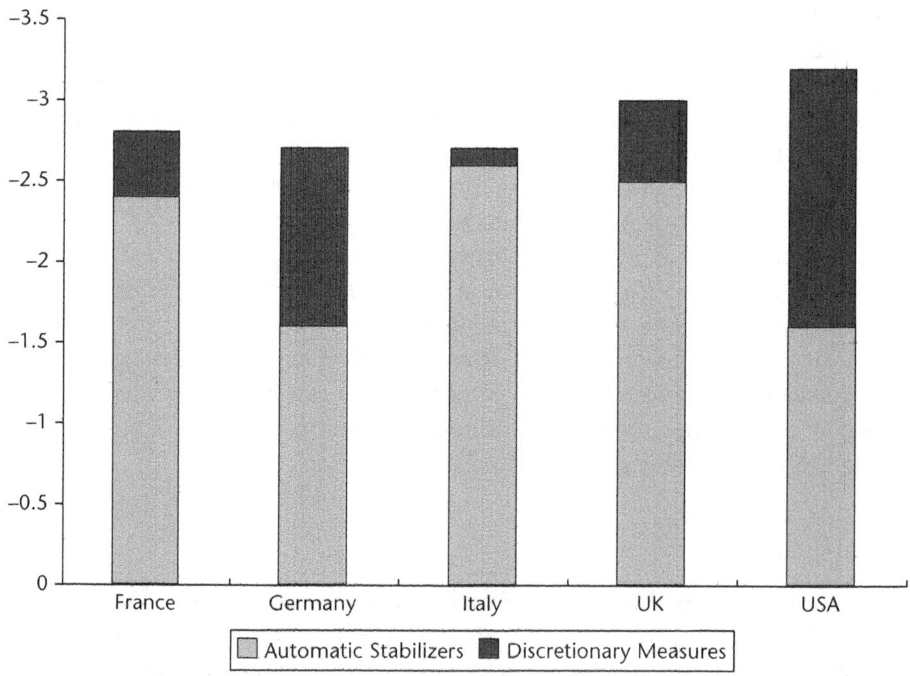

Figure 3.8 Changes in budget balances, October 2008
Source: International Monetary Fund (2009).

Given the lags in fiscal policy effectiveness, these estimates indicate that, though not procyclical, fiscal policy has not played much of a countercyclical role in the Eurozone. With interest rates tending toward the zero lower bound, the Eurozone governments are not actively trying to counter the ongoing contractionary forces. Resumption of growth will have to rely on private spending or exports.

The relatively limited use of fiscal policies in the three largest economies of the Eurozone may be related to the Stability and Growth Pact and the mandatory 3 percent ceiling on public deficits. As the recession deepened, the pact has been quietly put aside and, on the face of it, cannot be blamed for an insufficient provision of fiscal stimulus. Because the pact allows for some flexibility in "exceptional circumstances", this *de facto* suspension is very explicitly temporary. Since the circumstances are judged on the basis of GDP growth rates, a simple stabilization could trigger a reinstatement of the pact. With large negative output gaps, possibly slow to be closed, public budgets are therefore unlikely to recover spontaneously when the pact binds again. This may provide incentives to limit slippages in deficits that will be hard to correct once the recession is over. It can explain why most Eurozone governments have indicated little inclination to use fiscal policy as forcefully as other countries have such as the US, Japan, or the People's Republic of China (PRC).

3.5 The role of the euro

3.5.1 *The silent proof of success*

Never before have European countries gone through troubled times without undergoing sharp speculative attacks on some currencies. This is illustrated in Figure 3.9, which shows the exchange rates of the original founding countries relative to the deutsche mark. The shaded areas identify the two oil shocks and the recessionary episode of 1993, arguably the major macroeconomic events that occurred between the end of the Bretton Woods system and the creation of the euro. Each of these events was accompanied by sharp tensions within Europe and, in most cases, a few currencies faced acute speculative attacks.[7] In many respects, the single currency was adopted to rule out a repeat of these attacks. Since the adoption of the euro, there has been no currency attack within the Eurozone.

It is impossible to imagine what would have happened in the absence of the euro. One relevant observation is the behavior of the currencies of the

[7] In 1993, the Dutch, French, and Belgian currencies escaped mostly unharmed, but several other currencies (Irish, Spanish, and Portuguese) had to be devalued while Italy and the UK were forced out of the European Monetary System.

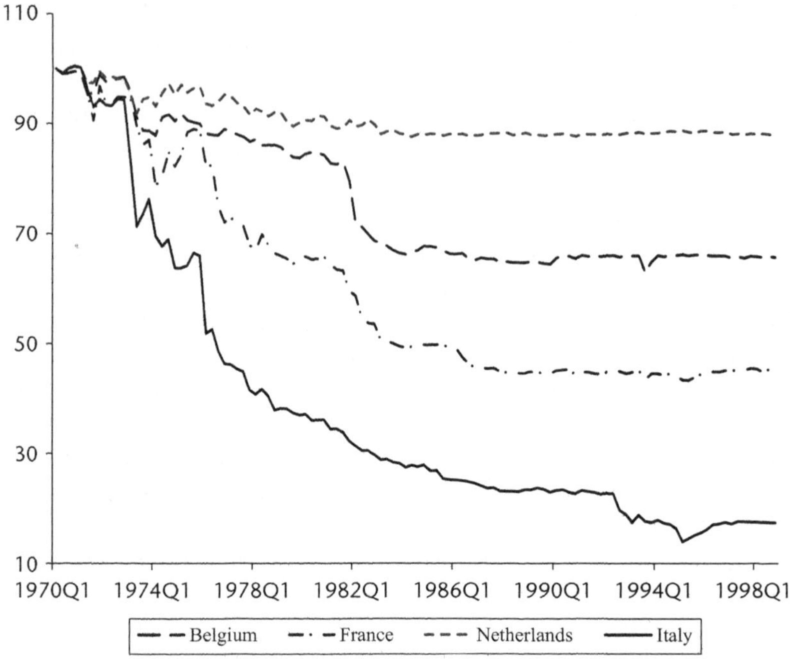

Figure 3.9 Exchange rates vis-à-vis the deutsche mark (Index: 1970Q1 = 100)
Source: International Financial Statistics, IMF.

countries that have not joined the Eurozone. Figure 3.10 shows that their exchange rates vis à vis the euro became unusually volatile once the financial crisis started.[8] Hungary has obtained emergency assistance from the IMF, while Poland has claimed support under the IMF's new Flexible Credit Line facility. Both have also received emergency credit lines from the ECB. The EU Commission also created a €50 billion balance-of-payment assistance fund for Eastern and Central European member countries. The freely floating Swedish and British currencies have both undergone deep depreciation.

3.5.2 *Pressure within the Eurozone*

Another indication that the single currency has most likely prevented several currency crises (or deep depreciations) is provided in Figure 3.11. The figure displays spreads of interest rates on national public bonds over the German bund rate. The largest spreads on Greek and Irish bonds reflect market con-

[8] Not shown are countries that peg to the euro, of which, Latvia, has obtained emergency funding from the IMF, as well as Romania, which is also under an IMF program.

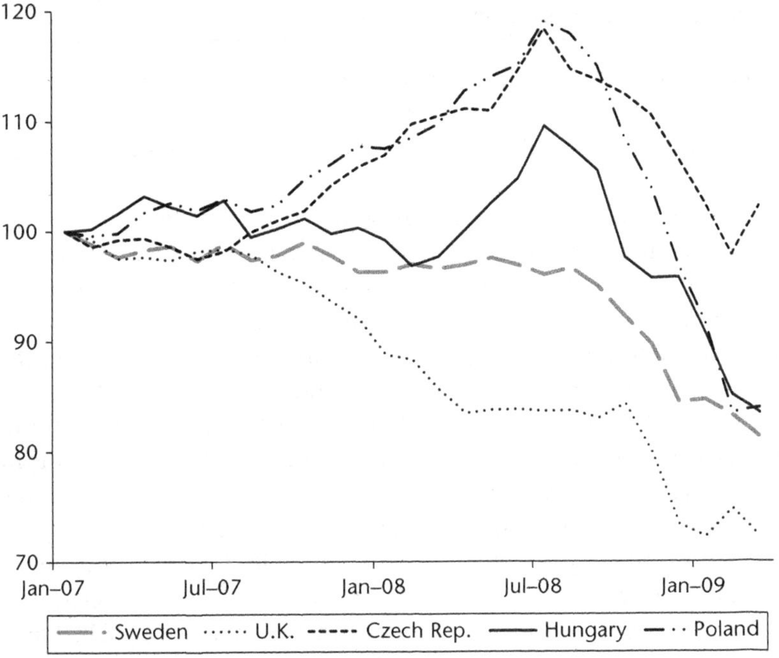

Figure 3.10 Exchange rates vis-à-vis the euro (Index: 2007m1 = 100)
Source: *Monthly Bulletin*, European Central Bank (ECB).

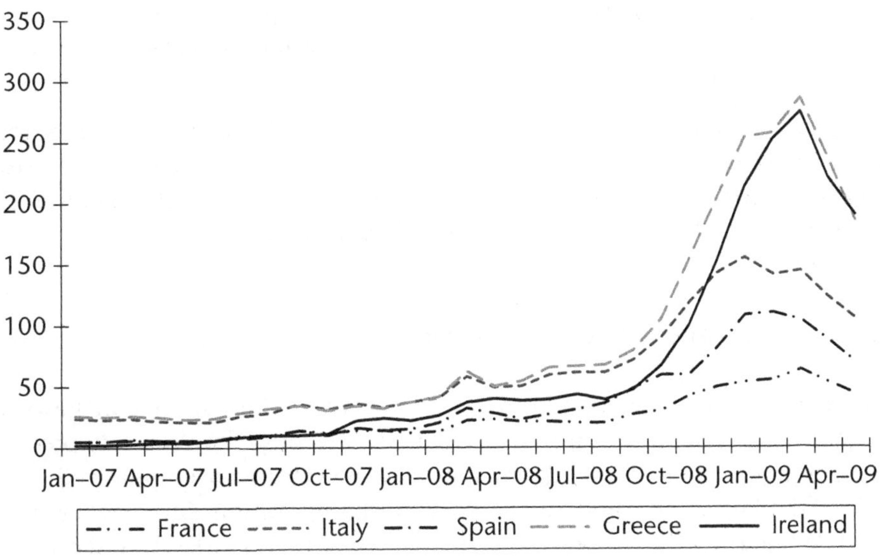

Figure 3.11 Treasury bond spreads (basis points)
Source: International Financial Statistics, IMF.

cerns that public debts could be unsustainable. Several other countries face large spreads too. It is not too farfetched to claim that, absent the euro, some of these countries would also have faced intense pressure on their exchange rates.

This evidence shows that belonging to the Eurozone does not shield member countries from country-specific financial pressure. This aspect was muted for a long period during which the spreads where very small and rarely exceeded 25 basis points. This even led the ECB to observe that the markets were not adequately monitoring national public finances or, worse, that the markets were wrongly expecting that the no-bailout rule, which prevents emergency lending to national governments by European institutions and by other governments, was not binding. As the recent episodes indicate, the markets do discriminate when they feel—rightly or wrongly—that some governments might face difficulties serving their public debts.

Strangely, perhaps, the debate on the no-bailout clause has emerged as spreads started to rise, when markets were indicating that the clause is credible. More strangely, a number of governments, even the ECB, have then suggested that some arrangements could be imagined without violating the no-bailout clause. The EU Commission President, José Manuel Barroso, even stated:

> The euro zone is prepared to help if one of its members is threatened with defaulting on debt. We are considering all options. If there is a problem in the euro area we will have the means to act.... We have instruments in Europe to react (Reported by Strupczewski 2009).

These may merely be statements made by anguished policymakers, presumably to reassure the markets. Yet they reveal the nature of integration forces. Within a currency area, it may be costly to let a government default, even partially, especially in a period of intense financial tensions.

3.6 Conclusions: any lesson for Asia?

The crisis is far from over and it may be too early to draw sharp conclusions. A few remarks may be of interest to Asian readers, but the customary precaution about policy recommendations needs to be vigorously emphasized.

First, the Eurozone comes out as extraordinarily cautious in its policy reactions. While the ECB has been forceful in dealing with market turbulence, its macroeconomic reaction has erred on the prudent side, perhaps because of its price stability mandate. Even though it has gone all the way to the zero bound, its actions have been delayed relative to those of the Fed and other major central banks. Similarly, perhaps because of the Stability and Growth Pact,

Eurozone member governments have relied on the automatic stabilizers to a greater extent than many other countries have and the region has made relatively little use of discretionary fiscal policy. As a result, its recession may be deeper than it would have been and may last longer than in other parts of the world. Collective pressure may encourage restraint, which may be a good thing in some circumstances and a bad thing in others.

Second, the key benefit from a common currency has been reaped. One thing that Eurozone member policymakers do not have to worry about is sudden and wide shifts in relative competitiveness. Since intra-EU trade is large, this is a major advantage.

Third, another benefit of the common currency is the limited extent of currency mismatch. This is greatly assisting the deleveraging process of banks. It also allowed the ECB to act forcefully in providing liquidity in euro. This stands in sharp contrast with Asia where the world liquidity shortage has severely impacted many countries and, in some cases, led to sharp currency depreciation which heightened the inflation–output tradeoff, severely complicating the task of central banks.

Fourth, beyond the benefits of a common currency, European governments have shown a great deal of solidarity. Some of it has led directly to significant financial support to countries that have not joined the euro. The ECB thus recognizes the central role played by the euro and the risks posed by large exchange rate fluctuation to the smooth functioning of the single market. Even though within the Eurozone markets can and do pressure individual countries, solutions are being imagined.

Fifth, while exports to partners outside the Eurozone have declined as much as elsewhere, the impact has been limited simply because much trade takes place within Europe. Since the onset of the financial crisis, the real effective euro exchange rate has appreciated slightly by about 5 percent without apparently generating much anguish. As a result, Europe knows, or should know, that exiting from the recession depends on internal demand, and hence internal macroeconomic policies. Little use has been made of this advantage so far, but the possibility exists and may be put to good use if and when policymakers recognize it.

Finally, a puzzling question: With limited direct exposure of households to financial events and a limited impact of declining exports, why is the recession so severe? Policy reactions have been subdued and late, but this does not quite explain the rapid decline in consumption and productive investment. An intriguing possibility is that demand was reined in simply because households and firms became overly cautious, thus triggering a self-fulfilling prophecy. This has led a number of observers to recall Keynes' views on animal spirits.

References

Buiter, W. (2008). Housing Wealth isn't Wealth. Centre for Economic Policy Research Discussion Paper 6920. London: Centre for Economic Policy Research.

Doyle, B. and J. Faust (2005). Breaks in the Variability and Comovement of G-7 Economic Growth. *Review of Economics and Statistics* 87(4): 721–40.

European Commission (2009). *Quarterly Report of the Euro Area* 8(1). Brussels: European Commission.

Fatas, A. and I. Mihov (2001). Government Size and Automatic Stabilizers: International and Intranational Evidence. *Journal of International Economics* 55(1): 3–28.

——(2009). The Euro and Fiscal Policy. Working Paper 14722. Cambridge, MA: National Bureau of Economic Research.

Galì, J. and R. Perotti (2003). Fiscal policy and monetary integration in Europe. *Economic Policy* 37: 533–72.

Goodhart, C. and B. Hofmann (2008). House Prices, Money, Credit, and the Macroeconomy. Working Paper Series 888. Brussels: ECB.

International Monetary Fund (IMF) (2008). *World Economic Outlook*. October, Washington, DC: IMF.

——(2009). The State of Public Finances: Outlook and Medium-Term Policies After the 2008 Crisis. March 6, Washington, DC: IMF.

Strupczewski, J. (2009). EU's Barroso: can act if euro member in trouble. *Reuters*, March 4. Availabe: http://www.reuters.com/article/bondsNews/idUSBRU00731820090304 (accessed March 24, 2010).

Wyplosz, C. (2005). Institutions for Debt Sustainability in Brazil. In *Inflation Targeting, Debt, and the Brazilian Experience, 1999 to 2003*, edited by F. Giavazzi, I. Goldfajn, and S. Herrera. Cambridge, MA: The MIT Press.

Part III

Impacts of the Global Financial Crisis on Asia

4

Recessions and Recoveries in Asia: What Can the Past Teach Us about the Present

Souvik Gupta and Jacques Miniane

4.1 Introduction

Asia is in full recovery from the Great Recession. With external demand for Asia's products vanishing as a result of a sharp deleveraging in advanced economies, export and industrial production growth in the region plunged in late 2008 to unimaginable levels. In turn, weakness in exports spilled over to domestic demand, with investment in particular showing signs of decline at a high rate. Major policy efforts in Asia and abroad averted the worst, and paved the road for normalization in global trade and growth.

In this context, two key questions emerge: what is different about the current recession and recovery cycle in Asia, and what lessons can be drawn from this? This paper puts the current episode in the context of historical recessions and recoveries in order to shed light on these important questions.[1] In particular, we assess how long and deep the typical recession has been, why some recessions have been noticeably longer and deeper, if and why some countries within Asia have suffered deeper recessions than others, how strong or weak have recoveries typically been, and what leads these recoveries.

[1] While some papers such as Kim, Kose, and Plummer (2003) have looked at business cycle dynamics in Asia, there are fewer studies looking specifically at recession and recovery episodes in the region. One of these is Hong, Lee, and Tang (2009), who use annual rather than quarterly data as is done in this chapter. The use of annual data allows the authors to cover a longer data span, but at the cost of a less precise identification of business cycle turning points and hence the dynamics of different components around these key dates.

The key findings of this chapter can be summarized as follows:

- In the past, recessions accompanied by financial stress—notably, stress in domestic banking sectors—have been substantially longer and deeper than the norm. The fall in credit deprives corporations of working capital and households of the means to smooth consumption, greatly exacerbating the downturn that may have been under way.
- Recoveries in Asia have typically been weak because they were driven by a single engine: exports. In contrast, other emerging economies have tended to experience more vigorous recoveries because of a stronger contribution from domestic demand, notably investment.
- In Asia, deep recessions have resulted in substantial declines in potential output growth, meaning that their effects are not just cyclical but permanent.
- The export shock that led to the current recession was very large by historical standards, and as a result the recession was both longer and deeper (measured by cumulative output losses) than typical past recessions in the region.

Nonetheless, the recovery was also stronger, and not just because of vigorous exports: domestic demand in Asia also grew faster than in past recoveries. Not trivially, the policy response in the current episode was more vigorous than in past recessions.

These findings lead to several important considerations. First, had Asian banks not entered the recession with such strong balance sheets, the current recession, already among the most severe in recent decades, could have been substantially deeper and longer. Second, the aggressive fiscal and monetary response in the region was fully appropriate given the magnitude of the shock; it is hard to argue that things would not have been worse without it. Finally, looking into the medium-term, efforts to make the region's economies less export dependent should continue given ongoing concerns that weigh on advanced economies' prospects.

The rest of this chapter is structured as follows. Section 4.2 explains the methodology used to identify recessions and recoveries, and reviews some of their general characteristics. Section 4.3 looks at past recessions in Asia with an emphasis on two questions: what distinguishes the most severe recessions, and whether some countries are more vulnerable than others. Section 4.4 looks at past recoveries in Asia, showing in particular why they have tended to be weak compared with recoveries in other regions. Section 4.5 discusses policy responses and their effects in past recessions. Section 4.6 looks at the latest recession and recovery episode and sees to what extent it accorded to the stylized facts gleaned from history. Section 4.7 gives concluding remarks.

4.2 Preliminary considerations

In a study of recessions and recoveries, the first obvious question is: what type of recession? The academic literature typically distinguishes between classical recessions, which entail a decline in GDP *levels*, and growth slowdowns, which deal with declines in GDP *growth*. This chapter focuses on classical recessions, mainly because many economies in the region experienced declines in GDP levels in the current cycle.

Recession episodes are identified through an extension of the "two-quarters-of-negative-growth" rule. As general terminology, a "recession" begins when the level of GDP starts declining after a "peak" and ends when the level of GDP reaches a "trough". A "recovery" begins when the level of GDP starts rising after the trough and ends when the level of GDP returns to its peak level; an "expansion" lasts until GDP reaches its next peak. This chapter identifies peaks and troughs by means of the Bry and Boschan (1971) algorithm, which has become standard methodology in the study of classical recessions. Strictly speaking, the algorithm does not require two consecutive quarters of negative growth after a peak to identify a recession, but it does require GDP growth to be negative over the combined two-quarter period following the peak.

This chapter also differentiates recessions alongside various dimensions that appear relevant at the current juncture. We define a financial crisis recession as a recession episode associated with a domestic banking crisis (as identified in Laeven and Valencia 2008), or as a recession associated with higher-than-normal levels in our measure of global financial conditions (the financial stress index for advanced economies used in Cardarelli, Elekdag, and Lall 2009). We also differentiate between export recessions—defined as those during which export levels fall by at least 5 percent relative to peak level—and nonexport recessions. One objective of this chapter is to assess whether there are clear differences in length, depth, and dynamics between financial stress and nonfinancial stress recessions, and between export and nonexport recessions.

The sample of recessions identified here is quite diverse, with one surprising finding: export shocks have been an important but not the main cause of recessions in Asia. Limiting our analysis to the post-1980 but pre-2008 period, we identify thirty-three recessions in the Asian economies in the sample, excluding the 2008 recession in several of these economies. Of these thirty-three recessions, ten occurred in industrialized Asian and Pacific economies—

Japan, Australia, and New Zealand—and twenty-three in emerging Asian economies (Table A4.1 in the Appendix). Of note is that no classical recession occurred in the People's Republic of China (PRC) or India during the sample period. Seventeen out of the thirty-three recessions are associated with financial stress, but only seven of these seventeen coincided with a banking crisis. The latter have typically resulted from the bust of large imbalances in the domestic economy, as was the case in Japan in the 1990s or in the Asian crisis. Finally, eight of the thirty-three were export recessions according to our definition, suggesting that export shocks have been an important but far from exclusive driver of recessions in the region. Moving to the current cycle, we identify eight recessions, all of which are clearly export recessions.

Asia's business cycles appear increasingly coordinated with global business cycles. The incidence of recessions in Asia has by and large been uncorrelated with the incidence of recessions in advanced economies, either contemporaneously or with lags, when measured over the whole sample. At the same time, every US recession has coincided with at least 20 percent of the Asian economies in our sample being in recession, and often more. Moreover, the correlation between the incidence of recessions in Asia and globally has clearly increased over the past decade, a consequence of Asia's deepening integration with the global economy.[2]

Finally, recessions in Asia have had one common characteristic, regardless of the shock that caused them: investment tends to decline during a recession. Looking across all recessions, exports do not appear to have fallen on average, nor does consumption. Investment, however, falls with high probability (Figure 4.1). Why? The reason has to do with the fact that investment is tied both to exports and to domestic demand, and it suffers when recessions are caused by shocks to export demand, shocks to consumption, or shocks to financial conditions. Indeed, contrary to consumption and exports, investment fell in both the 1997–98 and the 2000–01 recession, which at their roots were very different.

4.3 Past recessions in Asia: how long and how deep?

4.3.1 *Are some recessions deeper than others?*

In Asia, recessions have typically been neither very long nor very deep. The median duration of recessions in Asia has been three quarters, similar to those

[2] See Guimarães-Filho, Hori, Miniane, and N'Diaye (2008) for discussion on Asia's deepening integration with the global economy.

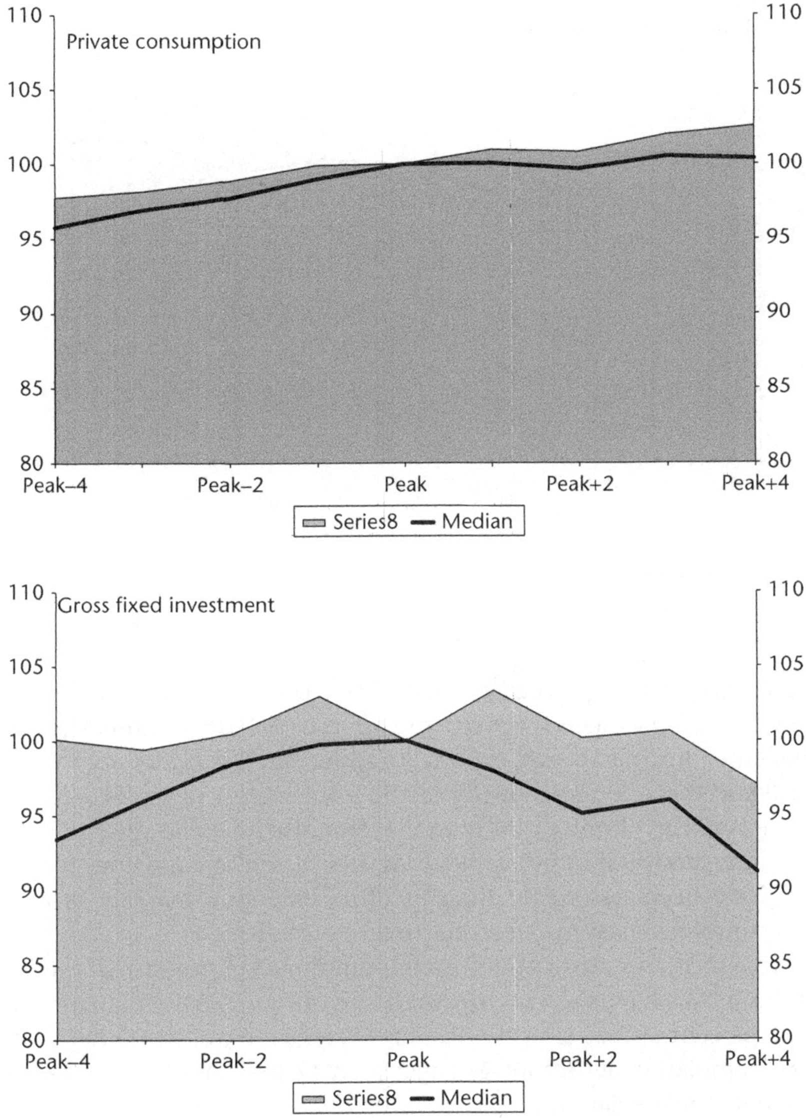

Figure 4.1 Asia: previous recessions since 1980 (median real level, peak of the recessions=100)
Source: IMF staff estimates.

in advanced economies as well as in non-Asia emerging markets.[3] In terms of the cumulative output loss during a recession, Asian episodes have been more costly than those in advanced economies—the median loss during an Asian

[3] Descriptive statistics in sections 4.3–4.5 pertain to recessions and recoveries up to but excluding the 2008–10 episode.

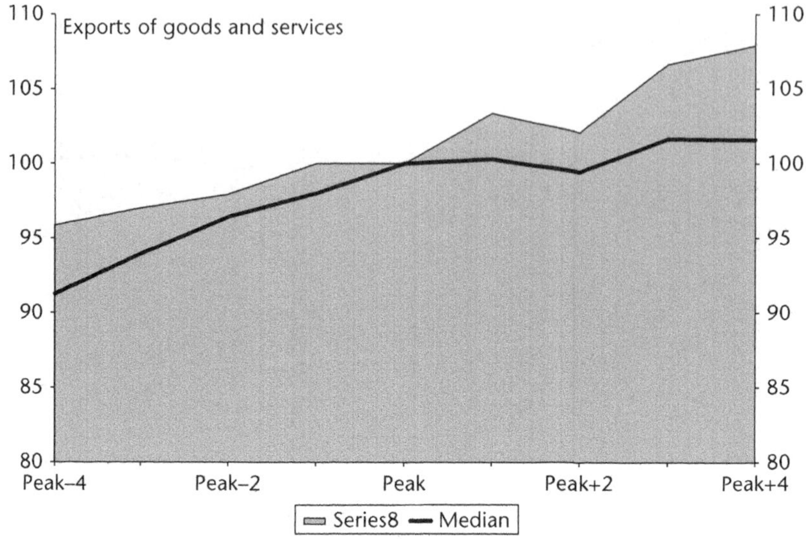

Figure 4.1 Continued

recession has been 5 percent of peak GDP, compared with 3 percent in advanced economies. This is consistent with the considerable literature showing that emerging markets are exposed to larger and more persistent volatility than advanced economies,[4] owing to the former's less diversified economic structures and their limited ability to use domestic financial systems or international markets to smooth the impact of shocks. At the same time, recessions in Asia have been less costly than in other emerging markets, where the median cumulative loss has been 10 percent of peak GDP.[5]

Yet these median statistics mask an important fact: a substantial number of recessions in Asia have been both long and very deep. In particular, nine of the 33 or 25 percent of recessions in Asia have lasted longer than a full year and entailed cumulative output losses larger than 12 percent of peak GDP, more than double the median loss.

These long and deep recessions are all associated with financial stress. Indeed, when we separate our sample between financial stress and nonfinancial stress recessions, the former led to output losses of 8 percent of GDP

[4] See Aguiar and Gopinath (2007) among others.

[5] Given Asia's higher trend growth pre-crisis, however, it is not clear that recessions in Asia have been less costly if measured not in terms of output loss relative to peak, but in terms of the output gap. We did not use the output gap as a measure of the cost of recessions because of the difficulty in properly estimating potential output during a recession.

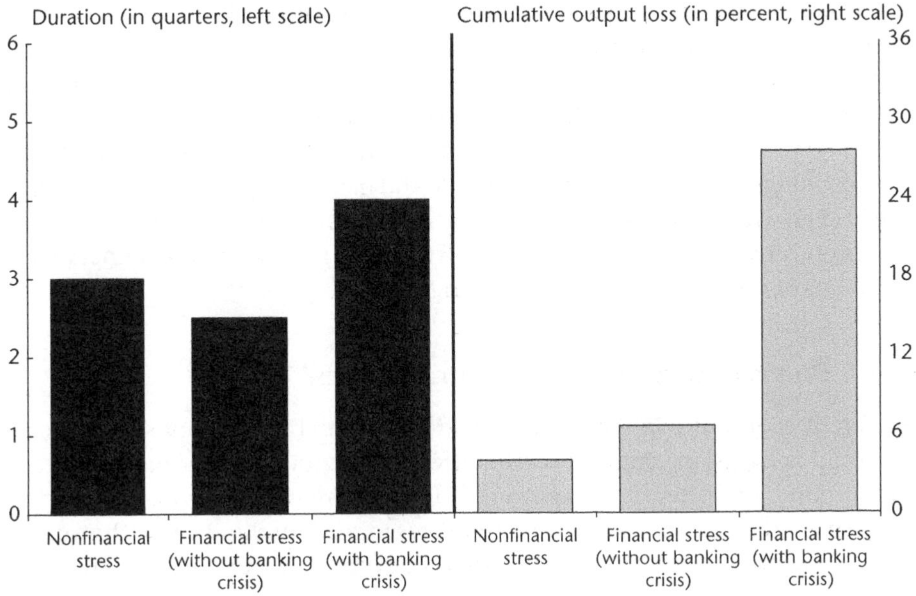

Figure 4.2 Asia: previous recessions since 1980 (median)
Source: IMF staff estimates.

higher in the median. At the same time, it is important to note that not all financial stress matters statistically for the length and depth of recessions. Recessions associated with global financial stress that were not accompanied by a domestic banking crisis are barely different in their severity to recessions with no financial stress, at least in our sample. It is recessions associated with banking crises that are of a more severe order of magnitude, entailing a 20 percent of GDP higher median cumulative output loss (Figure 4.2).[6] Indeed, the recessions in our sample with the largest 25 percent output losses were all associated with a banking crisis.

Credit curtailment appears to be the channel through which bank impairment amplifies recessions. In the case of Asia, credit growth remains by and large unaffected during standard recessions, but plummets during banking crises. At its lowest point during these recessions, median credit growth is 30 percentage points below its level before the recession started. Therefore, firms are deprived of working capital and consumers of the means to smooth consumption, explaining why the two decrease substantially more during banking crises. The relationship between credit and the real economy, however, should in no way be seen as uni-directional: banking crises are

[6] This result thus confirms for Asia what had been previously found for advanced economies in general in Cardarelli, Elekdag, and Lall (2009) and Reinhart and Rogoff (2009).

themselves caused by severe stresses in the real economy. What matters, then, is the feedback loops between real shocks and credit.

The lesson for the current cycle is clear. While the region suffered from the global reappraisal of risk in the form of capital outflows in 2008, declines in equity prices, and tight domestic liquidity conditions among other symptoms, core banking systems have remained stable and have been able to re-intermediate credit even when external funding was tightest. Without this stability, the current recession, already of historical proportions owing to the size of the external shock, would most certainly have been even longer and deeper.

4.3.2 *Do some economies suffer deeper recessions?*

Different economies in Asia seem to suffer comparable recessions on average. Decomposing Asian economies into different subgroups—regional groupings, commodity importers vs. exporters, high export exposure vs. low export exposure—does not signal major differences in median duration or the output loss of recessions across groups (Figure 4.3). Commodity exporters—Australia,

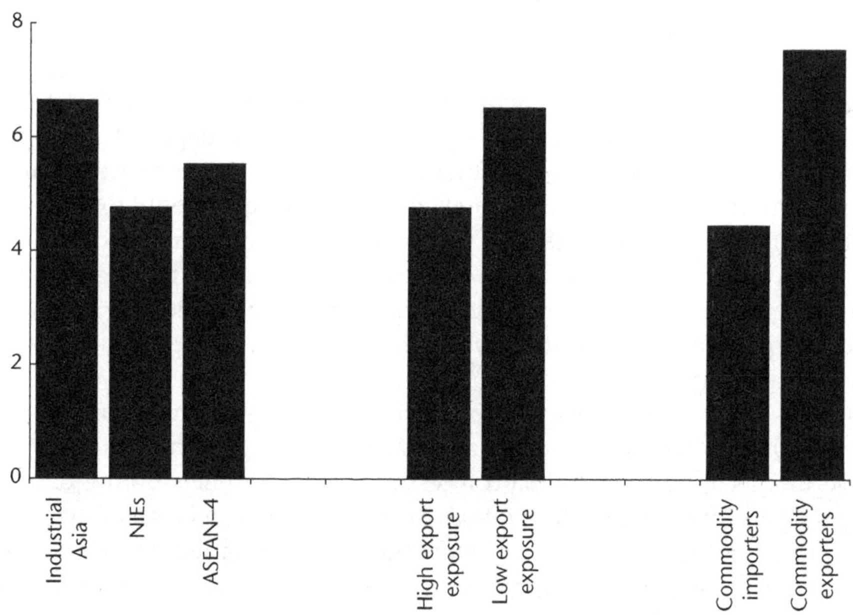

Figure 4.3 Asia by regional groups: cumulative output loss during previous recessions since 1980 (median, in percent)

Source: IMF staff estimates.

Notes: Industrial Asia = Japan, Australia, New Zealand; Association of Southeast Asian Nations (ASEAN) 4 = Indonesia, Malaysia, Philippines, Thailand; Newly industrialized economies (NIEs) = Hong Kong, China; Korea; Singapore; Taipei,China.

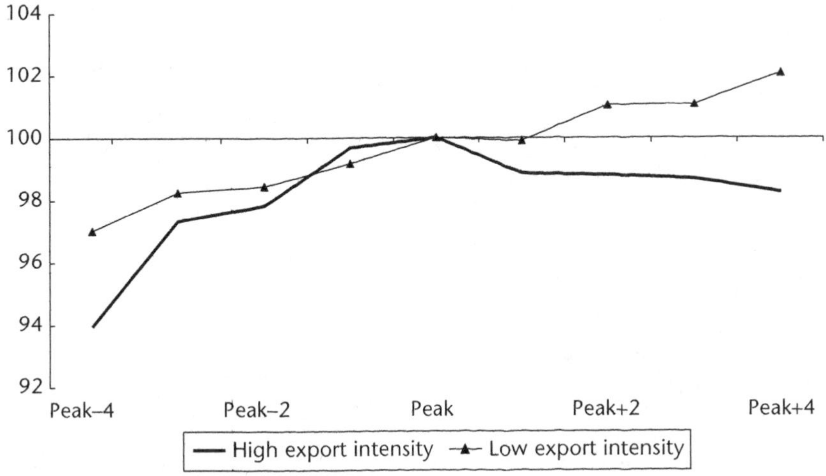

Figure 4.4 Asia by type of export activity: real gross domestic product during 2000–2001 recession (median level, peak of the recession = 100)

Source: IMF staff estimates.

Note: Includes countries that were not in recession in 2000–2001, excluding the People's Republic of China and India.

New Zealand, Indonesia, and Malaysia—seem to suffer deeper losses, but this is because two of the three recessions in Indonesia and Malaysia were banking crises.

However, of relevance to the current context, export-dependent economies are doubly vulnerable to export shocks because their domestic demand seems less autonomous from the export cycle.[7] Not only did GDP fall by more in these countries during export recessions, but consumption and investment fell as well (Figure 4.4).

We estimated the dynamic impact of export shocks on consumption and investment growth in the two sets of economies over the entire sample, by means of a panel vector autoregression (VAR). The results confirm that export shocks have substantially larger effects in the high export exposure group. In terms of magnitude, a 15 percentage point decline in year-on-year growth of real exports—a decline of similar magnitude to that experienced in Asia in the latest cycle—leads in the estimated model to a 6 percentage point decline in real investment growth in high export exposure countries, vs. a 2 percentage

[7] Highly export dependent economies are the newly industrialized economies (NIEs) and Malaysia. Low export dependent economies are Australia, Indonesia, Japan, New Zealand, Philippines, and Thailand. This classification uses data on Asian countries' direct and indirect export exposure to the US and the euro area presented in Guimarães-Filho, Hori, Miniane, and N'Diaye (2008).

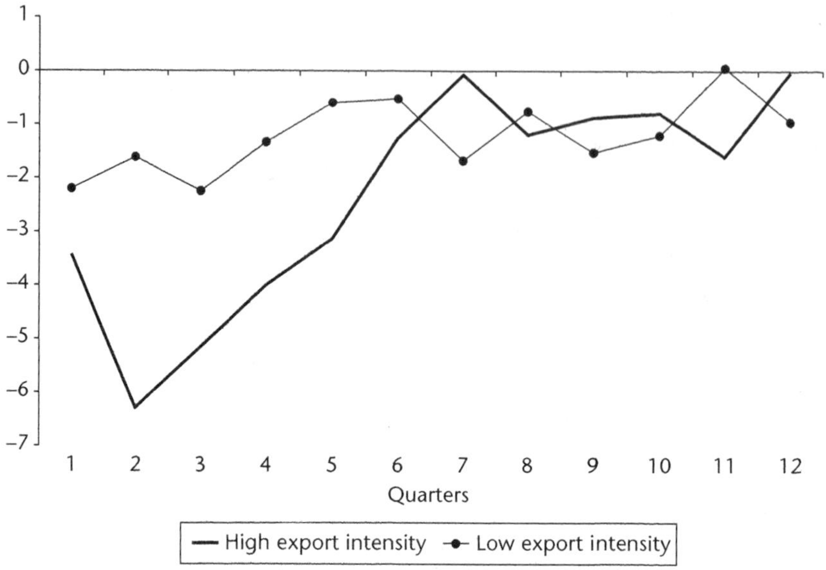

Figure 4.5 Asia: response of real gross fixed investment growth to a shock to real export growth (in percentage points)

Source: IMF staff estimates.

Note: A shock of 15 percentage points is considered here.

point decline in low export exposure economies (Figure 4.5). Moreover, the impact in the former group is persistent, with investment growth returning to pre-shock levels only a year and a half after the shock. The impact on consumption growth is smaller in magnitude but still not trivial: in trade-dependent economies, consumption growth declines by 1.5 percentage points following the shock.

Thus, past recession patterns yield two meaningful insights: (1) export-dependent economies are more vulnerable in the face of external demand shocks, and (2) banking sector stress greatly amplifies recessions. What lessons can be learned from the pattern of past recoveries? This is the purpose of the next section.

4.4 Past recoveries: how vigorous?

Patterns of recovery in Asia are relatively more homogeneous than those of recessions, and tend to be characterized by a strong rebound in exports and a relatively weak contribution from domestic demand. More specifically:

Exports have been the main engine of recoveries in Asia. In the recovery phase, exports tend to rebound strongly, with export volumes typically more than

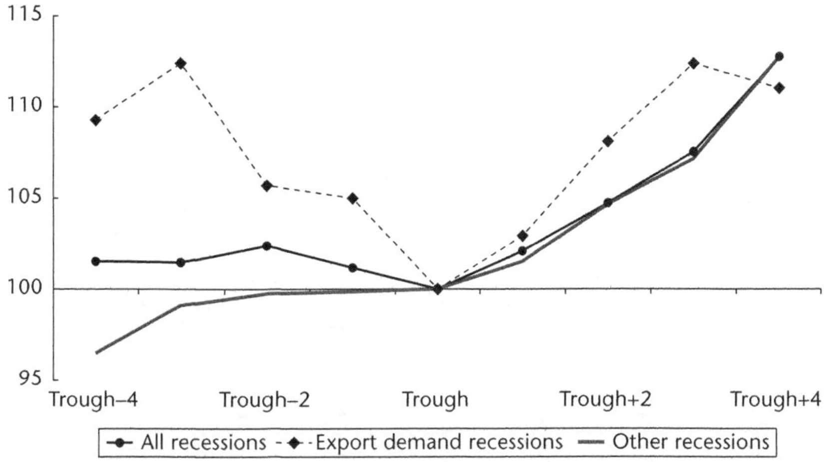

Figure 4.6 Asia: real exports of goods and services during previous recessions since 1980 (median level, trough of the recessions = 100)
Source: IMF staff estimates.

10 percent higher than their trough levels four quarters on (Figure 4.6). Not only was the rebound in exports key to the recovery in many export recessions, but growth in exports also led GDP and the other demand components in sixteen out of the other twenty-five recoveries.[8] Export rebounds appear to have been helped by currency depreciations, a common feature of Asian recessions, with stronger export recoveries associated with larger real effective depreciations in our sample.

Many recoveries in Asia have been "investment-less." In the typical recovery, investment remains flat post-trough for about three quarters, and then picks up the pace very gradually (Figure 4.7). Moreover, only four out of the thirty-three recoveries in the sample were led by a recovery in investment, defined as an upturn in investment post-trough that preceded the upturn in consumption and exports. Why has investment been so sluggish to recover? Excess pre-recession capacity may be part of the answer. Numerous studies have pinned excess investment before the Asian financial crisis as one reason investment appeared to be so weak after the crisis.[9] In fact, the collapse of investment in Asia following the 1997–98 crisis has often been cited as one of the root causes of the current account imbalances that have dominated the global economy in the past decade. Yet this crisis was not the only one during which investment failed to recover strongly. For instance, the recovery after the 2000–01

[8] To summarize, 60 percent of recoveries were led by exports, 30 percent by consumption, and 10 percent by investment.
[9] See IMF (2006) among others.

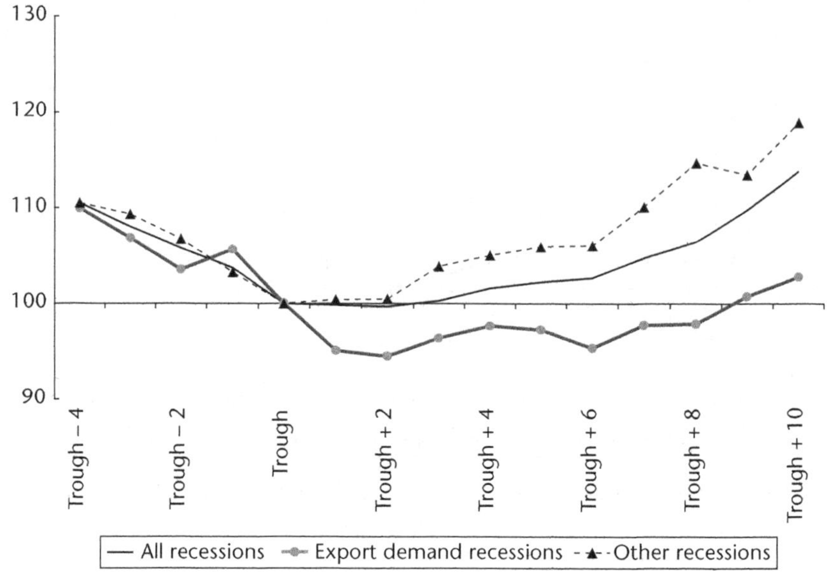

Figure 4.7 Asia: real gross fixed investment during previous recessions since 1980 (median level, trough of the recessions = 100)

Source: IMF staff estimates.

recession was even weaker, with investment stuck at trough levels for a full three years. Once again, excess capacity before the crisis, in this case concentrated in the information technology (IT) sector, led to weak investment after the crisis. It is an open and important question why investment in Asia appears to follow such pronounced boom and bust cycles.

Consumption played an important role in a limited number of recoveries. Consumption recoveries led about nine of the thirty-three GDP recoveries in the sample. Surprisingly, consumption led the recovery in several of the Asian-crisis episodes, for example in the Republic of Korea (hereafter Korea) and Singapore, and to a lesser extent in Thailand (Figure 4.8). This is in contrast with received wisdom that countries exited the Asian crisis thanks to sharp depreciations and export rebounds. This being said, it is doubtful that these consumption recoveries would have been sustainable had exports not recovered sharply soon after.

Given the importance of export growth in the recovery phase, this presents the question of whether export-dependent economies experience sharper recoveries. The answer is yes, both because the recovery in exports is sharper—perhaps owing to a higher elasticity of exports to foreign demand in these countries—and because the recovery in exports translates into a stronger recovery in domestic demand. Median GDP levels are 5 percentage

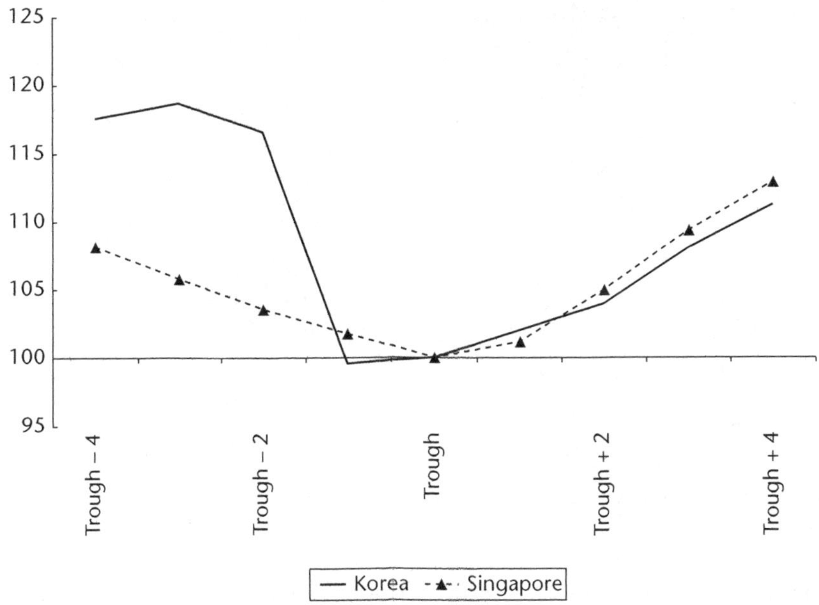

Figure 4.8 Selected Asia: real private consumption expenditure during the Asian Crisis (trough of the recession = 100)
Source: IMF staff estimates.

points higher one year after the trough in high export exposure economies, and the difference cannot be explained by higher trend growth in this group.

Because recoveries in Asia have typically relied on a single engine, they have tended to be weaker than in other regions. It typically takes emerging Asia three quarters to recover its recession output loss, when other emerging markets take two quarters to recover an output loss that was on average greater. Put differently, growth in the recovery phase in Asia is typically 0.5 percentage points lower per quarter (non-annualized) than in other emerging economies. A key difference is that non-Asia emerging economies typically benefit from a strong V-shaped recovery in investment.

Finally, are deeper recessions followed by sharper recoveries? The answer is a clear no. If output was trend stationary, a deeper recession could be followed by a sharper recovery. But the key is that deep recessions appear to entail permanent rather than just cyclical losses, violating the assumption of trend stationarity. In the deepest recession episodes, quarterly (annualized) potential output growth falls by some 1.5 percentage points, compared with about a one-third percentage point in the median recession (Figure 4.9). The cumulative impact of such a decline is significant: a 1 percentage point decline in annualized quarterly trend growth means that GDP would be 10 percent lower after ten years.

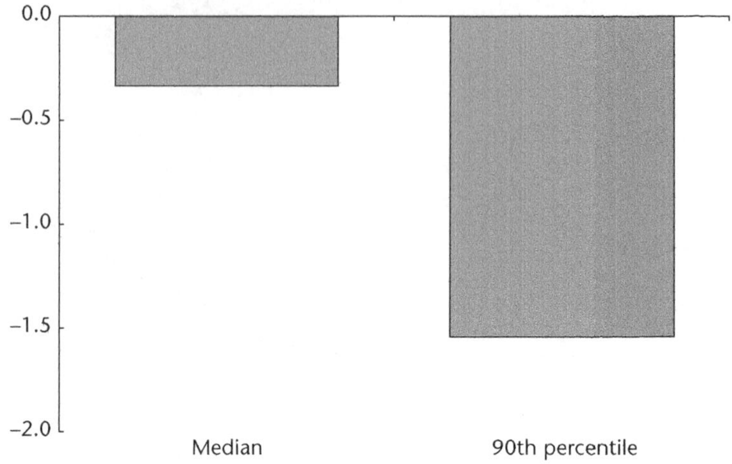

Figure 4.9 Asia: change in trend GDP growth during previous recessions since 1980 (in percent)

Source: IMF staff estimates.

Note: Difference in average annualized quarterly growth between eight quarters before peak and eight quarters after trough of the recessions.

4.5 Policy responses and impacts

Asia *did* take advantage of countercyclical tools in pre-2008 recessions. Despite a large literature documenting the procyclicality of fiscal and monetary policies in emerging economies,[10] our event study analysis shows that monetary and fiscal policies in Asia tend to loosen in response to recessions. Looking at monetary policy, interest rates have typically been reduced by 50 basis points (bp) over the full year after the recession (Figure 4.10). Needless to say, this was simply the median response: some recessions were met with higher policy rates to defend exchange rate pegs (as during the Asian crisis), whereas others were met with very aggressive policy loosening. Declines in nominal rates were enough to outpace falling inflation, as witnessed by the fact that median real interest rates fell as well. And, as mentioned earlier, exchange rate depreciations have been a common feature of recessions in Asia.

Although monetary policy is often thought of as the first line of defense, fiscal policy has also played its part in Asia. In past recessions, fiscal balances have typically been more than 1.5 percent of GDP lower a year after the peak. This was in part due to falling revenues in the recession, but expenditures

[10] See Kaminsky, Reinhart, and Vegh (2004), among others.

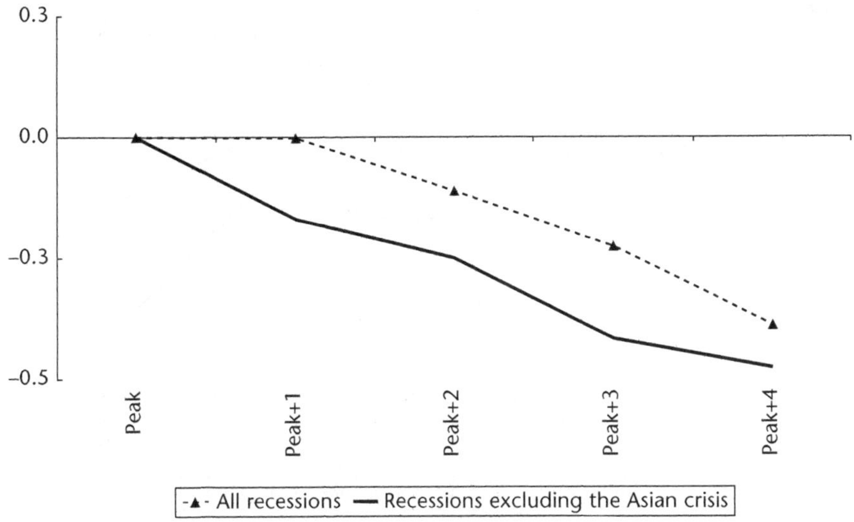

Figure 4.10 Asia: nominal policy rates during previous recessions since 1980 (median, in percent, peak of the recessions = 0)
Source: IMF staff estimates.

also tended to rise—by 1 percent of GDP over one year (Figure 4.11).[11] Equally noteworthy, the response of fiscal policy has typically been quite timely, with expenditures 0.5 percent of GDP higher one quarter after the recession started.

Has countercyclical monetary and fiscal policy been effective in the typical recession? Reverse causality hampers a proper answer to this question, because stronger policy responses tend to be observed during deeper recessions. To circumvent this problem, we constructed a counterfactual scenario. Specifically, we borrowed from the academic literature standard values for the dynamic impact of monetary and fiscal policy on GDP, and used these multipliers together with the actual policy changes during recessions to compute how much lower GDP would have been had policy not been loosened. The results show that, in the absence of observed policy changes, GDP would have been somewhat lower and the recovery shallower and more delayed. Because policy impacts operate with lags, the gap between the actual and counterfactual paths does not become substantial until one year after the start of the recession, but after two years the GDP counterfactual is 3 percentage points lower than actual GDP.

[11] We do not have enough data to determine how much of this jump is due to discretionary spending and how much is due to automatic stabilizers, but the latter tend to be small in Asia.

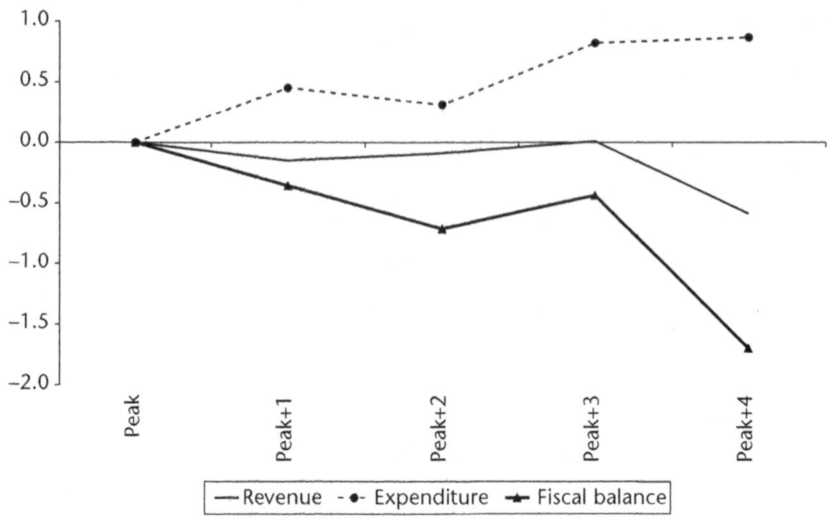

Figure 4.11 Asia: fiscal indicators during previous recessions since 1980 (median, in percent of GDP, peak of the recessions = 0)
Source: IMF staff estimates.

4.6 The current episode in historical context

Like other recessions in the past, the 2008 recession was caused by a shock to foreign demand, one that for all intents and purposes was exogenous to Asia. But the size of the shock was noteworthy, with the decline in exports *twice as large* as in past export recessions. In the latest episode, exports (national accounts definition) had declined by a massive 20 percent relative to peak levels four quarters into the recession, and in some countries by more.

Given such a large shock, it is not surprising that the latest recession was both long and deep by historical standards. In particular, the median cumulative loss was a high 7 percent of GDP, versus 5.3 percent in past recessions including the Asian crisis. Cumulative output losses in 2008–09 were far from uniform across countries, however, ranging from 1.5 percent in the Philippines to more than 10 percent in Japan. The degree of export dependency mattered again, with more export oriented countries suffering losses twice as large on average (Figure 4.12). Although Japan is not among the most export dependent economies in Asia, the large decline in GDP owed to the country's heavy orientation towards durables and capital goods, the global demand for which plummeted during the crisis.

Just as the recession was deep by historical standards, so the recovery was vigorous. Median cumulative GDP growth in the year after the trough, at some 8 percent, was twice as high as it had been in past recoveries (Figure 4.13).

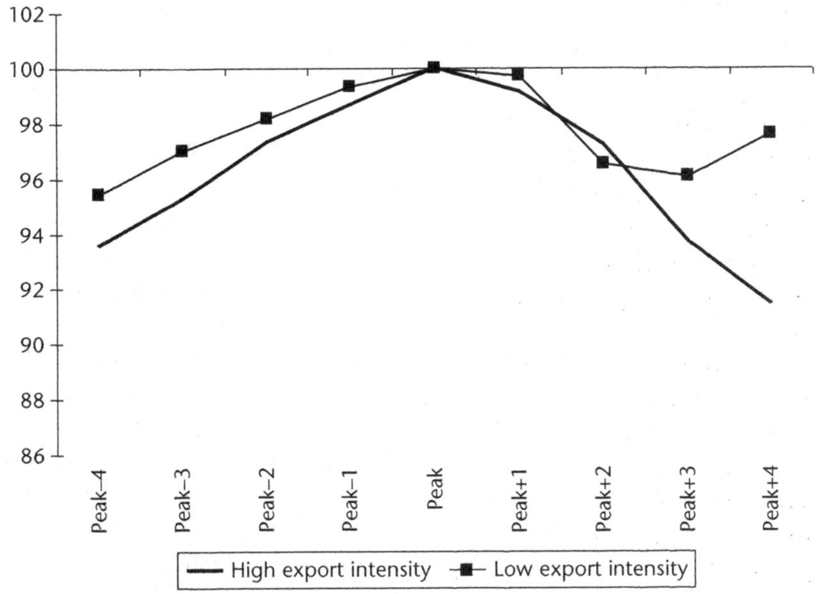

Figure 4.12 Asia by type of export activity: real gross domestic product during 2008–2009 Recession (median level, peak of the recessions = 100)

Source: IMF staff estimates.

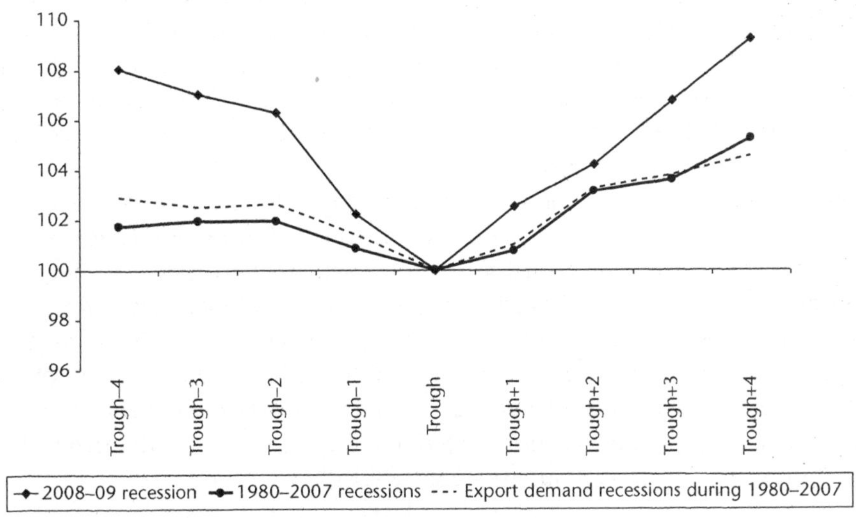

Figure 4.13 Asia: real gross domestic product during 2008–2009 recession vis-à-vis previous recessions since 1980 (median level, trough of the recessions = 100)

Source: IMF staff estimates.

There are two key reasons for this. First, the recession itself had been caused by a collapse in global trade that exceeded values warranted by fundamentals, hence the normalization in trade brought about unusually rapid export growth. This is borne out by the data: four quarters after the early 2009 trough, real exports in the recession-stricken countries in Asia had risen by more than 20 percent, vs. 12 percent in past median recessions. Second, domestic demand and particularly investment contributed substantially to the recovery. This is a significant development, as sluggish domestic demand had historically been the "Achiles' heel" of Asia's recoveries. While in previous recessions investment had remained flat for a full year after the trough, in 2009–10 investment in Asia grew by more than 10 percent cumulative.

This begs the question: why was the behaviour of domestic demand different this time around? Part of the credit has to fall on the vigorous policy response implemented in the region. Nominal policy interest rates were lowered more aggressively than in the past, some central banks moved decisively towards unconventional monetary policy, and fiscal balances in the recession-affected countries were allowed to deteriorate as much as in the Asian crisis, and twice as much as in the 2001 IT recession.[12] Moreover, some countries which were not officially in recession, such as the PRC, implemented large stimulus packages designed to bolster their own domestic demand and which had sizeable stimulative effects on other countries' exports. According to our calculations, GDP in the recession-affected countries would have been a massive 10 percentage points lower at the end of 2010 had they not implemented counter-cyclical macro policies over 2008–10 (Figure 4.14). Needless to say, such efforts would not have been possible without prudent policies during the pre-crisis period, which created the space for the subsequent crisis response.

The strong balance sheet of Asia's banks and non-financial corporates at the onset of the recession also played a key role in cushioning domestic demand in the downturn and later contributing to a swift recovery. Balance sheets did not bolt under pressure and averted negative feedback loops between the real and financial sectors which, if history is any guide, would have led to an even longer and deeper recession.[13] In contrast to various other regions of the world, overall credit to the private sector grew in Asia during the recession including in those countries most affected by the downturn, notwithstanding initial pressures on trade financing (Figure 4.15).

[12] The computation for the Asian crisis refers to standard fiscal outlays and excludes bank recapitalization costs.

[13] At the onset of the crisis, IMF (2009a) had predicted that the risks posed by the crisis on the region's financial systems were significant but manageable, thanks to strong balance sheets. IMF (2009a) had also argued that non-financial corporate sheets were in good stead and would help avoid widespread defaults despite the large decline in demand. Both proved to be true.

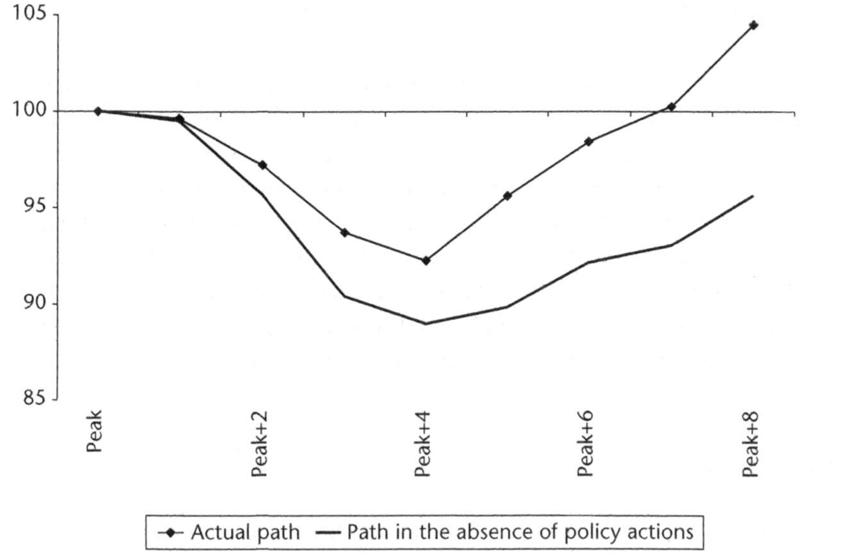

Figure 4.14 Asia: impact of policy actions on real gross domestic product during 2008–2009 recession (median level; peak of the recession = 100)

Source: IMF staff estimates.

Note: This includes economies in recession.

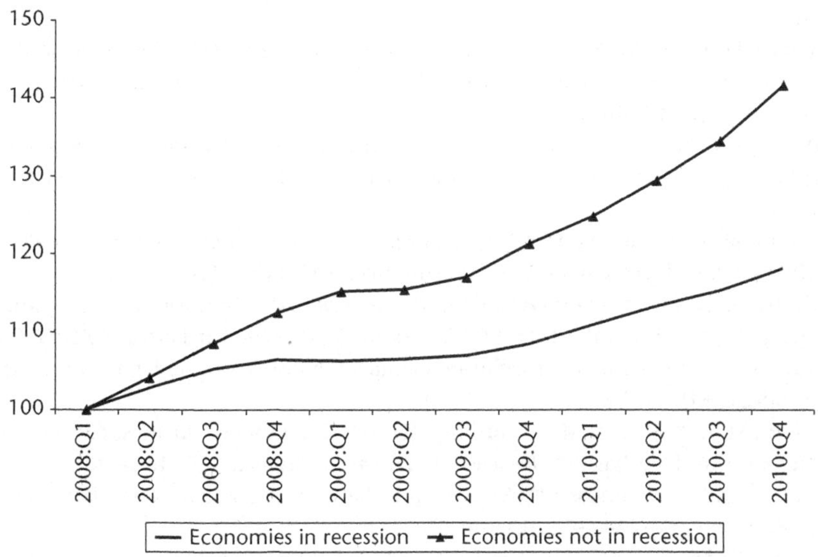

Figure 4.15 Asia: credit to private sector, 2008–2010 (nominal level; based on median quarter-over-quarter growth; peak of the recession = 100)

Source: IMF staff estimates.

4.7 Concluding remarks

Just as the region's reliance on exports is a key reason it has suffered greatly in this recession, timely countercyclical policies and strong balance sheets in the financial and non-financial sectors paved the way for a vigorous recovery. At the same time, households and sovereigns in advanced economies will need to repair their over-leveraged balance sheets over time. In such an environment, the structural growth rate of Asian manufacturing and exports could be lower. Structural reforms, such as expansion of social safety nets and deepening of domestic financial markets, some of which are ongoing, will be needed if Asia wants to diversify its sources of growth more durably.

References

Aguiar, M. and G. Gopinath (2007). Emerging Market Business Cycles: The Cycle Is the Trend. *Journal of Political Economy* 115: 69–102.

Bry, G. and C. Boschan (1971). Cyclical Analysis of Economic Time Series: Selected Procedures and Computer Programs. NBER Technical Working Paper No. 20. Cambridge, MA: National Bureau of Economic Research (NBER).

Cardarelli, R., S. Elekdag, and S. Lall (2009). Financial Stress, Downturns, and Recoveries. IMF Working Paper 09/100. Washington, DC: International Monetary Fund (IMF).

Guimarães-Filho, R., M. Hori, J. Miniane, and P. N'Diaye (2008). Can Asia Decouple? Investigating Spillovers from the United States to Asia. In *Regional Economic Outlook: Asia and Pacific*. Washington, DC: IMF. April.

Hong, K., J.-W. Lee, and H. C. Tang (2009). Crises in Asia: Historical Perspectives and Implications. ADB Economics Working Paper Series No. 152. Manila: Asian Development Bank.

International Monetary Fund (IMF) (2006). Asia's Investment Decline. In *Regional Economic Outlook: Asia and Pacific*. Washington, DC: IMF. May.

——2009a. *Regional Economic Outlook: Asia and Pacific*. Washington, DC: IMF. May.

Kaminsky, G., C. M. Reinhart, and C. A. Vegh (2004). When It Rains, It Pours: Procyclical Capital Flows and Macroeconomic Policies. NBER Working Paper No. W10780. Cambridge, MA: NBER.

Kim, S. H., M. A. Kose, and M. G. Plummer (2003). Dynamics of Business Cycles in Asia: Differences and Similarities. *Review of Development Economics* 7: 462–77.

Laeven, L. and F. Valencia (2008). Systemic Banking Crises: A New Database. IMF Working Paper 08/224. Washington, DC: IMF.

Lall, S., R. Cardarelli, and S. Elekdag (2008). Financial Stress and Economic Downturns. *World Economic Outlook*. October. Washington, DC: IMF. pp. 129–58.

Reinhart, C. M. and K. S. Rogoff (2009). The Aftermath of Financial Crises. NBER Working Paper No. 14656. Cambridge, MA: NBER.

APPENDIX 1

Data coverage

The sample of Asia and Pacific region economies includes Japan; Australia; New Zealand; PRC; India; Hong Kong, China; Korea; Taipei,China; Indonesia; Malaysia; Philippines; and Thailand, although no recessions were identified in the PRC or India.

Table A4.1 Asia: identification of previous recessions since 1980

	Recession episodes	Recessions identified with		
		Financial stress	Domesitc banking crisis	Export demand shock
Hong Kong, China	1982Q1–1982Q2	√		
	1989Q1–1989Q2			
	1995Q2–1995Q3			
	1997Q4–1998Q4	√		
	2001Q1–2001Q4			√
	2003Q1–2003Q2			
	2008Q2–2009Q1			√
Indonesia	1998Q1–1998Q4	√	√	
Japan	1992Q2–1992Q3	√		
	1997Q2–1999Q1	√	√	
	2001Q2–2001Q4			
	2008Q2–2009Q1			√
Korea	1979Q3–1980Q2			
	1997Q4–1998Q2	√	√	
Malaysia	1998Q1–1998Q3	√	√	
	2001Q1–2001Q2			√
	2008Q3–2009Q1			√
New Zealand	1982Q4–1983Q1	√		
	1985Q2–1986Q1			√
	1989Q3–1990Q2			
	1991Q1–1991Q2	√		
	1997Q4–1998Q1	√		
	2008Q1–2009Q1			√
Philippines	1983Q3–1985Q3	√	√	
	1990Q4–1991Q2	√		
	1992Q1–1992Q2			
	1998Q1–1998Q2	√	√	√
	2000Q4–2001Q1			√
	2008Q4–2009Q1			√
Singapore	1985Q2–1985Q4			√
	1997Q4–1998Q3	√		
	2001Q1–2001Q3			√
	2002Q3–2003Q2			
	2008Q2–2009Q1			√
Taiwan, China	2000Q4–2001Q3			√
	2003Q1–2003Q2			
	2008Q2–2009Q1			√
Thailand	1996Q4–1998Q3	√	√	
	2008Q3–2009Q1			√

Sources: Laeven and Valencia (2008); Lall, Cardarelli, and Elekdag (2008); and IMF staff estimates.

The sample of advanced economies includes Austria, Belgium, Canada, Denmark, Finland, France, Germany, Greece, Ireland, Italy, the Netherlands, Norway, Portugal, Spain, Sweden, Switzerland, the United Kingdom, and the US.

The sample of non-Asian emerging economies includes Argentina, Brazil, Chile, Colombia, Costa Rica, Croatia, Ecuador, Islamic Republic of Iran, Latvia, Lithuania, Mexico, Peru, Poland, Russia, South Africa, Serbia, Slovak Republic, Turkey, Uruguay, and Venezuela (other economies were part of the sample but no recession was identified for them).

The data are quarterly, and we focused on the post-1980 period because of the dramatic changes in the structure of Asian economies over the past four decades.

5

Intra-Regional Trade in East Asia

The Decoupling Fallacy, Crisis, and Policy Challenges

Prema-Chandra Athukorala and Archanun Kohpaiboon

5.1 Introduction

The "decoupling" thesis, the notion that the East Asian region has become a self-contained economic entity with potential for maintaining its own growth dynamism independent of the economic outlook for the traditional developed market economies, was a popular theme in Asian policy circles in the first decade of the new millennium until the onset of the recent financial crisis.[1] The empirical basis for this was provided by studies of trade patterns based on readily available trade data, which revealed a continuous increase in trade among the countries in the region (intra-regional trade) since the late 1980s, a process which received added impetus from the subsequent emergence of the People's Republic of China (PRC) as a world export powerhouse. A few studies questioned the validity of this inference in a context where international production fragmentation and the related network trade had been rapidly expanding with East Asia as its centre of gravity (Roach 2009; Bergsten et al. 2006; Athukorala 2005; Garnaut 2003). However, the decoupling thesis continued to dominate the policy scene, presumably because it fitted well with the East Asian growth euphoria of the day.

The global financial crisis (GFC) has served to reveal the fragility of the decoupling thesis since all major East Asian economies, including the PRC, have experienced precipitous trade contractions. Consequently, the policy debate in East Asia has made a U-turn from the complacency of the decoupling thesis to call for the rebalancing of East Asian growth with a view to reducing

[1] See Urata (2006), Yoshitomi (2007), and Park and Shin (2009) and the works cited therein.

its susceptibility to the vicissitudes of the global business cycle (ADB 2010; IMF 2010).

What went wrong with the decoupling thesis? Was the trade integration story that underpinned the decoupling thesis simply a statistical artifact, resulting from a failure to incorporate the realities of an era of global production sharing? What are the policy challenges faced by the East Asian economies in the post-GFC era? This chapter aims to probe these and related issues through a comparative analysis of the export experiences of PRC and other East Asian economies in the aftermath of the crisis against the backdrop of a systematic analysis of pre-crisis trade patterns.

The decoupling thesis is based on the traditional notion of horizontal specialization according to which international trade is an exchange of goods that are produced from start to finish in just one country. It ignores the implications for trade flow analysis of the ongoing process of global production sharing[2]—the breakup of the production processes into separated stages, with each country specializing in a particular stage of the production sequence—and the increasingly important role played by the PRC and other East Asian economies in the resultant global production network. In a context where production-sharing based trade is growing rapidly, trade flow analysis based on the assumption of horizontal specialization can lead to misleading inferences about the nature and extent of trade integration among countries for three reasons.

First, in the presence of global production sharing, trade data are double-counted because goods in process cross multiple international borders before becoming embodied in the final product. Thus, the total amount of recorded trade could be a multiple of the value of final goods. Second, and perhaps more importantly, trade shares calculated using reported data can lead to wrong inferences as to the relative importance of the "region" and the rest of the world for the growth dynamism of a given country, even controlling for double counting in trade. This is because "fragmentation trade" and trade in related final goods "final trade" are unlikely to follow the same patterns. Third, the intra-regional trade ratio estimated by lumping imports and exports tends to hide a significant asymmetry in regional trade patterns of imports and exports in a context where network related trade is growing rapidly.

Given these concerns, a meaningful analysis of trade patterns requires systematic separation of parts and components (henceforth referred to as "components" for short) from final (assembled) products in reported trade data. We do this through a careful disaggregation of trade data based on

[2] In the recent literature, an array of alternative terms have been used to describe this phenomenon, including "international production fragmentation", "vertical specialization", "slicing the value chain", and "outsourcing".

Revision 3 of the Standard International Trade Classification (SITC, Rev 3) extracted from the United Nations trade data reporting system (UN Comtrade database).[3]

For the purpose of this paper, East Asia is defined to include Japan and developing East Asia (DEA), which covers the newly industrialized economies (NIEs) of North Asia (Republic of Korea (hereafter Korea); Taipei,China and Hong Kong, China), the PRC and members of the Association of Southeast Asian Nations (ASEAN). Among the ASEAN countries, Myanmar is not covered because of a lack of data and Brunei, Cambodia and Lao PDR are treated as a residual group because of data gaps. The East Asian experience is examined in the wider global context, focusing specifically on the comparative experiences of the North American Free Trade Agreement (NAFTA) and the European Union (EU).

The chapter is structured as follows. The first section examines trade patterns in East Asia in the global context, paying attention to the nature and extent of production sharing and network-based trade, East Asia's role in this new form of international exchange and its implications for regional vs. global economic integration. In the next section the latest available data are used to examine the impact of the GFC on the export performance of East Asian economies. The following section deals with post-crisis policy challenges, focusing on the emerging debate regarding rebalancing (or reshaping) development strategies. The final section summarizes the key findings and draws some general inferences.

5.2 Pre-crisis trade patterns

Rapid export growth has been the hallmark of East Asia's rise in the global economy. The combined share of East Asian economies in world non-oil exports recorded a three-fold increase between 1969–70 and 2006–07 from 11 percent to 33 percent.[4] Rapid export growth has been underpinned by a pronounced shift in the region's export structure away from primary commodities and toward manufacturing. By 2005–07 manufacturing accounted for 92 percent of total exports from Asia, up from 78 percent four decades ago. Within manufacturing, machinery and transport equipment (SITC 7),

[3] For details on the decomposition procedure, and the list of parts and components used in the analysis, see Athukorala (2009).

[4] Trade magnitudes throughout the paper are measured in current US dollars unless otherwise indicated. Inter-temporal comparison calculations are made for the two-year averages relating to the end points of the period under study, so as to reduce the impact of year to year fluctuations of trade flows. All data reported, unless otherwise stated, are compiled from the UN Comtrade database.

particularly information and communication technology (ICT) products and electrical goods, have played a pivotal role in this structural shift. By 2006–07, over 58 percent of total world ICT exports originated from Asia, with the PRC alone accounting for 23 percent. In electrical goods, the PRC's world market share increased from 3.1 percent to 20.6 percent between these two years. Export dynamism in these product lines has been driven by the ongoing process of global production sharing (international production fragmentation) and the increasingly deep integration of East Asian countries into global production networks.

The best available indicator of the intensity of global production sharing is the share of components in total manufacturing trade. Reflecting the rapid growth of global production sharing, the share of components in manufacturing trade has sharply increased across all major countries in the region (Table 5.1). In 2006–07 components accounted for 34.1 percent of East Asia manufacturing exports (42.1 percent of manufacturing imports) compared to a world average of 27.1 percent (27.3 percent of imports). The share of components is particularly high among the ASEAN countries. There is a

Table 5.1 Share of parts and components in manufacturing trade, 1992–1993 and 2006–2007 (%)

	Exports		Imports	
	1992–93	*2006–07*	*1992–93*	*2006–07*
ASEAN	22.7	44.2	36.0	47.9
Indonesia	3.8	21.5	27.0	21.8
Malaysia	27.7	53.6	40.5	50.0
Philippines	32.9	71.7	32.6	61.3
Singapore	29.0	49.3	39.9	60.4
Thailand	14.1	29.9	30.6	36.1
Vietnam	—	11.0	—	19.1
EA	20.2	34.1	27.2	42.1
Japan	23.9	34.4	19.3	29.9
DEA	17.3	34.0	29.0	44.2
PRC	7.4	25.6	20.4	44.0
Hong Kong, China	15.8	33.3	24.1	48.5
Taipei,China	24.7	44.2	29.5	38.9
Korea	18.1	47.3	30.1	31.9
SA	2.3	8.2	16.6	23.8
India	3.0	10.4	17.5	22.9
EU15	18.3	22.4	21.2	23.2
NAFTA	28.4	31.2	37.4	28.8
Mexico	42.1	34.6	29.4	36.1
Developed countries	20.4	25.2	22.6	23.4
Developing countries	14.6	29.2	11.9	33.6
World	19.3	27.1	19.6	27.3

Source: Compiled from UN Comtrade database.

Notes: "—"—means data not available.
DEA = Developing East Asia; EA = East Asia; SA = South Asia.

remarkable similarity in component share figures in both exports and imports across countries, reflecting overlapping specialization patterns in component assembly among countries in the region.

The rapid increase in the component intensity (percentage shares of components) in East Asian trade is closely associated with cross-border component trade within regional production networks. Components account for a much larger share in intra-regional trade in East Asia compared to these countries' shares of world trade and trade with the EU and NAFTA (Table 5.2). Moreover, the share of components in total intra-regional imports is much larger than in exports, and has increased at a faster rate. This reflects the fact that the region relies more on the rest of the world as a market for final goods than as a market for components. The conventional trade-flow analysis which does not distinguish between components and final goods is therefore, bound to yield a misleading picture as to the relative importance of intra-regional trade, as compared to global trade, for growth in East Asia.

To illustrate this point, intra-regional trade shares are estimated separately for total manufacturing, components, and final goods (total manufacturing net of components), and reported in Table 5.3. The table covers trade in East Asia and three sub-regions therein which relate to contemporary Asian policy debates on regional integration. Data for NAFTA and the EU are reported for comparative purposes. Estimates are given for total trade (imports + exports) as well as for exports and imports separately in order to illustrate possible

Table 5.2 Share of parts and components in bilateral trade flows, 2006–2007 (%)

Reporting country	EA	Japan	DEA	PRC	ASEAN	NAFTA	EU15	World
(a) Exports								
EA	47.6	32.9	50.1	51.6	54.5	25.1	24.1	34.1
Japan	42.0	0.0	42.0	41.5	47.9	31.5	30.4	34.4
DEA	48.1	33.4	53.9	0.0	65.2	22.7	21.6	34.0
PRC	36.2	25.2	40.6	0.0	49.1	17.1	16.3	25.6
Korea	61.9	51.5	63.5	57.3	63.7	36.6	26.8	44.2
Taipei,China	51.5	59.0	50.5	39.5	61.2	35.0	37.6	44.2
ASEAN10	58.2	39.9	61.4	64.0	56.0	32.1	33.9	44.2
EU15	31.4	18.7	34.8	30.4	46.5	22.1	22.0	22.4
NAFTA	46.7	36.5	49.8	34.8	67.9	28.8	30.6	31.2
(b) Imports								
EA	51.7	48.8	52.8	34.8	68.3	54.7	33.1	42.1
Japan	34.2	0.0	34.2	23.1	44.9	41.0	18.9	29.9
DEA	55.5	47.7	59.5	0.0	74.3	40.3	31.7	44.2
PRC	55.2	47.5	59.2	0.0	74.0	40.1	31.6	44.0
Korea	33.0	26.6	38.1	26.1	55.7	38.9	22.9	31.9
Taipei,China	46.7	33.8	58.3	44.1	68.8	40.2	28.0	38.9
ASEAN10	50.3	47.2	51.4	40.1	55.9	67.5	41.7	47.9
EU15	25.0	33.6	22.8	14.9	37.9	34.1	22.1	23.4
NAFTA	29.4	39.3	26.0	17.7	40.5	36.3	25.1	28.8

Source: Compiled from UN Comtrade database.

Table 5.3 Intra-regional shares of manufacturing trade: total, parts and components, and final trade, 1992–1993 and 2006–2007 (%)

	EA		ASEAN + 3	ASEAN	NAFTA	EU15
(a) Total trade						
Exports						
1986–87	28.4	25.1	17.3	17.4	49.1	65.5
1992–93	47.2	38.2	15.3	20.7	44.4	61.2
2006–07	43.9	33.4	21.9	18.4	48.1	56.9
Imports						
1986–87	48.6	22.9	34.4	11.0	29.9	69.7
1992–93	58.2	34.9	43.0	15.5	36.3	64.1
2006–07	64.4	46.7	49.3	20.8	32.0	57.9
Trade (exports + imports)						
1986–87	35.8	24.0	22.9	13.5	37.1	67.5
1992–93	53.2	36.5	27.0	17.8	39.9	62.6
2006–07	55.1	40.0	30.4	20.1	38.4	57.4
(b) Components						
Exports						
1992–93	50.2	42.6	33.7	30.3	43.5	62.3
2006–07	61.1	53.9	35.3	25.4	46.9	55.9
Imports						
1992–93	65.9	35.3	39.6	20.2	39.5	58.0
2006–07	66.9	50.9	47.8	22.9	39.9	55.2
Trade (exports + imports)						
1992–93	57.0	38.7	35.4	24.2	41.4	60.1
2006–07	62.9	52.1	40.2	23.1	43.2	55.5
(c) Final goods						
Exports						
1992–93	46.0	36.8	11.4	16.1	44.7	60.9
2006–07	36.9	28.3	17.0	15.9	48.7	57.0
Imports						
1992–93	55.4	34.7	43.4	12.9	35.3	65.6
2006–07	63.0	42.8	50.2	20.6	30.2	58.5
Trade (exports + imports)						
1992–93	50.3	35.7	25.4	14.3	39.4	63.2
2006–07	46.4	34.0	29.1	18.0	37.3	57.7

Source: Compiled from UN Comtrade database, and Trade Data CD-ROM, Council for Economic Planning and Development, Taipei (for data on Taipei,China).

Notes: Intra-regional trade shares have been calculated excluding bilateral flows between the PRC and Hong Kong, China. ASEAN + 3 = ASEAN + Japan + Korea + the PRC. Final Goods = Total (reported) trade (a)—parts and components (b).

asymmetries in trade patterns resulting from East Asia's increased engagement in fragmentation-based international exchange.

Trade patterns depicted by the unadjusted (standard) trade data affirm the perception underlying the decoupling thesis that Asia, and in particular East Asia, has become increasingly integrated through merchandise trade. In 2006–07 intra-regional trade accounted for 55.1 percent of total manufacturing trade, up from 35.8 percent in 1986–87. The level of intra-regional trade in East Asia was higher than that of NAFTA throughout this period and was rapidly approaching the level of the EU-15. For developing East Asia (Asia excluding Japan) and ASEAN + 3, the ratios are lower than the aggregate regional figure, but they have increased at a much faster rate. The intra-regional trade share of ASEAN has been much lower compared to the other two sub-regions.

However the picture changes significantly when components are netted out: the intra East Asian share in final trade in 2006–07 was 46.4 percent, down from 50.3 percent in 1992–93. The estimates based on unadjusted data and data on final trade are vastly different for East Asia, particularly for DEA and ASEAN. Both the level of trade in the two given years and the change over time in intra-regional trade shares are significantly lower for estimates based on final trade. Interestingly, we do not observe such a difference in estimates for NAFTA and EU.

The intra-regional shares calculated separately for imports and exports clearly illustrate the risk of making inferences about regional trade integration based on total (imports + exports) data. There is a notable asymmetry in the degree of regional trade integration in East Asia. Unlike in the EU and NAFTA, in East Asia the increase over time in the intra-regional trade ratio (both measured using unadjusted data and data for final trade) has emanated largely from the rapid increase in intra-regional imports; the expansion in intra-regional exports has been consistently slower. The dependence of East Asia (and country sub-groups therein) on extra-regional markets (in particular those in NAFTA and EU) for export-led growth is far greater than is revealed by the standard intra-regional trade ratios commonly used in the debate on regional economic integration. For instance, in 2007 only 43.9 percent of total East Asian manufacturing exports was absorbed within the region, compared to an intra-regional share of 64.4 percent in total manufacturing imports. For DEA the comparable figures were 33.4 percent and 46.7 percent respectively. This asymmetry is clearly seen across all sub-regions within East Asia. The asymmetry between intra-regional shares of import and exports is much sharper when components are netted out. This is understandable given the heavy "component bias" in Asian intra-regional trade and the multiple border-crossing of parts and components within regional production networks. On the export side, the intra-regional share of final goods declined continuously from 46 percent in 1995 to 37 percent in 2007, whereas the intra-regional import share increased from 56 percent to 63 percent between these two time points.

In sum, these estimates suggest that extra-regional trade is much more important than intra-regional trade for continued growth in East Asia. Thus the rising importance of global production sharing seems to have strengthened, rather than weakened, East Asia's link with the wider global economy. As we will see in the next section, this inference is basically consistent with the behavior of trade flows in East Asia following the onset of the GFC.

5.3 Trade performance in the aftermath of the crisis

A striking feature of the global economy following the onset of the in late 2007 GFC has been the precipitous drop in global trade at a faster rate than during the Great Depression (Almunia et al. 2010; Krugman 2009). From April 2008 to June 2009 world trade contracted by 20 percent which amounted to almost the total contraction in world trade during the first 30 months of the Great Depression (starting in April 1929).[5] Interestingly, the trade contraction experienced by the East Asian economies during this period has been even greater than the contraction in total world trade (Figure 5.1).

Krugman (2009) points to the increased vertical integration of global production (the rise of globe production sharing) as a possible explanation for the surprisingly large trade contraction in the present crisis compared to the Great Depression. Vertical integration of production implies that a given degree of contraction in demand for a final (assembled) product has ramifications over trade flows between the many countries involved in the production chain. Also, demand for components is susceptible to rapid stock adjustment by producers compared to final goods. Given that global production sharing is much more important for trade expansion in East Asia, this explanation also seems relevant for East Asia's greater trade contraction compared to overall trade contraction at the global level. However, a number of other factors are also relevant for explaining the larger contraction in trade volume in the current crisis. These include the much larger contraction of trade credit, a greater share of consumer durables in contemporary world trade compared to the 1930s, and the effect of recent advances in communication technology on inventory cycle and just-in-time procurement practices. The current state of data availability does not permit us to systematically delineate the impact of production sharing on trade contraction while appropriately controlling for these other possible factors. Instead, this section puts together some readily available data that have some bearing on this issue in order to set the stage for further analysis.

All major East Asian economies (including the PRC, which was expected by the decoupling enthusiast to cushion the rest of East Asia against a global economic collapse) experienced a precipitous trade contraction from about the last quarter of 2008 (Table 5.4). The remarkably synchronized nature of the trade contraction across countries in the region, both in imports and exports, is generally consistent with the close trade ties among the East Asian economies forged within regional production networks and the unique role of the region within global production networks.[6]

[5] Numbers derived from Figure 5 in Almunia et al. (2010).

[6] Discussion on export performance of individual countries in this section is based on monthly export data extracted from the CEIC database (not reported here for want of space).

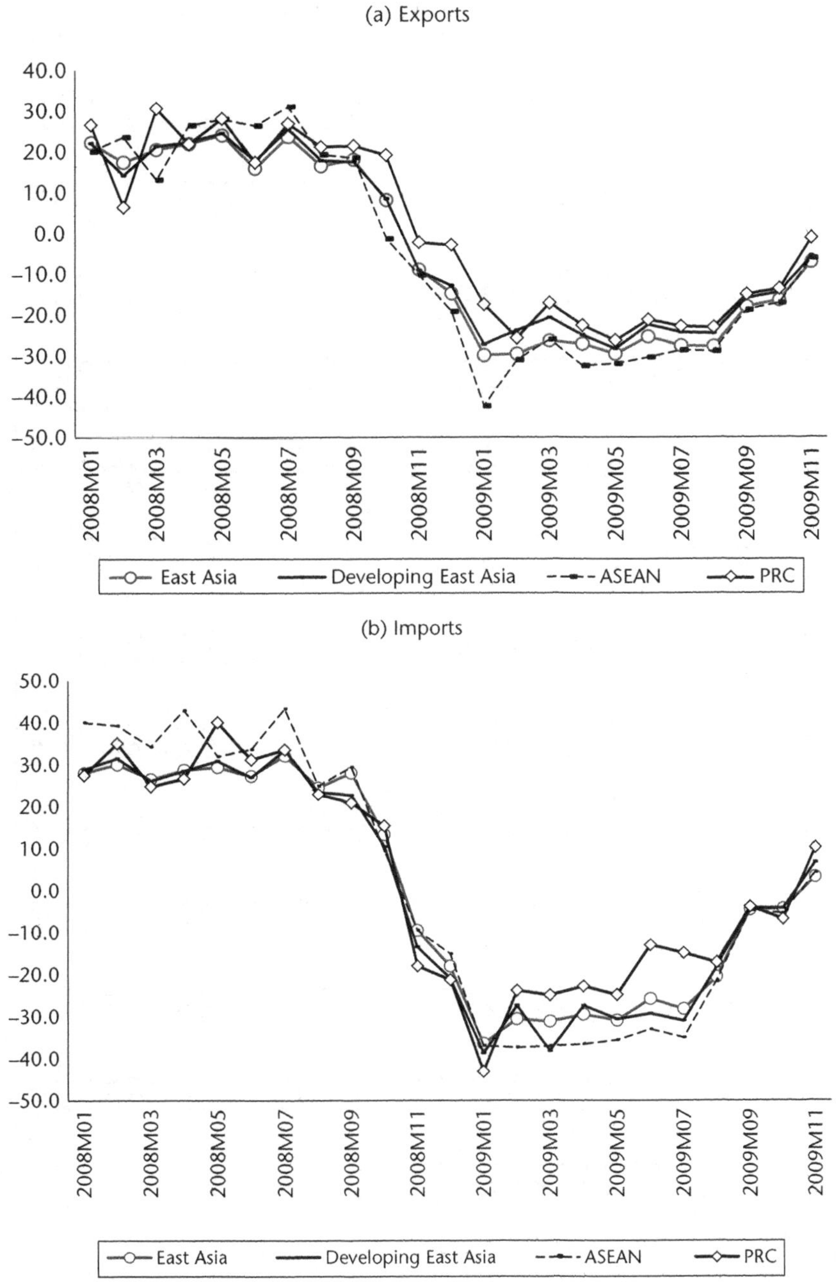

Figure 5.1 Growth of merchandise trade: East Asia, Developing East Asia, the PRC, and ASEAN (Y-O-Y, %)

Source: Based on data compiled from CEIC Asia database.

Table 5.4 East Asia: growth of total merchandise exports and imports (Y-O-Y, percent change)

	2007Q1	2007Q2	2007Q3	2007Q4	2008Q1	2008Q2	2008Q3	2008Q4	2009Q1	2009Q2	2009Q3	2009Q4	2010Q1	2010Q2
Exports														
ASEAN	14.5	13.1	10.6	18.1	19.5	23.3	22.1	−8.6	−22.8	−24.7	−20.0	10.7	32.4	34.3
Indonesia	22.2	19.9	8.8	13.1	21.8	18.9	22.4	1.4	−22.3	−14.8	−11.1	17.5	38.9	27.6
Malaysia	7.3	7.4	6.9	16.2	19.5	29.2	21.2	−12.5	−28.9	−33.3	−26.3	9.8	40.5	33.1
Philippines	9.4	4.6	2.3	9.9	2.8	5.5	4.1	−22.3	−36.8	−28.9	−21.5	6.0	42.9	33.3
Singapore	9.9	7.4	8.6	14.7	21.4	26.0	21.4	−13.4	−32.7	−30.6	−22.5	11.5	38.1	36.5
Thailand	16.3	17.4	13.7	25.2	23.7	28.6	26.1	−10.4	−20.1	-26.2	−17.6	12.0	32.1	41.8
Viet Nam	21.9	21.9	23.1	29.3	27.8	31.8	37.6	5.7	4.2	−14.7	−20.9	7.2	2.0	33.7
EA	14.3	13.3	11.6	17.4	19.0	20.8	18.1	−7.7	−24.1	−25.3	−20.0	6.0	32.9	35.6
Japan	9.7	6.9	9.1	14.0	20.2	18.0	13.0	−9.6	−41.5	−35.5	−25,5	−6.2	53.2	44.0
DEA	14.7	13.9	11.9	17.7	18.9	21.1	18.6	−7.5	−22.4	−24.2	−19.4	7.2	30.9	34.7
PRC	27.3	27.6	26.4	25.8	24.6	22.4	19.1	17.6	3.5	−22.2	−18.0	−16.1	−2.3	35.5
Hong Kong, China	8.4	11.1	7.8	8.6	11.0	8.2	6.0	−1.4	−20.9	−12.1	−13.5	−1.9	24.9	24.6
Korea	16.4	14.8	11.4	19.4	19.2	22.4	20.7	−14.2	−32.3	−27.6	−22.3	8.9	37.2	35.7
Taipei,China	8.6	6.8	9.7	15.2	16.9	18.2	7.5	−25.1	−37.5	−31.9	−20.5	16.9	54.8	45.3
Imports														
ASEAN	12.4	13.6	15.4	21.8	34.8	32.0	25.1	0.3	−28.0	−23.4	−14.6	9.1	40.7	31.8
Indonesia	11.6	19.2	20.6	7.4	41.2	44.1	44.7	31.9	−28.8	−27.0	−24.3	−8.3	42.8	35.9
Malaysia	12.8	9.0	8.6	18.3	15.7	17.5	14.6	−15.8	−36.6	−31.6	−22.6	12.5	45.1	44.0
Philippines	−1.1	12.0	22.4	25.2	13.8	2.9	−5.3	−3.0	5.0	9.3	14.4	13.9	16.4	11.3
Singapore	8.2	7.3	4.9	21.7	33.9	37.2	34.5	−8.0	−32.2	−33.3	−25.0	3.4	34.7	33.2
Thailand	5.4	6.9	7.7	16.1	35.0	30.0	39.4	5.3	−38.3	−33.1	−28.4	1.5	63.6	44.8
Viet Nam	37.6	27.5	28.5	42.4	69.0	60.1	22.7	−8.9	−37.2	−24.8	−1.5	31.9	41.5	21.8
EA	11.1	12.5	12.8	19.8	29.7	28.2	25.3	−0.6	−26.9	−26.4	−18.6	4.2	38.6	37.7
Japan	4.0	3.5	3.4	15.6	25.6	29.1	35.2	7.4	−29.1	−37.3	−31.6	−19.2	25.9	40.4
DEA	11.8	13.4	13.7	20.2	30.1	28.1	24.3	−1.4	−26.7	−25.3	−17.3	6.5	39.9	37.5
PRC	19.1	18.0	19.6	20.3	24.0	30.6	22.4	18.7	2.4	−25.2	−15.8	−11.1	6.4	53.3
Hong Kong, China	8.7	12.1	8.9	11.3	12.3	9.9	7.6	−3.3	−21.1	−14.1	−9.7	3.2	32.9	31.9
Korea	14.0	15.2	7.0	26.1	30.0	31.2	43.2	−7.8	−32.6	−35.7	−30.8	0.6	36.6	44.3
Taipei,China	2.3	7.3	9.0	13.1	25.9	18.0	19.1	−22.7	−47.8	−37.4	−28.7	18.1	78.9	54.3

Source: Compiled from CEIC Asia database.

Note: Growth rates calculated using current US$values.

Among the East Asian economies Japan has been by far the worst hit. A large share of Japan's exports consists of capital goods and high-end durable consumer goods, such as cars and electrical machinery, machine tools, and their components. Exports of capital goods and high-end consumer durables are heavily concentrated in the United States (US) and other developed-country markets and are therefore directly exposed to the global economic decline. On the other hand, contrary to the predictions of the decoupling enthusiasts, Japan's growing exports to the PRC have been indirectly affected by declining final (assembled) exports from the PRC (Fukao and Yuan 2009). The degree of export contraction suffered by Taipei,China and Korea has been smaller compared to Japan but, on average, notably higher compared to the other East Asian economies. As in the case of Japan, growing exports to the PRC do not seem to have provided a cushion against collapse in world demand for these two countries. The relatively lower degree of export contractions experienced by Korea, Taipei,China and the second-tier exporting countries in the region compared to Japan could possibly reflect consumer preferences for price-competitive low-end products in the crisis context.

An inspection of growth rates of exports of individual East Asian economies by destination provides no support for the view that East Asian economies have become less susceptible to the worldwide trade contraction because of regional growth dynamism. Intra-East Asia trade flows have in general contracted at a faster rate compared to these countries' exports to the US and EU.

A notable pattern in the PRC's foreign trade following the onset of the crisis is the relatively sharper contraction in the category of machinery exports (in which network trade is heavily concentrated) compared to other product categories, in particular traditional labor-intensive products (textile and garments, footwear and other miscellaneous manufactures). Exports belonging to the machinery category, in particular ICT products and consumer electronics are also predominantly consumer durables which, as already noted, are generally more susceptible to income contraction. In traditional labor-intensive products, developing country producers have the ability to perform better purely on the basis of cost competitiveness even in a context of depressed demand.

5.4 Policy options

As of mid June 2010 "the global recovery is proceeding better than expected" (IMF 2010 p. 1). Industrial production in the US and other major developed countries has begun to recover and the downward spiral in world trade volume has abated. However, the economic forces unleashed by the crisis will probably run rampant for years. The recovery has so far been driven largely by unprecedented fiscal and monetary stimulus and there is considerable downside risk of sustainability stemming from fiscal fragility. Over the medium term the US and other crisis affected developed countries will have to save more and spend less in order to wind down the massive accumulated household and public debts. Given this global economic outlook, what are the policy options available to governments in the PRC and other East Asian economies which have depended largely on export driven growth?

There has been a growing emphasis in Asian policy circles on the need for rebalancing growth—engineering a structural shift in aggregate demand away from exports and towards domestic markets (ADB 2010). The policy measures under consideration include measures to redress the export bias in the incentive structure, to reduce high saving propensities with a view to boosting domestic consumer demand and other measures directly aimed at promoting domestic non-tradable (services) production. The major focus of this policy advocacy is on the PRC.

The PRC's degree of export dependence is unusually high for a continental economy of the PRC's size. The PRC's export to GDP ratio (40 percent) grossly exaggerates its export dependence because of the heavy import dependence of assembly exports which accounts for over two-thirds of total merchandise exports. However, even the available adjusted estimates (20 percent) seem too high for the PRC's potential economic size. Moreover the unusually high domestic saving rates, the vast population base, highly repressed domestic financial system, excessively high (massive) urban–rural household income gap, all indicate the vast potential for policy-induced domestic demand-led growth in the PRC. Growth rebalancing will not only enable the PRC to deal effectively with massive external imbalances while cushioning growth momentum against external demand shocks, but also to engineer a critical shift in the focus of national development policy from the quantity to the quality of growth, with a view to redressing urban–rural disparities and achieving social harmony.

The need to embark on a major structural transition from export-led to domestic-demand led growth was recognized by the Chinese leadership well before the onset of the global financial crisis (Roach 2009 pp. 229–33). The 11th Five-Year Plan enacted in March 2006 stressed the imperatives of an enhanced, broad-based social safety net (encompassing not just social security but also rural health care and education) to improve income security, thereby reducing the excess precautionary saving that continues to inhibit the expansion of private consumption. However, the Chinese authorities have so far failed to put this policy into action, presumably because of the strong domestic political pressure to maintain the momentum of employment-intensive growth through export orientation (Yu 2007; Gang 2008).

The success on the rebalancing front will naturally involve an appreciation of the PRC's real exchange rate,[7] a reduction in the profitability of tradable production relative to non-tradable production. But this is unlikely to impede, at least over the medium term, the PRC's role as the premier assembly centre within regional production networks. Even after three decades of rapid growth, the average hourly wage rate overall in Chinese manufacturing (US$3.2) still (as at 2007) amounts to only 13 percent of the US hourly wage rate (US$24.4).[8] About half of the PRC's massive labor force (about 745 million) is still engaged in agriculture where productivity is, on average, barely one-eighth of that in industry and about a quarter of that in the service sector. This, coupled with the high skilled–unskilled wage differential (which, according to some estimates, has risen from 1.3 percent to 2.1 percent over the past decade (Blanchard and Giavazzi 2006) suggests that the PRC still has much potential for moving unskilled workers out of agriculture and into manufacturing and other productive urban sector activities.[9]

The pressure for maintaining export competition in a context of slow-growing world demand could provide a fertile setting for the rise of trade friction and protectionism (Bhagwati 1988; Erixon and Ražeen 2009). Fortunately, there has not yet been a protectionist backlash in the form of erecting tariff walls, as happened during the Great Depression. However, there are already signs of countries increasingly resorting to disguise (or just disguising) means of protection such as filing anti-dumping complaints and imposing a stringent implementation of technical and sanitary and phytosanitary standards, in addition to the massive financial support extended by the US and some other countries to automobile manufacturers (Gamberoni and Newfarmer 2009). The number of legislative measured introduced in the US Congress which involve some forms of sanction on PRC trade have multiplied in recent years (Roach 2009 p. 241). There is therefore a strong case for devising strategies to fight this new protectionism as part of a long-term commitment to non-discriminatory multilateral and unilateral liberalization. The Information Technology Agreement which came into force in 1997 seems to be a promising example to follow. There is also a case for Asia's G-20 countries and the

[7] Whether it would be preferable to achieve this by adjustments to nominal exchange rate than by adjustment to domestic prices remains a subject of controversy which is beyond the scope of this paper.

[8] Data from the US Bureau of Labor Statistics website (ftp.bls.gov).

[9] In recent years there have been many scattered cases of rising wages and worker shortages in industrial cities in the PRC. However, one cannot realistically infer this evidence as indicative of a broader macroeconomic trend of emerging labor shortages, given that the PRC economy is still a long way away from having a fully functioning labor market. These cases could well reflect skill mismatches and frictional dislocations in a highly imperfect labor market rather than genuine labor shortages.

ASEAN Secretariat to consolidate their positions against protectionist tendencies.

One option under consideration in Asian policy circles for sustaining regional trade growth in face of slow growth in world demand is to form a region-wide free trade area (FTA), encompassing ASEAN, the PRC, Japan, and Korea (and possibly India) (Kawai and Wignaraja 2008; ADB 2009). In our view this is a risky strategy, given Asia's heavy reliance on extra regional markets for its export dynamism. Such a move would invite swift retaliation by the US and the EU. In particular, given the importance of extra-regional markets for final goods for the growth dynamism of production networks in Asia, maintaining barriers to trade against non-members (while allowing free trade among members) can thwart the "natural" expansion of global production sharing. A firm commitment as part of the FTA not to increase existing tariff and non-tariff barriers against non-members is unlikely to avert this threat because an Asia-wide FTA, given that it encompasses a number of significant world trading nations, is likely to involve significant trade diversion even under the existing extra-regional tariffs. In any case, the chances of negotiating a region-wide FTA look rather slim in the context of the on-going crisis. In particular, the PRC may not want to get involved in such an endeavor not only because of its new emphasis on domestic-oriented growth but also because of its official commitment to averting protectionist backlashes against its exports from developed countries.[10] Governments in Southeast Asian countries are also concerned that any region-wide attempt to liberalize trade would give unfair advantage to the PRC in attracting FDI involved in global production networks, given its vast domestic economy characterized by regional differences in the costs of production.[11]

In reality, the trade effects of any FTA would depend very much on the nature of the rules of origin (ROO) built into it. However, formulating ROOs for trade occurring within global production networks trade is a rather complicated business. The conventional value-added criterion is not virtually applicable to this trade because tasks undertaken by each country in the value chain normally contain rather thin domestic value addition. The only viable option is to go for a "change in tariff lines"-based ROOs, but this leads to insurmountable administrative problems because trade in electrical and electronics goods and the related parts and components belong to the same tariff codes at the HS-6 digit level, which is the normal base for designing this type of ROOs (Kohpaiboon 2010, Appendix 2). Moreover, the process of global production

[10] See for instance the recent article written by the Chinese Minister of Trade to the *Wall Street Journal* (Deming 2009).

[11] This point is based on interviews with high-ranking officials at the Thai Ministry of Foreign Affairs.

sharing is characterized by the continuous emergence of "new" products. Given the obvious administrative problems involved in revising ROOs in tandem, these product inventions and innovations naturally open up room for unnecessary administrative delays and/or tweaking of the rules as a means of disguised protection.

Finally, it is important to note that the available evidence on the operation of FTAs in operation in the region (and beyond) augur well for the potency of a new region-wide FTA. Presumably because of the operational complications noted above, the actual utilization rates of tariff concessions provided under these FTAs are rather low, ranging from 5 percent to 20 percent across different product categories (Takahashi and Urata 2008; Kawai and Wignaraja 2008; Kohpaiboon 2008). More importantly, there is evidence that the utilization rates are often firm or industry specific: normally large firms and firms with close trade and FDI ties or those located in particular industries where meeting ROO requirements are simple and straightforward use FTAs. The upshot is that FTAs are unlikely to have the potential to promote trade in a neutral and broad-based fashion.

5.5 Conclusions

Intra-regional trade shares based on conventional trade data are generally consistent with the view that East Asia has become increasingly integrated through merchandise trade. However, when the on-going process of international production fragmentation and East Asia's unique role in the PRC-centered global production networks are appropriately taken into account, it is clearly evident that the region's dependence on the rest of the world for its trade expansion has in fact *increased* over the time. This inference is basically consistent with the remarkably synchronized nature of the trade contraction across countries in the region.

The rise of global production sharing has strengthened the case for a global, rather than a regional, approach to trade policymaking. Given the global orientation of the region's economies, we question whether there would be any significant positive payoff from forming a region-wide FTA. It is doubtful whether an FTA approach to trade liberalization is feasible in a context where global production networks are rapidly expanding, seamlessly encompassing many industries and countries.

The recent and prospective developments in the global economy following the global financial crisis make a strong case for the PRC to go ahead with the speedy implementation of the growth-rebalancing policy embodied in the 11th Five Year Plan. Given the nature of domestic factor market conditions and the on-going changes in the process of global production sharing, promoting domestic demand-oriented growth and engagement in global production sharing are not mutually exclusive policy priorities for the PRC over the medium term. Successful growth rebalancing has the potential to facilitate the further expansion of network trade by averting trade friction with and retaliation from the US and other major trading-partner countries. An enlarged domestic market would also have the potential to improve the international competitiveness of exporting firms within production networks by reducing unit costs of production. Looking further ahead, an increase in domestic income and wages under a successful balanced growth strategy would provide the setting for the PRC to move up the value ladder within global production networks. After all, the bulk (more than 60 percent) of international exchange within global production networks takes place among developed countries and, in the future, the PRC has the potential to become one of them.

References

Almunia, M., A. Benetrix, B. Eichengreen, K. H. O'Rourke, and G. Rua (2010). From Great Depression to Great Credit Crisis: Similarities, Differences and Lessons. *Economic Policy*, April 2010: 219–65.

Asian Development Bank (ADB) (2009). *Asian Development Outlook 2009: Rebalancing Asia's Growth.* Manila: Asian Development Bank.

——(2010). *Asian Development Outlook 2010: Macroeconomic Management Beyond the Crisis.* Manila: Asian Development Bank.

Athukorala, P.-C. (2005). Product Fragmentation and Trade Patterns in East Asia. *Asian Economic Papers*, 4(3): 1–27.

——(2009). The Rise of China and East Asian Export Performance: Is the Crowding-out Fear Warranted? *World Economy*, 32(2): 234–66.

Bergsten, C. F, B. Gill, N. R. Lardy, and D. Mitchell (2006). *China: The Balance Sheet.* New York: Public Affairs.

Bhagwati, J. (1988). *Protectionism.* MA: MIT Press.

Blanchard, O. and F. Giavazzi (2006). Rebalancing Growth in China: A Three-Handed Approach. *China and World Economy*, 14(4): 1–20.

Deming, C. (2009). China Calls on the World's Governments to Learn from History. *Wall Street Journal*, February 20.

Erixson, F. and S. Razeen (2009). Fighting the Urge for Protectionism. *Far Eastern Economic Review*, 172(1) (January/February): 28–31.

Fukao, K. and T. Yuan (2009). Why is Japan so heavily affected by the global economic crisis? Available: www.voxeu.org, June 8.

Gamberoni, E. and R. Newfarmer (2009). Trade Protection: Incipient but Worrisome Trends. Available: www.voxeu.org, March 4.

Gang, F. (2008). Renminbi Revaluation and US Dollar Depreciation, in *Debating China's Exchange Rate Policy*, edited by M. Goldstein and N. R. Lardy. Washington, DC: Peterson Institute for International Economics.

Garnaut, R. (2003). Australia and Japan: Time to be Important to Each Other Again. Address to the Australia-Japan Business Committee conference, Kyoto, October 5.

International Monetary Fund (IMF) (2010). *Global Economic Outlook: Rebalancing Growth*, Washington, DC: IMF.

Kawai, M. and G. Wignaraja (2008). Multilateralising Regional Trading Agreements in Asia, in *Multilateralizing Regionalism: Challenges for the Global Trading System*, edited by R. Baldwin and P. Low. Cambridge: Cambridge University Press.

Kohpaiboon, A. (2008). Exporters' Response to AFTA Tariff Preferences: Evidence from Thailand. Paper presented at the East Asian Economic Congress, Manila.

——(2010). *Product Fragmentation Phenomenon and Production Networks of Multinational Enterprises: Implication on Thai Manufacturing*. Bangkok: Misterkopy Publisher.

Krugman, P. (2009). The Return of Depression Economics. Lionel Robbins Lecture (PPT presentation and the summary by Geoff R., "Paul Krugman at LSE"). Available: http/ cep.lse.ac.uk/_new/events/special_post.asp.

Park, Y. C. and K. Shin (2009). Economic Integration and Changes in the Business Cycle in East Asia: Is the Region Decoupling from the Rest of the World? *Asian Economic Papers* 8(1): 107–40.

Roach, S. (2009). *The Next Asia: Opportunities and Challenges for a New Globalization*. Hoboken, NJ: John Wiley, 172–88.

Takahashi, K. and S. Urata (2008). On the Use of FTAs by Japanese Firms. *RIETI Discussion Paper o8-E-002*, Graduate School of Asia-Pacific Studies, Waseda University.

Urata, S. (2006). A Shift from Market-driven to Institution-driven Regionalization in East Asia. Paper presented to Conference on Economic Policy Reform in Asia, June, Stanford University.

Yoshitomi, M. (2007). Global Imbalances and East Asian Monetary Cooperation, in *Towards and East Asian Exchange Rate Regime*, edited by D. Chung and B. Eichengreen. Washington, DC: Brookings Institution Press, 22–48.

Yu, Y. (2007). Global Imbalances and China. *The Australian Economic Review*, 40: 3–23.

6

Decoupling of East Asia: Myth or Reality?

Yung Chul Park

6.1 Introduction

There has been much discussion about the "decoupling" of East Asia[1] from its economic interactions—both in trade and finance—with the rest of the world, in particular from the advanced economies of North America and Europe. Decoupling is a term that defies precise definition, yet there is considerable controversy about its causes and significance.[2] In the context of East Asia, decoupling often refers to the phenomenon of a weakening of the impact of demand and supply shocks emanating from the advanced countries on the economic performance of East Asian economies or their growth, which has become more independent from cyclical developments of the global economy. To some it is a reality; to many it is a myth.

During much of the postwar period, most of East Asia's developing economies and Japan had relied heavily on the growth of domestic demand from the United States (US) and Europe for their growth. As most of these countries had adopted an export-led growth strategy, this dependence had persisted until the late 1990s. During this period, the causal direction of economic interlinkages between East Asia and the advanced countries had largely been asymmetric. Demand and supply shocks originating in the advanced countries had been transmitted to East Asian economies, through the trade and financial channels, to have a significant effect on their growth. In contrast,

[1] In this chapter, East Asia refers to the ten ASEAN member economies, namely, Brunei Darussalam, Cambodia, Indonesia, Lao PDR, Malaysia, Myanmar, Philippines, Singapore, Thailand, and Viet Nam, and three other economies, namely, Japan, Republic of Korea, and the People's Republic of China. They are collectively called ASEAN + 3. Emerging Asia or emerging economies in Asia includes twelve countries of ASEAN + 3 excluding Japan. East Asian economies or countries refer to some or all of ASEAN + 3 depending on the context in which they are used.

[2] See World Bank (2006), Anderson (2007), IMF (2007), Park and Shin (2008), Athukorala and Kohpaiboon (2010 and Chapter 5).

however, the impact of similar disturbances occurring in East Asia on the advanced economies had been negligible.

Since the early 2000s, this uni-directional causality, it is argued, has undergone a change to one that is more bi-directional. Output shocks from East Asia's emerging economies have had a more pronounced effect on cyclical fluctuations in the advanced economies than before and the effects of external shocks on East Asia have become stronger in the 2000s (Kim, Lee, and Park 2009). Many other studies have pointed to an absence of empirical evidence of the development of East Asia as a self-contained region.[3]

Most of these studies cover the period before the 2008 global financial crisis. In view of the faster recovery of East Asia from the 2008 global economic crisis, it would be interesting to examine whether the crisis has changed the structure of trade linkages and financial spillovers between East Asia and the rest of the world to lend credence to the decoupling thesis. For this purpose, Section 6.2 of this chapter identifies some of the factors that are likely to cause such decoupling. Section 6.3 is devoted to an analysis of East Asia's experience with the 2008 global crisis, to examine whether the crisis has strengthened the case for decoupling. Section 6.4 discusses the prospects for decoupling in lieu of conclusions.

6.2 Causes of decoupling

A causal inspection of Figure A6.1 and Figure A6.2 in Appendix 1 leaves little doubt that the economic growth of the US and the European Union (EU) has had a significant effect on the growth of East Asia. More rigorous studies confirm this observation. In the three US recessions of 1982, 1991, and 2001, a 1 percentage point fall in US growth was accompanied by a decline of 0.5 percentage points on average in median growth of East Asia, comprising the People's Republic of China (PRC); Indonesia; the Republic of Korea (hereafter Korea); Malaysia; the Philippines; Taipei,China; and Thailand (IMF 2007).

Another more recent study estimates that a 1 percent decline in US and euro area growth could lower gross domestic product (GDP) growth across Asia by 0.3 percentage points, with estimates ranging from a low of 0.1 percentage points for Indonesia to a high of 0.6 percentage points for Malaysia (IMF 2010).[4]

[3] Representative of these studies are Athukorala and Kohpaiboon (2009 and 2010).

[4] In this study Asia includes Singapore and Japan, in addition to the sample countries of the 2007 study.

Park and Song (2011) present a somewhat different picture in their estimates of the effects of external shocks on the output of nine East Asian economies—Association of Southeast Asian Nations (ASEAN) + 5; the PRC; Japan; Korea; and Taipei,China.[5] Global shocks account for relatively large output variations only in the PRC and the Philippines, whereas regional shocks tend to cause relatively large changes in the domestic output of Korea; Singapore; Taipei,China; and Thailand. The two shocks are equally important in Japan; Malaysia; and Taipei,China.

If decoupling is defined in terms of the growing idiosyncrasy of East Asia's business cycle, it depends on a number of factors that include East Asia's growth strategy, intra-regional trade, and financial linkages with the global financial system. They are of particular interest from the perspective of this study.

6.2.1 *Rebalancing growth: relying more on domestic demand*

Throughout East Asia, there has been a reexamination of the viability of the region's preoccupation with export-led growth. The export-led development strategy would not have worked had it not been for the voracious appetite of US consumers for Asian exports. Now that demand for Asian manufactures by consumers in the US and Europe is likely to remain weak for years to come, even when the global economy recovers and financial stability is restored, export-led growth may no longer be a practical option. This awareness has led to an emerging consensus that emerging Asia should take steps to restructure the economies and change existing institutions to try to break away from export dependence and rely more on domestic demand as a source of growth.

According to the Asian Development Outlook (ADB 2009 p. 66), "rebalancing represents a return to the generally more balanced structure of demand and growth that prevailed in the region prior to the 1997 Asia crisis," implying that in the context of the Asian economy, rebalancing means restoring the current account balance. Economic restructuring for rebalanced growth would in general lead to a decline in the share of exports in GDP and that of the current account surplus.

[5] For each country, regional output is measured by a trade-weighted average of the output of the other eight countries. Global output is a trade-weighted average of the output of the US, Canada, Australia, and five European advanced countries (France, Germany, Italy, the Netherlands, and the UK).

6.2.2 *Importance of intra-regional trade*

The argument for decoupling on the trade side is founded on the belief that business cycle co-movements are a function of trade linkages.[6] There is some analytical support for this conclusion. Frankel and Rose (1998) demonstrated that business cycle correlations increase as trade integration deepens. The decoupling would then be observed if the share of intra-regional trade in East Asia's total trade rises. Shin and Wang (2004) showed that this point applies to Asia in particular. Imbs (2004) and Calderón, Chong, and Stein (2007) documented that business-cycle transmission is especially powerful when trade is intra-industry—which is increasingly the fact in Asia.

An increase in intra-regional trade would not necessarily be associated with decoupling in East Asia. This is because decoupling depends not only on the share, but also on the degree of horizontal integration of intra-industry trade. East Asia's intra-regional trade structure is often compared to a conveyor belt carrying parts, components, and other industrial materials produced by Japan and other East Asian emerging economies to the PRC for assembly and export to the rest of the world. This structure is known as international "production fragmentation" within a vertically integrated production process. The product fragmentation has been an important driving force behind the rise in intra-regional trade in East Asia, but not the decoupling.

In this vertical integration, the PRC serves as the processing and assembly platform for the final goods destined for the global market. According to Athukorala and Kohpaiboon (2010), the share of parts and components in total exports of Japan and other East Asian emerging economies to the PRC had been rising in the run-up to the 2008 crisis. This means that its trade with the rest of the world had been critical to East Asia's growth and that a negative shock in the US or Europe would reduce imports of final goods from East Asia, thereby affecting the region's business cycles.

Following the argument of international production fragmentation, the Asian Development Bank (ADB 2008) concluded that the story of decoupling (or uncoupling in their terminology) was no more than a myth. The report shows that emerging Asia is closely tied to global goods markets and that impulses run from the US, the EU, and Japan backward through the region. In this view, the PRC has become a more independent source of demand in recent years, but it still remains largely a conduit for importing parts and components from other countries in the region and assembling them into final goods to be exported.

[6] Representative of this view are statements by Anderson (2007 p. 1) about the PRC, to the effect that "There's no reason to argue over whether the mainland is 'decoupling' from the global cycle—as far as macro growth is concerned the economy is and always has been effectively 'decoupled,' and the PRC has little to fear from a global demand slowdown."

6.2.3 *Financial integration*

Beginning in the early 1980s, many of East Asia's emerging economies have embarked on reforms to deregulate and open their financial markets and intermediation industries. Financial liberalization has deepened and diversified linkages of these economies with financial markets of the US and other industrialized countries, although it has made a relatively limited contribution to regional financial integration in East Asia.[7] As East Asia's financial linkages with the rest of the world have increased, so have capital flows to the region. The tighter linkages have also enlarged the scope of spillovers from external shocks to the region, with the attendant increase in the correlation of asset prices of East Asia with those of the US and European countries.[8]

As far as East Asia is concerned, however, the direction of spillovers from an external financial shock has mostly been uni-directional. That is, the variation in the asset prices of the US and Europe has exerted a significant effect on the asset prices of East Asia, but the reverse has not been the case. This asymmetry stems from the fact that compared with industrialized economies, holdings of external assets as a share of GDP in East Asia are relatively small. Furthermore, a large share of these assets is held in foreign exchange reserves where demand is insensitive to changes in financial market conditions.

A high degree of volatility of capital flows to East Asia has its causes in some of the salient features of East Asia's financial systems. One such feature is that the financial markets of East Asia's emerging economies are relatively small, shallow, and lack liquidity. They have a limited capacity to absorb capital inflows. When large global investors enter these economies in search of high returns, they often overwhelm domestic financial markets, raising stock prices and causing currency appreciation beyond a level consistent with the economy's fundamentals. When they leave unexpectedly, as they often do, the domestic markets suffer from a shortage of reserve currency liquidity, precipitating the collapse of asset prices and in some cases even endangering the safety of the financial system itself.

Another feature to emerge is East Asia's heavy dependence on global financial intermediation conducted in reserve currencies—the dollar and the euro—and dominated by global financial institutions headquartered in the US and Europe. Few of East Asia's commercial banks and investment banks are global players, although they may be large in terms of assets. As a result, when a sudden reversal of capital inflows takes place, East Asia's commercial banks cannot easily fill in to supplement shortages of liquidity in reserve currencies.

[7] The average measures of financial integration with the US are much higher compared with those with other countries in the region (Park and Shin 2008).

[8] According to the IMF (2007), financial linkages serve as an important channel through which demand and supply shocks are transmitted from one country to another in the global economy.

For instance, when foreign lenders and investors sell off their East Asian assets and refuse renewal of their short-term loans, US dollar or euro liquidity dries up. If financial market participants overreact to an event like the failure of Lehman Brothers, the liquidity shortfall could provoke a currency crisis and a run on central bank reserves, as it did in Korea in 2008.

To be sure, East Asia's central banks are able to make additional liquidity available by dipping into their foreign exchange reserves.[9] During the six-month period beginning in September 2008, when the crisis was in full force, the central banks stepped in to ease the liquidity shortage. But the subsequent loss of foreign exchange reserves precipitated further currency depreciation, thereby setting off a chain of reactions in which the depreciation ended up in a further reserve loss and threatened the solvency of those banks unable to roll over their external loans.

A third feature is related to the asymmetric risk structure of capital flows in which the region as a whole imports safe financial assets—to be held monthly as reserves—while exporting risky ones. This asymmetry leaves East Asia highly susceptible to crisis contagion. When a crisis or a disturbance occurs in an emerging economy, investors with exposure in other markets become conscious about the possibility of a spread of the crisis to other emerging economies. When they hold risky assets like those issued by East Asia's emerging markets, foreign investors leave these markets simultaneously, even though their fundamentals are strong, shifting their portfolio investments to high quality riskless assets, as they did when the 2008 crisis broke out.

6.3 The 2010 global economic crisis and decoupling

If the decoupling had taken root before the crisis, one would expect that East Asia could have remained relatively immune to or had been spared, partially at least, the effects of adverse disturbances originating in countries outside the region, such as the US subprime crisis.

Following the bankruptcy of Lehman Brothers in September 2008, many economies in East Asia slid into a deeper recession than had been anticipated and some of them were pushed to the brink of a breakdown of their financial

[9] It is true that East Asia collectively holds more than US$4 trillion in foreign exchange reserves, but the bulk of these reserves are held by the PRC and Japan. Other East Asian economies may not have held enough reserves to prevent currency speculation. ASEAN + 3 has established a reserve pooling scheme for liquidity support for its members, but it has played little role during the crisis, thereby failing the market test. Except for Hong Kong, China; Singapore; and Japan, financial markets of other East Asian economies are far less integrated into the global financial markets than those in Europe.

systems. The overall macroeconomic deterioration was serious enough to refute the decoupling thesis and for hopes to be dashed that East Asia would serve as a regional engine of growth strong sufficient to moderate the downturn of the global economy.

Against all the odds, however, beginning in the second quarter of 2009, East Asia has staged an impressive rebound, which has been followed by a sustained recovery. This recovery has raised the expectation that emerging Asia would return to its pre-crisis path of growth and stability, in line with the IMF forecast (IMF 2010). The PRC's economy grew by 9.2 percent in 2009 and by 10.3 percent in 2010—more than the Chinese authorities had forecast—to the point where it is threatened with asset and consumer price inflation. The Asian NIEs (Hong Kong, China; Korea; Singapore; and Taipei,China), which were battered most by the crisis, have been making a strong comeback, posting average growth of 8.2 percent (IMF 2010) in 2010. Do these developments add up to provide any empirical evidence supporting the decoupling phenomenon?

6.3.1 *Domestic demand-led recovery*

A recent IMF *Regional Economic Outlook Asia and Pacific* (2010) shows that economic growth in East Asia except for Japan has been driven first by fiscal and monetary stimulus and then sustained by the subsequent expansion of private demand since the recovery began in 2009. Perhaps it is premature to conclude whether rebalancing growth has been taking root or the domestic demand-led output growth is likely to be a short-run development, or whether emerging Asia will return to export-led growth once the global economy recovers fully from the crisis. However, there is considerable evidence to suggest that domestic demand will continue to be a more important source of growth in East Asia in the coming years. One such piece of evidence is that in all East Asian economies, except Korea, the ratio of exports to GDP has been declining since 2005 (World Bank Database 2011); another is that the current account surplus as a proportion of GDP of ASEAN + 3 has also been declining since 2007 (Figure 6.1).

In addition to these developments, the PRC will undergo structural changes that will bring about rapid growth in the demand for consumer goods, including imported ones, as it sustains rapid growth. In fact, the draft of its 12th five-year plan (2011–15) highlights a policy shift toward boosting domestic consumption as one of the engines of growth, which will lead to a "moderate" increase in imports of consumer goods.[10] In the PRC, private consumption as

[10] A recent study suggests that if increases in income are complemented by exchange rate appreciations, East Asia will see a steady increase in imports of consumer goods (Thorbecke 2010).

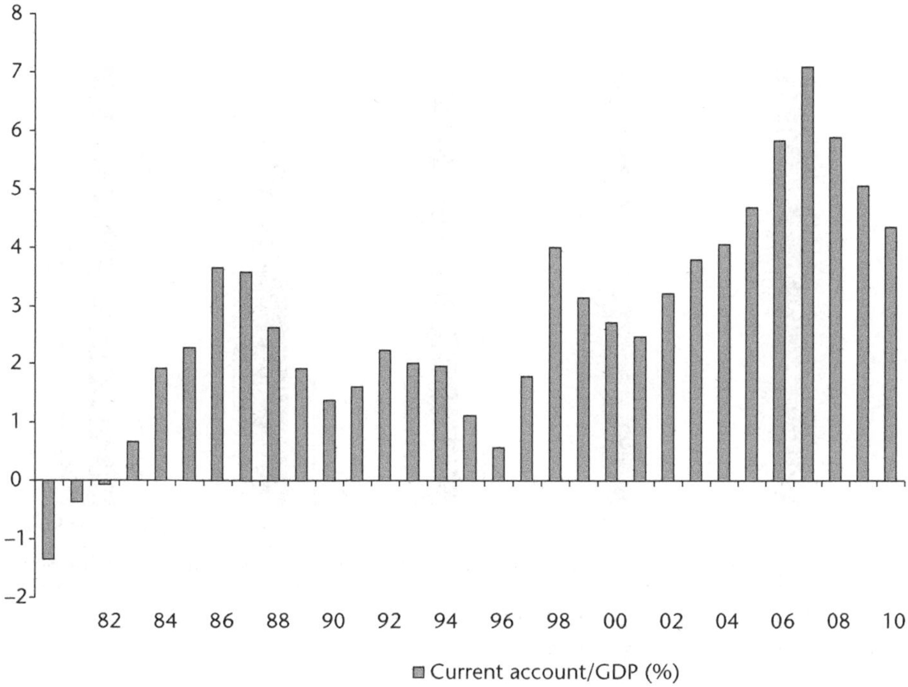

Figure 6.1 Ratio of current account balance to GDP of East Asian region (%)

Source: IMF, World Economic Outlook Database, 2011.

Note: The region includes ASEAN5; Hong Kong, China; Taipei,China; the PRC; Korea; and Japan.

a proportion of GDP has stabilized since 2009 after years of decline. The reform of retirement pensions and extended health care coverage are likely to reduce precautionary incentives to save (IMF 2010). At the same time, a number of East Asian countries including the PRC, Indonesia, Malaysia, the Philippines, and Thailand have given high priority to investment in infrastructure development. These changes in policy are in line with a new mandate that East Asia's emerging economies need to steer themselves to a more balanced growth strategy.

6.3.2 *Intra-regional trade integration*

The share of intra-regional trade in East Asia rose to an all time high of 42.5 percent in 2005. For the next three years, it declined before turning up again in the first quarter of 2009 (Figure 6.2). By the second quarter of 2010, it had returned to the level of 2005. Much of this increase has come from the PRC's growing absorption of exports of other East Asian countries. In expanding its capacity to import from East Asian countries, the PRC has strengthened its foothold as a hub for East Asia's regional trade.

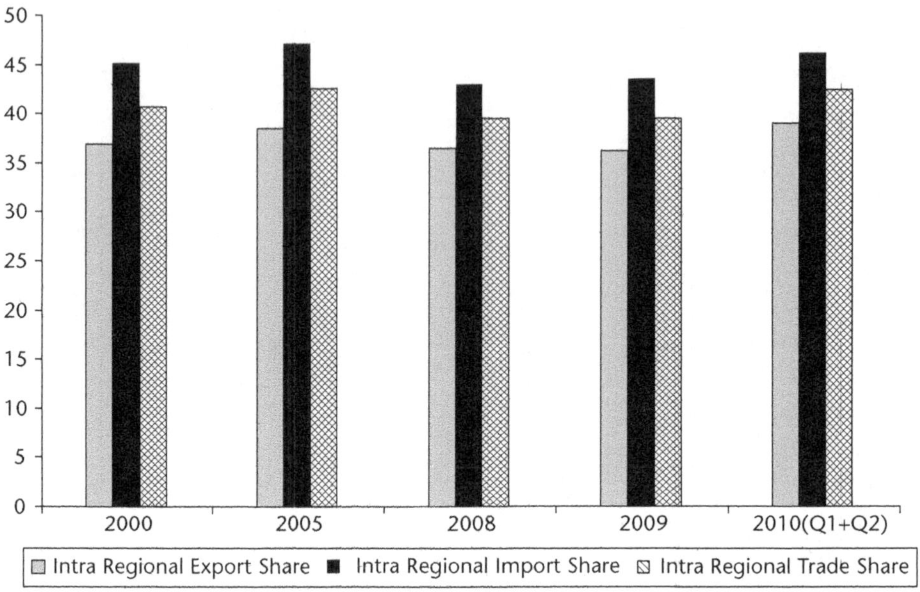

Figure 6.2 Share of intra-regional trade in ASEAN + 3

Source: IMF, *Direction of Trade*, various issues.

Available data on intra-industry trade are somewhat sketchy. Estimates of five-year averages of the Grubel and Lloyd (1975) index for intra-industry trade for eight East Asian economies from 1990 to 2004, where the intensity is estimated in manufacturing against the PRC, show that the indices of the eight economies vis-à-vis the PRC almost doubled on average over the ten-year period from 1990–94 and 2000–04. In contrast, with regard to the US the same indices barely changed between the two periods.

In a recent study, Athukorala and Kohpaiboon (2010) show that the share of parts and components imports in the PRC's total manufacturing imports rose from 18 percent in 1994–95 to more than 46 percent in 2006–07. This increase is presented as evidence for the rise in vertical integration in East Asia's intra-industry trade and the region's dependence on external trade for growth. Data on the trade in parts and components for East Asian economies for the recent periods are not available, but some of the recent macroeconomic and trade developments in the region since 2007 suggest that the share has declined and will continue to do so.

Like many other East Asian economies, intermediate inputs account for a lion's share of Korea's total exports to the PRC. However, since 2005, when it reached an all time high of 82 percent, the share has been declining: in 2008 the share fell below 70 percent (Jeong 2009). It would not be surprising if a

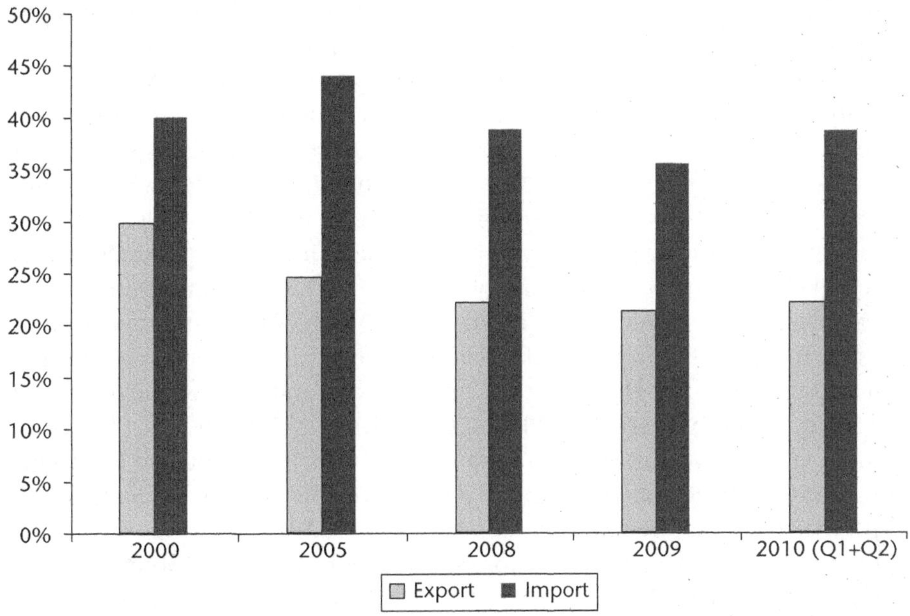

Figure 6.3 Shares of major Asian countries in the PRC's total exports and imports
Source: IMF, *Direction of Trade*, various issues.
Note: ASEAN5, Japan, Korea, and Taipei,China

similar development has taken place elsewhere in East Asia, largely because throughout East Asia countries have been moving towards embracing, to varying degrees, a new growth strategy depending more on domestic demand than before. This rebalancing suggests that integration in intra-regional trade is likely to proceed not just through trade in parts and components, but also through trade in final goods. In this regard, the PRC holds the key to future progress in the decoupling of East Asia.

The 2008 crisis hit the PRC's export oriented industries hard, slashing total exports by more than 12 percent in 2009. It also cut the PRC's imports from other East Asian economies as well as from the rest of the world by 10 percent. However, beginning in the first quarter of 2009, the PRC's imports have been increasing. By the first half of 2010, its imports from the East Asian economies had returned to the level of 2008 (Figure 6.3).

Using vector auto-regression (VAR) models, Park and Shin (2010) show that the PRC's imports have had a significant positive effect on the GDP of other East Asian economies in the post-Asian crisis period. The positive effect was more pronounced during the period from the last quarter of 2008 to the first quarter of 2010, supporting the claim that the import demand from the PRC has contributed to the region's speedy and robust recovery from the global crisis.

Park and Shin (2010, p. 18) go on to argue that the PRC is "beginning to become an engine of growth for other Asian countries."[11] The 12th five-year plan projects a somewhat moderate pace of annual growth of 8 percent. It remains uncertain whether the PRC would be able to achieve the target if exports continue to decline as a share of its GDP and the fiscal stimulus is phased out, although the IMF (2011) is bullish about the PRC's growth prospecst, forecasting more than 9 percent growth for both 2011 and 2012.

Taking a longer term perspective, the increase in intra-regional trade in East Asia is likely to be powered by the proliferation of free trade agreements (FTAs) in the region. ASEAN member states have 5–10 year plans to remove most of the structural and institutional obstacles to creating an economic community that visualizes the free trade of goods and services, and the free movement of labor and capital by 2020. The PRC-ASEAN FTA, which is the third largest in terms of GDP, came into effect in January 2010. The PRC signed an Economic Cooperation Framework Agreement (ECFA) with Taipei,China on June 29, 2010, which is a preferential trade agreement (PTA) between the governments of the two sides. Both Japan and Korea concluded FTAs with ASEAN.

Even before these FTAs entered into force, the total trade of ASEAN, Japan, and Korea with the PRC was growing at a double digit rate. Since 2010, there has been a phenomenal increase in trade between the PRC and other countries in East Asia. During the first six months of 2010, ASEAN's total exports to the PRC rose by more than 86 percent and its imports by 63 percent year on year. For Japan and Korea the rate of growth was 48 percent and 60 percent, respectively. This trade expansion is likely to bring about a synchronization of output movements in East Asia. Such a process would be a natural evolutionary outcome of trade expansion and geographical proximity among the members of the group.

6.3.3 *Financial spillovers*

The huge shock waves of the 2008 global financial crisis shook East Asia's financial markets to the core. During the period from the collapse of Lehman Brothers in September of 2008 to the first quarter of 2009, throughout the region stock prices nosedived and the exchange rates except for those pegged to the dollar depreciated against the US dollar and exhibited a higher degree of volatility than before. The sovereign spreads widened and the credit default swap premia, a measure of the quality of financial liabilities denominated in US dollars, sharply increased. Despite its initial virulence, the crisis was

[11] When the VAR model is modified to account for the PRC's imports from East Asia derived from the US demand for the PRC's final goods, much of the PRC's positive impact disappears over a longer horizon (Park and Shin 2010).

short-lived. By the end of the first quarter of 2009, stability had returned to East Asia's financial markets.

In retrospect, however, East Asia's financial systems were better able to withstand the onslaught of the 2008 crisis largely because, unlike those in other parts of the world, the region's financial institutions did not hold large amounts of US "toxic" assets. A series of financial reforms undertaken by the crisis-hit countries in the wake of the 1997–98 Asian financial crisis appear to have improved the efficiency and stability of their financial systems, allowing them to better weather the crisis.[12]

Since the recovery began, however, East Asia has once again been inundated with a flood of capital inflows. Ample global liquidity, the relatively robust growth and low public debt in East Asia together with expectations for low interest rates in mature markets, and a shift in global asset allocation have all come together to fuel capital flows to the region. Compared with 2009, total inflows into the region more than quadrupled in 2010. This massive increase is feared to exacerbate the risk of inflation, asset price bubbles, financial sector instability, excessive appreciation, and risks associated with a sudden stop of capital flows.

There is also the risk of the financial turmoil in Europe spreading to other regions including East Asia. Given the financial linkages with countries in East Asia, financial spillovers from Europe through higher risk aversion and lower equity prices could lead to an abrupt reversal of capital flows and a slowdown in growth and demand that would negatively affect the growth prospects of East Asia.

As long as emerging Asia is unable to mitigate a high degree of volatility of capital flows and asset prices, financial spillovers will bar any further decoupling of East Asia. Therefore, if emerging Asia is serious about erecting a buffer against external disturbances, it needs to consider instituting some of the remedies for controlling vagaries of capital flows. One such remedy is to impose controls on capital inflows. While the controversy on the effectiveness of such controls persists, there has been a reexamination of some of the control measures emerging Asia could adopt to reduce the volatility of capital inflows at the IMF (Ostry et al. 2011).

Regardless of its effectiveness, the capital controls alone will not be enough to restrict capital inflows. In particular, emerging economies will need to take precautionary measures to safeguard against large and unexpected capital outflows caused by the market's overreaction, which could trigger a reserve currency liquidity crisis.

[12] Park and Shin (2010) claim that the 2008 crisis did very little in undermining the safety and soundness of East Asia's financial systems.

To prevent a liquidity crisis, East Asia's emerging economies would benefit from consolidating the regional liquidity support system—the Chiang Mai Initiative Multilateralization (CMIM)—and from joining forces to help create a global liquidity safety net that could provide short-term liquidity when they suffer from a reserve currency liquidity crisis caused by a sudden reversal of capital inflows. The G-20 has been working on creating a liquidity safety net, and if such a net were complemented by capital control measures, East Asia's financial markets and institutions will be better equipped to insulate themselves from any unpredictable shocks emanating from global financial markets.

6.4 Prospects for decoupling

Emerging East Asia's rapid and robust recovery from the 2008 crisis has reopened the debate on decoupling. In this chapter, it has been shown that the available evidence from recent changes in intra-regional trade and financial linkages with global financial markets together with the 2008 crisis does not confirm either decoupling or re-coupling.

Much of emerging Asia's current recovery has been powered by the expansion of domestic demand bolstered by fiscal stimulus. It is too early to tell whether this domestic demand-led growth would be sustainable and, if it could be, whether it will boost intra-regional trade enough to develop a firmer base for decoupling. It also remains uncertain whether the PRC will be able to absorb a large share of imports from other emerging economies to help it withstand a future slowdown in the US and the EU. However, these uncertainties need to be weighed up against the background of a number of recent developments in East Asia that point to the formation of a region more self-contained than before.

Emerging Asia appears to be on the way to pre-crisis dynamism and growth. This, which will be further supported by the three FTAs of the PRC, Japan, and Korea with ASEAN (which have entered into force), will spur intra-regional trade. In addition, the PRC and Korea have expressed an interest in starting negotiations for a bilateral FTA between themselves. Japan and Korea are expected to resume their FTA negotiations, which have for some years been stalled by disagreements over agricultural trade. A long debated proposal for creating an FTA among the PRC, Japan, and Korea is no longer idle speculation.

With increases in income throughout the region, East Asia will witness continuing expansion in intra-regional trade, much of which will consist of intra-industry trade that is more horizontal than before. At the same time, if East Asia succeeds in instituting an efficient capital control regime and in strengthening the CMIM, which will be part of a global liquidity safety net, it will be able to better cope with the volatility of capital flows to the region. Together these developments will then help speed up economic integration among ASEAN + 3 member states to build a region that is more self-contained than before, as it will be less affected by the cyclical movements of the industrialized countries in North America and Europe.

References

Anderson, J. (2007). Is China Export-Led? *UBS Investment Research Asian Focus*. Hong Kong: Global Economics Research. September 27.

Asian Development Bank (ADB) (2008). *Asian Development Outlook*: Update. Manila: ADB.

——(2009). *Asian Development Outlook: Rebalancing Asia's Growth*. Manila: ADB.

Athukorala, P. and A. Kohpaiboon (2010). East Asia in World Trade: The Decoupling Fallacy, Crisis, and Policy Challenges. FIW Working Paper 52. Vienna: the Austrian Institute of Economic Research (WIFO), the Vienna Institute for International Economic Studies (wiiw) and the Computing Centre for Economics and Social Sciences (WSR).

Calderón, C., A. Chong, and E. Stein (2007). Trade Intensity and Business Cycle Synchronization: Are Developing Countries Any Different? *Journal of International Economics* 71(1): 2–21.

Frankel, J. A. and A. K. Rose (1998). The Endogeneity of the Optimum Currency Area Criteria. *The Economic Journal* 108(449): 1009–25.

Grubel, H. G. and P. J. Lloyd (1975). *Intra Industry trade: The Theory and Measurement of Internationally Trade in Differentiated Products*. London: Macmillan.

Imbs, J. (2004). Trade, Finance, Specialization and Synchronization. *Review of Economics and Statistics* 86(3): 723–34.

International Monetary Fund (IMF) (various issues). *Direction of Trade Statistics*. Washington, DC: IMF

——(2007). *World Economic Outlook*: Decoupling the Train? Spillovers and Cycles in the Global Economy. Washington, DC: IMF.

——(2010). *Regional Economic Outlook Asia and Pacific*: Consolidating the Recovery and Building Sustainable Growth. Washington, DC: IMF.

——(2011). *World Economic Outlook*: Tensions from Two-Speed Recovery, Unemployment, Commodities, and Capital Flows, Washington, DC: IMF.

Jeong, W. (2009). *Changes in the Commodity Structure of Trade between Korea and China in 2008 and Their Implications*. Institute for International Trade, Korea International Trade Association (in Korean).

Kim, S., J. Lee, and C. Park (2009). Emerging Asia: Decoupling or Recoupling. ADB Working Paper Series on Regional Economic Integration No. 31. Tokyo: Asian Development Bank Institute.

Ostry, J. O., A. R. Ghosh, K. Habermeier, L. Laeven, M. Chamon, M. S. Qureshi, and A. Kokenyne (2011). Managing Capital Inflows: What Tools to Use? IMF Staff Discussion Note SDN/11/06. Washington, DC: IMF.

Park, D. and K. Shin (2008). Economic Integration and Changes in the Business Cycle in East Asia: Is the Region Decoupling from the Rest of the World? *Asian Economic Papers* 8(1): 107–40.

——(2010). People's Republic of China as an Engine of Growth for Developing Asia?: Evidence from Vector Autoregression Models. ADBI Working Paper Series 175. Tokyo: Asian Development Bank Institute. (Forthcoming *Asian Economic Papers* 10 (2), 2011).

Park, Y. and C. Song (2011). RMB Internationalization: Prospects and Implications for Economic Integration in East Asia. Forthcoming in *Asian Economic Papers* 10(3).

Shin, K. and Y. Wang (2004). Trade Integration and Business Cycle Comovements: the Case of Korea with Other Asian Countries. *Japan and the World Economy* 16(2): 213–30.

Thorbecke, W. (2010). How Elastic is East Asian Demand for Consumption Goods? ADB Working Paper Series No. 260. Tokyo: Asian Development Bank Institute.

World Bank (2006). *East Asia Pacific Update: Managing Through a Global Downturn.* Washington, DC: World Bank.

World Bank (2011). Exports of goods and services (% of GDP). Washington, DC: World Bank. Available: http://data.worldbank.org/indicator/NE.EXP.GNFS.ZS.

APPENDIX 1

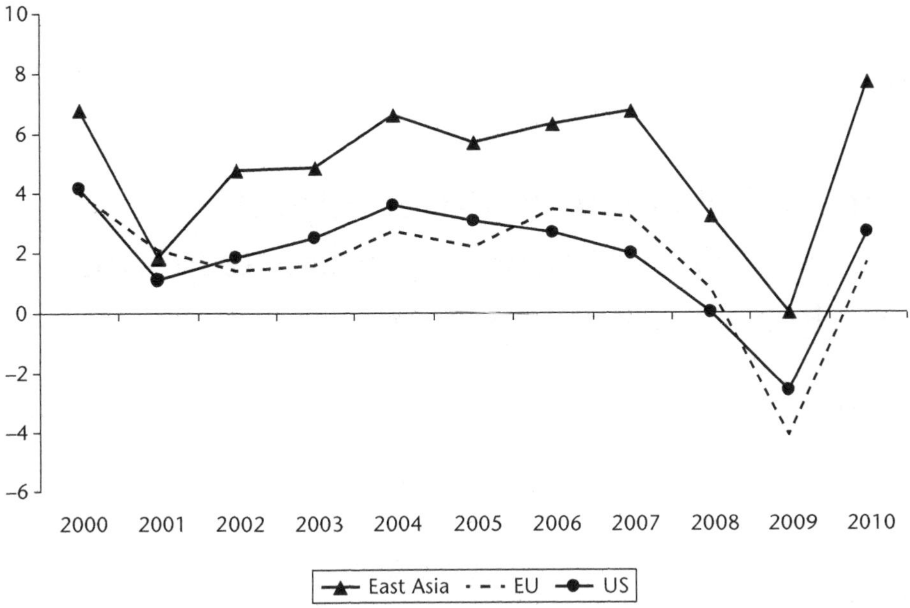

Figure A6.1 GDP growth rate for major regions (2000–2010)—including Japan (%)
Source: IMF, *World Economic Outlook* Database, October 2010.

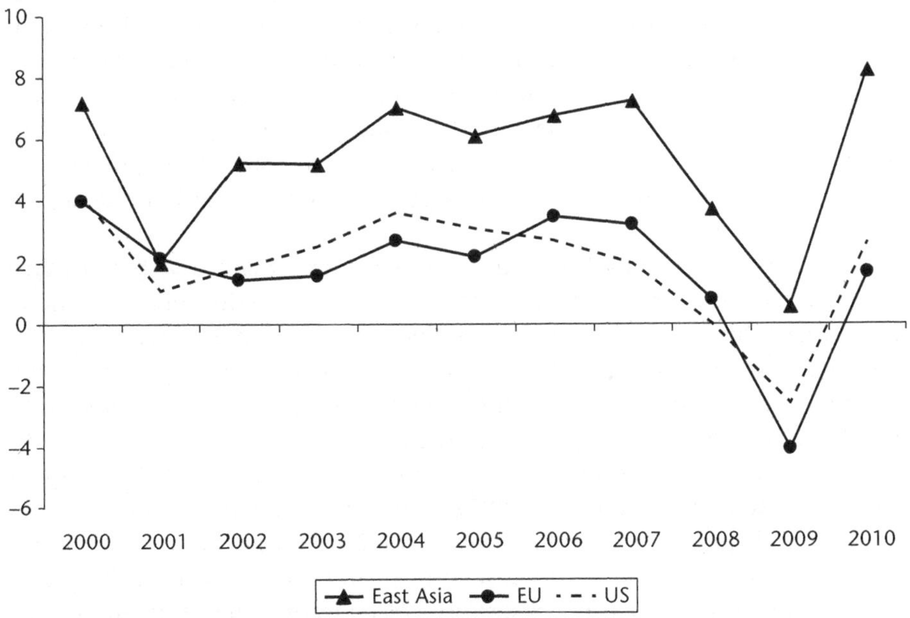

Figure A6.2 GDP growth rate for major regions (2000–2010)—excluding Japan (%)
Source: IMF, World Economic Outlook Database, October 2010.

Note: In Figures A6.1 and A6.2 major regions include the EU, the US, and East Asia (ASEAN5; the PRC; Hong Kong, China; Taipei,China; Korea; and Japan).

7

The Global Financial Crisis: Impact on the Chinese Economy, Policy Responses, and Rebalancing Approach

Bin Zhang and Yongding Yu

7.1 Introduction

Since the second half of 2008, the economy of the People's Republic of China (PRC) has experienced dramatic fluctuations. The global financial crisis, together with a cyclical downward adjustment that started at the end of 2007, resulted in an extreme reduction in inventories and production during the fourth quarter of 2008. The magnitude of the slowdown in the real economy was much greater than most economists had expected and led to policymakers paying significant attention to the issue. The government quickly adopted a number of stimulus policies to avoid further slowing of the real economy.

In the first quarter of 2009, the economy experienced a better-than-expected recovery. In contrast to many financial institutions elsewhere, which were threatened by bankruptcy and were therefore forced to reduce their business, commercial banks in the PRC—the dominant players in the PRC's financial market—were running healthy balance sheets and increased their loans by more than 20 percent in the first quarter of 2009. In contrast to the downturns in asset prices and dramatic currency depreciations in some emerging market economies, the PRC's composite share index rebounded by more than 20 percent in the first quarter of 2009, and international confidence in the currency was strong. In contrast to the downturn in the global real economy, the PRC's industry sector has seen improvements in an increasing number of indicators, such as the purchasing managers' index (PMI) and electricity production.

Does this mean that the PRC's economy has fully recovered from the effects of the global financial crisis? If this is indeed the case, what were the impacts of the global financial crisis on the economy? What policy responses did the government adopt and how can their effectiveness be evaluated? And finally, what should the PRC learn from its experience during the global financial crisis and what further policy changes should the government implement to improve the PRC's economic performance? The succeeding sections attempt to address these questions.

7.2 Impacts of the global financial crisis on the economy of the People's Republic of China

The impacts of the global financial crisis were concentrated mainly in the real sector of the economy. In the fourth quarter of 2008, the economy underwent an unexpected collapse in the industry sector and approximately 20 million rural migrant workers lost their jobs, or 15.3 percent of the total 130 million rural migrant workers (Xiwen 2009), an outcome that was influenced by domestic factors as well as the international financial crisis. During the first quarter of 2009, despite export and import growth rates plunging at double-digit rates, overall economic activity was weakly positive. Fortunately, given the limited involvement of the private sector in overseas financial markets, domestic financial institutions, households, and enterprises in the PRC, along with the government, generally remained healthy and the domestic financial market continued to function.

7.2.1 *Real variables*

The tradable sector was severely affected by external demand shocks. The manufacturing PMI and the PMI for new export orders dropped to less than 50.0[1] by July 2008 and continued to decline until November 2008, when the manufacturing PMI stood at 33.8 and the PMI for new export orders stood at 29.0.

Import and export growth rates became negative in November 2008 and continued to decline sharply in the first quarter of 2009 (Figure 7.1). Confronted with worse-than-expected external markets, most exporters took dramatic action by using up their inventories, lowering production, and

[1] A PMI of more than 50 represents an expansion of the manufacturing sector, compared with the previous month. A reading under 50 represents a contraction, while a reading of 50 indicates no change.

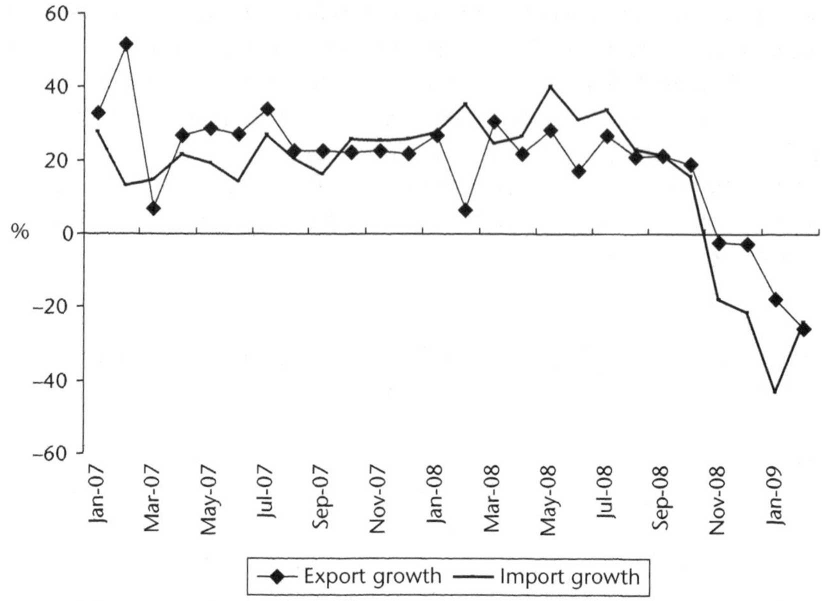

Figure 7.1 Export and import growth
Source: PRC Economic Information Database.

suspending the new training of employees. Thousands of enterprises went into bankruptcy and millions of migrant workers lost their jobs.

Investment in the real estate sector, which used to be a major economic growth engine, started to fall in mid-2008 in response to macroeconomic policy tightening, and fell from 33 percent in the middle of 2007 to 20 percent by the end of 2008 (Figure 7.2).

The sudden deterioration of two traditional economic growth engines—investment in fixed assets and in real estate—led to a drop in the year-on-year growth rate of the PRC's gross domestic product (GDP), which fell from 13 percent in 2007 to 6 percent by the fourth quarter of 2008. Some economists argue that, if the annualized seasonal adjusted quarter-on-quarter rate is applied to the GDP growth rate in effect during the fourth quarter of 2008, the corresponding annual GDP growth rate falls to 1 percent, or even becomes negative. We find that estimating the PRC's quarter-on-quarter GDP growth using publicly available statistics yields unreliable results because of contradictions in the data (Zhang 2009). In Zhang's estimation, the annualized quarter-on-quarter GDP growth rate could vary significantly from 1.0 percent to 5.6 percent depending on the analytical method used.

Instead of examining the GDP growth rate to understand the dramatic changes in overall economic activity, we could instead look at changes in

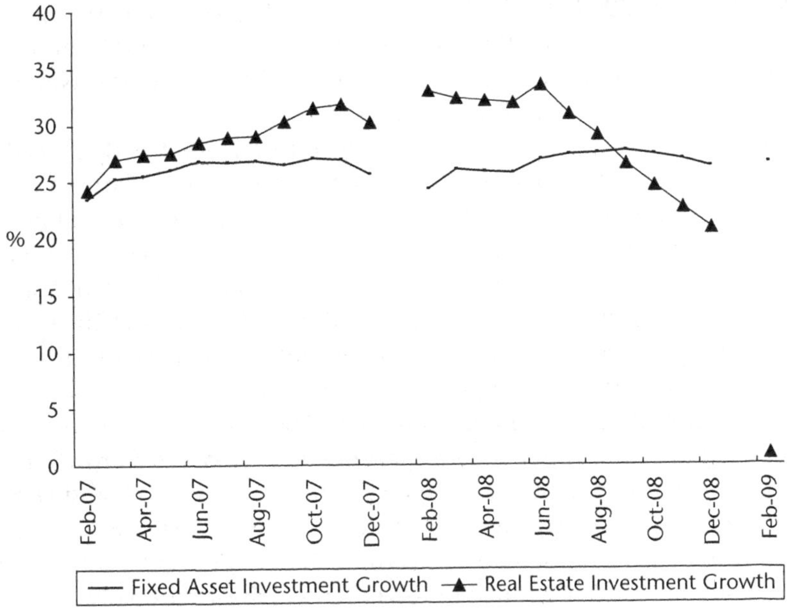

Figure 7.2 Growth in fixed asset investment and real estate investment
Source: PRC Economic Information Database.

the production of proxies: electricity and cement. We used seasonal adjusted production after deleting their time trend to assess the impacts of cyclical and external factors on the real economy. We found that both electricity and cement production experienced a dramatic adjustment in the fourth quarter of 2008. The negative effects of cyclical and external shocks were particularly severe in the case of electricity production; the adjustment in cement production was not as strong, revealing that the effects were greater in the industry sector than in the construction sector. A correction to the excessive reduction in inventories and the fiscal stimulus package both helped electricity and cement production to recover in the first quarter of 2009.

7.2.2 *Nominal variables*

The PRC's financial institutions remained healthy in the short run and were not seriously affected by the global financial crisis. Because of cautious deregulation in the PRC's capital account, the involvement of private financial institutions in overseas financial markets is limited. Despite a lack of complete statistics on total losses during the period of the global financial crisis, various sources indicate that total losses by the PRC's three main listed domestic commercial banks could amount to less than US$3 billion from the middle of 2008 to early 2009. In 2008, the capital adequacy ratio of the major commercial banks stood at 10 percent and the ratio of non-performing loans was 2 percent. To date, no financial institutions have gone into bankruptcy because of losses in overseas financial markets.

Money supply (M2) and credit growth began to decline in early 2008 due to macroeconomic tightening policies, but rebounded spectacularly in the first quarter of 2009. As with real variables, M2 and credit growth attained their lowest levels in November 2008 as a result of external shocks. However, as a result of the monetary authority's easing of its monetary policy stance and the government's huge fiscal expansion plans, the banks dramatically expanded the availability of credit, especially to large state-owned enterprises, which benefit from government-supported projects. Bank loans amounted to CNY1.60 trillion (US$234 billion) in January 2009 and CNY1.07 trillion (US $156 billion) in February 2009, corresponding to year-on-year growth rates of 18 percent in January 2009 and 20 percent in February 2009, and were 3–4 percent higher than average levels during the previous 20 years. As the economic outlook continues to be uncertain, banks are still cautious about making loans to small and medium-sized enterprises, especially enterprises in the tradable sector. The liquidity of financial institutions is good and the interbank overnight lending rate has remained low, ranging from 0.9 percent to 1.5 percent.

Capital outflows totaled around US$120 billion–US$140 billion in the fourth quarter of 2008 (Wright 2009). Despite a record quarterly trade surplus of US$114.3 billion and additional sources of capital inflows, the PRC's foreign exchange reserves rose by only US$40.4 billion during this period. Capital outflows were caused by a sudden reversal of renminbi appreciation against the United States (US) dollar.

7.2.3 *Mid- to long-term impacts*

The impacts of the global financial crisis on the PRC's economy could last for some time. The crisis that started in the US clearly signaled that the growth in consumption and the trade deficit in the US could not catch up with export growth in East Asia, especially in the PRC. The increasing trade imbalances and financial links since 2002 have proven to be unsustainable. Thus, in the foreseeable future, export growth will no longer contribute as significantly to overall economic growth in the PRC. The changing external environment is a major challenge not only for exports but also for the PRC's growth model. Unlike many other sectors, the private sector dominates the PRC's exports and accounts for the bulk of efficiency improvements. The PRC's economic growth is highly dependent on the growth nexus among exports, money creation, export-related investment, labor income, and tax revenues. One issue with this nexus is the government's inability to design incentives that will expand the domestic services sector.

The global financial crisis forced the government to seek new growth engines within domestic markets. Fiscal stimulus and reforms in many areas—such as health care, education, and pricing for energy and other natural resources—are under way. The reforms are intended not only to compensate for the slowdown in export growth but also to improve the sustainability of export growth. The old economic cycle has been broken but the new one is not yet completely in place.

7.3 Government policy responses and their effectiveness

Confronted with an unexpected worsening of global financial markets and severe downward pressure on the domestic economy, the government adopted ambitious stimulus policies, eased monetary and industry policies, and introduced a number of reforms, as noted earlier.

7.3.1 *Fiscal stimulus package*

In November 2008 the government announced an ambitious CNY4 trillion (US$585 billion) fiscal stimulus package. This was beyond the market's expectations and critics voiced numerous concerns. According to the government, this stimulus package was intended to boost economic growth by improving domestic demand and the economic structure. As Figure 7.3 shows, infrastructure accounts for the bulk of the package. The package's structure is different from that originally announced in November 2008, the major difference being the share of expenditure going to health care (which was increased by 2.75 percent), industrial innovation and upgrading (increased by 5.25 percent), and low-income housing (increased by 3 percent). The expenditure share of roads, railways, airports, and the power grid was decreased by 7.5 percent, and the share of environmental conservation was decreased by 3.5 percent. These adjustments reflected doubts about the effectiveness of devoting too much of the package to infrastructure and concerns about industrial upgrading and social welfare inadequacies.

The government used a number of different channels to finance the stimulus package. The central government was responsible for 25 percent of the total amount, while local governments were responsible for the remainder by means of sources such as taxes, land sales, bank loans, debt, and joint investment from the private sector. The central government's fiscal position has been good, with around CNY100 billion in 2008 and an outstanding treasury bills to GDP ratio of 22 percent. The government announced that in 2009 the

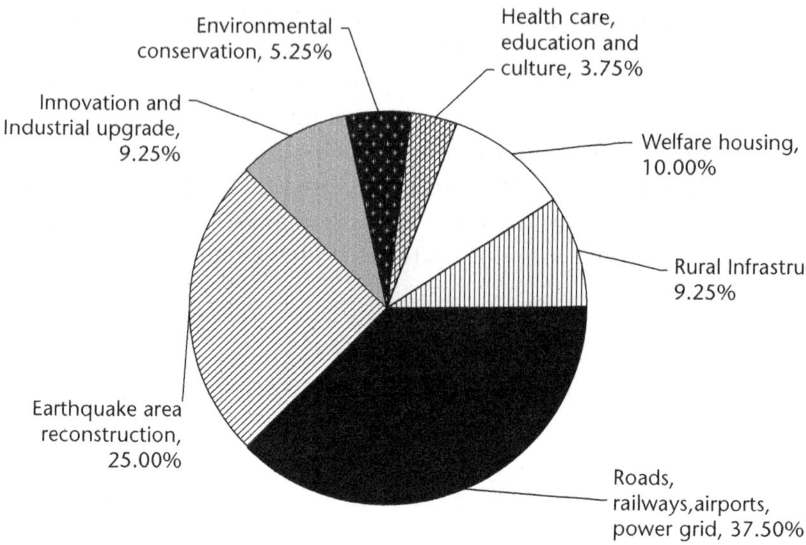

Figure 7.3 Fiscal stimulus package, 2008
Sources: National Development and Reform Commission, author's calculation.

total fiscal deficit would be CNY950 billion (including CNY200 billion for local government debts) and that the deficit–GDP ratio would be 3 percent (GDP is around CNY33 trillion, and the fiscal deficit close to CNY1 trillion), which is acceptable.

Access to financing has been less straightforward for local governments. Not only have they had to deal with slower growth in local income taxes because of the slowdown of the overall economy, but also their income from land sales—their major source of funds for local infrastructure construction—has fallen dramatically since 2008 because of the contraction in the real estate sector. As a result, local governments are looking for help from commercial banks and the central government. While large commercial banks have been extremely interested in making loans to the central government for big projects that were selected by the National Development and Reform Commission and are partly supported by central government financing, local governments have had to approach local commercial banks for some local government projects that were not on the commission's list and had no financing support from central government.

In academic circles, the major concerns about the fiscal stimulus package relate to its expenditure structure. These concerns include the following:

- The efficiency of such a large amount of infrastructure investment is not guaranteed. The number of non-performing loans in the banking sector will increase rapidly in the future, along with the extent of corruption.

- The package will delay the necessary adjustment of the real sector, such as phasing out outdated production capacity in the industry sector and transferring resources from the excessively large industry sector to the underdeveloped services sector.
- The government's excessive involvement in the industry sector, such as its provision of subsidies for industrial innovation and upgrading, will impair market competition and squeeze out private investment.

Many economists argue that instead of engaging in so much investment, the government should cut taxes rather than increase spending, give direct subsidies to the poor and to those who have lost their jobs, and increase the share of expenditure directed toward public health and social safety nets. Policymakers paid attention to these concerns and made some pertinent changes to the fiscal stimulus package.

Despite the concerns, the fiscal stimulus may prove to be extremely helpful by increasing employment opportunities and securing economic growth, at least in the short run. Dong, Zhang, and Zhang (2009) estimate the effects of the fiscal stimulus package on output and employment for the mainland PRC. Using an input–output table as the analytical framework, they argue that the announced fiscal spending of CNY2.0 trillion in 2009 could lead to a direct increase in output of CNY1.7 trillion, implying a fiscal multiplier of 0.84 in the short run, and could potentially generate 18–20 million new jobs in non-farming sectors. As the input–output analysis is static and does not consider the endogenous relative price changes, the long-run effects of the fiscal stimulus package could be quite different.

The fiscal stimulus plan encourages import growth with a focus on machinery and equipment and mining and quarrying. According to Dong, Zhang, and Zhang (2009), total intermediate imports amount to CNY316.8 billion (approximately US$46 billion), or 16 percent of the fiscal package. Intermediate imports for machinery and equipment will increase by CNY97.7 billion, about 1.2 times the value added induced in that sector. Mining and quarrying accounts for the second-largest increase in intermediate imports, CNY74.8 billion (approximately US$11 billion), as coking, gas, and petroleum industries use a good deal of imported mining and quarrying products as inputs.

7.3.2 *Monetary policy*

As the global financial crisis unfolded, the monetary authority took comprehensive measures to ensure liquidity in domestic financial markets and to lower the cost of credit. The easing of the monetary policy stance, which was initially introduced in the third quarter of 2008, included, among other measures, quantity measures, interest rate cuts, and stabilization of the renminbi–US dollar exchange rate.

Quantity measures included cutting the required reserve ratio, increasing base money supply through open market operations, and lifting restrictions on loan growth for commercial banks. In the fourth quarter of 2008, the People's Bank of China (PBC) lowered the required reserve ratio four times. The accumulated reserve ratio cut amounted to 2 percent for large commercial banks and 4 percent for small and medium-sized commercial banks. By the end of 2008, the total amount of liquidity released was CNY800 billion (PBC 2009). The PBC lowered its issuance of central bank bills in the fourth quarter of 2008 by CNY371 billion, equivalent to 8 percent of the total issuance of central bank bills in 2008. Quota management, which used to be the most effective instrument for restraining loan growth, was abolished.

The PBC announced five interest rate cuts in the fourth quarter of 2008. The 1-year base deposit interest rate decreased from 4.14 percent to 2.25 percent and the 1-year base lending rate decreased from 7.47 percent to 5.31 percent. The interest rate for required reserve deposits fell from 1.89 percent to 0.99 percent and that for excessive reserve deposits in the central bank decreased from 1.62 percent to 0.72 percent.

Thanks to the PBC's actions with respect to quantity and interest rate policies, liquidity shortages are not apparent, at least in the interbank markets. The interbank overnight lending rate decreased dramatically (Figure 7.4) and the interbank transaction volume remained stable. Liquidity injections from the central bank did not automatically translate into immediate faster M2 growth. Commercial banks, which had been facing deteriorating values of collateral and worsening of the real economy, were cautious about making new loans and leaving more money in the form of excessive reserves in the central bank. According to the PBC (2009), the average excessive reserve ratios of commercial banks was 5.11 percent by the end of 2008, an increase of 1.81 percent over 2007, resulting in a decline of the money multiplier and slower broad money growth.

Growth in bank loans rebounded spectacularly in the first quarter of 2009; year-on-year growth in bank loans was 21.3 percent in January and 24.5 percent in February. This sudden change resulted from the fiscal stimulus package, which provided for partial financing of many projects by the government, abundant liquidity, and the release of quota management of loan growth for commercial banks. The major contributors among the new loans were long-term loans for government-backed infrastructure projects and short-term commercial paper. As noted earlier, commercial banks remained cautious about making loans to private small and medium-sized enterprises.

In the second half of 2008, the PBC kept the renminbi–US dollar exchange rate constant, while allowing the nominal effective exchange rate to

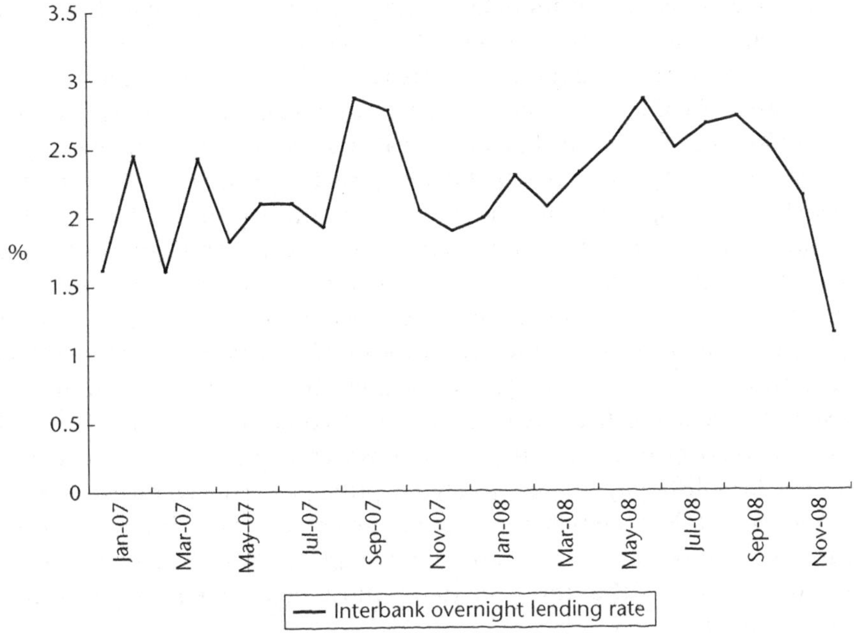

Figure 7.4 The interbank overnight lending rate (January, 2007–February, 2009)
Source: PRC Economic Information Database.

appreciate. The renminbi's appreciation against the US dollar, which started in July 2005 and accelerated in the first half of 2008, was suspended in June 2008 and has remained stable since that time. In the meantime, given the appreciation of the US dollar against other currencies, the renminbi's nominal effective exchange rate appreciated by 7–10 percent.

The objectives of the exchange rate policy have not changed. In the context of the global financial crisis and the appreciation of the US dollar, the PBC views a stable renminbi–US dollar exchange rate as attractive for a number of reasons, including:

- stabilizing international capital flows, as further appreciation or depreciation of the renminbi against the US dollar is perceived as attracting speculative capital flows and damaging domestic macroeconomic stability; and
- achieving the renminbi's move toward a reasonable equilibrium level.

To date, despite the rapid slowdown of export growth in the PRC, the government has not used the exchange rate as a policy instrument to promote export growth.

The moderate easing of monetary policy has facilitated financing for the fiscal stimulus package and recovery of the economy in the short run at the possible expense of giving rise to an increase in non-performing loans held by the commercial banks. The spectacular growth in loans and the weak recovery in the industry sectors in the first quarter of 2009 point to the positive impacts of the easing of monetary policy; however, such a growth in loans is unsustainable and dangerous. On the one hand, the commercial banks have adequate liquidity but, on the other hand, they direct the bulk of this liquidity into loans to government-supported infrastructure projects. As a result, the structure of commercial banks is being reshaped by an increasing share of low-yield reserve deposits in the PBC, other forms of government debt, and loans to infrastructure projects or other government-backed projects, and decreasing shares of loans to the private sector. This could be unsustainable in the long term as government revenue growth, which is the only way the government will be able to pay interest and repay principal to the commercial banks, will not occur unless the private sector has greater access to financial support. Until the private investment and consumption growth nexus are well developed, loans to the government or those guaranteed by government revenues are not safe.

7.3.3 *Other policies*

The government views its industrial policies as instruments for ensuring industrial upgrading and quality growth. In early 2009, the government announced ambitious industry reinvigoration plans that include ten major industries: automobiles, steel, textiles, machinery, shipbuilding, electronics and information, petrochemicals, nonferrous metals, logistics, and light industry. These industry invigoration policies, which make use of acquisitions and mergers, tax cuts, and investment in innovation, aim to get rid of outdated production capacity, boost domestic demand, and upgrade the industry sector.

The government seeks to deepen reforms in many fields to strengthen the sustainability of economic growth and to enhance social welfare. The government and academia are particularly interested in

- reforms in the health care sector, in which the government plans to take on more responsibilities in providing fundamental services and undertaking deregulation; and
- pricing of rural land, energy, and natural resources, which is thought to be ineffective and a factor underlying structural distortions and which should be market based.

The government's industry invigoration plans and reforms reflect its search for new economic growth engines. As many policies are under discussion and have not yet been implemented, we cannot evaluate them. Instead, in the next section we draw lessons from the global financial crisis and propose policies that the Government of the PRC should regard as priorities to rebalance the economy and to contribute to the sustainability of global economic growth.

7.4 Recovery, inflation, and contingent liabilities

7.4.1 *Moderate growth and tamed inflation*

Fiscal stimulus packages and loose monetary policy in both the PRC and other systemically important countries paved the way for real economy recovery as well as inflation in the PRC. The real economy is recovering very well. In 2009 GDP growth was 9.2 percent and in 2010 it was 10.3 percent, which are close to the PRC's 20-year average GDP growth. In the first half of 2011, GDP growth was 9.6 percent. In line with recovery of the real economy, the year-on-year consumer price index (CPI) rebounded in the autumn of 2009, and continued to climb in 2010 and the first half of 2011. In June 2011, the year-on-year CPI reached 6.4 percent (Figure 7.5).

Real estate prices responded more aggressively to the loose monetary policy. Year-on-year real estate price growth jumped from 3.0 percent in the global financial crisis period to 15.2 percent by the end of 2009. In the first-tier cities, such as Beijing and Shanghai, some newly constructed and secondary market residential property prices increased by more than 100 percent (Figure 7.6).

In the context of robust real sector recovery and rising property prices and CPI pressure, the PRC monetary authority has changed its monetary stance since early 2010. In February 2010, the monetary authority increased the required reserve ratio from 15.0 percent to 15.5 percent, and there were another eight required reserve ratio hikes from February 2010 to June 2011. In November 2010, the PRC monetary authority increased the 1-year nominal lending rate from 5.3 percent to 5.6 percent, and there were another three interest rate hikes in the next half year. In June 2011, the required reserve ratio was 20.5 percent and the 1-year nominal lending rate was 6.3 percent.

In addition to interest rate hikes and required reserve ratio policies, the PBC resumed renminbi exchange rate reform in June 2010, and the renminbi began to appreciate against the US dollar after that. However, appreciation of the renminbi against the US dollar cannot catch up with depreciation of the US dollar against other major currencies. The nominal effective exchange rate of the renminbi depreciated by 5.35 percent from June 2010 to June 2011; the

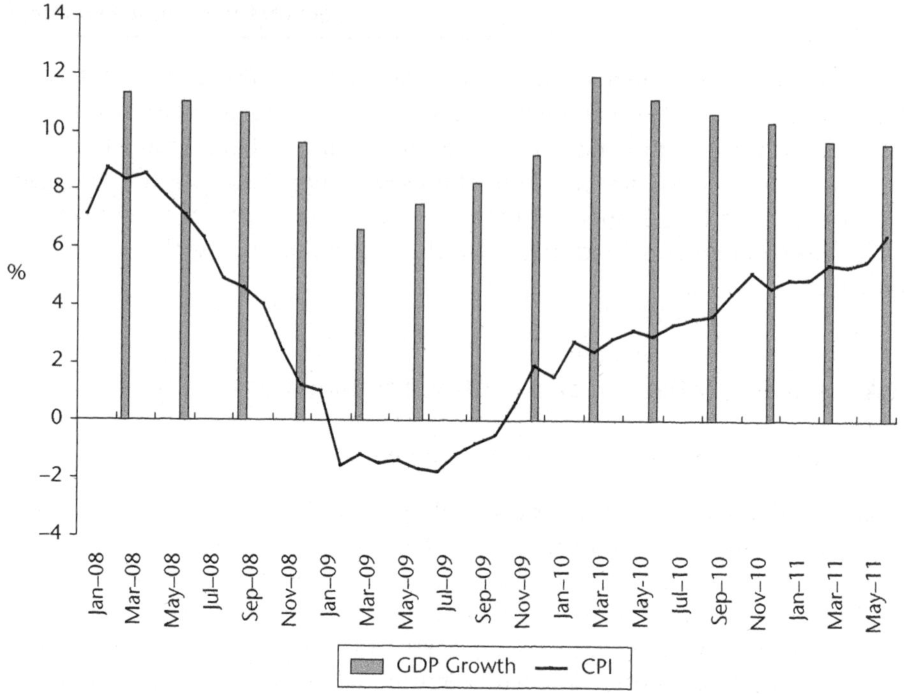

Figure 7.5 The PRC's CPI and GDP growth
Source: PRC Economic Information Database.
Note: GDP = Gross Domestic Product; CPI = Consumer Price Index

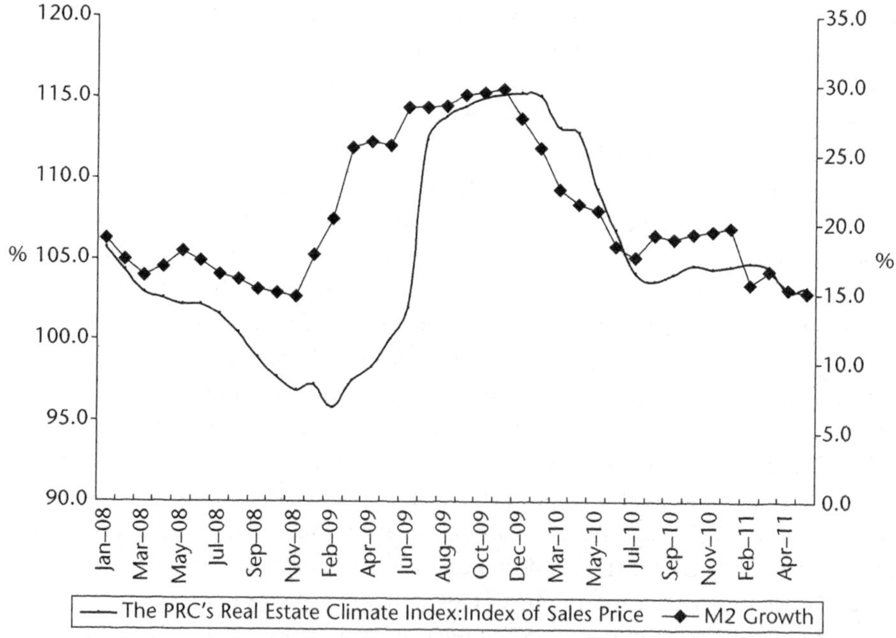

Figure 7.6 The PRC's real estate price index and M2 growth
Source: CEIC Data

real effective exchange rate depreciated by 2.72 percent in the same period. The difference between the nominal effective exchange rate and the real effective exchange rate is mainly due to rising domestic inflation.

Central and local governments in the PRC took other measures to cool down the economy and real estate markets. In 2010, credit control was reintroduced. Commercial banks had new loan growth quotas for each month imposed on them. From early 2011, in more than twenty first- and second-tier cities, local governments imposed property purchasing limitations on residential properties. Moreover, local government investment vehicles (LGIVs), which were flourishing at the end of 2008 and in 2009, were under severe investigation. Commercial banks were prohibited from providing new loans to local government financing platforms (LGFPs).[2] Thanks to the changing monetary stance and many other measures, broad money growth slowed down and converged to the historical average level. M2 growth, the most popular representative indicator of broad money growth in the PRC, peaked at 29.7 percent at the end of 2009 and then started to fall. In June 2011, M2 was 15.9 percent, which is close to its twenty-year average level.

Since M2 growth is under control and commodity prices have stabilized in 2011, worries on inflation have weakened. The mainstream forecast about the year-on-year CPI in the second half of 2011 is 5 percent. In line with tightening policies and a drop in M2 growth, the real estate price growth rate started to fall from early 2010; by the middle of 2011 it was 3 percent, which is lower than the average level in the past ten years.

7.4.2 *Imbalance remains*

On the supply side, there is no significant change in economic structure in the PRC—disproportional growth between secondary industry and tertiary industry remains. Secondary industry was affected more than tertiary industry in the period of financial crisis, leading to a decreasing share of secondary industry in GDP growth and an increasing share of tertiary industry in GDP growth in 2009. However, the shares of secondary and tertiary industry in GDP growth went back to their pre-crisis trend two years later. In 2010 and the first half of 2011, the average share of secondary industry in GDP growth was 53 percent, which is 7 percentage points higher than the past ten-year average; the average share of tertiary industry in GDP growth was 40 percent, which is 6 percentage points lower than the past ten-year average.

On the demand side, investment remains the major contributor to GDP growth. In 2010 and the first half of 2011, the average share of gross capital

[2] We will come back to LGIVs later.

formation in GDP growth was 54.5 percent, which is 1.0 percent higher than the past ten-year average; the average share of final consumption expenditure in GDP growth was 44.4 percent, which is 2.0 percent lower than the past ten-year average.

On the external side, the share of net export of goods and services in GDP growth declined after the financial crisis. During 2002–08, the average share of net export of goods and services in GDP growth was 10.1 percent; in 2010 and in the first half of 2011 it was 1.1 percent.

Two years after the global financial crisis, the PRC's external imbalance has declined due to stimulus policies in the PRC and the changing external environment, but internal imbalance remains. Since the low level of external imbalance in the past couple of years was largely a result of stimulus policies, it is not certain that the external imbalance will remain at a low level when stimulus policies cease. At least, International Monetary Fund (IMF) economists don't think so; they predict that the current account surplus to GDP ratio in the PRC will continue to increase from 2011 to 2015 (IMF 2011).

Policymakers in the PRC understood well the threats of external and internal imbalance to the sustainability of the PRC's economic growth. In March 2011, the 12th Five Year Plan was published, which gives high priority to switching the means of economic growth and rebalancing the PRC economy. Development of the service sector, improvement of basic housing and the medical system, nationwide coverage of the social safety network, adjustment of income distribution, further reform of the PRC's financial system, and many other objectives are listed in the plan.

7.4.3 *Contingent liability matters*

Local governments in the PRC always have strong incentives to invest, but they need approval from central government and loans from banks. During the global financial crisis, the central government relaxed controls over local government investment projects, and banks, in the context of loose monetary policy, were running excessive liquidity and were glad to provide loans to projects backed by local governments. Thousands of LGIVs were established in 2008 and 2009. Those LGIVs borrow money from banks and invest the money in infrastructure projects, such as roads, irrigation systems, and airports. According to the National Audit Office, the LGIV debt was CNY4.9 trillion at the end of 2010, which is 13 percent of GDP. However, observers think that the National Audit Office underestimates the level of LGIV debt because its estimates are restricted to formal local government liabilities and excludes informal commitments of projects supported by local government. The China Banking Regulatory Commission estimates outstanding LGIV bank loans at close to CNY9 trillion.

The LGIVs are having difficulties with debt payment. According to the National Audit Office, CNY2.6 trillion is due in 2011 of a total of CNY10.7 trillion local government debt, which includes CNY4.9 trillion of LGIV debt. If we use the China Banking Regulatory Commission's definition of LGIVs, the due amount could be larger. In addition to principal, local government has to pay CNY0.6 trillion–CNY0.9 trillion in interest payments every year. Tax revenue is growing strongly but most income is already allocated; little is available to service debt. Land sale income will be between CNY1.0 trillion and CNY1.3 trillion in 2011, but no more than 20 percent of it can be used for debt payment. LGIVs could generate some revenue, such as road tolls, but the overall revenue from finished projects is limited and much of it is used for other purposes. Due to lack of sufficient statistics, we could not present a very detailed picture on the expenditure and revenue of local governments and LGIVS in the PRC, but the general picture is clear—many local governments and LGIVs are not able to meet their debt payments. According to the China Banking Regulatory Commission, approximately CNY2 trillion–CNY3 trillion worth of LGIV loans (30 percent of total LGIV loans and 5–7 percent of GDP) are already in trouble, and it is very possible that more loans will be in trouble in the near future. Stephen Green from Standard Chartered predicted that between CNY8 trillion and CNY9 trillion (22 percent of GDP) in debt within commercial banks will ultimately have to be resolved (SinoCast Daily Business Beat 2009).

A bailout plan is needed for LGIVs. LGIV debt repayment failure may increase and spread across the country in the coming quarters. Some small local commercial banks are in danger of bankruptcy; PRC commercial banks as a whole are not capable of digesting such a large number of problematic debts. A national bailout plan is unavoidable. Before any bailout plan is released, debt repayment failure will have strong impacts on financial markets. LGIVs are important players in the credit markets as well as the production network; their debt repayment failures damage their credibility as well as that of their business counterparties. If not properly managed, this may generate a credit crunch and seriously affect the real economy. Fortunately, the government of the PRC and finance-related ministries pay close attention to this issue. More importantly, the central government has enough room to deal with the challenges.

The overall level of public debt in the PRC is not high by international standards. The major public debt consists of central government debt (CNY6.7 trillion), policy bank debt (CNY3.2 trillion), local government debt (CNY14.8 trillion, according to the China Banking Regulatory Commission's broad estimate of LGIVs), high-speed railway debt (CNY1.8 trillion), and some other small components. We don't include central bank bonds (CNY4.0 trillion) in the public debt since they are backed by more than US$3 trillion of assets. Putting all the public debts together, the overall public debt–GDP ratio is 70–75 percent, which is not high compared with other economies. Since growth in average fiscal revenues in the PRC has been greater than 20 percent in the past ten years and this trend is continuing, and given that the PRC economy is expected grow by 8–9 percent in the coming years, the government of the PRC still has room to deal with the local government debt problems.

7.5 Lessons learned from the global financial crisis and the economic rebalancing policies of the People's Republic of China

As the global financial crisis unfolded, the trade imbalance between Asia and the US was reduced. Given the huge losses in its nominal financial wealth, the US was forced to reduce both its consumption and its imports, thereby increasing its saving rate. As a result of the sudden drop in external demand, the PRC and its East Asia neighbors were forced to lower production in their tradable sector, as well as reduce their exports, thereby decreasing their saving rates at the expense of GDP growth. Even though the PRC and its East Asian neighbors were not at the center of the global financial crisis, and their finance sector losses were limited, their losses in real terms are comparable to those of the economies whose financial markets faced more serious problems.

Cyclical and structural factors amplified the negative effects of the global financial crisis on the PRC's economy. The PRC's GDP growth rate averaged 10.0 percent in 2003, 10.1 percent in 2004, 10.4 percent in 2005, 11.6 percent in 2006, and 13.0 percent in 2007, above the potential GDP growth rate of 9.0–9.5 percent. GDP growth was particularly dependent on investment in the tradable and real estate sectors. The tradable sector's huge production capacity meant that the gap between production and domestic demand increased, enhancing the importance of exports to overall economic growth. In other words, once external demand—an indicator of both cyclical and structural adjustment—collapsed, the domestic economy suffered more. A high saving rate used to be the most important factor explaining both cyclical and structural problems. On the other hand, the large trade surplus induced by the high saving rate gives rise to expectations of currency appreciation, speculative capital inflows, and asset bubbles along with an overheated economy.

The formula of "saving – investment = net export" is an accounting identity rather than an equation that describes behavior. With regard to the PRC, the high saving rate should not be treated as a result of household decisions. Explaining savings through net exports is more consistent with reality and has much more complex policy implications. As discussed in more detail below, we argue that policy distortions that boost the trade surplus will have many other side effects, such as worsening the distribution of income, increasing the saving rate, and causing GDP growth and welfare improvement to be unbalanced.

The following subsections describe certain aspects of the PRC's economy and a relevant model, and then propose a rebalancing strategy that is relevant not only for the PRC but also for other East Asian economies that have been running trade imbalances for an extended period.

7.5.1 *Two pertinent aspects of the economy of the People's Republic of China*

As Table 7.1 shows, the first relevant aspect of the PRC's economy is that the tradable sector experienced faster total factor productivity (TFP) growth than the nontradable sector. This is particularly true for the TFP growth differentials between export sectors and domestic monopoly sectors.

The most important factor that helps account for TFP growth differentials between the tradable and nontradable sectors is the different policies governing the two sectors. Since the early 1980s, the tradable sector has experienced systematic market reform, especially with respect to the following:

- *Market suppliers*: Many private enterprises were established and became the major force behind growth in the tradable sector. At the same time, state-owned enterprises were reorganized, including with respect to their shareholders. By the end of 2004, 1,464 of 2,903 large state-owned

Table 7.1 Comparison of TFP growth between selected tradable and nontradable sectors, average growth rate 1982–2000

Sector	Average TFP growth (%)
Tradable	
Electrical machinery	4.04
Fabricated metals	2.88
Instruments	3.8
Motor vehicles	2.9
Nonelectrical machinery	2.53
Primary metals	6.46
Nontradable	
Construction	(0.25)
Financial services	(11.18)
Oil and gas extraction	(9.96)
Other private services	(2.36)
Public services	(0.54)
Transportation	(4.65)

Source: Cao et al. (2008).

Note: TFP = Total Factor Productivity

enterprises had been reorganized as corporate enterprises with multiple shareholders.

- *Market building*: The price system was thoroughly reformed in most tradable sectors and barriers to market entry were relaxed. As a result, competition in most industry sectors has increased.
- *External environment*: Tariff and non-tariff barriers have been reduced and policy incentives are directed toward attracting foreign direct investment.

These market reform measures have had a positive influence on technological advancement, improved resource allocation efficiency in the tradable sector, and helped to realize rapid TFP growth in the tradable sector.

In contrast to the rapid and complete market reforms in the tradable sector, market reforms in the nontradable sector have been limited. In nontradable service sectors—such as education, health care, the environment, finance, communications, and railways—limited improvements have been made with respect to technology upgrading and resource allocation efficiency. The principal suppliers in these sectors are state-owned enterprises, and the private sector faces high barriers to market entry. Price controls and market entry controls are pervasive, market competition is insufficient, and industrial monopolies are widespread.

The second relevant aspect of the PRC's economy in the context of this chapter is the lack of a mechanism to facilitate adjustment in the relative prices of tradables and nontradables. According to the Balassa–Samuelson hypothesis, faster relative TFP growth in the tradable sector than in the nontradable sector will result in higher relative prices of nontradables compared with tradables and resultant resource reallocation.

Under the assumption that the PRC is a price taker in international markets, there are two ways to increase the relative price of nontradables compared with that of tradables. The first way is through currency appreciation. Given the international market prices of tradables, currency appreciation lowers the domestic prices of tradables—such as exports, potential exports, imports, and import substitutes—and the price of nontradables rises relative to the price of tradables. The second way is through inflation. As the nominal exchange rate is unchanged and the international market price of tradables is given, inflation will translate into a higher relative price for nontradables than for tradables. Either of the two ways results in appreciation of the internal real exchange rate in accordance with the definition of real exchange rates.

Given the high policy priority accorded to both low inflation and a stable renminbi–US dollar exchange rate, the ability to adjust the relative prices of nontradables to tradables required by TFP changes is limited. From 1995 to 2005, the renminbi–US dollar exchange rate was stable and movement of the renminbi's real effective exchange rate closely followed the exchange rate of the US dollar against other major currencies. Since July 2005, when the PRC's monetary authority announced exchange rate reform, the renminbi has steadily appreciated against the US dollar, as has the real effective exchange rate. However, given the rapid increase in the trade surplus at the same time the real effective exchange rate was increasing, one can conclude that adjusting the real effective exchange rate is insufficient to reallocate resources from the tradable sector to the nontradable sector, and therefore to redress the PRC's growing trade surplus.

7.6 The rebalancing policies of the People's Republic of China

Confronted with the global financial crisis, the government's ambitious stimulus package to boost domestic demand was timely and effective with respect to avoiding excessive adjustment of the real economy. However, the stimulus package did relatively little to redress the PRC's structural distortions and to provide sustainable economic growth engines. Excessive use of fiscal resources can be problematic if their use is not effective and sustainable. Thus, for the next stage of dealing with the global financial crisis, we recommend that the government gives priority to comprehensive domestic reforms and further international cooperation instead of increased government spending. Our proposal for a rebalancing strategy is described in the following paragraphs.

First, the government should introduce further deregulation in the nontradable sectors, such as railways, health care, education, finance, telecommunications, energy, and express delivery. Deregulation policies should focus on relaxing market entry restrictions for private investment and reducing government intervention in pricing. In the short run, such deregulation measures will help inspire confidence among private sector investors interested in the potentially huge domestic market, which has been depressed for a long time. This would also help meet the large unsatisfied demand in the domestic market and create job opportunities. In the long run, by improving TFP growth in those sectors undergoing deregulation, such deregulation measures will increase the ratio of marginal returns to labor to marginal returns to capital, and therefore enhance both income distribution and domestic consumption, and will direct more resources to the nontradable sector than to the tradable sector. We regard such deregulation policies as the top priority to lower the PRC's saving rate and trade surplus, and thus to rebalance the economy.

Second, the government should direct more resources toward reducing poverty by, for example, increasing its provision of public health care, basic education for the poor, and low-income housing. The government should be careful when expanding infrastructure such as highways and the power grid, given uncertainty about their effectiveness in the future, and therefore leave more resources for poverty reduction. State-owned enterprises, which are largely monopolies, should remit a substantial portion of their profits to the government. Such actions are aimed at increasing both the welfare and the purchasing power of the poor, and could thus help boost domestic demand and rebalance the economy.

Third, the government should continue with pricing reform and the reduction of favorable policies toward the tradable sector. The government has already taken active measures with respect to reform of the renminbi exchange rate, interest rates, energy prices, and prices in many other sectors. The essence of pricing reform is to reduce the government's influence on price making and therefore leave more room for market influence on prices. In addition, favorable policies toward the tradable sector, such as lower land prices and high tax rebates for enterprises financed by foreign direct investment and enterprises that contribute significantly to local GDP growth, have contributed to an increasing share of the industry sector in the overall economy. Yet the government has been taking gradual measures to overturn such favorable policies since 2005. It should reverse this latter approach and regard such policies as an indispensable part of the country's rebalancing strategy.

Fourth, the PRC needs to cooperate more extensively with other countries in East Asia and participate in reforms of the international financial architecture. In this chapter we focus on the PRC's domestic issues, especially its high saving rate and structural distortions, and suggest pertinent domestic reforms. However, when taking a global perspective, the PRC's contribution to global economic recovery and rebalancing is limited. Loose monetary policies in the US and an overdependence on the US dollar in East Asia increase the global imbalance and the fragility of East Asian economies. As a result of its bailout of financial companies, the US is running an exceptionally high budget deficit, which along with its loose monetary policy has given rise to concerns about high commodity prices. If expectations of high commodity prices result in expectations of inflation and force the US monetary authority to increase interest rates, this would put the recovery of the world economy in a more difficult situation. Thus, the PRC needs to not only address its internal structural distortions but, along with its East Asian neighbors, it also needs to reduce dependence on the US dollar and US monetary policy. To this end, the PRC and its East Asian neighbors should improve regional cooperation to develop regional financial markets and enhance policy coordination.

References

Cao, J., M. Ho, D. Jorgenson, R. Ren, L. Sun, and X. Yue (2008). Industrial and Aggregate Measures of Productivity Growth in China, 1982–2000. *Review of Income and Wealth* 53(2): 390–4.

Dong, H., Z. Zhang, and W. Zhang (2009). How Large Will Be the Effect of China's Fiscal Stimulus Package on Output and Employment. Hong Kong Monetary Authority Working Paper 05/2009.

International Monetary Fund (IMF) (2011). *2011 World Economy Outlook*. Washington, DC: IMF.

People's Bank of China (2009). *China Monetary Policy Quarter Four* (in Chinese). Beijing.

SinoCast Daily Business Beat (2009). China Considering Doubling CNY4trn Stimulus Plan. March 3. High Bean Business News Website, available: http://business.highbeam.com/436195/article-161-194757692/china-considering-doubling-cny4trn-stimulus-plan.

Wright, L. (2009). *The End of China's Liquidity Cycle? Part I: Capital Outflows in Q4 2008*. Beijing: Stone and McCarthy.

Xiwen, C. (2009). Speech to the State Council. February 2.

Zhang, B. (2009). The Confused China's Quarterly GDP Growth Rate. Research Center for International Finance at Chinese Academy of Social Sciences Policy Brief 09005.

8

The Global Economic Crisis: Impact on India and Policy Responses

Rajiv Kumar and Pankaj Vashisht

8.1 Introduction

The Indian economy looked to be relatively insulated from the global financial crisis that started in August 2007 when the sub-prime mortgage crisis first surfaced in the United States (US). In fact, the Reserve Bank of India (RBI) was raising interest rates until August 2008 with the explicit objective of cooling the economy and bringing down the gross domestic product (GDP) growth rate, which had visibly moved above the rate of potential output growth and was contributing to the buildup of inflationary pressures in the economy.[1] But when the collapse of Lehman Brothers on September 23, 2008 morphed the US financial meltdown into a global economic downturn, the impact on the Indian economy was almost immediate. External credit flows suddenly dried up and the overnight money market interest rate spiked to above 20 percent and remained high for the next month. The credit crunch was followed by a collapse in external demand for merchandise and services exports, which pulled down GDP growth by two percentage points during the second half of FY2008–09. Nonetheless, in line with the expansionary fiscal and monetary policy measures taken in the wake of the global recession, the Indian economy recovered quickly in the FY2009–10, before slowing down once again in FY2010–11. Against this backdrop, this chapter attempts an in-depth analysis

[1] Several observers, led by Surjit Bhalla (2008), had been pointing out since May 2008 that inflation, which had gone as high as 12.3 percent at the end of June 2008, was largely imported and a result of global commodity price hikes. Therefore, inflation had little to do with India's own rate of economic growth, which started to slow down in the third quarter of FY2007–08 after reaching its highest level of 10.6 percent in the second quarter of the same fiscal year.

of the impact of the global financial crisis on the Indian economy and suggests some policy measures to put the economy back on track.

Broadly, this chapter is divided into six sections. After dealing with the impact of the global financial crisis on the Indian economy in Section 8.2, Section 8.3 discusses the monetary and fiscal policy responses to the crisis, while Section 8.4 provides a critical assessment of the policy responses. Section 8.5 provides an overview of recent development in Indian economy. In the final section we recommend some policy measures that are needed to put the economy on a fast growth track.

8.2 Impact of the crisis on the Indian economy

8.2.1 *Global integration of Indian economy*

In response to its balance of payments (BOP) crisis in the early 1990s, India implemented a series of trade, industry, and investment reforms. These reforms effectively liberalized the economy, ending a long period of relative isolation from global markets and financial and technology flows. Since then the Indian economy has become increasingly integrated with the world economy.[2] Consequently, current account flows (receipts and payments of merchandise and invisibles) as a proportion of GDP increased from 20 percent in FY1990–91 to 53 percent in FY2007–08 (Figure 8.1). However, the most significant change can be witnessed in the capital account. Due to the rationalization of procedures and conditions for foreign investment, India has emerged as an attractive investment destination. This is reflected in an increase in foreign portfolio investment inflows from US$2 billion in FY2001–02 to US$29 billion in FY2007–08. Foreign direct investment (FDI) inflows have also gone up significantly during last seven years, having risen to US$34.3 billion in FY2007–08 from US$6.1 billion in FY2001–02. At the same time, Indian corporations have also entered the global market for mergers and acquisitions, resulting in some capital account outflow from India. As a result, two-way flows of portfolio and direct foreign capital have gone up from a mere 12 percent of GDP in FY1990–91, to 64 percent of the GDP in FY2007–08, registering a five-fold increase. Interestingly, these ratios are significantly higher than those in the US, for which trade in goods and services constituted only 41 percent of GDP in 2007 and capital flows another 25 percent in the same year.

[2] The peak import duty on manufactured products was slashed from more than 200 percent in FY1990–91 to about 10 percent in FY2007–08. Quantitative restrictions on imports have also been gradually phased out.

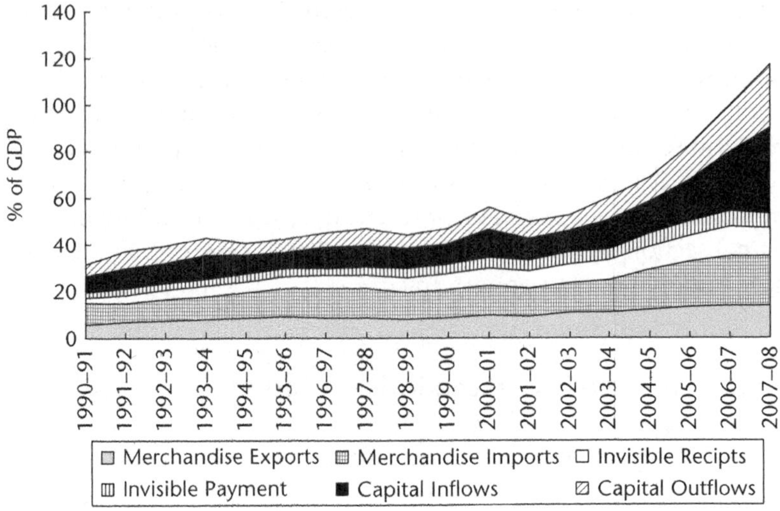

Figure 8.1 Deepening global linkages
Source: Authors' calculations compiled from Reserve Bank of India (2009b).

8.2.2 *Transmission of the crisis to the Indian economy*

With India's increased linkage with the world economy, India could not be expected to remain immune to the global crisis or be decoupled from the global economy. While it is true that the Indian banking sector remained largely unaffected because of its very limited operations outside India or exposure to subprime lending by foreign investment banks, the global crisis has affected India through three distinct channels. These channels are financial markets, trade flows, and exchange rates.

The financial sector includes the banking sector, equity markets (which are directly affected by foreign institutional investment (FII) flows), external commercial borrowings (ECBs) that drive corporate investments, FDI, and remittances. The global crisis had a differentiated impact on these various sub-sectors of the financial sector.

Given prudent regulations and a proactive regulator,[3] the Indian banking sector remained more or less unaffected, at least directly, by the global crisis. The imposition by the RBI of a higher provisioning requirement on commercial bank lending to the real estate sector helped to curb the growth of a real estate price bubble. This is one of the few global examples of a countercyclical capital provisioning requirement by any central bank. In general, Indian

[3] The RBI, under the leadership of Dr Y. V. Ready, has acted very proactively many times. In 2006, when land purchases were skyrocketing, he imposed a ban on the use of bank loans for land purchase.

banks were not overly exposed to subprime lending. Only one of the larger private sector banks, ICICI Bank, was partly exposed but it managed to thwart a crisis because of its strong balance sheet and timely action by the government, which virtually guaranteed its deposits. The banking sector as a whole has maintained a healthy balance sheet. In fact, during the third quarter of FY2008, which was a nightmare for many big financial institutions around the world, banks in India announced encouraging results. Against an absolute decline in the profitability of non-financial corporate enterprises, the banking sector witnessed a jump of 43 percent in its profitability. A ban on complex structures like synthetic securitization coupled with a close monitoring of appropriate lending norms by RBI also ensured a better quality of banking assets. The non-performing assets as a ratio to gross advances have remained well within prudential norms (Figure 8.2). Further, with an average capital risk weighted assets ratio (CRAR) of 13 percent, Indian banks were well capitalized and better placed to weather the economic downturn.

However, the indirect impacts of the crisis have affected Indian banks quite badly. The liquidity squeeze in global markets following the collapse of Lehman Brothers compelled Indian banks and corporations to shift their credit demand from external sources to the domestic banking sector. This move exerted a lot of pressure on liquidity in the domestic market and consequently short-term lending rates shot up abnormally. The interbank call money rate spiked to 20 percent in October 2008 and remained high for the next month. This credit crunch, coupled with the loss of confidence that followed the Lehman Brothers episode, increased the risk aversion of Indian banks and eventually hurt credit expansion in the domestic market. Contrary to

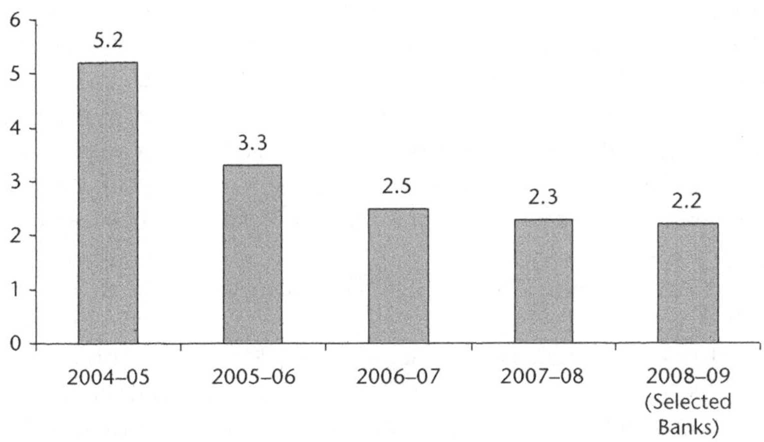

Figure 8.2 Non-performing assets percent to gross advances

Source: Reserve Bank of India (2008). Available: http://www.cmie.com/database/?service=database-products/firm-level-data-services/prowess-corporate-database.htm (accessed May 20, 2009).

the trend, non-food credit expansion started declining in November 2008 and became negative in January 2009. The magnitude of the impact of the crisis can be understood from the fact that non-food credit expansion during the last five months of FY2008–09 declined by more than 68 percent compared with the same period in the previous financial year.

After an impressive performance for nearly five years, foreign capital inflows lost their momentum in the second half of 2008. The most significant change was observed in the case of FIIs, which saw a strong reversal of flows. Against a net inflow of US$20.3 billion in FY2007–08, there was a net outflow of US$15 billion from Indian markets during FY2008–09 as foreign portfolio investors sought safety and mobilized resources to strengthen the balance sheet of their parent companies. This massive outflow of FII created panic in the stock markets. Consequently, equity markets lost more than 60 percent of their index value and about US$1.3 trillion of market capitalization from an index peak of about 21,000 in January 2008 to 8,867 by March 20, 2009. This bad run at Dalal Street[4] wiped out the primary market completely, despite its having been flourishing before the onset of the crisis. Between FY2007–08 and FY2008–09, fund collection through the primary market declined by 63 percent. In 2007, 106 initial public offerings (IPO) were issued and raised a total amount of about US$11 billion. In contrast, only 38 IPOs were issued in 2008 and resulted in accumulations of only US$3.8 billion.

The economic boom in India from FY2004–05 to FY2007–08 has also been accompanied by a substantial increase in the inflows of FDI and ECBs. The inflows of FDI increased from US$6 billion in FY2004–05 to US$34.3 billion in FY2007–08 (Figure 8.3). The surge in FDI not only improved the domestic rate of capital formation but also helped many industries improve their technological capacity due to the technology inflows that accompanied the FDI. Like FDI, the inflows of ECBs also went up from US$9 billion in FY2004–05 to US $30.3 billion in FY2007–08, registering a three-fold increase over four years. The spurt in ECBs benefited Indian entrepreneurs in two different ways. First, it supported them in their overseas mergers and acquisitions, making it easier for them to gain a market presence in target countries. Second, the influx of ECBs allowed Indian firms to finance their domestic capacity expansion at relatively lower capital costs.

Both FDI inflows and ECB volumes have been adversely affected by the turmoil in the financial markets in advanced economies. Given the credit crunch in the global markets since September 2008, Indian corporates managed to raise only US$15.2 billion in FY2008–09 as commercial credit from the overseas market, which is 49.8 percent less than the amount raised in the

[4] The Bombay stock market is often referred as Dalal Street.

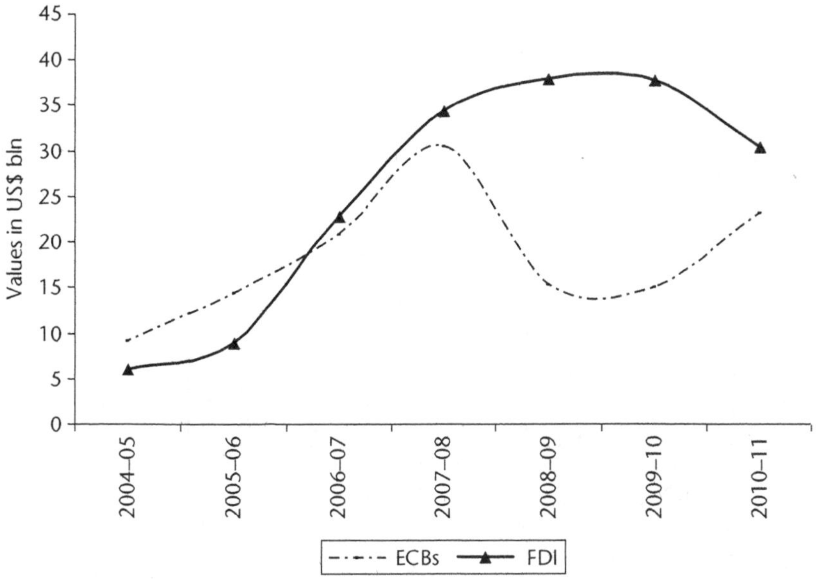

Figure 8.3 Annual ECBs and FDI inflows
Source: Reserve Bank of India (2011a and 20011b).
Note: ECBs – external commercial borrowing.

previous year. The fall was rather phenomenal during the second half of FY2008–09 (Figure 8.4), when monthly ECB approvals[5] declined from US$3 billion in September 2008 to less than US$0.5 billion in February 2009. Likewise, though not to the same extent, FDI inflows have also taken a hit. For the first time in the last few years, FDI inflows witnessed a modest growth of 10 percent in FY2008–09, which was followed by negative growth in FY2009–10 and FY2010–11.

Remittances are another source of inward foreign capital flows that in the past have helped to balance India's large trade account deficit and keep the current account deficit at a reasonable level. The remittances from overseas Indians started to feel the impact of the global crisis during the third quarter of FY2008–09 when, on a year-on-year basis, they declined by 0.5 percent. The impact becomes more evident in the fourth quarter of FY2008–09 when the inflow of remittances declined by more then 29 percent as compared to the same period in previous year.

The sluggishness of the inflows of FDI, ECBs, and remittances combined with the massive outflow of FII resulted in the significant deterioration of India's capital account in FY2008–09. From its peak in September 2007, the

[5] Monthly inflows of actual ECB are not available.

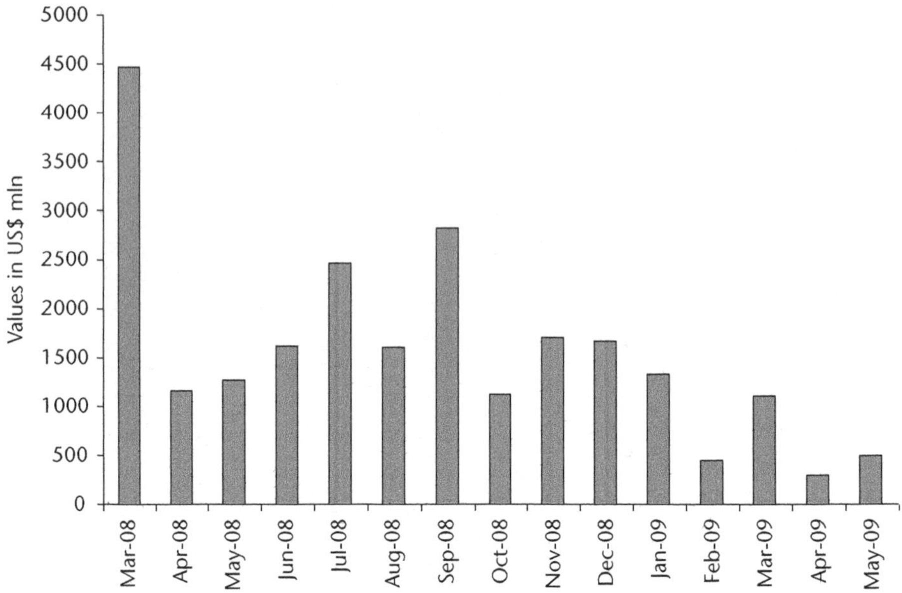

Figure 8.4 Monthly external commercial borrowing, approvals

Source: External Commercial Borrowings, Reserve Bank of India. Available: http://rbi.org.in/scripts/ECBView.aspx (accessed June 20, 2009).

capital account surplus as a percentage of GDP started to decline and disappeared completely by December 2008 (Figure 8.5). This was the first time after a long period that the capital account component of India's BOP has been negative.

The second transmission of the global downturn to the Indian economy has been through the steep decline in demand for India's exports in its major markets. Gems and jewelry was the first sector to feel pressure at the very beginning of the global meltdown. In November 2008, it witnessed a sharp decline in export orders from the US and Europe, which resulted in a retrenchment of more than 300,000 workers. After this, the negative impact expanded to other export-oriented sectors such as garments and textiles, leather, handicrafts, marine products, and auto components. As a result, merchandise exports registered a contraction of 17 percent from October 2008 to May 2009 (Figure 8.6).

Like merchandise, exports of services also witnessed a steep downturn. During the third quarter of FY2008–09, growth in service exports declined to a mere 5.9 percent as compared to 34.0 percent in the corresponding period a year before. The earnings from travel, transportation, insurances, and banking services contracted, while the growth rate of software exports declined by more than 21 percentage points. The real shock came in the fourth quarter

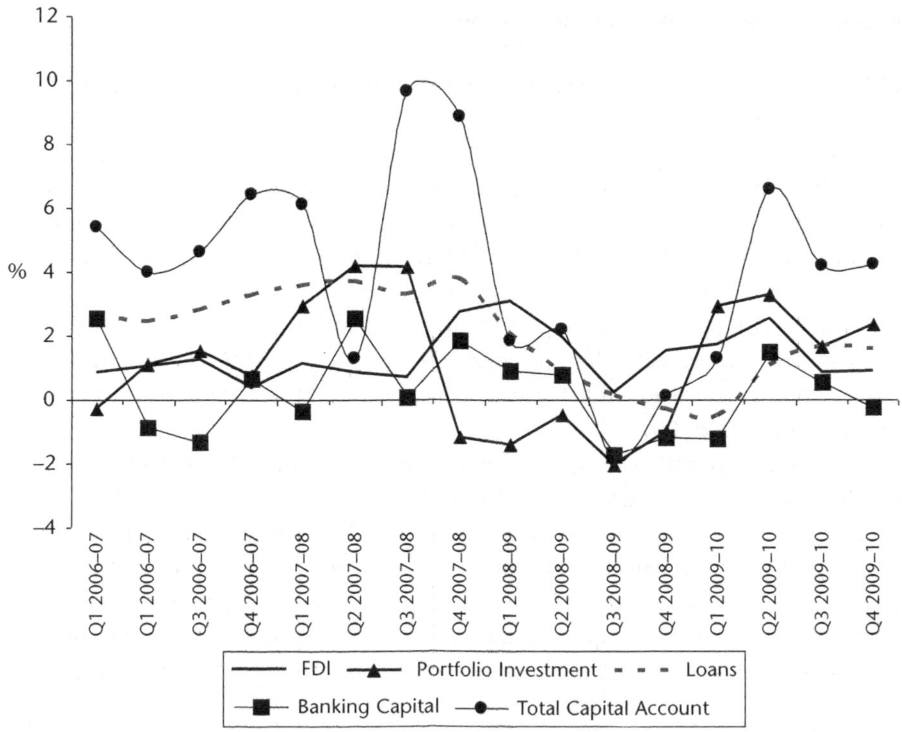

Figure 8.5 Capital account BOP (% of GDP)

Sources: Authors' calculations compiled from Reserve Bank of India (2011b) and Central Statistical Organization (2011).

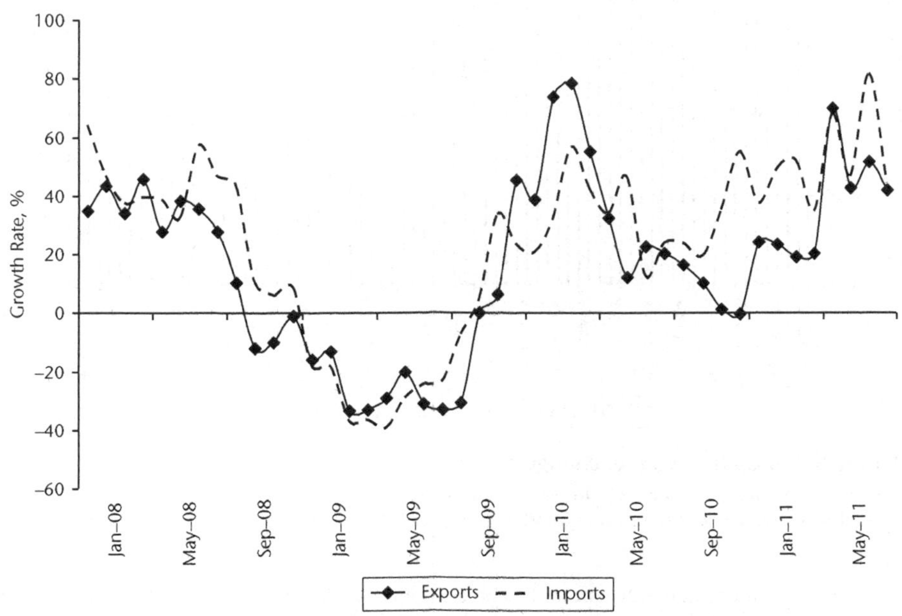

Figure 8.6 Recent trend in imports to and exports from India

Source: Ministry of Commerce, Government of India, 2008–11.

of FY2008–09 when service exports witnessed a contraction of 6.6 percent as compared to the same period in the previous year (RBI 2009c).

Though exports of both goods and services still account for only 22 percent of the Indian GDP, their multiplier effect for economic activity is quite large as the import content is not high, unlike Chinese exports. This is reflected in the manufacturing sector output experiencing a sharp slowdown in the months during which exports witnessed a decline. The index of manufacturing sector output (Manufacturing IIP), which had grown at 9.6 percent during FY2007–08 and by 5.3 percent in the first half of FY2008–09, slowed down to 0.5 percent in the third quarter and fell further to –0.16 percent in the fourth quarter of FY2008–09.

The third transmission channel is the exchange rate. With the outflow of portfolio investments and higher foreign exchange demand by Indian entrepreneurs who were seeking to replace external commercial borrowing by domestic financing, the Indian rupee came under pressure. From April 2008 to March 2009, the Indian rupee tumbled by 27 percent vis-à-vis the US dollar. At the same time, foreign exchange reserves also fell by US$60 billion[6] (Figure 8.7). The nearly 25 percent depreciation in the Indian rupee's

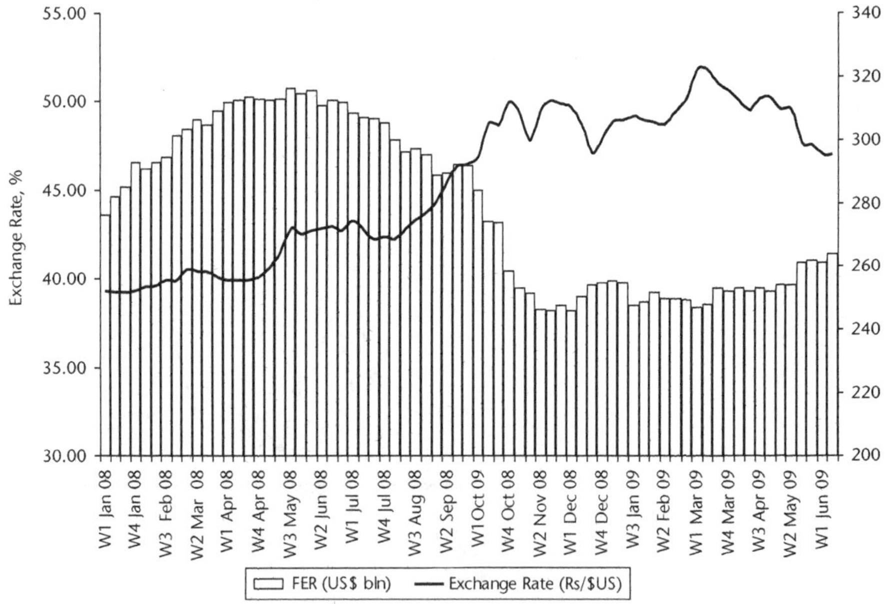

Figure 8.7 Indian foreign exchange reserves (FER) and exchange rate
Source: Reserve Bank of India 2009b. Weekly Statistical Supplements-Extracts. Available: http://www.rbi.org.in/scripts/BS_ViewWSSExtract.aspx (accessed June 30, 2009)

[6] Here it should be noted that around 63 percent of the decline in the foreign exchange reserve can be attributed to valuation, hence the actual decline in reserves is just around US$20 billion.

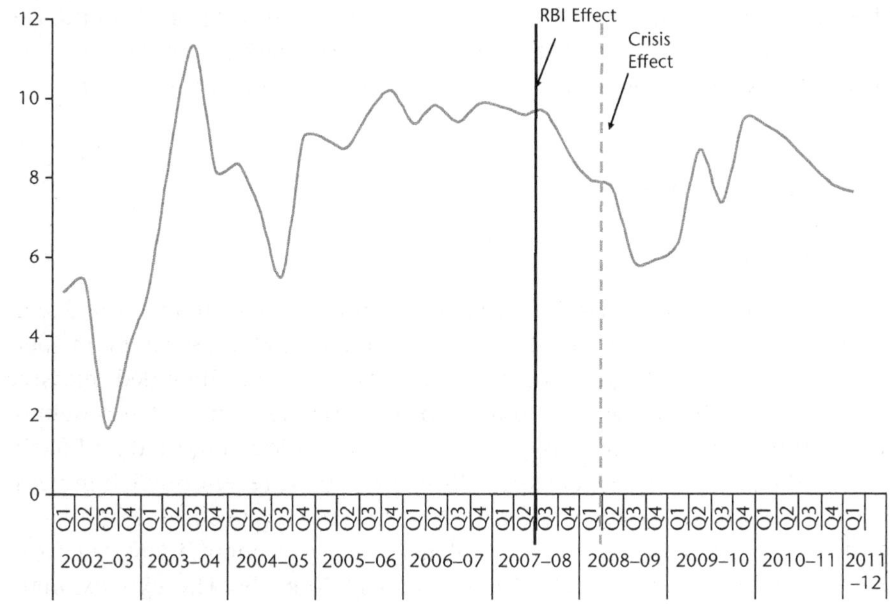

Figure 8.8 Quarterly GDP growth
Source: Central Statistical Organization (2011).

exchange rate partially nullified the benefits from the decline in global oil and gas prices and also increased the cost of commercial borrowings.

The timing of the external shock arising from the global economic downturn has been rather unfortunate. The Indian economy was already in the middle of a policy-induced slowdown (Figure 8.8) and the crisis aggravated this further. The impact of the global crisis on the real economy became evident in the second half of FY2008–09, when, belying the optimistic official pronouncements and expectations of some economists,[7] the Indian economy registered a modest growth rate of 5.8 percent, significantly lower than the 8.9 percent achieved in the corresponding period in FY2007–08, and after having achieved 7.8 percent growth in GDP in the first half of FY2008–09. At the sectoral level, robust growth in community, social, and personal services (17.5 percent) and financial, real estate, and business services (8.9 percent) enabled the services sector to maintain healthy growth despite the sharp decline in trade, hotel, transportation, and communication services. The secondary sector in general and the manufacturing sector in particular performed

[7] Until September 2008, a few economists, along with some forecasting agencies, were projecting a very healthy growth rate for the financial year 2008–09. During a seminar organized by ICRIER on September 19, 2008, Bhalla predicted that India would grow by 9.0 percent while in the same seminar Mahesh Vayas of CMIE projected a growth rate of 9.4 percent.

extremely badly. In the wake of a decline in domestic and export demand, the manufacturing sector witnessed a contraction of 0.3 percent, while growth in construction slowed down significantly from 8.3 percent to 5.5 percent.

8.3 Policy responses

8.3.1 *Fiscal stimulus*

It should be pointed out that the initial fiscal stimulus was actually provided in the budget for FY2008–09, announced in February 2008. Electoral considerations made this into an expansionary exercise that included massive increases in public outlays in support of employment guarantee schemes, farm loan waivers, pay commission rewards, and increases in food and fertilizer subsidies. This fiscal expansion is illustrated by the revenue deficit increasing from 1.4 percent of the GDP in FY2007–08 to 4.3 percent in FY2008–09. At the same time the fiscal deficit of central government increased from 2.6 percent in FY2007–08 to 6.0 percent in FY2008–09. The expansionary public outlays included some measures that implied a hefty transfer of purchasing power to farmers and to the rural sector in general. These included farm loan waivers, funds allocated to the National Rural Employment Guarantee Program (NREGP), Bharat Nirman (targeted for improving rural infrastructure), the Prime Minister's Rural Road Program, and a large increase in subsidies for fertilizers and electricity supplied to the farmers (Table 8.1). All of these measures were taken because of political considerations and not in response to the global crisis. Nevertheless, they have helped to shore up rural demand for both consumer durables and non-durables. In effect, the higher than expected GDP growth rate in both the third and fourth quarters of FY2008–09 could be attributed to the budgetary splurge announced in February 2008. While this has succeeded in shoring up GDP growth by raising rural

Table 8.1 Budget outlay on rural sector (values are in US$billion)

Ser. No.	Item	FY2008–09 (RE)	FY2009–10 (BE)
1	Bharat Nirman	6.25	8.18
2	Farm loan waiver	13.06	—
3	Fertilizer subsidies (a + b + c)	15.17	10.00
	a. Concession on decontrolled fertilizers	9.67	6.72
	b. Imported urea	2.20	1.56
	c. Indigenous urea	3.30	1.72
4	NREGA	6.00	6.02
5	Total	40.49	24.20

Source: Ministry of Finance, Government of India (2009).

Note: BE = budget estimates, NREGA = National Rural Employment Guarantee Act, RE = revised estimates.

demand, it did not leave much fiscal space for the Government of India to respond in any significant manner to counter the impacts of the global downturn.

However, some efforts were mounted to counter the effects of the global economic slowdown. Three fiscal stimulus packages—one each in the months of December, January, and March—were announced. These amounted in aggregate to Rs106,050 Crore or US$21 billion,[8] which is 2 percent of GDP. This can be compared to the 4 percent of GDP that was provided as a stimulus in the FY2008–09 budget discussed in the paragraph above. The three post-December 2008 stimulus packages were mainly comprised of increased government spending on infrastructure, a reduction in indirect taxes, and some assistance for export-oriented industries. In an attempt to boost the infrastructure spending that has been acknowledged as the most effective tool to counter economic downturn, the Government of India increased its planned spending by US$4 billion and also allowed the state governments to borrow an additional amount of US$6 billion from the market. In addition to this, the India Infrastructure Finance Company Limited (IIFCL), a special purpose vehicle (SPV) established in 2007, was allowed to issue interest free bonds worth US$6 billion to refinance long-term loans for various infrastructure projects.

Second, to prop up domestic demand the central excise duty was gradually slashed from 14 percent in December 2008 to 8 percent in March 2009 on all products except petroleum products. Likewise the services tax rate was also brought down from 12 percent to 10 percent. The government also provided some relief to export-oriented industries through subsidizing interest costs of exporters by up to 2 percent, subject to a minimum rate of 7 percent per annum. It also allocated US$240 million for a full refund of terminal excise duty or central sales tax, wherever applicable, and another US$80 million for various export incentives schemes. The direct fiscal burden of all the aforementioned measures adds up to 2 percent of total GDP. This looks rather small in comparison to the size of the stimulus in some other economies like the People's Republic of China (the PRC) and the US. However, if we include the stimulus provided in the FY2008–09 budget, the Indian government has in effect expanded its fiscal outlay by 6 percent of GDP during FY2008–09. It can be argued that the economy may have fared better if more fiscal space were available to boost domestic demand to counter the collapse of external demand that started in November 2008.

[8] This is the direct fiscal burden of the three fiscal stimuli and does not include the indirect burden.

8.3.2 *Monetary policy response*

With the objective of maintaining price stability alongside a reasonable rate of economic growth, the last few years have been very hectic for policymakers at the RBI. After a comfortable period of low inflation, the Indian economy started feeling the pressure of rising global commodity prices in the first quarter of FY2004–05. In response to this rise in inflation, the RBI started tightening monetary policy in September 2004, raising the cash reserve ratios from 4.5 percent to 5 percent. As the inflationary situation worsened in the subsequent period, the tightening of monetary policy became even more aggressive. Consequently, inflation declined from 8 percent in the middle of 2004 to less than 4 percent in September 2007. Nevertheless, coinciding with the rising global inflation trends, domestic inflation once again started increasing towards the end of 2007 and became a major headline in the first week of June 2008 when it entered the double-digit range for first time since the 1991 BOP crisis. It drew a sharp reaction from the RBI and the speed of monetary tightening was further increased. This credit tightening from FY2004–05 onward ensured a soft landing for the Indian economy, which had begun overheating during the previous three years with the actual growth rate exceeding its potential growth rate. As a result the growth rate began to slow down from the middle of FY2007–08.

In the wake of the global financial crisis and its potential adverse effects on the Indian economy, monetary policy shifted gear and became expansionary from October 2008. The rapid decline in Wholesale Price Index (WPI) inflation, which came down from its peak level of 13 percent in August 2008 to less than 1 percent in April 2009, allowed the RBI to completely shift its focus from inflation to growth. From October 2008 to April 2009, the RBI injected a considerable amount of liquidity into the economy through a series of policy rate cuts. The cash reserve ratios of banks was brought down from 9 percent to 5 percent, while the repo rate[9] was slashed by 425 basis points. Further, in order to discourage the banks from parking overnight funds with the RBI, the reverse repo rate[10] was gradually reduced from 6.0 percent in November 2008 to 3.25 percent in April 2009. The statutory liquidity ratio (SLR) was lowered by one percentage point. Apart from this, some special refinancing schemes were also announced to improve the liquidity for certain sectors (Table 8.2). The cash reserve ratios reduction of 400 basis points since September 2008 alone led to an injection of US$32.7 billion. In addition, another sum of US $12.9 billion was injected through unwinding the market stabilization

[9] The repo rate is the rate at which the RBI offers overnight liquidity to banks.
[10] The reverse repo rate is the rate that RBI pays on overnight funds deposited with it.

Table 8.2 Actual/potential release of primary liquidity since mid-September 2008 (values are in US$billion)

1	CRR reduction	32.7
2	Increase in export credit refinance	5.2
3	Liquidity facility for NBFCs through SPV	5.1
4	MSS unwinding	12.9
5	Refinance facility for SIDBI/NHB/EXIM Bank	3.3
6	Special refinance facility for SCBs (non-RRB)	7.9
7	Term repo facility	12.2
Total (1 to 7)		79.2
Memo: SLR reduction		8.2

Source: Compiled from Reserve Bank of India (2009d).

Note: CRR = cash reserve ratios, EXIM = export import, MSS = market stabilization scheme, NBFCs = non-banking financial companies, NHB = national housing bank, RRB = regional rural banks, SCBs = scheduled commercial banks, SIDBI = small industries development bank of India, SLR = statutory liquidity ratio, SPV = special purpose vehicle.

scheme. As of April 2009, a cumulative amount of nearly US$80 billion was pumped into the system (RBI 2009d).

As a result of the policy rate cuts, the prime lending rates of commercial banks came down from 13.75–14.0 percent in October 2008 to 12.0–12.5 percent in January 2009. The call money rates also remained stable at low levels and the overnight money market rate remained within the liquidity adjustment-facility corridor.

Apart from the above-mentioned initiatives, the RBI also liberalized the ECBs and FII related norms. To attract foreign portfolio investors, the FII limit on corporate bonds was increased from US$6 billion to US$15 billion. At the same time, in an attempt to boost the construction sector, developers were permitted to raise ECBs for integrated townships projects, while NBFCs dealing exclusively with infrastructure financing were also allowed to access ECBs from multilateral or bilateral financial institutions.

It could be argued that the three fiscal stimulus packages, in conjunction with the transfer of purchasing power to the rural economy through increased budget outlays on the rural sector and the hike in minimum support prices of various crops, saved aggregate demand and prevented a potential big decline in GDP growth. This was also helped by the quick monetary policy response discussed above. In fact, in hindsight, our shock-augmented leading indicator model that some experts at ICRIER have been using to forecast GDP growth for India[11] verifies this hypothesis. With the full impact of the external shock, we were expecting a growth rate of 5.3 percent in the fourth quarter of FY2008–09. Nevertheless, with an actual growth rate of 5.8 percent, our calculation suggests that the fiscal stimulus neutralized nearly 20 percent of the impact of the external shock.

[11] For details see Kumar et al. (2009).

8.4 Assessment of the policy responses

The Indian fiscal policy response to the crisis can at best be summarized as having been preempted by political considerations that resulted in a fiscal expansion ahead of the global crisis and left only limited space to respond in the aftermath of the crisis. Hence, it could be argued that the fiscal response after December 2008 was not as large as required.[12] Given a high fiscal deficit (central and state combined) of 4.1 percent in FY2007–08, India had limited fiscal maneuverability to begin with. However, due to electoral considerations a fiscal stimulus of nearly 4 percent of GDP was induced in the FY2008–09 budget. This raised the combined fiscal deficit to 8 percent, leaving barely any room for further fiscal stimulus after the crisis.

The fiscal stimulus, though very small in size when compared to other countries, worsened the fiscal deficit further, increasing it to 8.4 percent in FY2008–09. The increase in fiscal deficit had two implications. First, it drew a strong response from international credit rating agencies and the sovereign credit rating of India was in danger of being lowered. Second, the high fiscal deficit naturally led to an increase in government borrowing. Higher government borrowing also put a lot of pressure on the interest rate, as reflected in the 10-year bond yield rate going up along with the announcement of the new stimulus packages (Figure 8.9). The debt to GDP ratio was 75 percent in FY2008–09. The rise in public debt to GDP ratio can be worrisome as it is now well above levels reached in 1991 when the country faced a major crisis. However, the present situation is not as serious primarily due to the strong external sector balance that India has been successfully building up since the beginning of this decade.

In sharp contrast to the fiscal policy response, the monetary authorities in India acted aggressively once it was clear that inflationary pressures had subsided and growth was beginning to slacken. Unfortunately, because of the government's large borrowing requirement and the stickiness in deposit rates that keep the cost of funds high for the banks, the policy rate cuts did not filter into the retail credit market. The commercial bank's lending rates, in real terms despite some reduction, remained very high and banks were not able to push up the credit off-take. This was reflected in the continued decline in the growth of non-food credit off-take from commercial banks in the first half of FY 2009–10.

[12] It is argued by some observers that the policy response was delayed because the government was initially in something of a state of denial, believing that the global crisis would not affect the Indian economy as its banking sector was not at all affected. It was argued that the net contribution of trade to GDP growth is negative and hence the turmoil in the global market would not have any major impact on India. However, a sharp deterioration in some key sectors came as an eye opener for the government and it finally started responding to the crisis in December 2008.

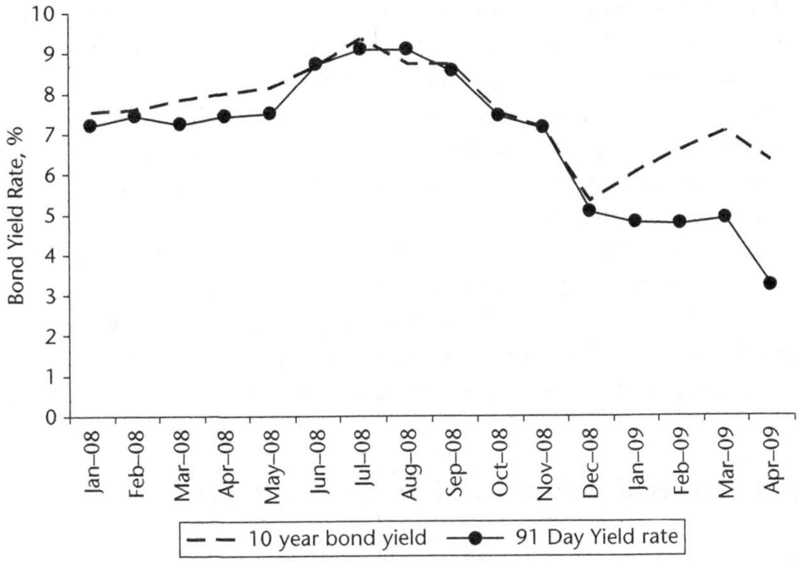

Figure 8.9 Trends in short-term and long-term interest rates
Source: Reserve Bank of India 2009a.

8.5 The Indian economy after the crisis

The Indian economy recovered fairly quickly from the downturn that saw GDP growth slump to 5.8 percent in both the third quarter of FY2008–09 (October to December 2009) and the fourth quarter of FY2008–09 (January to March 2009). The equity markets were the first to recover. Given the presence of unutilized liquidity in the global market, and India being one of the few countries with positive growth, FIIs started flowing back to India in April 2009. During FY2009–10, Indian equity markets received net FII inflows of more than US$32.2 billion. Consequently, equity markets gained their lost value. However, owing to prevailing uncertainties, the primary market has still not shown any major sign of recovery. The revival in equity markets was followed by a revival in external demand. After a steep decline, merchandise exports started increasing towards the end of 2009 (Figure 8.6). It was also accompanied by a reversal in the trend of services exports. In line with these changes, the GDP growth rejuvenated in the first quarter of FY2009–10 when it grew by 6.3 percent against 5.8 percent in the previous quarter. The upward momentum was sustained in the following quarters as the GDP growth continue to improve with each quarter (Figure 8.8). This was in line with global trends and clearly a result of the expansionary fiscal and monetary policy measures taken in the wake of the global recession.

However, the Indian economy once again started slowing down from mid FY2010–11 onward. This slide in growth could primarily be attributed to the partial withdrawal of fiscal stimulus in FY2010–11 and the policy of monetary tightening which RBI has been perusing since January 2010. The moderation in GDP growth is expected to continue even in FY2011–12. The fear of a further slowdown was confirmed during the first quarter of FY2011–12, when the Indian economy grew by just 7.7 percent, its weakest performance in the last six quarters. According to official estimates, the Indian economy is expected to grow by 8.2 percent in the current financial year, which is lower than the 8.6 percent growth registered in the previous year. Nonetheless, with continued high inflation and fast deteriorating global economic environment, attaining even 8 percent growth in 2011–12 would be very challenging.

8.6 Potential policy measures to reignite growth

The developments during last few years have shown that the Indian economy has entered a different phase. With a sustained high rate of economic growth, the purchasing power of a certain section of society has increased, which has virtually redefined the dynamics of inflation in India. In these changed circumstances, RBI has continuously struggled to strike a balance between growth and inflation. In the wake of the global crisis, inflation subsided in FY2008–09 giving RBI a chance to peruse an expansionary monetary policy. However, the ghost of inflation returned as soon as the crisis bottomed out and forced RBI to raise the interest rate from the very beginning of 2010. Since then, RBI has raised policy rates 11 times. However, these upward revisions have failed to provide any significant relief as headline inflation continues to be more than 9 percent. Therefore, monetary policy has little to offer in the current phase of economic slowdown. For the same reason, there is little room for fiscal policy action as the fiscal deficit is already very high. In fact, after running a high fiscal deficit in FY2008–09 and FY2009–10, the government of India started to contain its spending in 2010–11 and brought down the gross fiscal deficit by two percentage points. Nonetheless, it is still much higher than the limit imposed by the Fiscal Responsibility and Budget Management (FRBM) Act 2003 and needs to be reduced further. Any increase in fiscal deficit will imply an increase in public debt which has already increased to Rs.5,112,250 Crore in FY2010–11.[13]

[13] Here it should be noted that due to the fiscal consolidation in 2010–11 and GDP growth, the debt GDP ratio has declined to less than 65 percent in 2010–11 from more than 72 percent in 2008–09.

With very limited fiscal maneuverability and the monetary policy constrained by the tradeoff between holding down interest rates and preventing inflationary tendencies, the focus of policy measures must be to further raise India's potential output growth rate (Figure 8.10). Various agencies have set the target growth rate between 8.5–9 percent. Raising the potential growth rate requires another round of structural reforms that will improve the investment climate, especially for small and medium enterprises (SMEs) that have suffered the most with the collapse of external demand and employ the majority of the work force. SMEs currently suffer from having to face a plethora of official procedures and licensing and regulatory requirements that raise their transaction costs significantly, making them uncompetitive in global markets and unable to withstand import competition in domestic markets. The government will do well to review all the policies that have an impact on "doing business" in India with the clear objective of improving the investment climate. The evidence for this will be best reflected in an improvement in India's rankings in the World Bank surveys in the coming year.

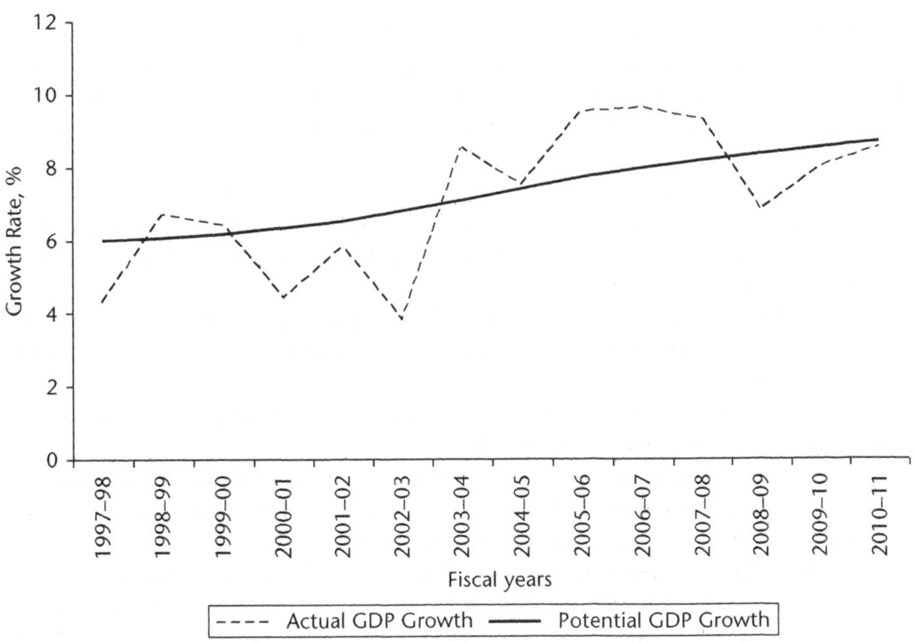

Figure 8.10 Potential GDP growth and output gap

Source: Authors' own calculation.

Note: HP filter technique has been used to calculate the potential GDP growth and output gap.

Other areas for policy attention that will help in removing some of the remaining structural bottlenecks on raising the potential GDP growth rate are the removal of entry barriers for corporate investment in education and vocational training, improving the delivery of public goods and services, and expanding physical infrastructure capacities, including a major effort at improving connectivity in the rural regions. These measures will constitute the second generation of structural reforms and will enable the Indian economy to climb out of the downward phase of the growth cycle and then to extend the upward phase for a longer period than was achieved in the last cycle. The two other areas that require attention and have been often discussed are an urgent improvement in the physical infrastructure and the delivery of public services, specifically urban utilities and law and order. Attention on these reforms will be far more effective and have a more permanent positive impact on raising India's potential rate of growth, which is essential if India is to achieve its goals of poverty reduction and rapid and sustainable growth to improve the overall welfare level of its people.

References

Bhalla, S. (2008). Inflation Control Chokes Growth. *Business Standard.* October 17.

Central Statistical Organization (CSO) (2011). *National Account Statistics.* New Delhi: CSO.

Kumar, R., M. Joseph, D. Allex, P. Vashisht, and D. Banerjee (2009). The Outlook of Indian Economy 2008–09 and 2009–10. ICRIER Working Paper 235. New Delhi: ICRIER.

Ministry of Commerce, Government of India (2008–2011). Press Release on India's Foreign Trade January 2008–October 2011. New Delhi. Ministry of Commerce. Available: http://commerce.nic.in/PressRelease/pressrelease_year.asp?year1=2011 (accessed October 4, 2011).

Ministry of Finance, Government of India (2009). Union Budget 2009–10. New Delhi.

Reserve Bank of India (2008). Report on Currency and Finance 2006–08. Mumbai: Reserve Bank of India.

——(2009a). Reserve Bank of India- Bulletin. Available: http://rbi.org.in/scripts/BS_ViewBulletin.aspx (accessed June 30, 2009).

——(2009b). Handbook of Statistics on Indian Economy. Mumbai: Reserve Bank of India. Available: http://rbi.org.in/scripts/AnnualPublications.aspx?head=Handbook%20of%20Statistics%20on%20Indian%20Economy (accessed June 2009).

—— (RBI) (2009c). Balance of Payment. Available: http://rbi.org.in/scripts/SDDS_ViewDetails.aspx?Id=5&IndexTitle=Balance%20of%20Payment (accessed June 30, 2009).

——(2009d). Macroeconomic and Monetary Development Third Quarter Review 2008–09. New Delhi: Reserve Bank of India.

——(2011a). Handbook of Statistics on Indian Economy. Mumbai: Reserve Bank of India. Available: http://www.rbi.org.in/scripts/AnnualPublications.aspx?head=-Handbook%20of%20Statistics%20on%20Indian%20Economy (accessed October 4, 2011).

——(2011b). Reserve Bank of India- Bulletin. Available: http://www.rbi.org.in/scripts/BS_ViewBulletin.aspx (accessed October 4, 2011).

9

The Republic of Korea's Economy in the Swirl of Global Crisis

Dongchul Cho

9.1 Introduction

The Republic of Korea (hereafter Korea) was one of the countries that was most severely hit by the global financial and economic crisis that originated from the United States (US). These recent events surprised many commentators who believed that the adverse impacts from the developed countries on Asia would be contained within a manageable range. Asian economies experienced painful restructuring processes during the recovery from the crisis that broke out in the late 1990s, and their economic structures were believed to have become sounder as a result. For example, the large foreign currency reserves in the region have often been referred to as comfortable safeguards against external shocks. As for the housing price bubble, which directly caused the current global crisis, the problem was far milder in Asia including Korea than in the US and Europe.

Having observed the current collapse of Asian economies some experts, for example Takatoshi Kato (2009), have declared that myths about Asian economies like "business cycle decoupling" have been dismantled. For the Korean economy in particular, the worse than expected performance of the fourth quarter of 2008 raised many issues. Should this collapse of economic activities be interpreted as a signal of another crisis like the one that hit Korea 10 years ago? Has Korea learned any lessons from the previous financial crisis? If so, why was Korea hit so severely by this global shock? How different are the policy responses this time from the previous crisis? What are the short-term prospects for the Korean economy? Will it be affected by the global rebalancing process?

It is impossible to rigorously answer all of these questions in a single chapter. However, this chapter will attempt to sketch the arguments related to these important issues with some circumstantial evidence. Following this introduction, Section 9.2 briefly explains the current situation of the Korean economy, focusing on what happened in the fourth quarter of 2008. Section 9.2 also discusses several factors that can help explain why Korea was hit so severely. Next, Section 9.3 compares the current recession with the currency crisis period from various perspectives, such as the depth of the recession, the structural aspects of the economy, and macroeconomic policy reactions. Section 9.4 discusses the prospects for the Korean economy, including the issue regarding exports vs. domestic demand and domestic savings rate. Section 9.5 summarizes the chapter with some comments.

9.2 Current recession of Korea's economy

9.2.1 *Collapse of economic activities in the fourth quarter of 2008*

Despite the global slowdown caused by the US subprime mortgage crisis, the Korean economy maintained a reasonable pace of growth until the third quarter of 2008. Domestic demand gradually slowed in the third quarter, mainly due to soaring oil prices and the resulting loss of purchasing power, but exports had maintained a solid expansion rate.

However, the Korean economy plunged into a severe recession in the fourth quarter, following panic in the global financial market. From the second half of September 2008, stock prices collapsed and the won/dollar exchange rate soared (expressing a sharp currency depreciation of the won). Credit markets became significantly crunched and the resulting impacts on domestic demand began to appear in October. Equipment investment collapsed and private consumption declined by a substantial margin.

On top of the contraction in domestic demand, exports also began to collapse in October 2008. Though export demand was expected to contract due to the global crisis, its rate of contraction during the fourth quarter was truly shocking. The year-on-year (month-to-month) growth rate of exports collapsed from 27.6 percent (–3.1 percent) in September to 7.8 percent (–2.6 percent) in October and further to –19.5 percent (–22.2 percent) in November (Figure 9.1). This collapse in export revenue raised concerns about Korea's capability to earn hard currencies and aggravated already unstable investor sentiment in the currency market. As a result, in the fourth quarter the Korean economy recorded a growth rate that was much worse than expected.

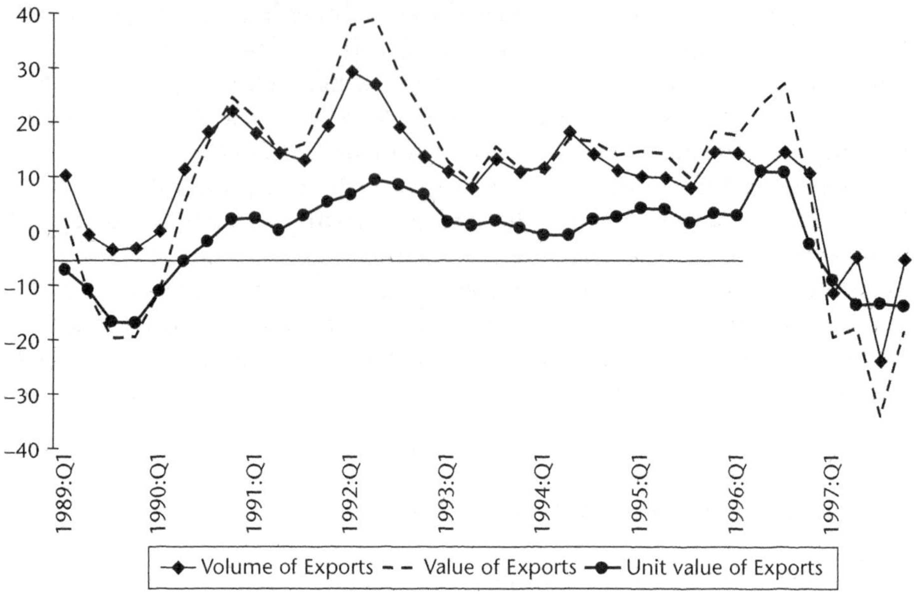

Figure 9.1 Export growth rate (year-on-year % change)
Sources: Korea Customs Service, Ministry of Knowledge Economy, Bank of Republic of Korea.

Upon the announcement of the fourth quarter growth rate (–5.6 percent quarter-to-quarter), the International Monetary Fund (IMF) substantially downgraded the forecast for Korea's 2009 growth rate from 2.0 percent in November 2008 to –4.0 percent in January 2009, while downgrading other countries' growth rates more mildly. The drastic downgrade of Korea's growth forecast showed the surprise with which the Korean fourth quarter growth rate was received.

9.2.2 *Factors for the collapse in the fourth quarter of 2008*

9.2.2.1 KOREA'S HIGH DEPENDENCE ON TRADE SECTORS

The most plausible explanation for the Korean economic collapse in the fourth quarter of 2008 is the economy's heavy reliance on exports, or more precisely, trade sectors. A leading example for this line of explanation is the IMF's position note written by Sommer (2009). Using the portion of (high-tech) manufacturing industries in a country's gross domestic product (GDP) as a proxy variable for the country's dependence on exports, he established a strong negative relationship between this variable and the fourth quarter growth rate, and provided a straightforward but convincing interpretation.

The result holds true if the whole manufacturing sector is used instead of a portion of high-tech manufacturing industries.

Clearly, Korea, along with other Asian countries, was heavily reliant on the manufacturing sector and was most severely hit in the fourth quarter of 2008. Nevertheless, the question still remains: could it be expected, *ex ante*, that Korea's GDP would contract three times as much as the crisis-originating countries, considering its heavy dependence on exports? Formal analyses indicate that there are no clear reasons to expect developing countries to respond more than proportionally with respect to the crisis of developed countries through trade channels alone. An estimate by the IMF (2001:80) shows that "a 1.0 percent change in real GDP growth in the G-7 countries is associated with a 0.4 percent change in growth in developing countries." As for Korea, simulation exercises conducted by the Korea Development Institute (KDI) using a macro-econometric model produced the result that Korea's GDP shrunk by approximately 0.8 percent when world GDP declined by 1.0 percent (KDI 2008). If Korea is twice as exposed to tradable manufacturing sectors as the average developing country, then this result appears to be consistent with the conclusions of the IMF report. In fact, the regression coefficient is close to one for the data set indicating that the growth response to a trade shock doubles when the share of manufacturing sectors doubles. Nonetheless, past experiences do not seem to systematically explain the more than proportional response of the Korean economy to the global crisis.

It also does not yield the impression that Korea should respond more than proportionally to the US recession. The recession in 2001 was triggered by the information technology (IT) bubble burst in the US, while the housing price bubble burst in the US triggered the current recession. The recession in 2001 was also accompanied by a contraction of global trade that severely affected Korea's export sector. More specifically, the 2001 recession saw a deep contraction in demand for IT products, a major export item for Korea as well as other Asian countries. Nevertheless, in 2001, Korea managed to maintain a reasonable 4.0 percent growth rate in spite of the sharp contraction in exports, which was far higher than those of advanced countries.

9.2.2.2 ADDITIONAL FACTOR #1: THE COLLAPSE OF THE CHINESE ECONOMY

Then why was Korea hit so severely this time? The factor of the People's Republic of China (PRC) is by far the largest trading partner of Korea and most Asian economies. While the PRC's growth was not greatly affected by the global recession in 2001, it collapsed with the current crisis along with its trade, and the adverse effects spread to neighboring Asian economies, including Korea.

A casual explanation for the sharp contraction of the Chinese economy in the fourth quarter of 2008 is that the recession in the US triggered the collapse of the PRC's export sector, which in turn caused the collapse of the PRC's growth as well as imports. This explanation, however, can hardly answer the same question—why not in 2001? It is not a general rule for Asian countries to respond more than proportionally to a US recession, even though their portions of GDP from manufacturing sectors are relatively large.

If the sharp decline of the PRC's growth rate in the fourth quarter of 2008 was not entirely induced by the recession in advanced countries, there must be an autonomous factor for it. The trend of the PRC's growth rate suggests a possible hypothesis. While there was no symptom of overheating in the PRC before the 2001 global recession period, it appears that the Chinese economy had overheated before the current global recession, particularly in 2006 and 2007 when the growth rates were over 10 percent. It may then be conjectured that, having accumulated internal fragility due to the overheating, the Chinese economy hysterically responded to the global shock this time, while it did not in 2001. In fact, with respect to basically the same sort of trade shock from the US in 2001, the PRC's trade did not contract as rapidly as that of the US. However, it did contract even more rapidly this time, suggesting a correction of the PRC's domestic economy from an overheated state (Figure 9.2). As

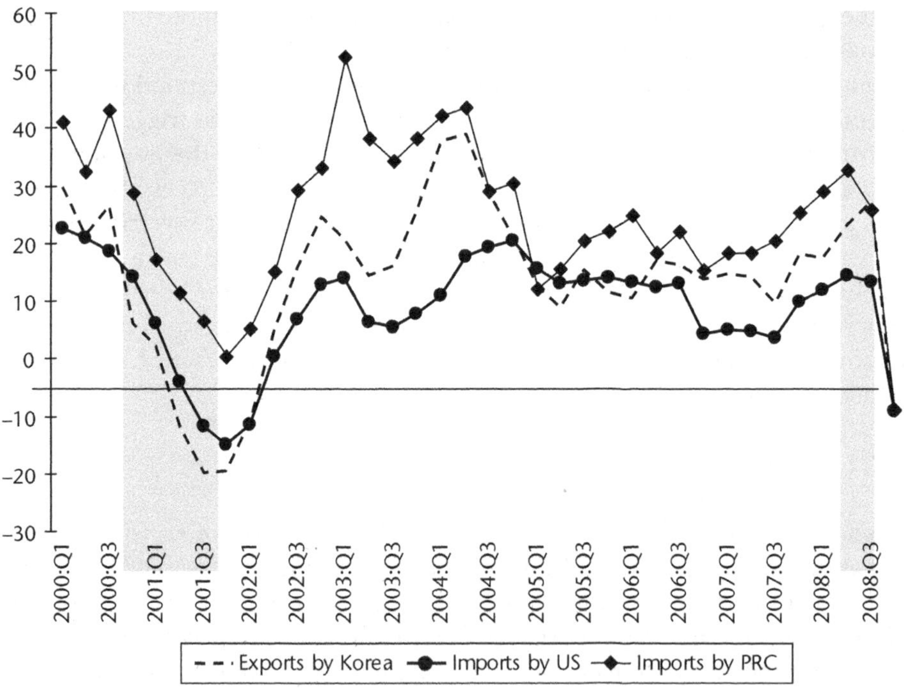

Figure 9.2 Growth of exports by Korea and imports by the US and the People's Republic of China (year-on-year % change)

Sources: Korea Customs Service (Republic of Korea), Foreign Trade Statistics (US), National Bureau of Statistics of China (People's Republic of China).

a reference, the export volume of the US contracted by 5.4 percent in 2001, but the PRC's export volume in the same year expanded by 9.6 percent.

Another piece of evidence for this hypothesis is the expansion of the PRC's trade surplus in the fourth quarter 2008. While the PRC's exports collapsed, its imports declined even more rapidly, boosting its trade surplus to its largest size ever during the fourth quarter. Apart from a terms-of-trade gain, the widening of a trade surplus is usually interpreted as a sign that domestic demand sectors have contracted more rapidly than export sectors. Thus, the increase in the PRC's trade surplus may have been surprising to many economists since the PRC, as an important counterpart to the US in terms of the global imbalance, was expected to experience a reduction in its trade surplus.

If there were an autonomous factor for the sharp decline of the PRCfs growth rate and imports, it would help to explain the more than proportional contraction of the growth rates in Asian economies, including Korea. A simple reduced-form regression of Korea's export growth rate (year-on-year) shows that, even after controlling for US imports, the PRC's imports maintain independent explanatory power, while those of the Eurozone and Japan do not:

$$\underset{}{EX_{Korea}} = \underset{(7.66)}{0.98\, IM_{US}} \underset{(-1.94)}{-0.20\, IM_{Euro}} \underset{(-0.52)}{-0.05\, IM_{Japan}} \underset{(7.49)}{+0.41\, IM_{PRC}} + residual$$

In the above equation, EX_i and IM_i are exports and imports of economy I (year-on-year growth rate), and numbers in parentheses are t-ratios. This result seems to suggest that at least the PRC's imports are not entirely induced by the economic fluctuations of the US. Also, the coefficient estimate for the PRC's import growth rate appears to be sizeable in determining Korea's exports, in that it is almost half of that for the US. All in all, the surprisingly drastic collapse of Korea's growth and exports in the fourth quarter of 2008 seem to be attributable not only to the import contraction of the US, but also to that of the PRC.

9.2.2.3 ADDITIONAL FACTOR #2: MASSIVE CAPITAL WITHDRAWAL FROM KOREA

While the PRC factor may help to explain the hysterical response of Asia's trade to the US crisis, it does not seem to be sufficient in explaining why Korea in particular was hit so hard. For this question to be answered, Korea-specific factors accounting for the collapse in the fourth quarter of 2008 need to be identified, in addition to the aforementioned PRC factor.

The abrupt capital withdrawal through the financial channel appears to be a plausible candidate for a Korea-specific factor. An enormous amount of foreign capital flowed out from Korea in the fourth quarter of 2008, depreciating the Korean won by more than 30 percent vis-à-vis the US dollar. This magnitude of depreciation was the largest among the Asian currencies.

The main reason for this drastic withdrawal of financial capital seems to be the Korean economy's heavy reliance on short-term foreign debt. While Korea holds the sixth largest official foreign reserves in the world, the size of short-term foreign debt is so large that its ratio to foreign reserves is greater than those of other emerging economies (Figure 9.3).

With this relatively fragile foreign liquidity front, the panic of the global financial market was directly transmitted to the Korean market through the abrupt reversal of foreign capital flow since October 2008. In fact, the size of net financial capital withdrawn from Korea during October 2008 was US$25.5 billion (more than 3 percent of annual GDP) which was far larger than the US $6.4 billion withdrawn in December 1997, the worst month during the Asian crisis. This flight of capital caused Korea's asset prices to collapse and credit to become severely crunched. Apart from the collapse of exports, disturbances in the financial market provided an additional shock to the Korean economy, particularly with respect to domestic demand such as private consumption and equipment investment.

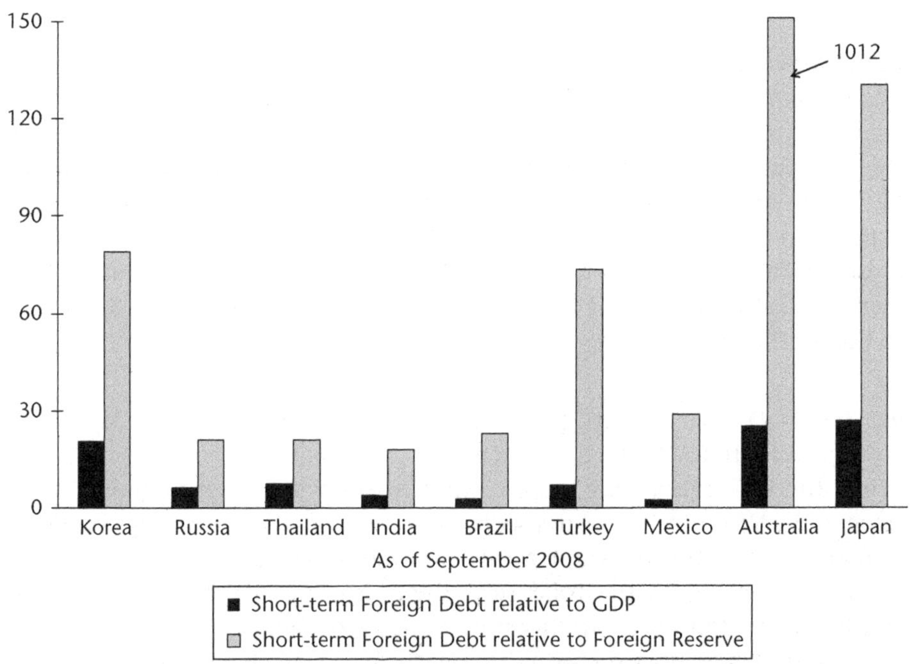

Figure 9.3 Short-term foreign debt relative to GDP or foreign reserve (%)
Sources: Joint External Debt Hub (BIS, IMF, OECD, World Bank) and Global Insight.

9.3 Comparison with the currency crisis period

9.3.1 *Major macroeconomic indicators: similarities and differences*

On surface, the current recession in Korea appears to be similar to the currency crisis period: in both periods, the growth rate and the currency value collapsed simultaneously. The quarter-to-quarter growth rate in the fourth quarter of 2008, –5.6 percent, was the second worst in the economic history of Korea since 1970, which was approximately two-thirds of the worst record, –7.8 percent, in the first quarter of 1998. The degree of recent currency depreciation was also approximately two-thirds of that during the currency crisis period.

Though the fluctuations of GDP and currency value appear to be similar, the current recession is qualitatively different from the currency crisis period in many respects. Above all, the responses of domestic demand and exports are totally different. During the currency crisis period, domestic demand drove the collapse of GDP, while export demand continued to expand. This time, however, it was export demand that drove the economic recession, while the contraction in domestic demand was relatively mild. This sharp contrast in the response of the economy clearly reflects the difference in the source of shocks. While the currency crisis was triggered by the implosion of the internal financial market, the current recession was mainly triggered by the explosion of the external financial market.

The difference in the responses of demand components has many important implications. Among them, probably the most important is its implication regarding employment. Previous research, for example Shin and Kim (2008), showed that most short-term employment fluctuation is determined by domestic demand, particularly private consumption, while the effect of export fluctuation is minimal or almost non-existent. This seems to be the main reason that the loss of employment remains within a manageable range in the current recession, while it explosively expanded during the currency crisis period.

For example, right after the currency crisis broke out, approximately 870,000 jobs (more than 4 percent of the total number of workers) were lost during the month of January 1998. The employment situation continued to be worsened until August 1998 when approximately 1.6 million jobs (7.4 percent of the total) were lost compared to the same month of the previous year. During the current recession, however, the loss of jobs has been relatively mild.

9.3.2 *Structural positions of the economy when the shock occurred*

Both the currency crisis and the current recession were triggered by external shocks, such as the Thai baht crisis in 1997 and the Lehman Brothers bankruptcy in 2008. However, the severity of the two external shocks is not comparable: the latter was definitely more severe than the former. Yet, the Korean financial market saw a meltdown in 1997 but not in 2008.

The improvement of financial market stability can be attributed to restructuring efforts since the currency crisis. First, the financial positions of the corporate sector were substantially improved in comparison with those during the currency crisis period. The average debt-to-equity ratio of the manufacturing sector was reduced from 424.6 percent in 1997 to 106.5 percent in 2008 and the profitability of the corporate sector was also greatly improved.

Second, the soundness of financial institutions was also strengthened. The average capital adequacy ratio (BIS ratio) of the banking sector was greatly improved, providing financial buffers to the system. Although the BIS ratio has been reduced since the global crisis, no Korean banks have yet received public money. There has been much progress in terms of profitability of the banking sector as well.

Third, the foreign reserve position has also improved since the currency crisis period. Although short-term foreign debts had increased rapidly since 2005 and triggered some disturbances in the foreign exchange market in the wake of the global financial panic, the amount of official foreign reserves has substantially increased compared to that in the currency crisis period in both absolute and relative terms (Figure 9.4).

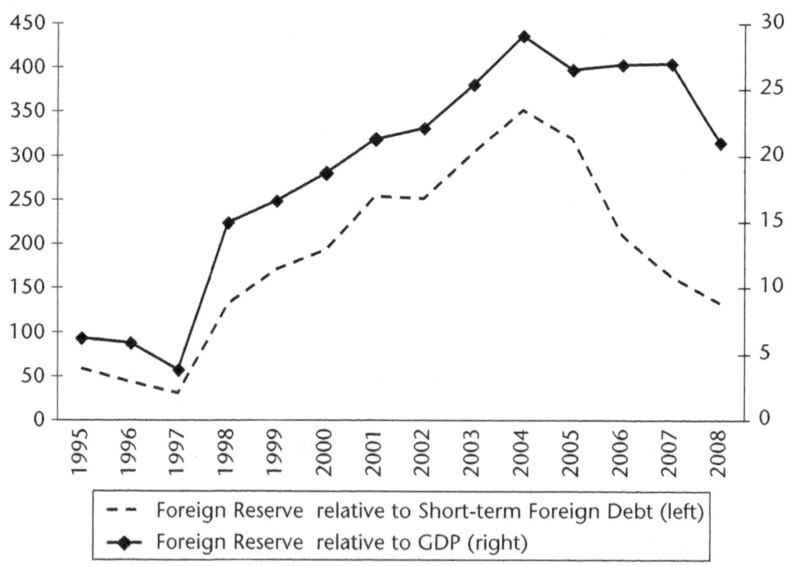

Figure 9.4 Foreign reserves relative to GDP and short-term debt (%)
Sources: Bank of Korea (Republic of Korea) and International Monetary Fund.

Fourth, there has been qualitative progress, though it is not readily measured quantitatively. For example, financial market supervision has been strengthened in many respects, and accounting practices and public announcement systems have become more transparent.

Of course, there are some aspects that have deteriorated. The size of household debt, which was extremely low during the currency crisis period, has increased to a level that concerns investors in the Korean market. The size of government debt has also increased, though it is still in far better shape than that of many advanced countries. Nevertheless, there is no doubt that the overall structure of Korea's financial market has become sounder than it was 10 years ago, which seems to have greatly helped maintain financial market stability and domestic demand.

9.3.3 *Macro-policy reactions*

The policy reactions to cope with the current crisis have also been very different. Above all, the use of exchange rate policy has completely changed since 1997. In 1997, the Korean government continued futile attempts to defend the currency value through direct market interventions until its foreign reserves became nearly depleted. When the Korean government asked the IMF for a bailout package, its remaining foreign reserves were below US$10 billion. This time, however, the government did not intervene, even when the exchange rate became extremely volatile right after the Lehman Brothers bankruptcy filing. Instead of clinging to the exchange rate, the Korean government tried to secure overall foreign currency liquidity in the market by negotiating currency swaps with the US, Japan, and the PRC. This policy stance greatly contributed to saving official foreign reserves as well as helping (or forcing) the private sector to quickly adjust itself to a new currency value and generate a current account surplus. In other words, the Korean government honored the floating exchange rate regime, and facilitated the necessary macroeconomic adjustments.

By letting the exchange rate float, the Korean government could maintain a flexible monetary policy this time, which it actually exercised. In response to the financial market panic, the Bank of Korea swiftly lowered the policy interest rate target from 5 percent to 2 percent within the four months from October 2008 to January 2009. This monetary policy reaction starkly contrasted with that of the currency crisis period when the Korean government (and the IMF) abruptly raised the interest rate target to around 30 percent. This contrast in the monetary policy reactions was mainly due to the difference in foreign currency liquidity situations during the crises. In December 1997, faced with the near-depletion of foreign reserves, minimizing the nation's default probability became the foremost policy objective, and all policy measures were aligned accordingly. Monetary policy was also mobilized for this purpose and the interest rate rose drastically. While previous research showed that the high interest rate policy contributed to the early recovery of foreign reserves and exchange rate stabilization, it was clear that this policy significantly deepened the economic recession and worsened the employment situation. This time, however, backed by more than US$200 billion in foreign currency reserves, monetary policy was used for economic stabilization.

Fiscal policy reactions were not as contrasting as monetary policy reactions. In both periods, expansionary fiscal stances were assumed, *ex post*. The size of the budget deficit, approximately 3 percent of GDP, is also similar. However, the processes leading to these similar reactions were different. In the crisis of the late 1990s, the IMF initially recommended that the Korean government maintain a balanced budget, but as the economic situation worsened in 1998 it revised its recommendation toward a budget deficit: 0.8 percent of GDP in the fifth agreement on February 7, 1.75 percent of GDP in the sixth agreement on May 2, 4.0 percent of GDP in the seventh agreement on July 24, and finally 5.0 percent of GDP in the eighth agreement on October 27. In contrast, the Korean government announced a fiscal expansion as soon as the current global crisis began. After the global financial panic was triggered, the Korean government announced a supplementary budget of W11.2 trillion (1.1 percent of GDP) in November 2008, which has already been implemented. In addition, the government submitted another supplementary budget plan of W28.9 trillion (2.8 percent of GDP) to the National Assembly in March 2009, which should be implemented soon. This difference in policy reaction flexibility may have a meaningful implication on the time lag problem that is typically associated with fiscal policy.

9.4 Prospects for the Korean economy

9.4.1 *Short-term prospects for growth rebalancing*

9.4.1.1 FACTORS FOR THE COLLAPSE IN THE FOURTH QUARTER OF 2008, REVISITED

If export reliance was the main cause of the collapse of Asia as well as Korea in the fourth quarter of 2008, there should not be any expectations for recovery in Korea, or more broadly in Asia, until the US and Europe begin to recover. In contrast, if the additional factors discussed earlier prove to be important contributors to the collapse of the Korean economy, it is worthwhile thinking about the possible impacts of those factors.

First, the severe capital withdrawal pressures are likely to be eased within a relatively short time period, though this easing will rely heavily on the capricious environment of the global financial market. Such a drastic capital withdrawal as seen in October 2008 does not seem to be sustainable: if Korea's short-term foreign debt continues to be withdrawn by as much as US$23 billion a month, it will almost disappear by the end of the first half of this year (the total short-term foreign debt was approximately US$150 billion at the end of last year). In fact, the pressures have already eased from US$23 billion in October 2008 to US$12 billion in November and to US$6 billion in December. In terms of the abrupt capital outflow being an additional factor dragging down Korea's domestic demand, one may hope for a partial normalization process of domestic demand even before global trade begins to recover.

Second, if the current global crisis eventually leads to the unwinding of long-accumulated global imbalances, its corollary should be a relatively small correction of final demand in Asia compared to that in the US. Therefore, it seems natural to expect Asian domestic demand to recover earlier than that of the US. To the extent that Asian intra-regional trade does not entirely rely on the final demand of the US, or as far as Asia's trade is at least partially related to its own final demand, a small correction of Asia's demand is likely to result in a relatively small correction in Asia's trade, though Asia as a whole should reduce the size of its trade surplus.

The major premise of this scenario is the boosting of domestic demand in the PRC, a key component in the global rebalancing process, as well as a critical driver for the revitalization of Asia's intra-regional trade. In this sense, what happened during the fourth quarter of 2008 was a correction of global overheating including the PRC, and the global rebalancing scenario has not yet begun, at least not on the part of the PRC. However, as the PRC begins to rebalance its overheated economy, prospects appear more positive, at least in relative terms, for Asia and Korea. Of course, the full-blown recovery of Korea will be in line with the global recovery in both the financial and real sectors.

9.4.1.2 POLICY REACTIONS, REVISITED

Unlike during the currency crisis period, macroeconomic policies immediately responded to the shock this time. The substantial depreciation of the won in the swirl of the global financial crisis will help the profitability of Korean exporters and relieve deflation pressures from abroad. The policy interest rate target has already been lowered to an unprecedented level of 2 percent, which will relieve the burdens of debt-ridden households and firms as well as the downward pressure on asset prices. Also, the government's proposal for a supplementary budget, which should be approved in the near future, will help to alleviate the declining trend of domestic demand. In short, all of the macroeconomic policy tools are consistently aligned for one single goal—boosting the economy.

9.4.1.3 RECENT ECONOMIC INDICATORS

In 2009, there have been some signs that investor sentiment has improved. For example, stock prices are rising and the currency value is appreciating. Both business and consumer sentiment indexes have turned around since February 2009. More solid signals can be confirmed from the monthly indicators of production. Service production, which takes up 55 percent of GDP and has close ties to domestic demand, began to increase month-on-month in December 2008, as the capital outflow pressures gradually eased. Industrial production, which takes up 30 percent of GDP and closely relates to export demand, also began to increase month-on-month in January 2009, as the collapsing trend of the PRC's imports stabilized. As for industrial sectors, it is also encouraging that inventory has been declining very rapidly despite the collapse in export demand. This implies that industrial production has adjusted promptly to the abrupt contraction in demand, and can rebound early if demand conditions do not deteriorate further in the future.

9.4.2 *Domestic demand vs. exports, or services vs. manufacturing*

It is often said that Asia should increase its domestic demand because its growth is too dependent on exports. This assertion may make sense for countries like the PRC that maintain a huge current account surplus. Faced with the presumably permanent decrease in demand from the US, it is necessary for Asia to seek other demand sources to make up for this gap. In this sense, the recovery of domestic demand in the PRC will play a pivotal role for the recovery of the whole Asia.

However, the same argument does not seem to be warranted for Korea, in which the current account fluctuates around a balanced level. Any permanent and sizeable increase in domestic demand, unless accompanied by a parallel increase in exports, would imply a current account deficit that would likely disturb the foreign exchange market as it recently did. The aggregate savings rate in Korea has also been in a declining trend since the currency crisis, as bank credits became readily accessible to consumers. In particular, the net savings rate of Korean households has declined rapidly from 20 percent before the currency crisis to 3 percent in 2007. In fact, the current savings rate of the Korean household is so low that many economists are worried about its negative implications on the financial market stability and future consumption potential.

A similar argument from a supply-side perspective, however, seems legitimate—Korea needs to boost its service sectors rather than its manufacturing sectors. Though this statement appears to be similar to the earlier demand-side arguments because most services are spent domestically, its implications are totally different. First, it does not have any implications for current account sustainability, while clearly recognizing the fact that the Korean economy relies heavily on manufacturing sectors in relation to exports. Second, typical measures for boosting domestic demand are expansionary macroeconomic policies (in particular, a fiscal expansion), but policy measures for boosting service sectors include microeconomic policies to enhance their productivities. According to the Organisation for Economic Co-operation and Development (OECD) (2004), Korea's productivity growth in the service sector relative to the manufacturing sector was the second lowest (next to Poland) among the OECD countries, which was largely attributed to many regulations that hampered service sector productivity, such as entry and exit barriers, mandatory licensing, and policy discrimination in favor of manufacturing. How to reform these regulations into efficient systems will be a key policy agenda for the government of Korea.

9.5 Concluding remarks

There has been debate about whether Korea, or more broadly Asia, can be "decoupled" from the business cycles of the US. This chapter argues that Korea, as well as Asia in general, is not immune to global crises. At the same time, however, a more than proportional response of GDP to global crises in Korea and Asia does not seem to be the general case either. In this line of reasoning, the extremely hysterical response of Korea during the fourth quarter of 2008 was attributed not only to the crisis in the US, but also to additional idiosyncratic components such as the extraordinary collapse of the PRC's imports and the drastic capital outflow from Korea.

The chapter also identifies the similarities and differences of the current recession in comparison to the currency crisis period. The current recession appears to be similar to the currency crisis period in that the growth rate and currency value collapsed simultaneously. However, the chapter argues that there are more differences than similarities. First, the currency crisis was mainly attributed to the internal fragility of Korea's financial market, but the current recession was mostly caused by external shocks. This difference in the causes of the two recessions was clearly reflected in the different responses of private consumption and exports, and hence employment. In the dimension of macroeconomic policy reactions, monetary policy was far more flexible this time than during the currency crisis period.

From this analysis, two implications can be drawn. First, as far as the economic response of the fourth quarter of 2008 being more hysterical than necessary for the rebalancing of macroeconomic fundamentals in Korea, it is expected that those economic losses can be recovered relatively soon. The most recent economic indicators appear to be encouraging in this context.

Yet, for a more visible recovery of the Korean economy, the recovery of the PRC's domestic demand seems necessary, which is also crucial for the global macroeconomic stability. Ultimately, a full-blown recovery in Korea will be in line with the global recovery.

A second implication is that structural aspects are critical for maintaining economic stability as well as employing flexible macroeconomic policies. While the Korean economy plunged into a historic crisis in 1997, triggered by the relatively small external shock of the Thai baht crisis, the economy is expected to remain relatively robust this time even in the midst of the most serious global crisis since the Great Depression. Behind this positive expectation stand the sound institutional fundamentals and flexible macroeconomic policy reactions of the Korean economy.

References

International Monetary Fund (IMF) (2001). International Linkages: Three Perspectives. In *World Economic Outlook: The Information Technology Revolution*. Washington, DC: IMF.

Kato, T. (2009). Implications for Asia from the Global Financial Crisis and Policy Perspectives. Presented at the Harvard Asia Business Conference, Harvard University, Cambridge, February 14–15.

Korea Development Institute (KDI) (2008). Effects of the Global Recession on the Korean Economy. Internal manuscript. Seoul: KDI.

Organization for Economic Cooperation and Development (OECD) (2004). *OECD Economic Surveys: Korea*. vol. 2004/10. Paris: OECD.

Shin, S. and H. Kim (2008). An Analysis on the Recent Slowdown of Employment. In *KDI Economic Outlook*. Seoul: KDI.

Sommer, M. (2009). 'Why Has Japan Been So Hard Hit by the Global Recession?' IMF Staff Position Note SPN/09/05. Washington, DC: IMF.

10

Thailand's Growth Rebalancing

Somchai Jitsuchon and Chalongphob Sussangkarn

10.1 Introduction

This chapter starts by reviewing some lessons from Thailand's 1997 crisis. Through macroeconomic mismanagement, by mid-1997 the country basically became insolvent in terms of not having enough useable foreign reserves to back up its foreign currency obligations, and had to abandon the basket peg and float the baht. Recovery was slow and was driven mainly by exports. Lessons learned from the crisis and post-crisis reforms led to a more risk-averse financial system, and this helped to shield the Thai financial system from the direct impacts of the United States (US) subprime crisis. However, the indirect impacts through the trade channel have been very severe.

Even though the Thai economy has showed a sharp recovery since the third quarter of 2009 and throughout most of 2010 (Figure 10.1), the impact of the current crisis is far from over. The weak recovery in the US economy in the past few years and the severity of public debt problems in Europe reflect deep-rooted structural problems of the global economy. Against this long-term gloomy backdrop, Thailand needs to seriously re-think about rebalancing its economy so as to increase its resilience to external shocks. What to do and how to proceed is the main objective of this chapter.

The chapter highlights the fiscal and monetary policy responses that have been carried out. It suggests that these measures are mainly short-term in nature and have not yet addressed the need to rebalance Thailand's growth path toward being sustainable and less dependent on exports in the future. The chapter ends by discussing some key strategies that could help Thailand achieve a more balanced and sustainable growth path.

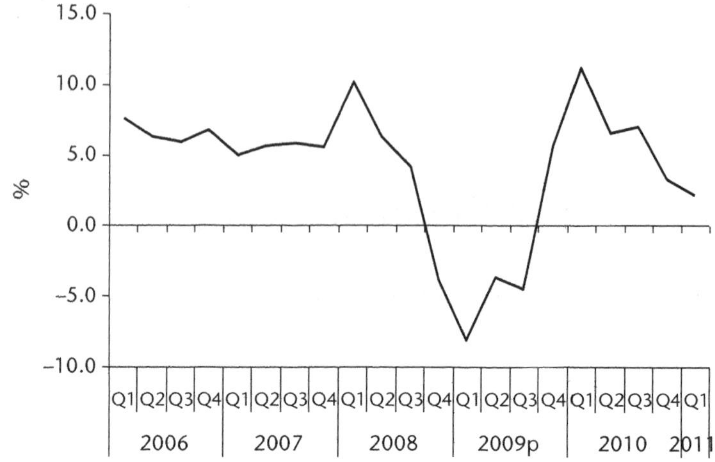

Figure 10.1 Real GDP quarterly growth

Source: National Economic and Social Development Board.

10.2 Lessons from the 1997 economic crisis

There are many important lessons that can be drawn from the 1997 crisis.[1] The most important is probably that while financial globalization can bring benefits from better access to financial resources, it can also bring about a lot of volatilities and risks, and needs extremely prudent management. Given Thailand's past development successes based on real sector globalization (through trade and FDI), the country was regarded as an example of the so-called "East Asian Economic Miracle" (World Bank 1993), and was praised internationally as being a model that other countries should emulate. Given these successes, the authorities may have become overconfident, and embarked on policies of financial liberalization in the hope of turning Bangkok into a major financial center for the region. Unfortunately, there was insufficient understanding of the implications of financial liberalization, and an incorrect policy regime was pursued and this eventually led to the crisis.

The crucial mistake of the authorities was to liberalize capital flows while sticking to a fixed exchange rate system and also trying to pursue an independent monetary policy; Mundell's classic "impossible trinity" (Mundell 1963). Thailand had successfully used a fixed exchange rate system since the end of the Second World War, and this had contributed to economic stability and growth for many decades. However, these successes were mostly achieved under an environment of modest financial capital flows. The mistake was to

[1] See Sussangkarn and Vichyanond (2007) for detailed discussions of the crisis and lessons.

stick to this old paradigm in the 1990s when capital flows became very large and very volatile.

Prior to the crisis, the baht was fixed to a basket of currencies with the US dollar having by far the largest weight in the basket. This resulted in a fairly stable baht/US$ rate for many years prior to the crisis. However, Thailand also tried to pursue an independent interest rate policy. This can be seen from the gap between the Thai overnight inter-bank rate and the US overnight federal funds rate. This gap averaged 4 percent between January 1989 and June 1997 (the last month before the float of the baht), and sometimes reached up to 10 percent with liberalized capital flows, this inevitably led to a large amount of capital flows into Thailand.

Most of these capital flows came in the form of external debt, which rose rapidly from US$29 billion in 1990 (34 percent of GDP) to US$108.7 billion in 1996 (59 percent of GDP). Even more dangerous was the fact that much of this debt was short-term debt (with a maturity of less than one year).[2] By the end of 1996, the total short-term foreign debt was about US$47.7 billion, which was larger than the amount of official foreign reserves at the time—roughly US $38.7 billion. Even after taking into account the foreign assets of the banking system, the total foreign assets (official and private) were less than the amount of short-term foreign debt of the country. If these short-term foreign debts were not rolled over, there would not be enough foreign assets in the country to service the debt.

These large capital inflows fueled the economic bubble in Thailand. There was excessive investment in non-trade sectors, particularly real estate. There was also a lot of crony capitalism. Persons sitting on the boards of financial institutions also sat on many of the boards of client companies. Banks were lending to clients without sufficient scrutiny. One bank, that eventually failed, lent almost 60 percent of its total lending to projects initiated by relatives and friends of the owners and managers. Clearly, corporate governance as well as risk management needed to be significantly improved in order to avoid a similar crisis in the future.

The authorities were also viewing the economic situation with the wrong paradigm. As capital flows increased, foreign reserves also increased, as foreign borrowings were converted into local currency to invest in the country. The authorities were viewing this as a sign of strength and were looking at the adequacy of foreign reserves in terms of the number of months of imports that they covered (a current account paradigm). The fact that foreign reserves were also needed to cover foreign debt, particularly short-term debt, (a capital

[2] This is related to the provisioning requirement of the Basel Capital Accord, see Sussangkarn and Vichyanond (2007).

account paradigm) was not well-understood. This was a painful lesson from the crisis. Since the crisis, the country's short-term debt has been carefully monitored to make sure that the country does not return to a situation anything like the one that existed pre-crisis. The ratio of foreign reserves to external short-term debt has increased substantially, to almost 5:1 at the end of 2008, from less than 1:1 just before the crisis (Figure 10.2).

To avoid a similar crisis, economic management needs to be much more prudent. The authorities need to understand and look out for various risks to the economy. Major policy changes (like financial liberalization prior to the crisis) need to be carefully studied to understand the full implications and risks involved. It is also very important to carry out appropriate sequencing of policy changes.

Another important lesson is the need to improve the country's social safety nets so that they are able to respond appropriately to an economic crisis. After the crisis, it was very apparent that the social safety nets available at that time had been very inadequate. Laid-off workers had little protection, and fiscal expenditure to cushion the impacts could not be disbursed quickly enough. Funds borrowed from multilateral organizations, such as the World Bank and the Asian Development Bank, could not be dispersed quickly enough because of many rules and regulations on procurement and disbursement imposed by the lenders. On this issue, Thailand was very grateful that the Japanese government came forward with the so-called Miyazawa Initiative, providing financial assistance in a way that could be disbursed very quickly. Since the crisis, the system of social safety nets has been improved in many areas, most

Figure 10.2 Ratio of foreign reserves to external short-term debt
Source: Bank of Thailand.

notably in the areas of a universal health care scheme and unemployment insurance under the Social Security System.[3]

10.3 Impacts of the US subprime crisis on the Thai economy

In the current subprime crisis, it is fortunate that the Thai financial system was not directly affected in a significant way. One small bank had to be re-capitalized because of exposure to toxic assets. Most other banks avoided exposure to these assets or were exposed only marginally. There were certainly people trying to sell various collateralized debt obligations (CDOs) to financial institutions. That the Thai financial system avoided falling prey to these toxic assets must be related to the lessons that had been learned from the 1997 crisis. From the painful experiences of that crisis, the Thai financial sector is now much more risk-averse than before. Also being a less sophisticated financial system than those in the West, there was little understanding of what these debt instruments were, and because of the risk aversion, financial institutions avoided them.

The stock market was, of course, affected, in line with stock markets around the world. As financial markets in the advanced economies experienced liquidity crunches, there was a massive liquidation of liquid investment assets in the emerging markets and a massive outflow of capital. Fortunately, Thailand had more than sufficient foreign reserves to cover for this capital outflow, and depreciation pressure on the exchange rate could be managed fairly easily. Other countries were not so fortunate, and some countries experienced a severe depreciation of their local currency. This shows that it is no longer sufficient to think about having enough foreign reserves to cover current account and short-term debt; reserves also need to cover other contingent liabilities, such as foreign holdings of stocks and bonds that can be quickly liquidated, converted to foreign currency, and then taken out of the country.

Even though the financial system managed to avoid the direct impacts of the subprime crisis, the country was seriously affected indirectly through the trade channels. This was apparent between the last quarter of 2008 until the third quarter of 2009 when exports volume shrank significantly.

After the 1997 crisis, the external sector (exports of goods and services) has provided the main impetus for growth. This was not surprising. Thailand was an export-led economy prior to the crisis, so that with further stimulus coming from the depreciation of the baht, the export sector was able to easily respond and provided the impetus for growth and the recovery of the economy. Even now, investment has not fully recovered, so the export sector has

[3] See Chandoevwit (2006) and NaRanong and NaRanong (2006) for discussions of the social security system and the health care scheme.

continued to be the main engine for growth, as evident by the strong resumption of exports in 2010–11. Thailand thus once again exhibited its strong dependence on external demand to maintain its overall economic growth. Table 10.1 expresses vividly how the Thai economy depends on exports, as the real quarterly GDP growth rates have moved along closely with export growth.

One of the indicators that points to a shrinking economy is the heavily depressed capacity utilization of manufacturing production. Figure 10.3 shows that capacity utilization rates fell across-the-board since the beginning of 2008 and particularly since around the end of the third quarter of 2008. As expected, the firms or industries more dependent on the export market experienced deeper production declines. Among highly export dependent firms (exports greater than 60 percent of total sales), capacity utilization is now less than 50 percent. Other indicators also move in the same direction; with private investment, private consumption, and employment, among other areas, all falling.

Obviously, the growth prospects of the Thai economy will depend on the prospects for growth and trade at the global and regional level, which have proved to be rather uncertain, and real recovery is likely to take a longer time. As in the case of the 1997 crisis, even when the economy bottoms out, this does not mean that the problems are over. While Thailand bottomed out five to six quarters after the start of the 1997 crisis, it took five years before output returned to its pre-crisis level. The decline of the non-performing loan ratio to less than 10 percent took even longer—about eight years. Thus, in the case of the subprime crisis, a quick return to business as usual appears as if it will be difficult.

Table 10.1 Exports and real GDP growth rates (%)

Years[a]	Export growth (Year-on-year growth in %;Nominal in US$)	Real GDP growth (Year-on-year growth in %)
2006	18.7	5.1
2007	17.0	5.0
2008 H1	23.3	5.8
2008 Q3	26.1	3.1
2008 Q4	-10.7	-4.1
2009 Q1	-20.7	-7.0
2009 Q2	-26.2	-5.2
2009 Q3	-17.7	-2.8
2009 Q4	11.7	5.9
2010 Q1	31.6	12.0
2010 Q2	41.4	9.2
2010 Q3	21.9	6.6
2010 Q4	20.8	3.8
2011 Q1	28.1	3.2
2011 Q2	19.4	2.6

Sources: Bank of Thailand and the National Economic and Social Development Board.
[a] H = Half year; Q = Quarter year

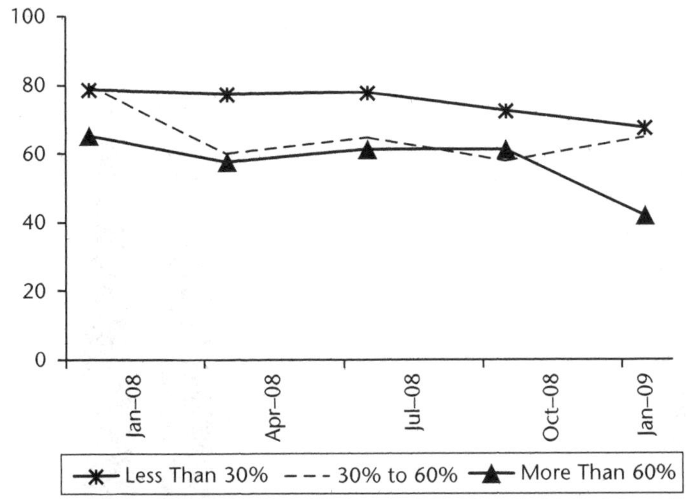

Figure 10.3 Capacity utilization rate of manufacturing. Firms classified by export ratio to total sales (%)
Source: Bank of Thailand.

10.4 Policy responses

Like governments all around the world that are facing the negative consequences from the subprime crisis fallout, the Thai government has responded to the crisis with various expansionary fiscal and monetary policies.

10.4.1 *Fiscal stimulus programs*

There have been six fiscal measures undertaken to stimulate the Thai economy, as shown in Figure 10.4. Increased government spending and tax cuts are the most common measures. A special Mid-year Budget Act amounting to baht1,16.7 billion was passed in early 2009, shortly after the current government took office. The details of this mid-year budget are in Table 10.2. There are two cash transfer programs amounting to around baht28 billion (about US $800 million); baht18.9 billion for living cost subsidies to low-income households and baht9 billion as supplementary income for the elderly).

Both the theory and the experience of some low-income countries indicate that cash transfers are among the most effective ways to both stimulate the economy and mitigate the negative impacts of a crisis on the poor and other vulnerable groups. One caveat is that the transfer must be made to the right target groups, that is, any leakage to ineligible recipients, such as high-income

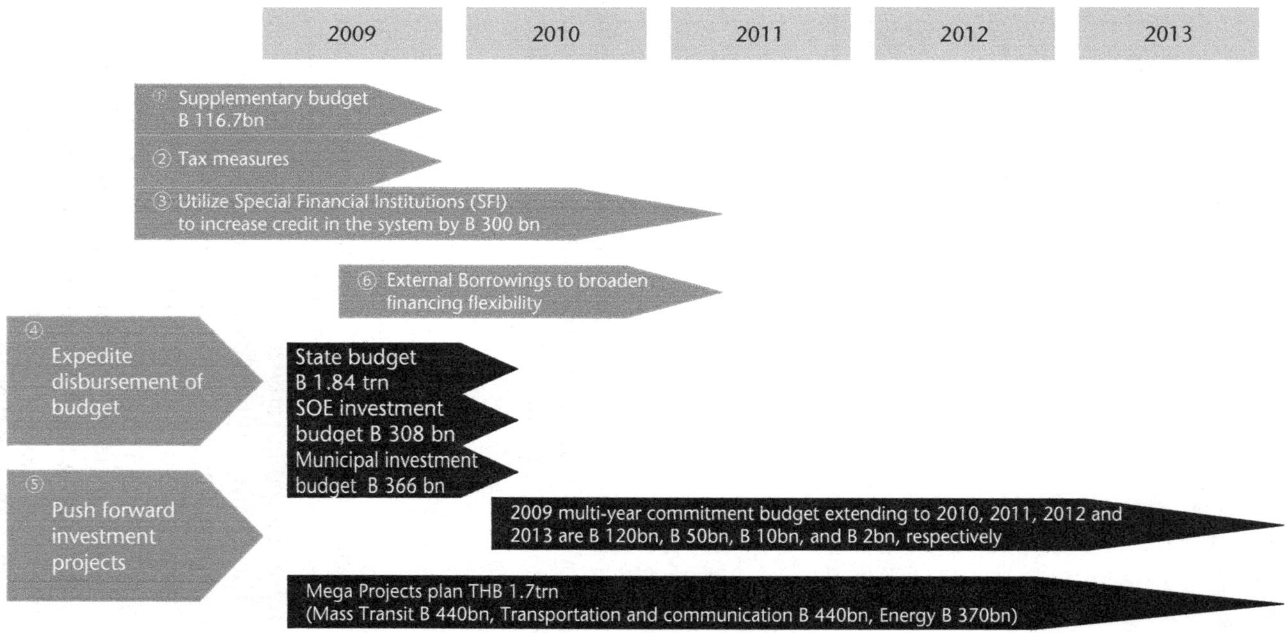

Figure 10.4 Fiscal stimulus programs

Source: Fiscal Policy Office, Ministry of Finance.

Table 10.2 Additional mid-year supplementary budget (millions baht)

Projects/expenditure items	Amount
Total mid-year supplementary budget	116,700.0
Economic recovery and confidence restoration	37,464.7
1.1 Living cost subsidy for low-income earners and government officials	18,970.4
1.2 Extension of five measures to reduce living costs	11,409.2
1.3 Water resources for farmers and agriculture	2,000.0
1.4 Road construction in villages and rural area	1,500.0
1.5 Commercial funds for low income earners	1,000.0
1.6 Tourism promotion	1,000.0
1.7 Small water resource and water management projects	760.0
1.8 Small- and medium-size enterprise promotion	500.0
1.9 Economic confidence restoration and national image promotion	325.0
Revenue creation, Quality of life enhancement and social security	56,004.8
2.1 Free education program for the first 15 years	19,001.0
2.2 Social development fund	15,200.0
2.3 Monthly allowance for senior citizens	9,000.0
2.4 Unemployment reduction and labor potential promotion	6,900.0
2.5 Health care promotion	3,000.0
2.6 Civil servant and police officers housing scheme	1,808.0
2.7 Clinic and health station development	1,095.8
Expenditure under emergency circumstances	4,090.4
Treasury cash repayment	19,139.5

Source: Fiscal Policy Office, Ministry of Finance.

people, must be kept to a minimum. However, the two transfer programs implemented by the current government do not strictly meet this criterion.

The living-cost subsidies were given to private employees included in the Social Security System who earn less than baht15,000 per month. Since all Social Security System workers receive wages at or above the minimum wage, and the minimum wage is about twice the official poverty line, it is likely that the subsidies did not to go the very poor, who account for 10 percent of the total population. Most of the poor are those working in the informal sector or in agriculture, and are not part of the Social Security System. As the subsidy tended to benefit urban low-income workers, albeit not the very poor, the stimulating effect could still be high, as the marginal propensity to spend among the urban low-income group is likely to be highest compared to other urban population sub-groups. The same leakage problem occurs with the monthly allowance for the elderly. Because the allowance is universal (given to rich and poor alike), most of it will benefit non-poor elderly people.

Table 10.3 summarizes the tax measures that have been initiated in response to the current crisis. The total tax loss from these measures is estimated at around baht 40 billion. The effectiveness of these measures in terms of stimulating the economy is expected to be lower than direct government transfers, as most taxpayers are not poor. Also, some sector-specific tax

Table 10.3 Tax measures

Sector	Policy details
Community enterprises	Income tax exemption for community enterprises with an annual income of less than baht1.8 million (previously baht1.2 million) for 58,000 community enterprises nationwide (only for income received between 2009 to 2010)
Debt restructuring	Exemption of income tax and stamp duty arising from debt restructuring that takes place in 2009
Individual taxpayers	Expand minimum taxable income from baht60,000 to baht1 million, which would be subjected to 0.5% tax rate
Investment fund	Exemption of income tax for dividend income and capital gains from sales of SME stock until 2012
Mergers and acquisitions	Exemption of income tax from merger or acquisition of businesses that takes place in 2009
Real estate	Personal income tax allowance of up to baht300,000 for houses or condominiums purchased or transferred in 2009 and tax allowance of up to baht100,000 for mortgage interest payment.
Tourism	Double tax deduction for conference and meeting expenses incurred in Thailand
Venture capital	Income tax exemption for any gains resulting from a transfer of stock from a small- and medium-sized enterprise (SME) to venture capitalists (only applicable for SMEs with assets worth less than baht200 million, or those with less than 200 workers)

Source: Fiscal Policy Office, Ministry of Finance.

incentives, such as those in real estate, are more likely to work only if the general economy is already on the path to recovery.

10.4.2 *Monetary easing*

Again, as in most other countries, monetary policy has also been eased in response to the looming economic crisis. In fact, the monetary authorities (the Bank of Thailand) switched its position quite abruptly from a fear of inflation following the rapid hike in fuel and food prices in early 2008 to a serious concern over an economic downturn in the fourth quarter, when indirect impacts from the subprime crisis began to hit Thailand's exports. The Monetary Policy Committee (MPC) decided to lower the policy interest rate on December 3, 2008 by 100 basis points. By the end of May 2009, there have been three other interest rate cuts, amounting to another 150 basis points (Table 10.4).

Most economists agree that loose monetary policy can only play a secondary role in revitalizing an economy suffering from rapidly shrinking external demand. The main cause of the problem is from vanishing orders from overseas, and lowering the financial cost will not do much to help. Actually, the main problem for most firms now is access to credit rather than the cost of credit. With the downturn, banks became much more stringent about lending. Existing loans may be trimmed or recalled completely and getting a new loan becomes very difficult. Loans from abroad, which were a part of the rapid

Table 10.4 Monetary policy decisions

Decision dates	Announced policy Interest rate (%)	Decision
January 16, 2008	3.25	Hold
February 27, 2008	3.25	Hold
April 9, 2008	3.25	Hold
May 21, 2008	3.25	Hold
July 16, 2008	3.50	Raise 25 bps
August 27, 2008	3.75	Raise 25 bps
October 8, 2008	3.75	Hold
December 3, 2008	2.75	Cut100 bps
January 14, 2009	2.00	Cut 75 bps
February 25, 2009	1.50	Cut 50 bps
April 8, 2009	1.25	Cut 25 bps
May 20, 2009	1.25	Hold

Source: Bank of Thailand.

capital inflows a couple of years ago, have also dried up as liquidity problems hit the financial system in the advanced economies. Thus, getting credit to those that can make productive use of it is probably the key problem at this time. This is not an easy problem to solve, as it is not straightforward to separate those who can make productive use of the credit from those that will quickly be added to the list of non-performing loans for banks. Of course, one area that will really benefit from the low interest rates is the fiscal cost of government spending, as the government will be able to finance its rapidly growing debt relatively inexpensively.

One area of monetary policy which is likely to become an issue of heated debate is exchange rate management. It is natural for an economy like Thailand, where exports are such an important part, that when problems arise for the export sector—such as rapid capital inflows leading to significant appreciation of the currency back in 2006–07 or contraction of export demand as in the current situation—there will be calls from the export sector (which is very vocal) for a weaker exchange rate. This influence is reinforced by the fact that there are, in the region, countries that can be regarded as competitive with Thailand for certain products whose currencies have weakened considerably as a result of the large withdrawal of capital resulting from the subprime crisis, for example Korea, Indonesia, and India. Some of these countries have fundamental problems such as a lack of sufficient reserves to back up the short-term debt as well as the contingent liabilities on reserves discussed earlier. However, whatever the reason for the large depreciation of other countries' exchange rates, the business sector can make a persuasive case that they should also be helped by weakening the local currency.

There is, therefore, a danger of the whole region, which is generally dependent on exports, descending into an episode of competitive depreciation. This would benefit no one. It would also make it much more difficult to make the adjustments needed to rebalance the region's growth path to one that is less dependent on exports, with an increased role for domestic demand in economic growth. For example, public infrastructure investment, which will be a very important component of growth rebalancing for many economies, will become much more costly because it normally has a high import content.

10.4.3 *Limitations*

Most of the policy responses to the crisis are directed toward the short-term need to shore up the economy in the face of economic contraction. Fiscal injections are expected to generate greater domestic consumption, which will ease the pain for domestic producers and consumers. Little attention has been paid to making these fiscal injections sustainable. Even less thought has been given to what a new "rebalanced growth path" for the country might look like and how it could be achieved.

Policymakers seem to hope that the crisis will be short and that fiscal injections can provide a temporary relief before everything returns to normal. This has already proved to be not true, as the global economy continues to be fundamentally weak. And it is unlikely that a full recovery will mean that East Asian exports can play as big a role in East Asian economies as it did before the Asian financial crisis. Thus, some fundamental restructuring of the Thai economy, as well as those of other East Asian countries, will be necessary in order to pursue a new growth path which is less dependent on exports. This will certainly not be easy and cannot be achieved in the short-term.

If recovery from the crisis is long and drawn out, then the sustainability of fiscal injections will become a major issue. Even though the fiscal position of Thailand improved during 2010, mainly due to high economic growth, the economic slowdown in 2011 and the looming recessions in some major economies will require further fiscal injection. The situation is likely to be made worse by the so-called "populist policies" of recent Thai governments, including the current one. Many of these policies create large market distortions and do not generate increases in productivity. As a result, fiscal resources will generate a purely short-term boost to the economy and are likely to be largely misused. It is likely that long-term fiscal sustainability will become a major concern in the near future.

10.5 Strategies to rebalance growth

For an export dependent economy like Thailand, the current crisis may be harder to deal with than the 1997 crisis. Thailand exported her way out of the 1997 crisis, assisted by the depreciation of the baht. This was a natural recovery path for the country, as Thailand, in a similar way to most of the other East Asian economies, is used to export-led growth. East Asia has pursued a path of export-led development for decades, following the successful example set by Japan. This was regarded as a "flying geese" pattern of development (Akamatsu 1962).

During the 1997 crisis, the advanced economies were not greatly affected (with the exception of Japan which has extensive economic links with other parts of East Asia). Thus, the main export markets for East Asian products could provide demand for increased exports from East Asia; from both the crisis affected countries as well as from newly emerging production powerhouses, such as the People's Republic of China (the PRC).

The current situation is very different. The crisis has led to a collapse of world demand for exports, which hits at the very heart of the East Asian model of export-led growth. Exporting their way out of the current crisis is out of the question for East Asian economies. Indeed, many economists view the global imbalance—with East Asia exporting its way to growth, creating a huge balance of payment surpluses, and vast accumulation of reserves, while the US runs bigger and bigger deficits—as being a partial cause of the subprime crisis and subsequent credit crunch. Of course, while the global imbalance may have provided excessive liquidity to the financial markets in the West, a much more fundamental cause of the subprime crisis, however, is regulatory failure in the West, particularly in the US, that allowed a huge explosion of toxic assets, built up from subprime mortgages, throughout the financial system.

It is likely that a sustainable solution to the current crisis will involve not only a strengthening of financial regulations everywhere, but also better mechanisms to prevent a buildup of vast global imbalances, as occurred in the past decade. However, correcting such deep-rooted global imbalances takes time, as many major economies or economic groups will have to undergo substantial restructuring. For example, economists know that the US economy must consume and import less and export more, while East Asia and other major trading partners to the US must do the opposite. However, switching from importing to exporting, and vice versa, does not involve just changing numbers on paper, but real adjustments at the firm level and other microeconomic policy changes, such as retraining laborers to be able to shift to new economic sectors, which may require very different skills.

Another important change that is likely to be needed in correcting the global imbalances is a substantial realignment of major currencies. The US dollar certainly needs to be much weaker against its major partners' currencies. Again, this is not an easy adjustment to make. East Asia is certainly facing a huge dilemma on this issue. On the one hand, not implementing changes that would prevent a reemergence of huge global imbalances in the future runs the risk that a future financial crisis will hit East Asian economies severely, as in the current crisis. On the other hand, working to bring about a realignment of currencies, particularly a significant weakening of the US dollar, will mean that East Asia will need to accept a book loss on the value of the huge amount of US dollar-denominated assets that are held by the region.

Whatever the solution might be to preventing a crisis like the subprime crisis in the medium to long term, it is clear that East Asia has been forced to make a significant adjustment to its development strategy in the short- to medium-term. In the short-term, countries have been making sizeable fiscal injections to try to shore up their economy, hurt by the collapse of the export engine. The Thai short-term response was discussed earlier. In the medium term, some form of growth rebalancing will be necessary. This does not mean that exports will no longer be important to East Asia, as it is very unlikely that much of the production base that feeds the global consumer demand for manufactured products can shift back to the advanced economies, or that another region could replace East Asia in this production role. What rebalancing means is that East Asia needs to rely less on the engine of exports and supplement it with other engines based on domestic demand. This, again, is not that easy to achieve. It will require a significant restructuring of various economies, and also the implementation of appropriate policies to make sure that domestic demand driven growth, such as through investment, does not generate large economic bubbles and current account deficits similar to those that occurred prior to the 1997 crisis.

In the case of Thailand, one can say that the economy has not grown in a well-balanced manner since the 1990s. During the economic bubble of the 1990s, growth was driven by excessive and speculative investment. When the 1997 crisis occurred, Thailand then had to rely too much on exports to restore growth and overall economic health. The present overreliance on exports makes the country highly vulnerable to the current global recession, as has been seen in recent export and growth figures. There have been discussions in academic and policy circles about rebalancing growth to be more dependent on domestic demand and less on exports. How to achieve these goals, however, is not clear and little serious analysis has been carried out on this issue.

Actually, the issue of Thailand being highly dependent on external trade was discussed seven to eight years ago, when the rapid rise in exports, which enabled Thailand to recover from that crisis, significantly increased exports' share of the economy. Many were already voicing concerns that the increased dependence on exports makes Thailand more vulnerable to the volatilities in both its trading partners' economic conditions and world trade. However, it is difficult to be precise when calculating whether or not a country depends too much on exports. Certainly, there are countries that have much higher ratio of exports to GDP than Thailand (Malaysia; Singapore; Hong Kong, China; and

Japan, to name a few), and the growth experiences in those countries have been very successful. It is true that when external conditions deteriorate, the more open economies experience greater transmission to the domestic economies (Rodrik 1996). However, volatilities from short-term external factors do not mean that these export driven economies do not, on average, perform well over time. Actually, the more open, export led economies tended to perform better than those which were more inward looking (Sussangkarn 1997). Certainly, having to compete in the export market can bring about efficiency spillovers. There is also evidence supporting the view that, for Thailand, the degree of openness positively affects total factor productivity (TFP) (Tinakorn and Sussangkarn 1998; Sussangkarn, Jitsuchon, and Vajragupta 2003).

Irrespective of the impacts of openness on volatilities and growth, it is clear that the fall out from the subprime crisis will mean that Thailand (and other East Asian export led economies) will have to accept a reduced dependence on exports over the next several years, and probably over the course of the medium term. It is therefore of interest to see what might be some of the important strategies enabling sustainable growth given lower export dependence.

One obviously important strategy is increased domestic investment, which will have to be mainly public investment as the private sector has been considerably weakened by the crisis and there is a large amount of excess capacity in the manufacturing and services sectors. It is not entirely clear, however, that an investment led growth strategy can be sustainable. If the investment is not excessive, then it should be sustainable. In that case, however, the growth generated may not be very high. If investment becomes excessive, then there is a danger of large adverse impacts on the current account and external stability. There is also a danger of creating a bubble, as was done just prior to the 1997 crisis. So managing the size of public investment to ensure that it is at an appropriate level will be important. The quality of these investments will be equally important. Thailand has made wasteful and inefficient investments in mega-projects in the past, including both purely public sector projects and those given out as concessions to the private sector. This is again a very important issue needing careful planning and monitoring.

There are other strategies that will be important parts of a growth rebalancing strategy. In the rest of this paper, we highlight three important strategies from analyses in Sussangkarn, Jitsuchon, and Vajragupta (2003). That paper used a computable general equilibrium (CGE) model of Thailand to carry out policy analyses on how to achieve moderate average growth, given an assumed decline in the role of exports in the Thai economy. It was assumed that the ratio of exports to GDP would decline by 10 percentage points over a five-year time horizon. The paper found that growth would slow down significantly. The paper then analyzed various strategies that could increase growth while ensuring sustainability in the sense of maintaining external stability. In the analyses, the current account was kept fixed for each scenario, with the level of investment being endogenous.

The analyses highlighted three strategies that will be important for growth rebalancing. These are (1) increasing total factor productivity; (2) deepening the production structure of the economy; and (3) lowering energy dependence.

10.5.1 *Improving total factor productivity (TFP)*

Improving TFP is the best way to make growth more well-balanced. With higher productivity, the country can compete better on a long-term basis. At the same time, higher productivity will translate into higher wage rates and higher real income of the working population, enhancing the purchasing power of the domestic market.

In the past, productivity gains in Thailand came primarily from resource mobilization between economic sectors, and from the accumulation of physical capital, usually in the form of imported technology (Tinakorn and Sussangkarn 1998). Resource mobilization had limits, as the country depleted its natural resources at an alarming rate. The ability of people to move from low-paid agricultural work to higher-paid industry and service jobs is also approaching its limit, as agriculture currently accounts for less than 10 percent of GDP, and most farmers already have substantial non-farm income. Relying on accumulating imported capital is not a sustainable way of improving productivity either, as the value-added tends to be small.

Real productivity gains should come from improving human capital. In this regard, there is plenty of room for Thailand to make more progress. The education and training system needs to improve a lot. Thailand's international rankings in education and training lag behind its performance in other areas, such as physical infrastructure. Table 10.5 shows that there are many sub-areas in education and training which are troublesome. For example, although Thailand has made much progress in secondary enrollment since 1990s, its ranking is still low.

Improvement in scientific and technological capabilities is another important area. Investment and expenditures on scientific research and development is low in Thailand compared to more advanced countries, and much of the investments that have been made have not yielded commercial benefits. There has been great difficulty in linking research and development to commercial products.

Table 10.5 International ranking of Thai education and training (selected indicators)

Indicator	World rank[a]
Education expenditure	46
Extent of staff training	51
Internet access in schools	42
Local availability of research and training services	58
Primary enrollment	61
Quality of math and science education	55
Quality of management schools	49
Quality of primary education	64
Quality of the educational system	53
Secondary enrollment	85
Tertiary enrollment	44

Source: The Global Competitiveness Report 2008–2009, World Economic Forum (WEF).[a] The total number of countries in the sample was 134.

10.5.2 *Deepening the production structure of the economy*

Deepening the production structure means reducing the import content of various sectors in the economy in order to increase domestic demand. The focus here is more on intermediate demand and the stress is not on protectionism, but rather on encouraging a deeper and more diversified production base.

The structural weakness of Thailand's reliance on exports is that most of the leading exports have high import content. As shown in Figure 10.5 almost

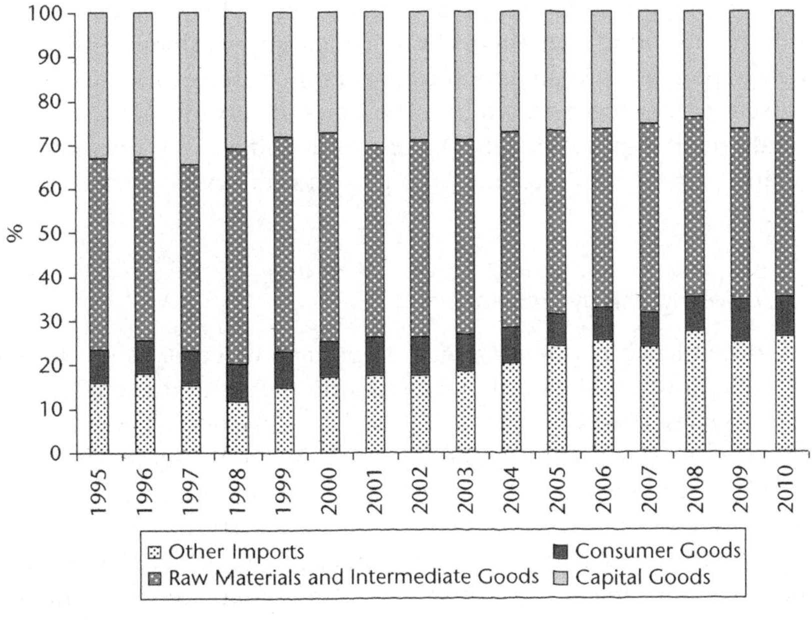

Figure 10.5 Import structure (in %)
Source: Bank of Thailand.

half of Thailand's imports are raw materials and intermediate goods. When combined with imports of capital, these two import groups account for two-thirds to three-quarters of total imports. Thailand is clearly a member of regional production networks that spread the production of parts to many countries. In theory, this international division of labor benefits all member countries. In practice, however, a country will benefit more if more parts are produced within that country, as this lowers the import volume while raising export volume. To increase parts production in Thailand, a highly developed domestic network of industry clusters must be put in place, and logistical arrangements must be efficient.

To reduce intermediate imports, the key issue is to increase the productive capacity of local producers so that they can increase links to the supply chain of various industries. Thailand has seen some successes regarding this in the past for certain industries, particularly the auto industry. In its early days in Thailand, most of the auto industry was simply the assembly of completely knocked down parts imported from abroad. Over time, the share of locally produced parts steadily increased. This occurred as local producers improved the quality of their products, up to international standards. More FDI in the parts industry, some as joint ventures with local companies, also helped this process. The auto sector in Thailand is now very competitive with a high local content, and some locally made parts are now exported.

The production deepening will reduce the ratio of imports to GDP. This reduction of import share brings the potential for higher growth. In the CGE analysis, it was found that a reduction of total import share of GDP by five percentage points across all import categories increased economic growth by an average of 1.6 percent per annum. The auto industry experience is one that Thailand can attempt to emulate in many other industries. This should be an important part of the medium-term growth strategy to craft rebalanced growth.

10.5.3 *Lowering energy vulnerability*

Import dependence is probably most important when it comes to energy imports. As shown in Figure 10.6, the proportion of imported energy to GDP went up from less than 4 percent in 1998 to 12–14 percent in 2006–08, a three-fold increase in less than a decade. As a result, the economy became very vulnerable when energy prices went up, and the vulnerability became more and more serious. Not having sufficient domestic energy sources is only a small part of the problem, using energy inefficiently is a much bigger problem.

A policy of lowering energy dependence can also be used to promote new industries and contribute directly to growth. For example, the Thai government initiated the so-called "Eco-car" project in 2007. These eco-cars are small

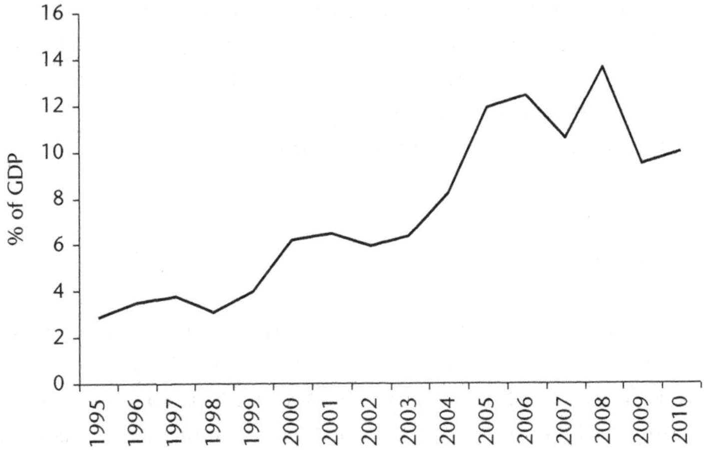

Figure 10.6 Dependence on imported energy (in %)
Sources: Bank of Thailand and the National Economic and Social Development Board.

cars (with an engine size, in cubic centimeters, of less than 1,300 for gasoline engines and less than 1,400 for diesel engines) that can achieve a mileage rate of more than 20 kilometers per liter, and comply with both the Euro 4 emissions standards and stringent safety standards. The main incentive for the development of eco-cars was a reduction in the excise tax from 30 percent to 17 percent. After the project was announced, seven manufacturers applied to the Board of Investment for promotional privileges to carry out an eco-car project. Output was initially due to come to the market in late 2009 or 2010. Unfortunately, with the current crisis, this will be postponed until market conditions improve. Nevertheless, these fuel efficient and environmentally friendly cars should be able to drive a new growth path for the auto industry in Thailand.

10.5.4 *Other rebalancing factors*

There are obviously many other important aspects of growth rebalancing strategies. For Thailand, income distribution is another important issue. In terms of income distribution, Thailand is among the most unequal countries in the world. The Gini coefficient has remained stubbornly above 0.5 throughout the past three decades. One of the important consequences of high inequality is the relatively small size of the domestic market, as wealth is concentrated among only a handful of the rich. A successful redistribution of wealth would therefore increase the domestic market size and make growth better balanced. This is especially true for a country such as Thailand with moderate average income levels. Measures to improve income inequality include fiscal measures, micro-credit policies, and equitable enforcement of rules of law, among others. Another important by-product of a more equal income distribution is the reduction in political polarization, which is damaging Thai politics and its economy at the moment.

10.6 Conclusions

The recovery from the 1997 crisis left Thailand more dependent than ever on exports as the main growth engine. Being highly dependent on exports, however, Thailand, along with other export oriented East Asian economies, was greatly affected by the indirect impact of the subprime crisis on exports. The lessons learned from the 1997 crisis led to a more risk-averse financial system, and this helped Thailand avoid the direct impacts of the subprime crisis. It thus remains crucial that Thailand rebalance its economy to be less dependent on external demand and more resilient to external shocks.

The Thai government has been using fiscal stimulus to try to shore up the economy. This stimulus also tended, increasingly, to be of a populist nature, bringing mostly short-term gains with little impact on productivity increases. This may quickly weaken Thailand's fiscal position, and more attention needs to be given to fiscal sustainability. In the medium to long term, Thailand needs to move toward more balanced growth that is less dependent on exports (although exports will still be important) and more focused on other, domestic sources of growth. The chapter suggests a number of key strategies that could help Thailand achieve a more balanced and sustainable growth path. The main strategies include (1) a focus on increasing total factor productivity; (2) further deepening the production structure of the economy; and (3) reducing the dependence on imported energy. In addition, improving the country's highly skewed income distribution will also help to increase demand from domestic consumption.

References

Akamatsu, K. (1962). A Historical Pattern of Economic Growth in Developing Countries. *Journal of Developing Economies* 1(1): 3–25.

Chandoevwit, W. (2006). Policy Challenges for the Social Security for Private Employees. *TDRI Quarterly Review* 21(4): 11–19.

Mundell, R. A. (1963). Capital Mobility and Stabilization Policy Under Fixed and Flexible Exchange Rates. *Canadian Journal of Economics and Political Sciences* 29(November): 475–85.

NaRanong, V. and A. NaRanong (2006). Universal Health Care Coverage: Impacts of the 30-Baht Health-Care Scheme on the Poor in Thailand. *TDRI Quarterly Review* 21(3): 3–10.

Rodrik, D. (1996). Why Do More Open Economies Have Bigger Governments? NBER Working Paper No. 5537. Cambridge, MA: National Bureau of Economic Research.

Sussangkarn, C. (1997). Thailand: Looking Ahead to 2020 in Light of Global and Regional Changes. *TDRI Quarterly Review* 12(2): 3–13.

Sussangkarn, C. and P. Vichyanond (2007). Ten Years After the Financial Crisis in Thailand: What Has Been Learned or Not Learned? *Asian Economic Policy Review* 2(1): 100–18.

Sussangkarn, C., S. Jitsuchon, and Y. Vajragupta (2003). Globalization of Thailand: Economic Impacts and Restructuring for Sustainability. Paper (in Thai) presented at TDRI's 2002 Year-end Conference, Thailand Development Research Institute, Bangkok.

Tinakorn, P. and C. Sussangkarn (1998). Total Factor Productivity Growth in Thailand: 1980–1995. TDRI Research Report No. M45. Bangkok: Thailand Development Research Institute.

World Bank (1993). *The East Asian Miracle: Economic Growth and Public Policy*. New York: Oxford University Press.

11

Malaysia and the Global Crisis: Impact, Response, and Rebalancing Strategies

Shankaran Nambiar

11.1 Introduction

The Malaysian economy has been hit by crises in the past, but the global financial crisis is quite unlike those it has been affected by in the last 10 years. Because the recent crisis was triggered by external sources, it demands a serious reconsideration of the country's growth strategy. The 1997 crisis, for example, required temporary measures (such as instituting capital controls) and some fundamental changes (such as the restructuring of the banking and financial system), but the global financial crisis will require new ways of thinking about how Malaysia should re-position itself, since the crisis undermines the assumptions on which the country's growth strategy is based.

The next section discusses the importance of trade to the economy and Malaysia's reliance on demand generated by developed economies. The third section analyzes the impact of the global financial crisis on the Malaysian economy. This is followed by an examination of the government's policy responses. Section 11.4 discusses the need for rebalancing and suggests possible strategies that could be adopted for economic recovery. Subsequently, the government's development strategies are examined for their focus on rebalancing. Finally, some concluding remarks are made.

11.2 The global financial crisis and the Malaysian economy

It has been observed that the global financial crisis has had an impact on developing Asia through the contraction of trade and FDI inflows (James et al. 2008). It is easy to see why the global financial crisis would have an impact on the Malaysian economy via the trade channel. Malaysia is a very open economy, with exports and imports totaling RM1.11 trillion, twice the national GDP. For a country that is as dependent on trade as Malaysia is, it is obvious that if demand from the country's dominant trade partners were to decrease, its repercussions would be felt throughout the economy. The evidence for the extent of the dependence on trade is striking when one notes the structure of Malaysian exports. This structure clearly indicates the dominance of manufactured goods which accounts for 81.3 percent of total exports for the period 2000–08 (Table 11.1). This is followed by minerals which contribute 8.5 percent of exports for the same period. The share of agricultural commodities accounts for 6.5 percent of total exports.

Table 11.1 Exports by sector (% share)

	2000	2001	2002	2003	2004	2005	2006	2007	2008
Agricultural commodities	4.8	4.7	6.2	7.3	6.6	5.8	6.2	7.5	9.0
Palm oil	2.7	3.0	4.2	5.1	4.3	3.6	3.7	5.3	6.9
Rubber	0.7	0.6	0.7	0.9	1.1	1.1	1.4	1.2	1.2
Manufactured goods	85.2	85.4	84.5	82.0	81.2	80.7	80.3	78.4	74.1
Electronics, electrical machinery, and appliances	61.7	59.9	59.4	56.0	53.4	52.7	51.1	47.6	41.8
– Electronics	44.7	41.8	44.0	42.1	39.2	38.9	37.6	35.3	29.5
– Semiconductor	19.1	18.1	20.4	21.4	18.5	16.8	15.9	15.9	13.5
– Electronics equipment and parts	25.6	23.7	23.6	20.7	20.6	22.0	21.7	19.3	16.0
– Electrical machinery and appliances	17.0	18.2	15.4	13.9	14.3	13.8	13.5	12.4	12.3
– Consumer electrical products	7.1	7.1	5.9	5.0	4.6	4.2	3.2	2.7	3.2
– Industrial and commercial electrical products	6.3	7.0	5.5	5.1	5.4	5.4	5.9	4.9	4.7
– Electrical industrial machinery and equipment	3.4	3.7	3.5	3.4	3.7	3.7	3.9	4.2	3.8
– Household electrical appliances	0.2	0.3	0.4	0.5	0.6	0.5	0.5	0.6	0.5
Chemicals and chemical products	4.0	4.5	4.8	5.3	5.8	6.0	5.6	6.2	6.2
Manufactures of metal	2.3	2.6	2.5	2.8	3.3	3.2	3.9	4.4	4.4
Optical and scientific equipment	1.8	2.3	2.3	2.3	2.4	2.3	2.3	2.2	2.3
Rubber products	1.3	1.3	1.3	1.3	1.3	1.3	1.5	1.7	1.9
Textiles, clothing, and footwear	2.8	2.7	2.4	2.2	2.2	2.0	1.9	1.8	1.6
Transport equipment	0.8	0.7	0.8	0.8	1.1	1.3	1.5	1.4	1.4
Wood products	1.8	1.8	1.8	1.7	1.8	1.6	1.8	1.6	1.5
Minerals	7.0	6.8	6.1	7.4	8.2	9.5	9.3	9.7	12.9
Crude oil	3.8	3.3	3.2	3.9	4.5	5.3	5.2	5.3	6.5
Liquefied natural gas	3.1	3.3	2.8	3.4	3.6	4.0	4.0	4.3	6.1
Other exports	3.01	3.20	3.16	3.34	3.94	4.01	4.18	4.31	4.00
Total exports									

Sources: Author's calculations compiled from Department of Statistics, Malaysia (2005–08) and Malaysian Institute for Economic Research (MIER) computations.

Within the category of manufactured goods, electronics, electrical machinery, and appliances are 53 percent of the exports share. This category of commodities drives the manufacturing sector. Again, as a component of this broad category, electronics goods are the most dominant. Exports of electronics products can be sub-divided into semiconductors and electrical equipment and appliances, both of which have roughly equal importance.

There is no doubt that the export of manufactured goods is particularly vulnerable to drops in external demand. Since the demand for electronics goods largely comes from developed countries (particularly the Unites States (US), the European Union (EU), and Japan), a decline in consumption in these economies is bound to have a negative impact on the exports of Malaysian manufactured goods. It is important to note that percentage share in total exports has slipped the most from the previous yearfs percentage in 2008 in goods such as semiconductors (2.4 percent) and electronics equipment (3.3 percent). The export of electronics, electrical machinery, and appliances fell by 5.8 percent from 2007 to 2008. While manufactured goods accounted for 78.4 percent of total exports in 2007, it dropped to 74.1 percent in 2008.

Other items such as chemicals and chemical products; textiles, clothing, and footwear; manufactures of metals; and optical and scientific equipment do not constitute a large share of Malaysian exports. In 2008, chemicals made up just 6.2 percent of exports and manufactures of metals contributed only 4.4 percent. Neither of them experienced any change from the previous year. The other items mentioned accounted for less than 2 percent in 2008, with the exception of optical and scientific equipment (2.3 percent), but they too were not affected by the global crisis.

The data strongly suggests that Malaysia's export structure is such that those goods exported to developed countries are more important to the economy than other goods. Not only must we note that the country's growth is largely dependent on trade, but also that the export structure is heavily weighted in favor of manufacturing goods. Further, Malaysia's export-driven manufacturing sector depends on goods derived from the electronics and electrical sector.

The vulnerability of Malaysian exports is also confirmed from an examination of trends in exports by Malaysia to its major trading partners. The US was the largest single destination for exports in the mid-1990s (Figure 11.1). However, it seems to have lost its favored position, as other countries have come to take a place of roughly equal standing. In 1995, 21 percent of exports were directed to the US, with a gentle decrease to 18 percent in more recent years.

After the US, the EU was next in importance in 1995, claiming 14 percent of exports. The share of exports heading for the EU has hovered around 12.5 percent in recent years. Japan, to which 13 percent of Malaysian exports went in 1995, now claims 9 percent. The biggest decline has been in Singapore. In the late-1990s, 20 percent of exports went to Singapore. Since 2006,

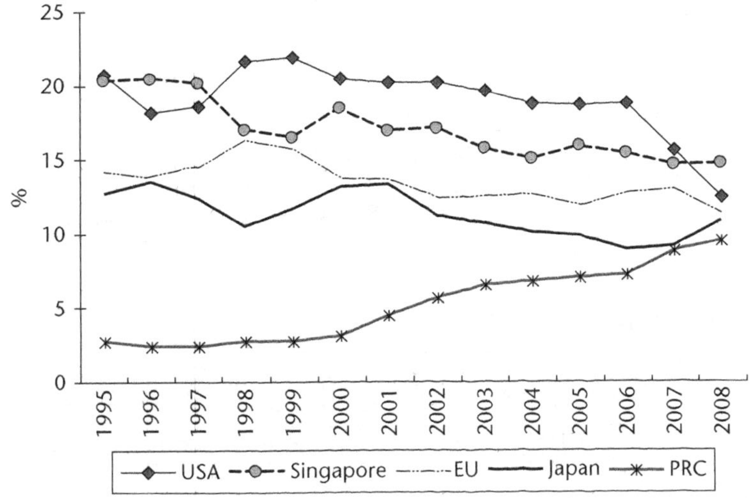

Figure 11.1 Exports to major partners

Source: Author's calculations compiled from Department of Statistics, Malaysia (2005–08).

Note: USA = United States of America, EU = European Union, PRC = the People's Republic of China

this figure has dropped to 15 percent. On the other hand, the People's Republic of China (PRC) has been assuming greater significance as a source for Malaysian exports. Three percent of exports went to the PRC in the late-1990s, but in the last two years, this figure has almost tripled. The five most important economies to which Malaysian exports now go are the US, Singapore, the EU, Japan, and the PRC.

There is some convergence in terms of import sources. In the mid- and late-1990s, Japan was the largest import source, followed by the EU and Singapore (Figure 11.2). While 27 percent of exports were directed to Japan in 1995, this dropped to 13 percent in 2007 and further in 2008 (12.5 percent). The US accounted for 16 percent of total imports between 1995 and 1997. In the years 2007 and 2008, only 10 percent of imports were from the US. Eleven percent of imports come from the EU. The PRC was the source of only 2.2 percent of imports in 1995, but shot up to 10 percent in 2005 and further to 12.9 percent in 2007.

There is a strong relationship in Malaysia between exports and imports in that the goods produced for export have a strong import content. Also, the same countries serve as destinations for exports and sources of imports. Again, these are the countries that have suffered severely from the impact of the global financial crisis. Given the fact that Malaysia's growth relies heavily on export-oriented manufacturing, the crisis has had a strong impact on the Malaysian economy.

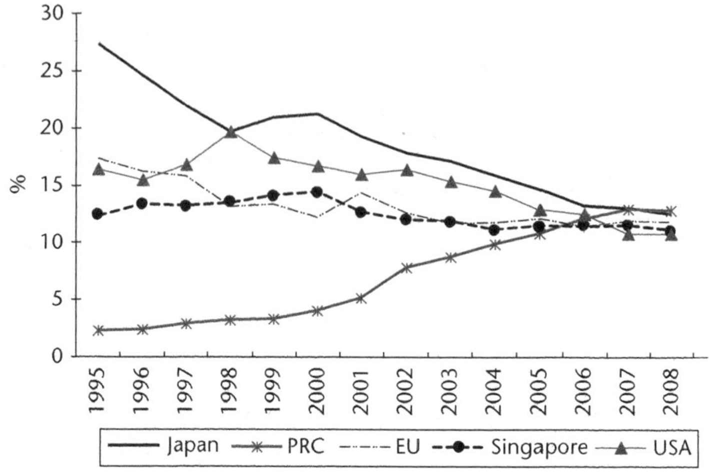

Figure 11.2 Import sources

Source: Author's calculations compiled from Department of Statistics, Malaysia (2005–08).
Note: EU = European Union, PRC = the People's Republic of China, US = United States of America

11.3 Impact of the crisis on the Malaysian Economy

Two economic indicators that show the impact of the current crisis are exports and the industrial production index. Export figures, which were doing well in the first three quarters of 2008, took a downturn towards the end of that year (Figure 11.3). In January 2008, exports increased by 10.4 percent (year-on-year),

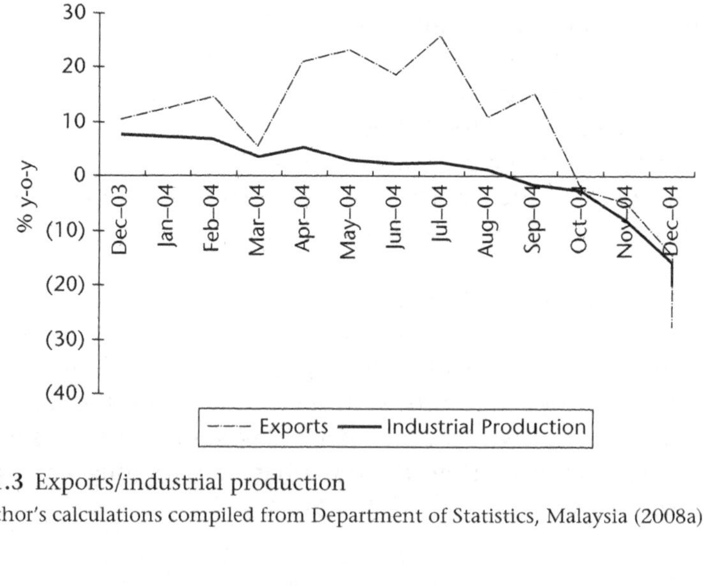

Figure 11.3 Exports/industrial production

Source: Author's calculations compiled from Department of Statistics, Malaysia (2008a).

and more-or-less doubled to 20.9 percent in April 2008. However, in October 2008, a negative figure was reported (–2.6 percent), only to decline more deeply as the months progressed. In December 2008 a decline was registered (–14.9 percent), which worsened in January 2009 (–27.8 percent).

Imports, which tend to follow export trends rather closely in Malaysia, reported a similar pattern. Imports increased by 11 percent (year-on-year) in February 2008 and exceeded 10 percent in the months of June and July 2008 (12.5 percent and 15.0 percent, respectively). Again, the change in imports fell into negative territory from October 2008, falling from –5.3 percent in that month to –23.1 percent in December 2008, and dropping to –32 percent in January 2009. It is understandable that imports should fall along with exports because imports of intermediate goods are required to meet the production of exports. The strong demand for exports that comes from Malaysia's major trading partners (US, Japan, and the EU) having fallen, it should be expected that exports from Malaysia would also fall.

Since most of the manufacturing sector is driven by the growth of exports, the industrial production index reflects the poor export conditions of the global environment and has been sinking since September 2008 (–1.7 percent, year-on-year), deepening towards the end of 2008, particularly in December, and into January 2009 (–15.9 percent and –20.2 percent, respectively) (Figure 11.3). These results are not surprising in view of Malaysia's heavy dependence on the environment and energy (E&E) sector and the fact that Malaysia's major trading partners were badly affected by the global financial crisis. Given these facts, claims that Malaysia has decoupled from the US do not seem valid. Others have claimed that Malaysia is shifting its trade towards the Association of Southeast Asian Nations (ASEAN). While there is evidence that trade with Singapore and Thailand has been increasing, this phenomenon must be contrasted with the nature of production networks. Units in other parts of ASEAN are a part of the production processes where the final products are ultimately exported to countries such as the EU and the US.

The effects of the crisis began to show in the GDP numbers by the third quarter of 2008. In no sector was this clearer than in manufacturing (Figure 11.4). The manufacturing sector had a 5.6 percent increase (year-on-year) in the second quarter of 2008. In the following quarter it was positive, but closer to 2 percent (1.8 percent), and it was negative (–8.8 percent) by the fourth quarter of 2008. The construction sector also showed negative growth in the fourth quarter of 2008. In fact, real GDP slid to a 0.1 percent growth rate in the last quarter of 2008.

Viewed in terms of real GDP by demand expenditure, the most striking decreases in the fourth quarter of 2008 were observed in gross investment (–10.2 percent), exports (–13.4 percent), and imports (–10.1 percent) (Figure 11.5). Private consumption also fell, but remained at a respectable

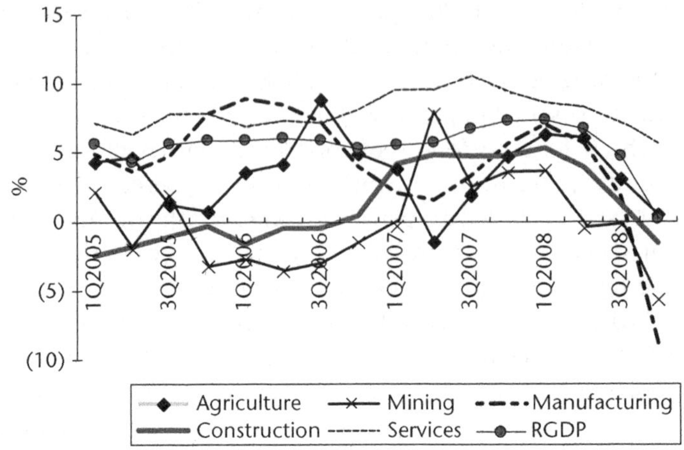

Figure 11.4 GDP by sectors
Source: Department of Statistics, Malaysia (2008b).
Note: GDP = gross domestic product, RGDP = real gross domestic product

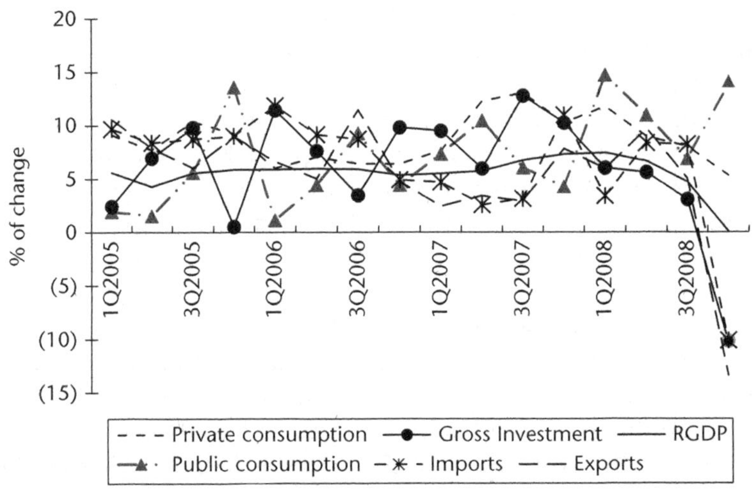

Figure 11.5 RGDP by demand expenditure
Source: Department of Statistics, Malaysia (2008b).
Note: RGDP = real gross domestic product

rate of 5.3 percent. Comparatively, in the first quarter of 2008, private consumption had increased by 11.7 percent and similarly, in the same quarter gross investment increased by 6 percent, with exports and imports showing increases as well (at 6 percent and 3.4 percent, respectively). The net effect of all the decreases in the various components was a decline in real GDP growth to 0.1 percent for the last quarter of 2008 compared to 7 percent in the first half of the same year.

The capital outflows from Malaysia increased with the onset of the crisis. First, reverse investments that were high in the second half of 2007 (about RM21.9 billion) slowed in the fourth quarter of 2008 to RM5.6 billion. The outflows of portfolio funds from Malaysian markets reflected the reality of the global crisis. There was a surge of portfolio flows into the country in the first quarter of 2008 (RM21.0 billion), and starting in the second quarter, the outflows continued to be extremely large. In the second quarter, portfolio outflows amounted to RM21.9 billion and in the third and fourth quarter, they were RM56.1 billion and RM33.2 billion, respectively.

FDI did not compensate for portfolio outflows during the same period. In fact, FDI has been hovering at around RM5.0 billion every quarter in recent years (2006–08). There have been occasional spurts of FDI inflows into Malaysia, particularly in the second quarter of 2007 and the second quarter of 2008. The large increases in FDI that took place in the second quarter of 2007 amounted to RM11.5 billion, increasing to RM15.9 billion in the second quarter of 2008. The first was due to foreign investors (from Japan, the US, Germany, and Singapore) making investments in E&E activities. The second was due to a large joint venture enterprise initiated by an Australian company relating to aluminum processing. There is no doubt that with the crisis and with Malaysia's traditional FDI sources being adversely affected, FDI inflows have also decreased. This can be seen distinctly in the third quarter of 2008 when FDI worth RM900 million was all that flowed into the country, although it recovered to RM5.0 billion the following quarter (Figure 11.6). The full

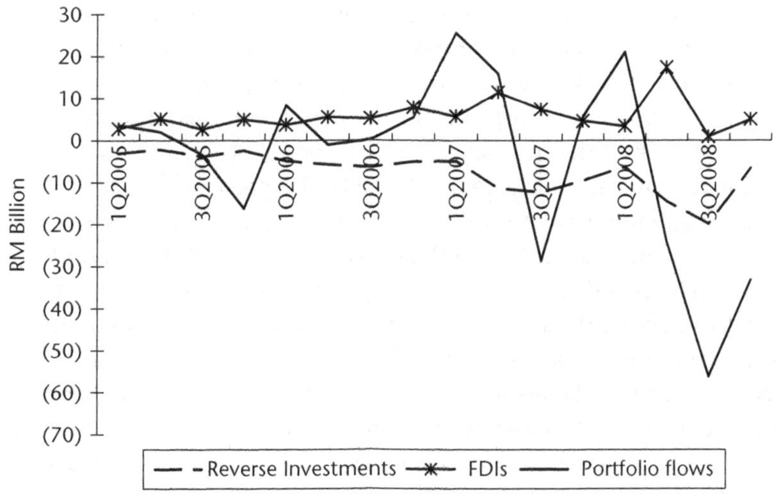

Figure 11.6 Capital flows

Source: Author's calculations compiled from Department of Statistics, Malaysia (2005–08).

Note: FDI = foreign direct investment

effects of the crisis on FDI are perhaps yet to be seen, since decisions by multinational corporations to invest in foreign countries will be made after the second half of 2008 and in the coming years.

The crisis has also prompted a drop in the value of Malaysia's foreign reserves. The economy held foreign reserves valued at US$82.4 billion in 2006. Reserves increased in 2007 (US$101.3 billion) and a further increase was noted in 2008 (US$91.5 billion). Although Malaysia's reserves have been high in the years following the 1997 crisis, the global financial crisis has taken its toll on reserves. Quarterly figures depict the reality of the crisis. In the second quarter of 2008, reserves were US$125.8 billion and fell to a limited extent in the following quarter of the same year to US$109.7 billion. However, in the last quarter of 2008, the fall was even sharper, reaching US$91.5 billion, a loss of US$18.2 billion.

The declines in FDI, foreign reserves, and portfolio funds had been cushioned by the relatively stable current account balance. In the fourth quarter of 2008, the current account balance dropped to RM29.8 billion from RM38.7 billion in the previous quarter. More striking, however, is the overall balance which has continued to drop drastically since the third quarter of 2008, falling from –RM31.5 billion to –RM61.9 million in the last quarter of 2008.

The impact of the global financial crisis has been felt most strongly in two sectors of the Malaysian economy: the manufacturing sector (discussed above) and the construction sector. The impact on the construction sector can be seen in several of its key indicators. The number of new sales permits has been falling since July 2008, but the figures have reflected the pessimism of the industry most distinctly since August 2008. The number of new sales permits, which earlier in the year reached eighty-seven per month, fell to fifty-eight in August and forty-one in December 2008. The number of housing approvals has also been trend downward. The change in the production of construction-related products shows the bleak outlook of the industry. In September 2008, there was a 6.8 percent increase (year-on-year) in this index. It fell by 1.9 percent in October 2008, but most alarmingly there was a contraction of 5.1 percent in November 2008.

The more prominent sectors in the economy have suffered from the impact of the global financial crisis. With the negative reactions that have been felt by the E&E sector, construction industry, and property development, the outlook for local markets is bleak. Not surprisingly, this bleak outlook has also had an impact on the financial sector. Given the uncertainty in the economy and declining consumer confidence, the credit market has been affected. As a consequence of this weak confidence, loan approval has fallen. Particularly since September 2008, the growth in loan approval has been negative (–2.9 percent) and has continued to decline, especially in the months of October 2008 (–14.4 percent) and November 2008 (–44.0 percent) as well as January 2009 (–35.6 percent). The caution exercised in the banking sector is indicated by the growth in loans disbursed. This too declined in the months of October 2008 (8.2 percent), November (7.6 percent), and December 2008 (0.6 percent), finally becoming negative in January 2009 (–10 percent).

The overall atmosphere of negativity has also led to unemployment. Not surprisingly, the manufacturing sector has suffered the most from the crisis in terms of retrenchments. This can be seen in the second half of 2008. In the third quarter of 2008 about 10,000 workers were retrenched and about 5,000 lost their jobs in the last quarter of that year. Retrenchments were also high in the services sector in the third and fourth quarters of 2008. Except for the agriculture sector, retrenchments have been high, and about 20,000 workers were retrenched in the second half of 2008, according to published statistics (Bank Negara Malaysia 2009).

11.4 Policy responses to the crisis

The immediate response to the global crisis was one of denial, expressed through arguments that included the following: the Malaysian economy was decoupled from the US economy, the subprime crisis would not affect Malaysia because Malaysian banks had no exposure to such financial instruments, and Malaysia could tap into the growth generated by the PRC. As if to produce evidence that the Malaysian economy would continue to grow despite the global slowdown, the Ministry of International Trade and Industry highlighted the fact that the Malaysian Industrial Development Authority was receiving an increasing number of applications for investment in Malaysia.

However, with the continued global slowdown, it became clear that Malaysia would be adversely affected. In response to the threat posed to the economy, the government reacted with the following measures:

1. a RM7 billion stimulus package, announced on November 4, 2008;
2. a second stimulus package of RM60 billion, announced on March 10, 2009; and
3. interest rate cuts by Bank Negara Malaysia, the central bank of Malaysia.

The introduction of these measures demonstrates that the government realized the seriousness of the problem and decided to use the full array of fiscal and monetary measures to mitigate the effects of the crisis. It was necessary to protect the economy against declining aggregate demand and to ensure that domestic spending did not recede. Further, there was an urgent need to protect the economy against any erosion of confidence. No less crucial was the recognition that social well-being could not be sacrificed should the effect of the crisis be severe.

The two principle objectives of the first stimulus package (SP1) as declared by the finance minister were to reinforce and stimulate the economy, and to bring relief to the public.

The principle allocations under SP1 are as follows:

- RM1.2 billion to build 25,000 units of low- and medium-cost houses.
- RM500 million to upgrade, repair, and maintain police stations and quarters, and army camps and quarters.
- RM500 million to construct roads, schools, and hospitals.
- RM500 million to construct roads in rural areas and villages.
- RM500 million to improve public transport systems in urban centers.
- RM200 million to revive abandoned housing projects.
- RM200 million to fund micro-enterprises.

The incentives extended under SP1 included:

- Extension of all housing loans for government servants to thirty years (from twenty-five years) and an increase in loan amounts for certain categories of government servants to buy cars.
- Employment Provident Fund members can reduce contributions by 3 percent for two years.
- Foreigners and foreign companies can buy commercial real estate valued at RM500,000 or more without seeking the approval of the Foreign Investment Committee.
- Hypermarkets can extend business operations until 11 p.m. on weekdays and until 1 a.m. on weekends. Hypermarkets in shopping complexes can apply to operate on a twenty-four-hour basis.
- Import duty on cement, long iron, and steel products will be abolished.
- Permits for foreign knowledge workers will be issued directly to workers rather than to employers.
- Government-linked companies will launch the Graduate Employability Management Scheme to help train 12,000 graduates in two years.
- Recruitment into the public sector to be expedited so as to fill vacancies in critical areas. (This is expected to include about 18,000 vacancies.)

The Second Stimulus Package (SP2), besides involving a far larger amount of funds than SP1, is more comprehensive. SP2 is more ambitious in terms of reach as it is directed at a wider range of target groups and covers a broader range of economic activities. SP2 promises to address four strategic issues: reducing unemployment and increasing job opportunities; easing the economic burden of the people, particularly those in vulnerable sections of society; supporting the private sector; and undertaking capacity building for the future.

Given the concerns the fund allocation addresses, the robustness of the private sector seems to be of top priority. The task of promoting private sector confidence and ensuring that this sector does not collapse due to the deepening of the crisis has attracted an allocation of RM29 billion, almost half the amount of the total budget. Next in importance is RM19 billion to build capacity for the future. This is followed by the concern for compensating individuals whose welfare has been adversely affected due to a recession, for which RM10 billion has been set aside. Reducing unemployment and creating job opportunities seems to attract the least funding (RM2 billion), but this is understandable as the other strategic thrusts will directly and indirectly result in the creation (or retention) of jobs.

SP2 works towards bolstering the private sector in a variety of ways, including direct financial assistance, incentive packages, and mega-projects that require private sector participation. The focus of this thrust is on small and medium enterprises (SMEs) since SMEs comprise 99 percent of total registered businesses in Malaysia. SMEs are an important link as they account for 56 percent of total employment and contribute almost 32 percent of GDP. The government is committed to extending several guarantee schemes that are specifically directed at SMEs. Through these schemes the government intends to provide guarantees to assist SMEs in raising funds for working capital, industry restructuring, and raising loans in the bond market. Most of these guarantee schemes are meant for companies with shareholder equity below RM20 million. The Industry Restructuring Guarantee Fund Scheme (which encourages the taking out of loans for productivity-increasing activities, value-added activities, and the application of green technology) will serve companies with equity below RM20 million as well as those with shareholder equity of RM20 million or more. Companies that fall into the latter category will enjoy a 50 percent guarantee from the government and an equal guarantee from financial institutions, whereas those with shareholder equity of RM20 million or less will receive a larger guarantee from the government (80:20).

In order to facilitate the proper financial functioning of the private sector during times of crisis, SP2 includes measures to enable companies to raise funds in the capital market with greater ease. To ensure that this is possible, the following is permitted: rights issued by listed companies now do not require application and approval of the Securities Commission (SC), the Code on Take-overs and Mergers 1998 no longer applies to private limited companies, bond and sukuk holders need only inform the SC of any amendments to the terms and conditions of their issuances without having to apply and await approval, unlisted public companies can proceed with issuance and offerings of equity securities without seeking the SC's approval, the SC need not be informed of revisions relating to terms and conditions of bonds and sukuk to be listed on Bursa Malaysia, and convertible and exchangeable bonds will be exempted from mandatory rating requirements.

SP2 also attempts to reduce the cost of doing business by exempting and reducing levy payments that companies must pay to the government. Companies in the E&E sector will not have to make levy payments to the Human Resource Development Fund for a period of six months. Further, levy payments will be reduced by 1 percent to 5 percent for a period of two years for all employers.

The transportation sector (particularly, the automotive and aviation industries) receives special attention under SP2. The aviation industry will benefit from a new low cost carrier terminal that will be built at the existing Kuala Lumpur International Airport for an estimated RM2 billion. A rebate of 50 percent on landing charges will be given for a period of two years to all airlines that operate from Malaysia. The government is also committing itself prominently to the sustenance of the domestic automotive sector. It is doing this by providing RM200 million to the Automotive Development Fund and has committed itself to establishing the Automotive Institute of Malaysia. A discount of RM5,000 will be given to car owners who trade in cars which are at least ten years old for the purchase of new Proton or Perodua cars. The tourism industry is also targeted by SP2, and the building of an extension to the existing airport and a decrease in landing charges will incentivize tourists. In addition, the government will allocate RM200 million to upgrade and develop the tourism industry. Areas such as eco, health, and education tourism are areas that the government would like to develop. Some of the allocation will be spent on promoting tourism through international conferences and exhibitions, and promoting second home ownership by foreigners in the country.

There are ample fiscal measures that have been created in this stimulus package for the resuscitation of the private sector. An accelerated capital allowance has been proposed. This deduction is applicable to investments in plant and machinery as well as expenses incurred from the renovation and refurbishment of business premises. Another tax instrument that is being made available to alleviate the effects of the crisis is allowing companies to set losses made in the current year against any profits that were made in the preceding year (2008). This arrangement will allow companies to pay a lower tax on the profits made in 2008, or enjoy a tax refund should they incur losses this year. Yet another fiscal instrument is a revision in the windfall profit levy on oil palm. At present, a profit levy is imposed on crude palm oil when the price exceeds RM2,000 per ton, but this will be raised to RM2,500 for peninsular Malaysia and RM3,000 for Sabah and Sarawak.

The intention to build capacity for the future is second in importance. The measures that come under this thrust include investments to be undertaken by Khazanah Nasional Berhad in sectors such as telecommunications, technology, tourism, agriculture, and life sciences. The Iskandar Development Project is scheduled to be a key beneficiary of funds under SP2, with the development of infrastructure, hotels, theme parks, and universities being specific areas of interest. RM3 billion has been earmarked for the development of the telecommunications sector, particularly for the improvement of the country's broadband infrastructure. Several off-budget projects have been listed under SP2 and these include: the building and expansion of airports (RM2.3 billion), projects to improve the telecommunications infrastructure (RM2.4 billion), and the construction of sky bridges and covered walkways (RM100 million).

Funds totaling RM2 billion have been set aside to boost private investment activities through private finance initiatives and public–private partnerships. These projects will be in areas such as education, health, and tourism. Other projects are expected to improve infrastructure (relating to traffic and the building of offices, hotels, and shopping complexes), develop new technologies (particularly biotechnology), and upgrade human resource development (with an emphasis on private tertiary education). The movement of skilled foreign labor will be eased to complement the investments in the aforementioned areas.

The institutional element has not been ignored in the thrust to build future capacity. First, the framework for government procurement will be improved with the promise that all government procurements will be made on the basis of open tenders or restricted tenders. Transparency has also been mentioned as an issue that will be addressed. Second, it is stated that the Standards and Costs Committee must approve any changes to project costs, scope, and plans. This committee will report to the cabinet on standards compliance and related issues. Third, the Foreign Investment Committee will restructure its outlook and adopt a more liberal stance. The Foreign Investment Committee will monitor investments and engage in micro-management only in projects that affect the national interest, such as ports, airports, defense, public transportation, and telecommunication.

The second thrust of easing the burden on the populace includes measures for the following: poverty eradication; a social safety net scheme to protect oil, palm, and rubber smallholders who may be affected in the event of a fall in the prices of these commodities; subsidies and assistance for fuel consumption, food security, and educational assistance; the provision of microcredit programs for small businesses; and the Fisherman's Welfare Fund. The third point will be directed at ensuring that basic necessities and transport costs do not erode the purchasing capacity of the population. An allocation of RM830 million is provided to implement social safety net programs for the elderly, disabled, and single mothers.

While an attempt is made to address the concerns of vulnerable groups, a range of issues that affect a broader portion of the population is also targeted. These include issues such as: repairing and maintaining drains and roads; improving the living conditions of those in public apartments; maintaining and repairing welfare homes, and fire stations and their quarters, and public toilets; improving school facilities, by building and repairing schools; and improving basic amenities in rural areas (especially public utilities and roads). The needs of retrenched workers is emphasized, with the government giving a tax exemption of RM10,000 (up from RM6,000) on retrenchment benefits for each year of service completed. Retrenched workers will also be able to defer the repayment of their housing loans for one year.

Although the budget allocation for reducing unemployment and increasing employment opportunities is not the largest, this thrust receives some attention in terms of the strategies that have been designed to tackle the economic problem. The strategies that have been created cover training and re-training, job placement, and job creation. Some of the prominent measures that have been proposed include the following:

1. providing training in skill-specific areas (e.g. robotics, welding, construction, and jobs in technology);
2. creating jobs in government-linked companies and employing graduates on a contract basis within the government service;
3. ensuring that private companies employing retrenched workers receive a double tax deduction;
4. establishing a sufficient number of job placement centers;
5. providing incentives for postgraduate education;
6. providing training for graduates to become entrepreneurs; and
7. restricting the employment of foreign workers in all areas except construction and plantation.

In the months leading up to the global crisis, the government insisted on increasing expenditure. The 2009 budget was expansionary and had increasing the welfare of the lower- and middle-income groups among other objectives. To achieve these aims, the government offered a one-month bonus for civil servants and reduced import duties for several consumer products. The personal income tax rate was reduced by 1 percent for those in the top income bracket as well as for those in the RM35,000–50,000 bracket.

The policy measures that have been announced by the government do not seem to recognize that the problem is structural and needs a deeper readjustment. First, the federal government has been running a deficit in its fiscal balance since the 1997 crisis. As has been discussed, with the financial crisis deepening the government has adopted a fiscal policy that is countercyclical in nature, both with the RM7 billion Economic Stabilization Plan on November 4, 2008 and with the additional stimulus package announced on March 10, 2009. The large stimulus packages have resulted in widening fiscal deficits. The fiscal deficit now amounts to 7.6 percent of GDP, but it will only add a 1 percent increase in growth.

Of the RM60 billion that has been allocated, only RM15 billion is direct expenditure, with RM10 billion being allocated for the first year (2009) and the remaining RM5 billion for the following year (2010). Much of the second stimulus package consists of government guarantees. This raises the question of whether or not the guarantees will work. It should be noted that the guarantees are meant to take away the burden of failed loans from banks, but under the difficult and pessimistic circumstances that presently prevail, the more pressing question is whether or not there will be demand for loans at all. The second question is whether or not banks will be encouraged to be less risk-averse with the guarantees being put in place by the government. With questionable effectiveness, this measure again avoids addressing the underlying problems of the crisis.

Many of the measures included in both stimulus packages treat the economic problem as one that will be short lived. Under this assumption, it is not useful to offer scholarships to students for postgraduate courses, nor give tax exemptions to companies that offer retrenchment benefits, as this does little beyond providing immediate relief. Similarly, granting contract employment in government-linked companies (GLCs) to the unemployed is, again, only a temporary benefit.

Some of the measures that have been designed are ill-conceived and will work against sustained economic recovery. The heavy emphasis on providing huge funds via the GLCs will do little to bolster the private sector's participation in the economy through the crisis and after. Even more unhelpful is the intention to assist the GLCs in stimulating investments that depend on foreign investment. A stark example of this is the idea of directing funds towards the Iskandar Development Project which depends very much on investment from foreign countries, such as Singapore, or from the Middle East.

Nevertheless, the government is correct to target SMEs and the development of infrastructure projects to stimulate the economy. This is a concern that needs a better planned approach for the long term. However, the manner in which the government has set out to accomplish the task of developing SMEs is inadequate since it relies on providing guarantees to raise loans. Clearly, this does not address the issue of building a robust SME sector. Indeed, a more comprehensive plan is needed to re-shift the focus to domestic investors and rebuild the robustness of domestic consumption. The concern for social protection, an issue which has long evaded the attention of policy makers, must be seriously revisited as part of a long-term plan to recover from the crisis.

11.5 Rebalancing for growth

Malaysian industrial policy in at least the last twenty years has been centered on increasing export growth. The government has tackled employment generation and poverty eradication through export-led economic growth, creating five-year plans and industrial policy largely premised on this assumption. The approach, however, must be re-evaluated and alternative scenarios must be devised to prepare for what could be a prolonged period of soft demand for Malaysian exports. Accomplishing this will be very difficult because some of the assumptions that have traditionally driven policymaking must be reexamined and replaced. Accordingly, new strategies to drive economic growth must be designed and implemented.

After the 1997 crisis, given the robust export trends that worked to Malaysia's advantage, the current account posted encouraging gains. In the years directly preceding the global financial crisis, the current account balance has enjoyed an upward trend (Figure 11.7). With favorable export figures, Malaysia has had a large current account surplus, and consequently, reserves have also been growing rapidly. There were decreases in reserves in the fourth quarter of 2005 and in the third quarter of 2008 due to capital withdrawals,

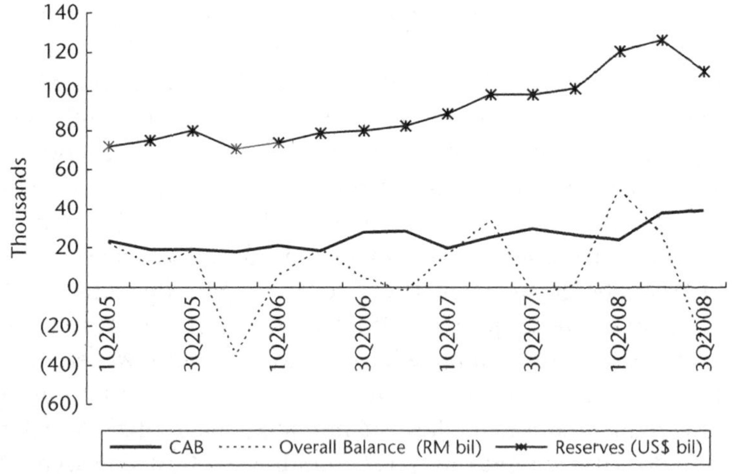

Figure 11.7 Current account, overall balance, and reserves

Source: Author's calculations compiled from Department of Statistics, Malaysia (2005–08).

Note: CAB = current account balance

but the reserves continued to be strong. These events attest to the importance of exports in the economy. Much has been done to assist growth in exports, through institutional support, fiscal incentives, and the undervaluation of the ringgit. As these strategies have been employed for more than 20 years, there will likely be some resistance to changing them.

The economic crisis challenges two assumptions that policymakers do not seem to have questioned so far: Malaysia's comparative advantage in E&E exports, and the prevailing predominance of the US, the EU, and Japan as sustained destinations for Malaysian exports. It is not clear when the US will fully recover from its recent crisis, how prolonged it will be, and whether the pattern of recovery will be "V-", "U-", or "L-shaped". Under these circumstances, Malaysia cannot expect to continue to depend on US-generated consumer demand.

These uncertainties also place additional pressure on the manufacturing sector. The initial challenge that the sector is facing—and has not yet come to terms with—is increasing competition from the PRC and Viet Nam. The comparative advantage of Malaysia's cheap, compliant, and well-educated labor force has disappeared and has led to concerns about the inflow of FDI. Malaysia cannot compete for FDI as it could ten years ago, since it has neither the unskilled labor advantage, nor an abundant supply of skilled, knowledge-intensive labor. The present crisis will continue to intensify the problem, particularly if the demand from developed economies that Malaysia has traditionally depended upon does not return to pre-crisis levels. If demand does not completely recover, Malaysia's growth rate will continue to fall, along with other macroeconomic variables including employment and well-being in the economy.

In view of the global financial crisis, Malaysia will have to readjust its growth strategies and shift away from its dominant emphasis on export-oriented growth, especially if the crisis is prolonged. Currently, support for the export-oriented policy comes from other elements in the policy landscape and involves a suitable industrial policy, export promotion institutions and strategies, and fiscal incentives.

A reorientation can only be successfully accomplished if the new goals are articulated and defended, and suitable alternative policies and strategies are selected and implemented. A reorienting strategy would function along three lines. First, resources would be shifted from manufacturing industries that are concentrated on exports to developed countries to industries and services that serve the domestic market. Second, strategies would have to be designed to improve the disposable income of individuals. Third, the government would strengthen the provision of public goods, particularly those affecting the well-being of individuals. These policies, if successful, would affect a rebalancing of economic growth. Growth rebalancing would also have an impact on the economy's macroeconomic variables. As a consequence of growth rebalancing, it is possible to expect that Malaysia will achieve a reduction in the savings rate as well as increases in domestic consumption and investment.

There are a variety of public goods, the provision of which desires more attention in Malaysia. The provision of health care, education, and social safety nets, are among the public goods whose provision leaves much to be desired. With the privatization wave of the 1980s, there has been a feeling that the government cannot bear the burden of making these services available to individuals. In the case of health care, it was argued that, with escalating costs, the government could not afford to fund health care in the way it previously had. This was also related to the rising cost of pharmaceutical products, medical equipment, and investigative procedures. Higher standards of living and education also led to a higher demand for specialized treatment. Further, the cost of retaining medical personnel within government employment was rising. The government reasoned that with greater demands on health care expenditure, the private sector needed to play a more active role in the health care market.

With the growing population, there was also more demand for education. The government assumed a bigger role in the provision of education for the Bumiputera (as the ethnic Malays and indigenous people are referred to) in keeping with the spirit of the New Economic Policy. The New Economic Policy was dedicated to improving the economic participation of the Bumiputera and necessarily required more investment in education, especially at the tertiary level. This obligation meant leaving larger numbers of non-Bumiputera without avenues to pursue post-secondary education. There was a political issue associated with this trend since the non-Bumiputera were excluded from public universities. In order not to aggravate non-Bumiputera discontent in being excluded from public institutions of higher learning, the government permitted the establishment of private colleges in the mid-1980s. This has led to large numbers of colleges, branch campuses of foreign universities, and private universities opening up in Malaysia.

The government has also been reluctant to create social safety nets and to ensure adequate social protection for the disadvantaged. There have been complaints from non-governmental organizations, activists, and citizen's groups that social safety nets are not being given enough consideration or being implemented, but the government has not been receptive. Although the trade unions have been arguing that there is an urgent need for a minimum wage, this has been ignored because of the belief that Malaysia's competitiveness is based on cheap labor costs. Similarly, the government has shown no interest in introducing unemployment benefits, nor has it introduced any scheme that supports workers who lose their jobs in times of economic downturns. The poor state of public transport has also been criticized, but has not been the focus of any action. Indeed, there is worry about the state of urban poverty and concern that the welfare reduction caused by the current crisis has been understated. There is concern that official definitions of poverty do not do justice to current living standards and living costs.

Unfortunately, the prevailing government sentiment goes against the provision of social safety nets and social protection because of the following: it is felt that the burden on government expenditure will be increased, provision of social protection for the disadvantaged will draw resources away from more profitable allocations, and growth rates will be compromised if unproductive investments are made in improving social welfare. However, policymakers fail to see that there are valid reasons why the provision of public goods and social protection programs should not be viewed as a drain on government resources and a misallocation of funds. As the capability approach has shown, state provision of education and health care on a wider basis has yielded better economic outcomes (Sen 1999). In fact, expenditure on such programs can better help combat poverty, reduce inequalities, and induce pro-poor growth. The question of growth is particularly important in the Malaysian context.

Although retrenchments occur regularly in Malaysia and often worsen with crises, no programs have been instituted to protect workers despite the economic downturns that have occurred in the past (most notably the crisis of 1997). There are three reasons why health, education, and unemployment benefits must be given more attention. First, the costs of private health care and education are rising and are a heavy burden on the middle class. Second, in times of economic crisis, the costs of these items, which cannot be avoided, weighs heavily on consumers. Third, after retirement and diminished earnings, these costs can lead to debt. A survey conducted by the Employers' Provident Fund (EPF) indicates that individuals tend to spend all the funds that they are entitled to from their EPF contributions within three years of retirement. This means that those over fifty-five have diminished consumption patterns after retirement, but also are unable to finance any unexpected expenses after using all of their funds. It is important to note the rising life expectancy rates. It follows that individuals are likely to have higher savings rates, in addition to their contributions to their EPF. Thus, they would have lower disposable incomes during their years of active employment. Malaysia does not yet have a problem due to its aging population. With a more significant aging population there would be a larger decrease in household consumption and savings rates would be higher, reducing aggregate demand. A large aging population would increase household savings, reduce consumption, and so dampen the prospects for growth.

The argument that public spending on education, health care, pensions, and social safety nets does not foster growth and encourages a welfare state is not without flaws. Well-designed social safety nets can minimize the disincentive effects that have been wrongly attributed to social safety nets. There is also evidence that the disincentive effect is not as severe as it is often portrayed in public debates (see Grosh et al. 2008; Coady, Grosh, and Hoddinott 2004). More importantly, socially oriented programs have the capacity to generate multiplier effects due to the investment they require (as in the construction of schools, better public transport, and health centers) and this may generate growth. With doubt being cast on the US as a continued source of vigorous demand for Malaysian exports, attention must be directed at generating domestic consumption. This can only take place if individuals have higher disposable incomes. The measures that have been taken by the government (as exemplified by SP2) do not have the capacity to act as solutions to increasing disposable income in the face of what may be an extended decline in export growth rates.

Malaysia should revise the focus of its development policies. The Ninth Malaysia Plan (2006–10) and the Third Industrial Master Plan (2006–20) were conceived at a time when the global economic scenario was buoyant, and Malaysia's only challenge was to be more competitive in the international trade environment. The issues that are at stake now are different and more complex. Among the problems that Malaysia would have to solve are: the higher risk that individuals and households have to manage in the face of global uncertainties, the higher demand for precautionary savings due to the receding role of the government in the provision of public goods, creating opportunities for domestic investors, generating employment through industries and services that are directed at domestic or regional markets, and finding more profitable uses for foreign reserves or reducing the tendency to induce export competitiveness by undervaluing the ringgit.

Finding solutions to the issues that have been suggested first requires a shift in developmental emphasis to small and medium enterprises that produce for the domestic and ASEAN markets. This in no way implies that the markets of developed economies would be excluded from consideration. Second, the government should favor the building of infrastructure. Many aspects of transportation that have been ignored in the last decade should be revisited. This includes improving urban transportation and rapid travel between cities. Third, the government should re-involve itself in education and training, as well as the provision of health care and low-cost housing. There are three aspects to government expenditure in these areas: improving human capabilities over the long term; enabling the economy to benefit from ensuing multiplier effects through the construction industry, by the building of clinics, schools, and community colleges; and releasing savings for consumption purposes.

The claim is often made that government support for health, education, and social protection is not the best allocation of resources because it is a straightforward drain on funds, since these are subsidies that the government cannot afford. However, this is not the case. In fact, export promotion and FDI attraction demand government investment. The government must allocate funds for the maintenance of free trade zones and fiscal incentives, not to mention the subsidies that are extended to multinational corporations. The changed export patterns and the lower inflow of FDI will free some of the resources that could then be directed to improving capabilities and the social welfare function.

11.6 Recovery and development strategies

The Malaysian economy recovered quickly from the crisis. A comparison of some of the basic macroeconomic indicators clearly shows the speed of recovery. While real GDP contracted by 1.7 percent in 2009, in 2010 it increased by 7.2 percent. Similarly, unemployment (as a percentage of the labor force) was 3.7 percent in 2009, but it declined to 3.2 percent in 2010. Perhaps the figures relating to trade were most striking in terms of the swiftness with which they improved. Exports decreased by 16.7 percent in 2009, and moved into positive territory by 15.7 percent the following year. No less impressive, were the change in imports, which shifted from 16.4 percent in 2009 to 21.7 percent in 2010.

The macroeconomic performance in 2010 clearly indicates that the economy had recovered from the crisis of 2008. Obviously, the strategies that were introduced in 2009 helped bring the economy back on track. An examination of the strategies that were implemented at that time shows that they were largely fiscal (and expansionary) nature. But as was discussed earlier, the crisis pointed to the fact that the Malaysian economy would gain from a rebalancing of its economy. Indeed, the recovery was engineered by an increase in consumption, largely spurred by expenditure in infrastructure, on vulnerable groups, and by targeting re-training, skills upgrading, and the unemployed. While this strategy was clearly well-suited to achieving economic recovery following the crisis, it also suggested the need for a rebalancing of the economy.

Rebalancing the Malaysian economy is an initiative that is necessary for the long-term economic growth of the country. Since Malaysia has traditionally been an export-oriented economy that has depended heavily on the external sector to generate demand, the adoption of rebalancing strategies would mark a shift in developmental focus. An examination of the strategies that have been announced subsequent to the recovery of the 2008 crisis would reveal the intentions of the government to rebalance the economy. Two documents were launched soon after the crisis: the New Economic Model (NEM) (National Economic Advisory Council 2010) and the Tenth Malaysia Plan (10MP) (Economic Planning Unit 2010). The seriousness of the government in pursuing rebalancing—though not necessarily at the cost of abandoning growth through trade—would be expected to surface in these documents.

The NEM report, which was published in 2010, acknowledges the weaknesses in the economy. First, current FDI inflows have not yet returned to the levels that were experienced prior to the 1997 crisis. Second, there is appreciation of the fact that the manufacturing sector is largely export-oriented. Third, the report points out that there is excessive dependence on exports to the G-3 markets (US, Europe, and Japan). Finally, the report explicitly states that the "bottom 40 percent of households have experienced the slowest growth of average income, earning an average of RM1,222 in 2008" (National Economic Advisory Council 2010, p. 58). It is also mentioned that income growth has been strong only for the top 20 percent of Malaysian income earners, with the Gini coefficient remaining high for the urban group. Clearly, there are strong indications that the domestic market has to be further developed, along with a shift from the strategy of promoting export-led manufacturing. Also, the lack of emphasis on creating more inclusive growth is striking. Growth seems to have missed the bottom 40 percent of the population; and a higher level of consumption could have been generated if this segment of the economy had received more attention.

The NEM identifies achieving a sustainable, inclusive, high-income economy as its objective. Broadly, the goal of the NEM is to remove obstructions to the proper functioning of markets, and to encourage more competition. The reform initiatives (referred to as the "strategic reform initiatives") that have been identified are expected to encourage private sector participation; improve the quality of labor and reduce dependency on foreign labor; create a competitive domestic economy, strengthen the public sector, introduce affirmative action policies that are market-friendly, build infrastructure, enhance the sources of growth, and ensure the sustainability of growth.

Some of the strategic reform initiatives (SRIs) address the goals of rebalancing, to a larger or lesser extent. The second SRI (SRI 2) is directed at improving the quality of labor in Malaysia. A sub-component within this initiative seeks to provide safety nets for workers. This is a useful feature in an environment where jobs in the manufacturing sector are subject to retrenchments. SRI 4, which is concerned with strengthening the public sector, has elements that will be of use in rebalancing the economy. One sub-component of SRI 4 aims at providing for safety nets that will stabilize and correct instances of market failure. However, the NEM document assigns a "residual role" for these safety nets (National Economic Advisory Council 2010 p.130). SRI 5 relates to creating market-friendly affirmative action. This SRI has a rebalancing aspect in so far as it is targeted at the disadvantaged groups and attempts to increase the income of the bottom 40 percent of households. SRI 8 pertains to sustainability issues and it considers the preservation of the environment, green technology, and green investment. This initiative is valuable because it will encourage investment that will create a more environmentally friendly economy. It can be expected that SRI 8 will address pollution and waste disposal, to take two examples.

The 10MP, a blueprint for Malaysia's development for the period 2011–15 was unveiled on June, 2010, shortly after the NEM. The 10MP is based on five key thrusts: (1) creating an environment to promote economic growth; (2) creating inclusive socioeconomic development; (3) establishing Malaysia as a talent base; (4) creating an environment that enhances the quality of life; and (5) undertaking government transformation. The Plan places considerable emphasis on achieving high growth, and it proposes to do this through productivity-led growth and innovation, while safeguarding the interests of the vulnerable groups.

The 10MP has identified twelve areas, known as the national key economic areas (NKEAs) in the plan document, in order to drive growth. These NKEAs are: oil and gas; palm oil and related products; financial services; wholesale and retail trade; tourism; information and communications technology (ICT); education; electrical and electronics; business services; private health care; agriculture, and establishing Kuala Lumpur, the capital, as a world-class city, which will be both a financial hub as well as a tourist destination. The NKEAs does not indicate any intention of shifting from previous economic strategies. Further, the 10MP commits itself to the expansion of Malaysia's growth through trade. It proposes achieving this goal by expanding export markets, entering into new free trade agreements and engaging more aggressively in export promotion. The emphasis on trade, and the willingness to continue directing public expenditure on trade promotion and subsidizing foreign investment, shows that the government is not wholly persuaded of the need for rebalancing.

Nevertheless, there are elements in the 10MP that will help in rebalancing the economy. The government is committing itself to improving health care and housing in the country. The 10MP has planned that during the designated 10MP period 78,000 units of new, affordable public housing will be built by the Federal Government for individuals with a household income of less than RM2,500 a month. A Housing Maintenance Fund is scheduled to be established with an initial capital of RM500 million. This is to assist public housing residents to repair and maintain their units. The 10MP has made allocations for health care. RM637 has been allocated for building 197 new clinics across the country; and RM600 million has been set aside for four new and four replacement hospitals. The government also wants to improve the doctor-to-population and the nurse-to-population ratios by 2015.

Aside from health and housing, the government will participate with the private sector in providing the following:

- attractive living spaces, particularly in the cities;
- a comprehensive public transport system;
- efficient public utilities and essential services;
- improvements to the environment and conservation of existing resources.

These initiatives have their limitations insofar as they are not going to be entirely funded by the government. Instead, they will be the outcome of public--private programmes.

The overall texture of the policies that have been announced subsequent to the recovery from the 2008 crisis does not seem to suggest that the government will rebalance the economy in a directed manner. Whatever rebalancing that is being undertaken is incidental and in response to the social responsibility function that the government is expected to perform. A more targeted approach would have emerged if the government had taken rebalancing as a macroeconomic policy imperative. The main thrust of the recent policy documents is not to rebalance the economy, however some of the incidental features will contribute, if only to a limited extent, towards encouraging consumption, and in building a robust domestic sector.

11.7 Conclusion

Malaysia's response to the economic and financial crisis of 1997 was a set of unorthodox policy measures, highlighted by the use of capital controls. This was complemented by institutional measures, some of which were temporary, such as the establishment of organizations to restructure debt, while others were of a more long-term nature. Among those in the latter category were actions taken to strengthen the banking sector through bank mergers and initiatives for the phased liberalization of the financial sector.

At the center of Malaysia's development plans is an export-oriented growth strategy. This has implied encouraging and providing incentives for export-oriented manufacturing and the promotion of exports. Closely related are efforts to attract FDI and support the location of multinational corporations in Malaysia. In view of the nature of the current crisis and the economies involved, there is an urgent need to reconsider the basis for these policies. The crisis requires a rebalancing of strategies and consideration of policies that could change the structure of the economy. The crisis indicates that it is necessary to undertake deeper changes that can be viewed not simply as an adjustment due to a possible decreased demand for exports, but as an attempt to enhance human security, and upgrade human capital for Malaysia's passage into a more knowledge-intensive era of economic development. However, policy documents that have been released in the aftermath of the crisis indicate an attempt to pursue familiar policies with rebalancing being addressed in an incidental manner.

References

Bank Negara Malaysia (BNM) (2009). Monthly Statistical Bulletin. Available: http://www.bnm.gov.my/index.php?ch=116&pg=352&ac=4&eId=box1 (accessed July 23, 2009).

Coady, D., M. Grosh, and J. Hoddinott (2004). *Targeting of Transfers in Developing Countries: Review of Lessons and Experience*. Washington, DC: World Bank and International Food Policy Research Institute (IFPRI).

Department of Statistics (1995–2008). External Trade Statistics. Kuala Lumpur: Department of Statistics, Malaysia.

—— (2005–08). Quarterly Balance of Payment Report. Kuala Lumpur: Department of Statistics, Malaysia.

—— (2008a). Index of Industrial Production. Kuala Lumpur: Department of Statistics, Malaysia.

—— (2008b). National Accounts, Gross Domestic Product: Fourth Quarter 2008. Kuala Lumpur: Department of Statistics, Malaysia.

Economic Planning Unit (EPU) (2010). *Tenth Malaysia Plan: 2011–2015*. Kuala Lumpur: Economic Planning Unit, Malaysia.

—— (2011). Official Portal of the Economic Plannning Unit. Available: http://www.epu.gov.my/home#=e (accessed October 20, 2011).

Grosh, M., C. del Ninno, E. Tesliuc, and A. Ouerghi (2008). *The Design and Implementation of Effective Safety Nets for Protection and Protection*. Washington, DC: World Bank.

James, W., D. Park, S. Jha, J. Jongwanich, A. Terada-Hagiwara, and L. Sumulong (2008). The US Financial Crisis, Global Turmoil, and Developing Asia: Is the Era of High Growth at an End? ADB Economics Working Paper Series No.139. Manila: ADB.

National Economic Advisory Council (NEAC) (2010). New Economic Model for Malaysia: Part 1. Kuala Lumpur: National Economic Advisory Council.

Sen, A. (1999). *Development as Freedom*. Oxford: Oxford University Press.

Part IV
Lessons and Emerging Issues in Asia

12

Lessons of the Crisis for Emerging Markets

Barry Eichengreen

12.1 Introduction

Unlike other recent financial crises, the seeds of this one were sown in the United States (US or America). This crisis erupted in America in the summer of 2007 and the shock waves radiated out from there. The crisis was rooted first and foremost in lax regulation and skewed incentives in US financial markets.[1] Within a few months, however, it had engulfed the entire world. It thus has important implications for high-, medium-, and low-income countries alike.

In this chapter, I focus on the lessons for middle-income countries, what are popularly called emerging markets. Given the origins of the crisis a large literature has already developed around the lessons for the advanced countries.[2] And organizations from the International Monetary Fund (IMF or Fund) to the United Nations and the Overseas Development Institute have focused on the plight of the poor countries.[3] The implications for middle-income countries have received less attention, for reasons that are not entirely obvious. For a time there was the belief that emerging markets might decouple from the advanced countries and consequently that the crisis had no first-order repercussions for them. While decoupling proved to be a mirage,

[1] There is a view that the crisis was due principally to large capital flows into the United States, which lowered lending standards and fueled credit market excesses, and that these large capital inflows reflected the excess of saving over investment in Emerging Asia and the oil-exporting economies. My own view, expressed elsewhere, is that this problem of global imbalances, while adding fuel to the fire, was not the spark. And as for the origin of the imbalances, it takes two to tango; the inadequacy of saving relative to investment in the United States was equally part of the story.

[2] My own take is Eichengreen (2009a)

[3] See IMF (2009), te Velde (2008), and Griffith-Jones and Ocampo (2009).

important emerging markets, starting with the People's Republic of China (PRC), have bounced back smartly from disruptions to their exports and growth. Again this may have created a mental inclination to minimize the implications.

The lessons for the US and the other high-income economies are clear. They need to strengthen supervision and regulation and address agency problems in their financial markets. They need to finish repairing their broken financial systems. When growth resumes they will have to address their gaping budget deficits and rising debts. For low-income countries the implications are also clear. They need to continue investing in education, health care and other basic human services, and building the physical and organizational infrastructure needed to penetrate foreign markets. There may be no question of the desirability of more help from outside, but they must be prepared to do these things under their own steam insofar as the more slowly growing advanced countries may now be less forthcoming with aid.

But what about emerging markets? More than the fact that the impact on their economies has been relatively muted, there is a lack of clarity about the policy lessons. How, in light of recent events, should emerging markets modify their terms of engagement with global trade and finance? What are the implications for the supervision and regulation of their financial systems, given that supervision and regulation in the high-income countries, traditionally regarded as role models in international standard setting, have been revealed as deficient? Should monetary, fiscal, and exchange-rate policies be rethought in light of new evidence on what has and has not worked? Now that recent events have given emerging markets more influence over reform of the international financial architecture, for what specific changes should they push?

The crisis also reminds us that it is appropriate for pundits from "advanced" countries to show modesty and restraint when sketching lessons for emerging markets. But I won't let this stop me.

12.2 Assumptions

Anyone seeking to draw lessons must confront the question: are the structural consequences of the crisis permanent or transitory? Will large capital flows resume, or will countries face significantly greater difficulty in accessing foreign finance? Will the financial sector no longer be the supercharged engine of growth in the US, United Kingdom, and other advanced countries? Will there be a permanent rise in US savings and fall in PRC savings or will global imbalances return? Will countries that have held down currencies and domestic demand in pursuit of export-led growth now modify their strategies? Will trade grow more slowly? Will other aspects of globalization be rolled back? Or will this too pass? Will the new normal in fact resemble nothing so much as the old normal?

For purposes of the present analysis, I assume the following. The globalization of finance will be partly rolled back, or at least gross capital flows will grow less rapidly. The crisis is a reminder of the risks when the domains of financial business and of supervision and regulation do not coincide—when banks and markets are global but regulation is national. National oversight then creates scope for regulatory arbitrage. No one national regulator will have the information and powers needed to avert and resolve problems of financial instability. One can imagine a global regulator, but governments remain unwilling to cede this authority to a supranational body. And loosely organized committees and colleges of regulators, no matter how frequently they meet, are unlikely to constitute a fully-adequate substitute. Unable to significantly expand the domain of regulation beyond national borders, there will consequently be a tendency for governments to roll back the domain of financial business to coincide with the scope of oversight. The cross-border operations of banks and other financial institutions will be more tightly restricted. More stringent capital and liquidity requirements for bank and nonbank financial institutions will make intermediation more costly and cause lending, both domestic and internationally, to grow more slowly. Forcing trading in derivatives into clearinghouses and onto exchanges will limit the growth of instrument diversity and make hedging foreign exposures more costly. This is not to imply that capital flows will evaporate, but assuming that the experience of the crisis is not forgotten they are likely to grow more slowly than in the recent past.

In contrast, the globalization of trade and production will not be rolled back. The logic of global supply chains, production networks, and outsourcing remains compelling. The growth of trade in parts and components in East Asia reflects advances in transport technology—containerization—and what we have learned about containerization is not about to be forgotten.[4] The outsourcing of call centers and back office services to India reflects the growth of global broadband and satellite communication, whose advantages the crisis has done nothing to diminish. To be sure, trade requires trade credit and the crisis severely disrupted access to such credit, for small firms in particular. But this disruption proved temporary, and credits fully collateralized by trade deliverables are the form of capital least likely to be diminished in availability as a result of the crisis.[5]

[4] Another illustration is advances in air freight that encourage the export of cut flowers from Latin America or of Maine lobsters to Japan.

[5] In addition, the official community has stepped in with a range of initiatives to maintain the supply of trade credit.

If trade grows more slowly, this will reflect protectionist pressures bequeathed by the crisis. High unemployment fuels protectionist sentiment. Governments are loath to see the benefits of expensive fiscal stimulus leak out to free riders in the form of increased domestic spending on foreign goods. Similarly, now that governments have larger stakes in domestic auto companies, they may become less committed to the maintenance of a level playing field for foreign motor-vehicle producers. Evidence of murky protectionism there has been. At the same time, the fact that a wide range of countries has proceeded with fiscal stimulus diminishes the free-rider problem. The problem of high unemployment will pass. Governments have committed to completing the Doha Round.

Similarly, world migration will not be rolled back. Cross-border migration has grown rapidly in recent years, reflecting the strong growth of the global economy but also the aforementioned advances in transportation and communication.[6] The increase in information about living standards and job opportunities in high-income countries that has flowed to low-income regions through everything from earlier migrants to soap operas will not now evaporate. Nor will the transport and logistical support for future migration provided by past migration. Demographic imbalances between certain parts of the high- and low-income world will continue to provide a logic for large-scale migration. Again, the kicker is whether tougher economic times in the high-income countries will precipitate a backlash against foreign workers. While there is some evidence of this in Europe, it is striking that, so far at least, the crisis has provoked little hostility toward foreign workers in the US.[7]

Neither the US nor the PRC—or for that matter any other major economy—will abandon its tried-and-true growth model. To be sure, a situation where the US runs a current account deficit of 7 percent of gross domestic product (GDP) and absorbs 75 percent of the collective current account surpluses of the rest of the world is unlikely to recur. There are a number of reasons for thinking that the increase in household savings in the US will be long lasting.[8] With US demand growing more slowly, the PRC authorities will continue to boost domestic demand. The aging of the PRC's population will reinforce the trend toward lower savings rates. More US and less PRC production of traded goods necessarily implies an adjustment in the real exchange rate between the two countries. But these developments are likely to be more gradual than abrupt.

[6] See International Organization for Migration (2008).

[7] Thus, while the crisis occupied center stage in the 2008 US presidential election, the issue of undocumented immigration largely fell off of the electorate's radar screen.

[8] See Carroll and Slacelek (2009) for a careful analysis.

Finally, I assume that this is not the last serious global financial crisis in our lifetimes.

12.3 Implications for trade and financial policies

A first policy lesson is that a strategy of export-led growth entails greater risks than appreciated previously. The point is not just that global demand is volatile; it is that trade appears to be more elastic with respect to the cycle and more vulnerable in downturns than previously thought. The decline of exports in emerging Asia in late 2008 and early 2009 was nothing short of catastrophic, with volumes down by as much as 40 percent year-on-year. The consequences for GDP were dramatic. In Singapore, an extreme case, GDP fell at an annual rate of 13 percent in the first quarter of 2009.[9] Unbalanced growth emphasizing exports creates vulnerabilities just like excessive dependence on foreign finance. Evidently, trade as well as finance can exhibit sudden stops.

The destabilizing macroeconomic impact is even greater to the extent that a growing share of investment in emerging markets is export linked. In the PRC, investment in gross fixed capital in the tradable sectors increased from 28 percent of total investment in the first half of the 1990s to 36 percent in 2003–07. In Brazil the comparable increase was from 19 to 56 percent.[10] Falling export demand therefore means falling domestic demand at the same time.[11] Some shift from the excessive inward orientation of investment in countries like Brazil was clearly desirable. The question is whether, given what we have now learned about the volatility of export demand, the shift has gone too far.

Determining the appropriate policy response requires first identifying the causes of the recent collapse of trade. This is an important topic for investigation since the root causes remain obscure. It could be that the collapse reflected despair about future demand leading to an exceptional drawdown of inventories for traded goods. With evidence now that governments are prepared to intervene to stabilize demand, equally violent inventory corrections may be unlikely. It could be that trade was hammered by disruptions to the supply of trade credit. To the extent that this is the explanation, then enhancing the public provision of emergency trade finance is an alternative to altering the composition of production and investment. Or it could be that production fragmentation and the elaboration of global supply chains, for the manufactured products in which emerging Asia specializes in particular, have

[9] This is according to the July 2009 revision of figures for 2009 Q1. GDP in 2009 Q1 was down 10 percent of GDP in 2008 Q1.

[10] Bank for International Settlements (2009, p.75).

[11] Absent offsetting government action.

somehow increased the sensitivity of trade with respect to the cycle, in which case more far-reaching policy adjustments may be called for.[12]

Second, the crisis serves as a reminder, if one was needed, of the risks of excessive dependence on foreign finance. Countries with large current account deficits and external financing requirements were disproportionately hit by the crisis as foreign investors deleveraged and capital flows dried up. Emerging Asian and Latin American countries have managed their current accounts and external financing requirements more carefully in light of prior experience. But the same cannot be said of Central and Eastern Europe. With the benefit of hindsight it is hard to conceive how the Latvian authorities, to take the most glaring example, could have permitted the country's current account deficit to soar to some 25 percent of GDP. It, as well as other countries in a less extreme version of this same position, saw domestic demand compressed violently when foreign finance for their deficits dried up. Latvian GDP is forecast (as of mid-year) to contract by an astonishing 18 percent in 2009—this despite a rescue package jointly financed by the IMF and the European Union equivalent to 34 percent of national income.

East Asia and Latin America may have avoided large current account deficits but they did not avoid currency and maturity mismatches. The Republic of Korea's (hereafter Korea) problem as I read it was essentially a maturity mismatch: banks that lent long-term to shipbuilders who had receivables in US dollars (which would accrue when the boats were floated) squared their currency books by borrowing short, offshore, in dollars. When the crisis hit, their short-term US dollar funding dried up, setting off alarms. In Mexico and Brazil, in contrast, the problem was essentially a currency mismatch. While on-balance-sheet foreign currency mismatches had been reduced, corporations in both countries had increased their off-balance-sheet foreign currency exposure through derivative positions. These corporations bet against depreciation of the local currency by selling foreign exchange options in the offshore market and were smashed when those currencies depreciated by more than 30 percent following the failure of Lehman Brothers.[13] These are arguments for why regulators should require banks to more closely match the maturity of their assets and liabilities when operating in foreign currency and why they should regulate firms' positions in forward and options markets.

The crisis also sheds new light on earlier arguments about foreign bank presence. Contrary to worries that foreign banks would cut and run at the first sign of trouble, foreign banks maintained support for their subsidiaries in

[12] That Latin American trade, which is more heavily in raw materials, held up better in the crisis is consistent with the notion that recent sensitivity is somehow connected to production fragmentation and global supply chains, but this observation still does not identify the mechanism.

[13] See Jara, Moreno, and Tovar (2009).

emerging markets to a remarkable degree.[14] Cross-border lending fell less in countries with significant foreign bank presence than in emerging markets where foreign bank ownership was not dominant, other things equal. If anything, domestic banks with shallower pockets were more likely to cut back in the crisis.[15] Here is one place where Asian countries that have been reluctant to open to foreign banks might take a cue from Central and Eastern Europe. Of course, whether home countries will now be as permissive in encouraging banks' foreign operations, given the difficulties of multinational supervision, remains to be seen.

Other positive aspects notwithstanding, foreign bank presence also appears to be associated with currency mismatches. In Central and Eastern Europe foreign banks were the vehicles for extending euro- and Swiss franc-denominated corporate, home, and car loans to firms and households with incomes in local currency—something that added to corporate and household financial distress when local currencies depreciated. Austrian, Italian, and Swiss regulators, seeing their banks with assets and liabilities both in their own currencies, happily looked the other way. The implication is that emerging markets, while encouraging foreign bank entry, should at the same time strictly regulate their local lending practices.

These banking-sector controversies bring us back to the argument for local bond markets. Bond markets provide an alternative to bank intermediation. There is evidence that countries with better developed bond markets experienced less negative fallout from the crisis as large firms in particular retained access to nonbank sources of finance.[16] Opening those markets to foreign investors, on the other hand, appears to have been a mixed blessing. Korea, the East Asian country with the largest share of its security market capitalization held by foreign investors, also experienced the sharpest price and exchange rate corrections as those foreign investors, forced to deleverage, desperately repatriated their funds. Encouraging foreign investor participation is a quick way of jump starting local bond market activity. But recent experience suggests that quickest is not necessarily best.

12.4 Implications for monetary, fiscal, and exchange rate policies

The crisis also underscores the advantages of policy space. Stronger budget balances and lower debt ratios gave emerging markets more room for

[14] Bank for International Settlements (2009, p. 83).

[15] That said, they appear to have cut back less than in earlier crises, reflecting greater capitalization, fewer non-performing loans and higher profitability on the eve of the event.

[16] Or at least had been able to finance their operations at longer tenors, obviating the need to go back to the markets once conditions deteriorated. Bank for International Settlements (2009, p. 84).

countercyclical fiscal policies. Discretionary fiscal stimulus of 2.9 percent of GDP in the PRC, 2.0 percent in Russia, and 1.5 percent in Mexico (all averages for 2009–10) has helped to buffer the effects of falling export demand, an experience that stands in sharp contrast to earlier crises.[17] There has also been room for automatic stabilizers; budget deficits associated mainly with more slowly growing tax revenues amount to some 3 percent of GDP in 2009 in G20 emerging markets. Again it would not have been possible to allow for this stabilizing impact had fiscal positions not been strong on the eve of the crisis. Finally it has been possible to expand social programs this time to help shelter society's most vulnerable members from the blow of the crisis as a result of the relatively strong stance of fiscal policy going in. All this is a reminder of the value of keeping one's powder dry.

Economists still like to debate the merits of IMF advice to jack up interest rates in 1997–98, but given how the interaction of foreign currency obligations with sharp currency depreciation could cause an outright financial meltdown, it is hard to see what else the countries concerned could have done.[18] In 2008–09, in contrast, lower inflation, greater central bank credibility, and less foreign currency debt facilitated the more active use of monetary policy. Essentially all G20 emerging markets in Asia and Latin America had room to cut policy rates. The PRC, India, Korea, and Turkey all cut theirs by more than two percentage points in the six months from August 2008. The reduction in policy rates was even more dramatic, if starting from higher levels, in Colombia and Brazil. Some might argue that the different response this time reflected differences in the nature of the crisis or better economic advice. But given how emerging markets with less policy credibility and more foreign debts (Pakistan, Jamaica, much of Eastern Europe) were forced to raise rates, it seems clear that the stronger position entering the crisis is the main explanation for the different response.

This more flexible use of monetary policy has been facilitated by the shift from exchange rate targeting to inflation targeting in Latin America and, to a lesser extent, East Asia. During the period when external demand was strong, countries were in a position to allow their currencies to strengthen to prevent overheating. They could then allow their exchange rates to adjust downward when the crisis struck and external demand slackened.[19] Currency depreciation when the economic backdrop deteriorates is not entirely welcome—it is a symptom of the fact that all is not well—but it helped to maintain export competitiveness at a time when exports were needed most. Brazil, Chile,

[17] It can be argued that the PRC is in fact doing more than this insofar as the authorities also directed the banks to increase their lending for infrastructure and other fixed-investment projects in the first half of 2009.

[18] Other than slap on controls or repudiate their debts.

[19] Here the counterexample of the Baltic countries is informative.

Colombia, and Mexico all felt benefits from this. Asian countries, as is their wont, were more reluctant to allow their currencies to fluctuate, although there were sharp declines in the Korean won and Indonesian rupiah. The existence of coherent inflation targeting regimes in all these countries allowed exchange rates to adjust without expectations becoming unanchored. In some cases, there was the feeling that fluctuations were excessive, leading the authorities to intervene in the foreign exchange market. This is a reminder that even a well-developed commitment to inflation targeting does not entirely allow for neglect of exchange rate fluctuations.

In the longer run, this episode of heightened currency volatility will undoubtedly encourage more discussion of collective currency pegs, common currency baskets, and regional monetary unions. These topics are hardy perennials, and recent events will do nothing to make them go away—nor bring discussions to an early conclusion. The more immediate policy question is how to modify the conduct of inflation targeting. Recent events suggest that the standard inflation targeting framework, where the monetary policy instrument is adjusted in response to deviations of expected future inflation and the output gap from their respective targets, is seriously incomplete; it has to be augmented by attaching a weight to financial-stability concerns. Monetary policymakers cannot treat threats to financial stability with benign neglect or dismiss those threats as the responsibility of the regulators. But the question of how, exactly, to modify the conduct of monetary policy to incorporate those macro-prudential concerns remains unanswered. Until analysis of that question at least has more structure, central bankers will be flying by the seats of their pants.

12.5 Implications for the international financial architecture

Dissatisfaction in emerging markets with prevailing international monetary and financial arrangements is not new. Earlier instances where they were caught in the cross-winds were met mainly by steps to bullet-proof their economies, although there were also subsidiary efforts, mainly in Asia, to build regional supports. Insofar as the lessons of earlier crises motivated efforts to strengthen budgets, work down public debts, limit current account deficits, and more carefully manage foreign currency exposures, the resulting reduction in vulnerabilities and increase in policy space have been profoundly advantageous, as documented above.

Whether the accumulation of foreign reserves, the other approach to bullet-proofing, has been equally beneficial is less obvious. The one thing it has clearly been is expensive. In the PRC reserves of more than US$1,500 per resident are the equivalent of 25 percent of per capita income. Devote those resources instead to physical investment where they would conservatively earn a rate of return of 8 percent, and the PRC would accrue the equivalent of another two percentage points of economic growth.[20] Or devote those resources to consumption, and living standards would be two percentage points higher. In Korea, where reserves were the equivalent of 20 percent of per capita income on the eve of the crisis, the implications are analogous. The situation is again similar in a variety of other high-reserve countries.

The problem with the strategy, besides the fact that it is expensive, is that it is not clear that the reserves in question can be used. When Korea's reserves threatened to fall below US$200 billion, a very high threshold, the markets showed alarm and the authorities were unable to access them further.[21] To obtain resources with which to replace the private-sector dollar liquidity that had dried up, the Bank of Korea had to negotiate a US$30 billion swap facility with the Federal Reserve.

None of this is to deny the value of insurance, but it does point to the need for more cost-effective ways of obtaining it. Regional reserve pooling is one possibility. ASEAN + 3 continues to elaborate the Chiang Mai Initiative, in the spring of 2009 taking another step toward its multilateralization and agreeing to the creation of a regional surveillance unit. But there has been reluctance on the part of the participants to activate their arrangement; if they were unwilling to do so in the wake of Lehman Brothers' bankruptcy, it is hard to imagine circumstances under which they will. The core problems are conditionality and repayment: countries are reluctant to lend reserves without assurance that they will be paid back, and repayment can be confidently expected only when loans come packaged with conditions. But sovereigns hesitate to demand conditions of their neighbors since doing so threatens to poison diplomatic relations.[22] ASEAN + 3 would address this dilemma by outsourcing the authority to determine conditionality and disburse funds to a board of experts independent of governments.[23] So far, however, this remains a political bridge too far. And as long as Asian governments remain reluctant to cross it, their regional reserve pool will remain untapped.[24]

[20] One can argue that one should apply such calculations only to a fraction of the PRC's total reserves, bringing down the sacrifice in income. On the other hand one can argue that the rate of return to physical capital is higher than 8 percent.

[21] US$200 billion was the ballpark for the country's external financing requirement over the next nine months on the assumption, hardly realistic, that none of its short-term external debt or maturing long-term external debt was renewed (Huang 2008).

[22] And not just in Asia. The EU has outsourced the negotiation of conditionality for Eastern European countries receiving joint assistance to the IMF.

[23] See Eichengreen (2009b). Unwilling to do so, ASEAN + 3 instead outsources the responsibility to the IMF, which means in effect not outsourcing it at all.

[24] European experience is revealing in this regard. So long as the decision over lending and conditionality remained in the hands of national governments and central banks, there was a reluctance to provide extensive support. The creditor countries took steps to limit their obligations,

In Latin America, where proto-reserve-pooling arrangements are at an even earlier stage, Colombia and Mexico have contracted for insurance with the IMF, qualifying for its new Short-Term Liquidity Facility. But the problem of stigma at the point of drawing evidently remains. When Mexico needed dollars late last fall it, like Korea, arranged a US$30 billion swap with the Federal Reserve. Evidently the Fed is the true reinsurer of last resort.[25] That in times of crisis such countries are at the mercy of the US is explanation enough for their dissatisfaction with the prevailing architecture.

The obvious vehicle for efficient reserve pooling is the IMF. Insofar as balance-of-payments shocks are more highly correlated within than across regions, global reserve pooling has advantages over regional reserve pooling. And reserve pooling was in fact one of the original rationales for creating the IMF. Thus the reluctance of emerging markets to make freer use of the Fund is a serious inefficiency. The question is what can be done to mitigate the stigma associated with IMF programs. Knowing that they have more voice and influence in the institution may reassure emerging markets: hence the case for quota reform, for restructuring the executive board to reduce the overrepresentation of the G10, and for an open leadership selection process that might someday produce a managing director from an emerging-market country.

But it is not clear that such incremental reforms will cause such countries to flock back to the IMF.[26] Emerging markets need to specify exactly what changes in the structure of the institution they require in order to regard accessing its facilities as attractive. My own suggestion is not further steps to redress the political balance—since such steps haven't produced results when pursued at the regional level.[27] Rather, it is to remove politics from the Fund's short-term decision making by strengthening the independence of the management team and empowering it to make key operational decisions. The IMF could then provide emergency liquidity quickly, as did the Federal Reserve in November 2008, but without the sour taste of politics. Officials from emerging markets may not like this idea, but then they are obliged to specify what alternative reforms would render the IMF attractive for pooling their reserves.

notably in the case of Germany and the Emminger letter. Arguably, now that the decision to provide emergency credits has been outsourced to an independent entity, the European Central Bank, the response to crises has been faster and more forceful.

[25] As is the ECB in Europe. Since December the PRC has also moved to provide yuan swap facilities for a variety of trading partners. But since the yuan is inconvertible, these swaps are mainly useful for importers who would otherwise find it difficult, given foreign exchange shortages, to settle their accounts with Chinese firms; yuan credits cannot be easily used in other financial-market operations.

[26] Especially in Asia, where turning to the IMF is seen as political poison by any self-respecting government.

[27] Thus, the Chiang Mai Initiative Multilateralization involved a formula for the voting shares of the PRC, Japan, Korea, and the Asian countries that have not obviously made activation of that arrangement more likely.

Finally there is what emerging markets should see as the priorities for reforming the international monetary system in light of the crisis. Recent events have pointed up the problems with a dollar-based reserve system. Here officials from emerging markets may have become more vocal, but they have yet to adequately specify their objectives. Thus while both the PRC and Russia have been campaigning for an enhanced role for the Special Drawing Rights (SDR), they have also been taking steps to encourage the expanded use of their national currencies in their countries' own cross-border transactions, with their immediate neighbors in particular. Absent a more coherent message, there will not be coherent reform.

This flurry of initiatives is clearly open to alternative interpretations.[28] Mine is that the PRC's long-run objective is to enhance the yuan's own international-currency role, initially as a regional reserve currency and ultimately as a global reserve currency. (Russia and Brazil have similarly made noises about enhancing the use of their currencies in their respective parts of the world.) This is the best way of understanding recent initiatives designed to encourage firms in the PRC's southern provinces to settle more cross-border transactions in yuan as well as the yuan swap arrangements that the country has negotiated with various trading partners. Of course, making the yuan an attractive form in which to hold reserves will require not just that more of the PRC's trade be invoiced and settled in its own currency but also that it develop deep and liquid markets in yuan-denominated securities and that the currency become convertible on capital account. The PRC has a plan for elevating Shanghai to the status of a major international financial center by 2020. Financial-center status similarly entailing capital-account convertibility, this suggests the relevant time frame for the associated steps.

To be sure, the US (and the euro area) will not have gone away. This points to the development of a multi-currency reserve system not unlike that which prevailed in the first era of globalization prior to 1914. With multiple countries possessing deep and liquid financial markets open to foreign investors, there will be multiple forms and places in which to hold reserves. In this multipolar world, not unlike the multipolar world that existed before 1914, no single issuer will monopolize the privilege of supplying the reserve unit.[29] And the fact that there will exist more than one country with deep and liquid

[28] For example, the SDR initiative could simply be addressed at domestic constituencies which are not pleased that so much of the national patrimony is invested in US dollars; the SDR proposal is thus a way for the People's Bank of China to signal its constituents that it is aware of its fiduciary responsibility. Or it could simply be a way for emerging markets to signal the G20 that it wants to be taken seriously in discussions of international monetary reform.

[29] Thus, I am pushing back against the argument that increasing returns owing to network externalities are so strong that there is only room in the market for a single dominant international currency.

markets in a position to supply reserves will be a constructive source of discipline on policy.

Where then does this leave the SDR and other more radical visions for international monetary reform—more regional monetary unions for example? The PRC, being aware that the longer it waits the more likely its economy and currency will dominate East Asia, is unlikely to evince much enthusiasm for pooling its monetary sovereignty. And if the PRC is serious about the yuan as a reserve currency, then surely it can't be serious about the SDR as well. My suspicion is that talk of an expanded role for the SDR is a way for the PRC and other emerging market to signal their concern that they might suffer losses on their existing dollar holdings. They would like to see a Substitution Account-like facility through which they could exchange some of their dollars for SDR-denominated claims on the margin. Alternatively they would like to see the US offer a guarantee against losses on their existing dollar holdings. To the extent that their cooperation is needed on other aspects of the global agenda (agreement on reduced carbon emissions, for example), one can imagine the outlines of a bargain. But it is implausible that the international community would agree to relieve the PRC of the entirety of its US$1 trillion-plus dollar reserve portfolio, much less that it would relieve emerging markets as a group of their dollar reserves. And it is even more implausible that the SDR could supplant national currencies as the main form of international reserves in our lifetimes.[30]

12.6 Conclusion

When I am told that the crisis will mark a fundamental break in the structure and management of the world economy, I am reminded of Hurricane Katrina. By laying bare the extent of American inequality, and also of the inadequacy of the public-sector response, Katrina, it was said, would mark a fundamental break in social policy and the role of government in the US. But it was not too long before America slid back into its comfortable old ways. Analogously, there is now the question of whether once the crisis passes business as usual will resume.

My suspicion, noted at the outset of the paper, is that there will be no return to business as usual when it comes to the regulation of finance. The demand for more stringent financial regulation will be enduring. Leverage, cross-border portfolio investment, and transactions in complex derivative securities will be rolled back or at least grow more slowly than in the recent past.

[30] I develop the argument why in Eichengreen (2009c).

Consequently emerging markets (recently, limited mainly to Central and Eastern Europe) that have relied heavily on foreign capital will have to finance more of their development at home. As the domain of bank operations is reorganized to coincide with the domain of regulation, they will be less able to outsource intermediation to foreign banks. Countries like Korea and the PRC that sought to harness finance as a growth engine, turning themselves into financial hubs for Northeast Asia, will have to look to other sectors.

By comparison, the crisis will have a much more limited impact on other dimensions of globalization. The fundamental social and technological factors supporting the rapid globalization of production and trade in recent years remain firmly in place. Emerging markets need to continue adapting their policies to take advantage of this "real existing globalization". This means making their economies more attractive for foreign investment by streamlining bureaucracy and imparting labor skills. It means continuing to run sound and stable monetary, fiscal and debt-management policies in good times so that they have space to deploy those policies in bad times.

More controversially perhaps, I have also argued that the crisis is unlikely to occasion fundamental changes in the structure of the international monetary system—in either exchange rate arrangements or the composition of reserves. To be sure, the system will continue to evolve. The dollar will become less dominant in the international monetary system for all the same reasons that the US will become less dominant in the international economy. But, barring even more serious crises, this evolution will remain gradual, as has typically been the case in the past. Thus, the policy problem for emerging markets is to deal with the international monetary system that actually exists, not the one they imagine might exist.

References

Bank for International Settlements (BIS) (2009). *Annual Report.* Basel, Switzerland: BIS, 75 and 83–4.

Carroll, C. and J. Slacelek (2009). *The American Consumer: Reforming, or Just Resting?* Baltimore, US: Johns Hopkins University, Department of Economics. Available: http://econ.jhu.edu/people/ccarroll/papers/ReformingOrResting.pdf.

Eichengreen, B. (2009a). Strengthening the Financial Architecture: Unanswered Questions. Paper for the Dubai Economic Council Annual International Conference, October.

—— (2009b). *Can Asia Free Itself from the IMF?* Prague, Czech Republic: Project Syndicate. Available: http://www.project-syndicate.org/commentary/eichengreen6.

——(2009c). The Dollar's Dilemmas: The World's Top Currency Faces Competition. *Foreign Affairs Magazine* 88(5), September/October.

Griffith-Jones, S. and J. Ocampo (2009). The Financial Crisis and its Impact on Developing Countries. Working Paper no.53, Brasilia: United Nations Development Program.

Huang, Y. (2008). Measuring Asia's External Vulnerability. Citigroup Global Markets, October 8.

International Monetary Fund (IMF) (2009). *Implications of the Global Financial Crisis for Low-Income Countries.* Washington, DC: IMF.

International Organization for Migration (IOM) (2008). *World Migration Report 2008.* Geneva, Switzerland: International Organization for Migration.

Jara, A., R. Moreno, and C. Tovar (2009). The Global Crisis and Latin America: Financial Impact and Policy Responses. *BIS Quarterly Review*, June: 53–68.

te Velde, D. W. (2008). The Global Financial Crisis and Developing Countries: Which Countries are at Risk and What Can Be Done? Background Note, October. London: Overseas Development Institute.

13

Growth Patterns in Asian Emerging Markets: Implication for Global Rebalancing

Eswar S. Prasad

13.1 Introduction

Rebalancing growth in developing Asia is an important component of the overall global rebalancing effort that will be required to stabilize the world financial and economic systems. There is little doubt that global macroeconomic imbalances served as tinder for the global financial crisis, although there are sharply contrasting views about whether it was the proximate determinant. This debate is not merely a semantic one and takes on particular importance in view of a plausible scenario in which the recovery from the financial crisis of 2008–09 is associated with a resurgence of global imbalances, particularly if the rest of the world relies on the US to lead the recovery of global demand. There is also a divergence of views about whether global imbalances themselves are mainly the result of regulatory failures and undisciplined macroeconomic policies that encouraged excessive consumption in the US and some other advanced economies or a savings glut caused by inappropriate policies in the People's Republic of China (PRC) and other emerging Asian economies. In any event, rebalancing growth in Asia may be in the direct interests of the countries in the regions themselves, and could also be important via feedback channels that involve greater stability of the world economy.

To make progress on this subject, we first need to consider what exactly is meant by rebalancing of growth. This in turn requires a characterization of growth patterns. In Section 13.2 of this chapter, I provide an empirical characterization of recent growth patterns in the main emerging market economies and a few less developed economies in Asia. In the context of the discussion of global imbalances, a key issue is the role of domestic demand vs. foreign demand in driving growth in these economies. In other words, how much are these economies relying on exports to drive domestic growth. A majority of Asian economies have recorded positive contributions of net exports to growth during this decade. Over the period 2000–08, net exports have on average contributed about 1.5–2 percentage points to GDP growth in Hong Kong, China; Singapore; and Taipei, China. For the PRC, this contribution has averaged only 1.1 percentage points relative to average annual GDP growth of about 10 percent, even though exports themselves have climbed from 21 percent to 33 percent of GDP over this period. In terms of sheer volumes, of course, the PRCs trade surplus of US$295 billion in 2008 (6.8 percent of GDP) dominates aggregate Asian trade (excluding Japan) with the rest of the world.

There are other aspects of potential growth imbalances that also need to be considered. For instance, even if domestic demand is the key contributor to overall growth, there are very different implications if that growth is driven by consumption or by investment. In particular, growth in household labor income and the overall welfare implications of GDP growth can be affected by this composition. There may also be ancillary implications for employment growth, which in turn could have distributional consequences.

This analysis shows some striking patterns in Chinese growth during this decade, with investment accounting for half of GDP growth, the share of private consumption in overall GDP dropping to about one-third (the lowest in the sample of Asian countries), and employment growth amounting to an anemic 1 percent per year despite strong GDP growth. India and Viet Nam also have relatively high contributions of investment growth to GDP growth, with one major difference relative to the PRC being that these two countries finance part of their investment through net inflows of foreign capital (India's current account deficit is small relative to its GDP, Viet Nam's current account deficit is much larger). These two countries also register among the highest GDP growth rates of the countries in the sample other than the PRC but report better average employment growth rates than the PRC.

In Section 13.3, I provide a different perspective on the balance of growth that ties together the domestic and international implications by examining patterns of national savings and investment. An analysis of the evolution of saving–investment balances is of course relevant for understanding the dynamics of global imbalances. I also explore the different components of national savings attributable to households, corporations, and the government.

One of the interesting results from this analysis is that corporate savings have risen markedly in the PRC and other major Asian economies. In economies such as the PRC and India, household saving rates have continued to rise (as a share of household disposable income) even as their shares in overall national savings have declined. In the PRC, both national saving and investment rates have risen sharply during this decade, with the former rising faster, resulting in an expanding current account surplus. India's saving and investment rates have risen in tandem, keeping the current account in deficit but at a low level relative to GDP.

In Section 13.4, I use the descriptive data from the previous section to anchor an analytical overview of the relative importance of the different forces that could affect household saving and consumption behavior. I discuss and evaluate the empirical evidence (both from the existing literature and, more specifically, for Asia) on the following channels/factors:

- consumption smoothing over the life cycle;
- demographic factors;
- cultural factors;
- habit persistence;
- precautionary savings;
- inderdevelopment of the financial system.

In Section 13.5, I provide a detailed case study of the PRC using some macroeconomic perspectives as well as household-level data to illustrate many of the analytical points in the previous section. From 1995 to 2008, the average urban household saving rate in the PRC rose by 11 percentage points, to about 28 percent of disposable income. Saving rates have increased across all demographic groups although the age profile of savings has shifted to an unusual pattern in recent years, with younger and older households having relatively high saving rates (i.e. a U-shaped age-saving profile rather than the normal hump-shaped one). Chamon and Prasad (2010) find that these patterns are best explained by the rising private burden of expenditures on housing, education, and health care. These effects and precautionary motives may have been amplified by financial underdevelopment, as reflected in constraints on borrowing against future income and low returns on financial assets. Drawing on the work of other authors, I also provide some comparative perspectives using micro data-based studies from other regional economies.

In Section 13.6, I broaden this discussion by examining possible reasons for the growth patterns and analyze policy choices that may account for them. Specifically, I consider how cross-country differences in saving rates (both changes and levels) can be attributed to certain policy choices. The discussion will also be tied to the effects of policies on investment rates and, hence, on current account balances. Specific policies and domestic factors examined will include:

- the level and nature of financial development;
- fiscal policies—government budget balance, spending on government consumption and investment;

- tax and transfer policies, including the social safety net (pensions, unemployment insurance);
- level and composition of government expenditure (with a particular focus on education and health care spending);
- capital account liberalization (insofar as it influences government borrowing, external financing for domestic investment, and opportunities for international portfolio diversification);
- other relevant macroeconomic and microeconomic policies.

I conclude the paper with a summary of the main findings and a discussion of policy implications in Section 13.7.

At the outset, it is useful to lay out the scope of the empirical analysis in this chapter. The analysis will largely focus on the developing economies of East Asia, Southeast Asia, and South Asia. In particular, I will focus on the major emerging markets in these regions, including relatively more advanced economies such as Hong Kong, China; Republic of Korea (hereafter Korea); and Singapore. The macroeconomic data used in this chapter are mostly at an annual frequency and are taken from one of the following databases: CEIC, the IMF's International Financial Statistics, the World Bank's World Development Indicators, and Penn World. In most of the analysis, I focus on developments since 1990.

I complement the macroeconomic data with household-level data from some of my earlier work on the PRC (undertaken with Marcos Chamon). To provide a comparative perspective, I will also discuss results from other micro data-based papers on household savings in Asia and present some preliminary results based on the Asian Development Bank's (ADB) analysis of household data from the Philippines.

13.2 Composition of growth

In this section, I characterize some of the key patterns of growth in the Asian economies and also examine related outcomes such as employment growth. It is useful to start off with a description of the evolution of the structure of GDP from a national accounts perspective.

The median share of private (household) consumption in Asian countries' GDP has fallen from 66 percent in 1995 to 57 percent in 2008. The shares of government consumption and investment have remained relatively stable. The big shift has been in net exports, which went from a median share of minus 6 percent in 1995 to 4 percent in 2008.

Among the major Asian economies, the most dramatic shift in the share of private consumption is recorded by the PRC, where its share in GDP fell from

46 percent in 2000 to 35 percent in 2008. Singapore is the only other Asian economy where private consumption accounts for significantly less than half of GDP. In the PRC, the shares of both investment and net exports rose markedly—by about 8 and 6 percentage points, respectively—from 2000 to 2008. There is a significant decline in the share of private consumption in India's GDP as well—the share fell from 64 percent in 2000 to 57 percent in 2008, with investment taking up the slack. In Viet Nam, there is a surge in the share of investment, which is largely offset by a corresponding expansion of the trade deficit. Consistent with evidence from micro data that individual saving propensities tend to rise with income levels, there does seem to be a positive correlation between per capita income levels and the share of private consumption in GDP, with countries like Bangladesh, Cambodia, Pakistan, the Philippines, and Sri Lanka having relatively high consumption ratios.

Table 13.1 shows average GDP growth rates over the period 2000–08 for each country in the sample. The next five columns show the contributions of different components—total consumption (which is further broken down into private and government consumption), investment and net exports—to overall GDP growth. The last column of the table shows employment growth in the formal sector.

Consumption is typically the largest component of GDP, so it is usually the case that consumption growth tends to track overall GDP growth. On average, total consumption growth (private and public) contributes about 3.7 percentage points to GDP growth, relative to median GDP growth in the sample of about 5.2 percent per annum.[1] In other words, consumption growth on average accounts for about three-quarters of GDP growth among the 15 countries in the sample.

There are three economies for which the contribution of consumption growth amounts to less than 50 percent of GDP growth, well below the sample average—the PRC; Hong Kong, China; and Taipei,China. In the PRC, the contribution of private consumption growth to GDP growth is less than one-third, lower than in any other economy in the sample. At the other extreme is Sri Lanka, where consumption growth contributes about 4.8 percentage points, relative to GDP growth of 5.2 percent.

What is the relative importance of private vs. government consumption in driving GDP growth? Private consumption growth clearly dominates total consumption growth in all countries, with the notable exception of the

[1] I show medians rather than means in these calculations to mitigate the effects of outliers in these small samples. In any event, using means rather than medians made little difference to the patterns I discuss in the text. The reported averages treat each country as a unit; there is no weighting for country size.

Table 13.1 Contributions to growth and employment growth, 2000–2008 (%)

		GDP growth contributions					
		Consumption					
Country	GDP Growth	Total	Private	Government	Investment	Net exports	Employment Growth
Bangladesh	5.8	3.6	3.2	0.4	2.1	0.0	3.3
Cambodia	9.0	6.9	6.6	0.3	2.3	–0.4	5.7
PRC	10.2	4.1	2.8	1.3	5.0	1.1	0.9
Hong Kong, China	5.0	2.3	2.1	0.2	1.3	1.7	1.4
India	7.2	4.1	3.5	0.5	3.6	–0.3	1.9
Indonesia	5.2	3.1	2.5	0.6	1.4	0.4	1.6
Korea	4.9	2.5	1.9	0.6	1.0	1.4	1.7
Malaysia	5.1	4.6	3.5	1.1	0.4	0.1	2.1
Pakistan	4.9	3.7	2.7	1.0	1.1	0.1	3.1
Philippines	5.0	3.9	3.8	0.2	0.7	1.0	2.3
Singapore	5.5	2.8	2.1	0.6	1.5	1.5	4.1
Sri Lanka	5.2	4.8	3.8	1.0	1.3	–0.8	1.9
Taipei,China	3.6	1.5	1.4	0.1	0.0	2.2	1.2
Thailand	4.8	2.7	2.4	0.4	1.5	0.5	1.6
Viet Nam	7.5	5.3	4.8	0.5	4.3	–2.4	2.3
Unweighted medians:							
All countries	5.2	3.7	2.8	0.5	1.4	0.4	1.9
All excl. China	5.1	3.6	2.9	0.5	1.3	0.2	2.0
International comparisons:							
Germany	1.4	0.5	0.3	0.2	0.1	0.9	0.4
Japan	1.5	1.0	0.6	0.4	0.2	0.5	–0.1
US	2.3	2.3	2.0	0.3	0.1	–0.1	0.7

Sources: CEIC, IMF's WEO, ADB, and author's calculations.

Notes: GDP growth rates (in percent) are annual averages over the period 2000–08. GDP growth contributions (in percentage points) are averages over the same period, except for Cambodia (2000–05), Indonesia and Malaysia and Pakistan (2001–08). Contributions may not sum exactly to GDP growth because of rounding error or, in the case of some countries like the Philippines, because the statistical discrepancy is large. Investment includes private and public investment. Employment growth rates (in percent) are also annual averages over the period 2000–08, except for Bangladesh (only 2000, 2003, and 2006), Cambodia and Viet Nam (2000–06). India's employment data are only available for 2000 and 2005 from ADB. In international comparison, Japan's investment does not include 2008 number due to lack of data. The unweighted medians are the cross-sectional medians of the data in respective columns.

PRC. On average (excluding the PRC), private consumption growth accounts for four-fifths of the total growth contribution of consumption.

Investment growth on average accounts for about 1.4 percentage points of GDP growth. The PRC, India, and Viet Nam all get high contributions from investment growth, nearly 5 percentage points per annum in the case of the PRC and close to 4 percent in India and Viet Nam. Nevertheless, it is worth noting that only in the PRC is investment growth the dominant source of GDP growth. Another key difference between the PRC, on the one hand, and India and Viet Nam on the other, is that in the PRC the investment is largely domestically financed while in the other two countries it is financed through foreign capital (as we will see later, the PRC now runs a large current account surplus while India and Viet Nam have a deficit).

Another aspect of the balance of growth is related to dependence on external trade for growth. Here it is important to be careful about the use of the term "export-led growth". Even if a country has a very high level of exports relative to GDP, it could have a balanced trade account, which would mean that *net* exports were not contributing much to the bottom line in terms of GDP growth.

The penultimate column of Table 13.1 shows that, on average, net exports account for only a small fraction (0.4 percentage points) of overall GDP growth among the countries in the region. But this conceals a wide disparity across the individual countries. For six of the fifteen economies in the sample, net exports contributed 1 percentage point or more per annum to GDP growth. The average contribution of net exports to growth is negative in the cases of Cambodia, India, Sri Lanka, and Viet Nam.

It is interesting to note that, despite the popular characterization of the PRC as relying on export-led growth, the direct contribution of net exports to GDP growth has amounted to only 1.1 percentage points per year over the period 2000–08, which is only about one-tenth of overall GDP growth. The data in this table certainly do not look like prima facie evidence of export-led growth among the Asian economies in general, or the PRC in particular. I will examine this issue in more detail below.

13.2.1 *Employment growth*

A different way to think about the composition of growth is about how much employment is generated in the process of achieving that growth rate. The last column of Table 13.1 shows that the cross-sectional median of employment growth over the period 2000–08 was about 2 percent. The two economies with the lowest average rate of employment growth are the PRC and Taipei,China. It is striking that in the PRC net employment growth, at barely 1 percent per annum, was only about one-tenth the pace of output growth.[2]

In other words, the Chinese growth model, which has relied to a great extent on investment growth, has resulted in limited employment growth and a substantial increase in the capital–output ratio. It would seem that a growth model that generates high GDP growth but only minimal employment growth is not welfare-improving, especially in a less developed economy like the PRC that has a high level of unemployment and underemployment.

[2] Prasad (2009) notes that, over the period 2000–06, growth in secondary and tertiary sector employment averaged a healthier 3 percent per annum, but this was largely offset by a decline in primary sector employment.

This is a subtle issue as high output growth and low employment growth together imply a high rate of labor productivity growth. This is certainly welfare-enhancing, especially if the growth in labor productivity is largely driven by growth in total factor productivity (TFP). Indeed, the calculations of Bosworth and Collins (2008) suggest that TFP growth has accounted for a substantial portion of labor productivity growth in the PRC during the first half of this decade. Nevertheless, the low rate of employment growth is clearly a concern even to the Chinese authorities, as it has implications for economic and also social stability.

13.2.2 *Dependence on trade*

Returning to the issue of dependence on export-led growth, The average ratio of exports to GDP has remained stable at about 45 percent during this decade, suggesting a high level of dependence on exports. But the average ratio of the trade balance (or net exports), which is of relevance to the GDP bottom line, is in fact much smaller and on average about minus 1 percent of GDP. This is down from an average of about half a percent of GDP in 2007, reflecting the sharp compression of net exports from the region during 2008.

There is again a wide disparity among countries. For nearly half of the countries in the sample—Bangladesh, Cambodia, India, Lao PDR, Pakistan, Sri Lanka, and Viet Nam—the trade balance has on average been negative during the 2000s. The largest average trade surpluses are recorded by Hong Kong, China; Malaysia; and Singapore. The PRC's exports and total trade have increased at a rate substantially higher than that of GDP over the last seven years. In part, this is due to WTO accession, which boosted the PRC's exports to advanced western economies and also promoted its role as a processing hub for trade going from other Asian countries to the west. The PRC's trade balance has risen sharply, from 2 percent of GDP in 2000 to 6.8 percent in 2008, although down from a peak of 9.3 percent in 2007.

What is the right way to look at a country's dependence on exports? This is again a subtle issue. It is true that for a country with a net trade balance of zero the direct contribution of external trade to GDP growth is zero. Nevertheless, even for such a country, the spillover benefits from the exporting sector and, indeed, from overall trade volumes could be quite large. Such benefits could include technology transfers associated with trade, scale efficiencies in production associated with larger market size, employment generation in downstream and upstream firms (suppliers, distributors), and increased efficiency in production due to greater competition. From this perspective, the average trade openness ratio of over 90 percent implies that Asian economies are in general very open to and are in a position to derive considerable benefits from international trade. While trade openness has increased in most Asian economies during the period 2000–08, the increase in the volume of trade has not kept pace with GDP growth in a few economies such as Indonesia, Lao PDR, Malaysia, the Philippines, and Sri Lanka.

In the case of the PRC, the high level of exports to GDP and also the large trade balance indicate that exports have become an important contributor to growth, both through the direct and indirect channels discussed earlier. But this is a relatively recent phenomenon. As shown in Table 13.1, the average contribution of the trade balance to GDP growth since 2000 was only 1.1 percentage points. So there has clearly been an important shift in the Chinese economy towards greater export orientation and also greater reliance on external trade for domestic growth. In the next section, I will explore the global implications of this shift.

13.3 Savings–investment balances

The connection between domestic and global imbalances is through the current account, which represents the difference between national savings and national investment. It is of interest to examine not just evolution of the current account but its components as well. Figure 13.1 shows aggregate savings and investment balances for Asia ex-Japan. The aggregate savings to GDP ratio is the sum of national savings across the countries in the sample divided by the sum of national GDP for those countries, with both variables expressed in a common currency, converted at market exchange rates from domestic currency. The aggregate investment and current account data are constructed in a similar manner.

The top panel of Figure 13.1 shows that aggregate savings and investment have been rising in Asia since the early 2000s. The rate of increase in savings has been higher than that of investment, leading to a rising current account surplus, which rose to 6.7 percent of aggregate GDP by 2007, but then fell to 5.7 percent in 2008. The lower panel of Figure 13.1, which excludes the PRC, shows that that country is a big driver of these patterns in the data (its current account balance to GDP ratio was 10 percent in 2008). The aggregates for the remaining countries show savings and investment rising gradually and in tandem, with the current account balance to GDP ratio remaining relatively flat in the 3–4 percent range since early 2000 (except in 2003, when it spiked up to nearly 5 percent) until 2008, when it fell to about 2 percent.

From the perspective of the discussion of global imbalances, the excess of savings over investment represents the contribution of the Asian region to the financing of current account deficits of industrial countries, including the US. It is interesting to note that the total excess savings of this region amounted to only about US$100 billion in the early 2000s. Excluding the

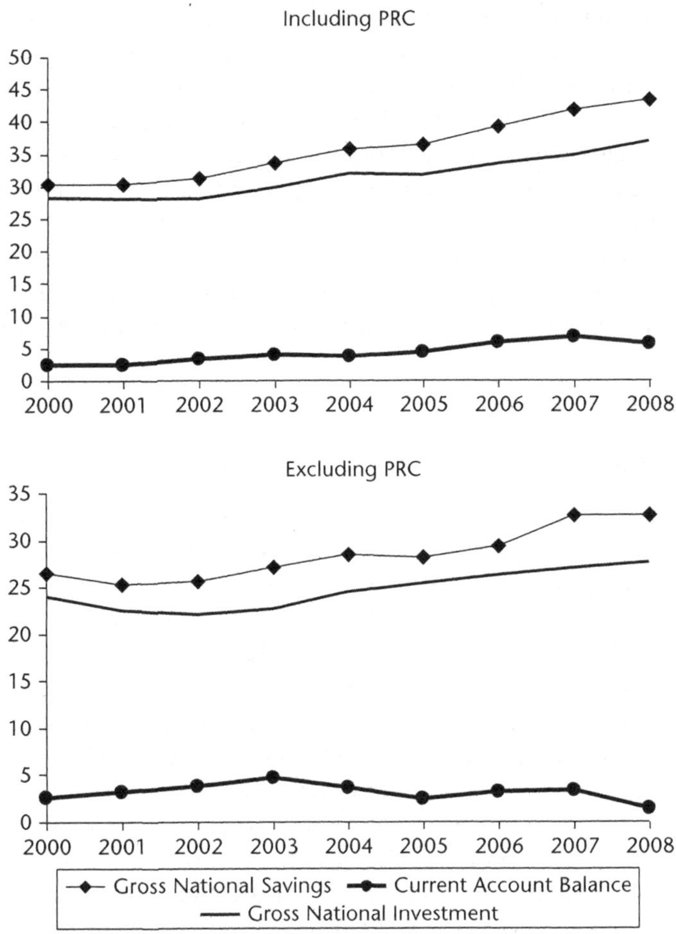

Figure 13.1 Aggregate saving–investment balance for developing Asia (% of GDP)

Sources: CEIC, ADB, and author's calculations.

Notes: This figure shows aggregate savings, investment, and current account balances for 15 developing Asian economies, expressed as ratios of the aggregate nominal GDP (in a common currency, at market exchange rates) for that group of economies. The 15 economies are as follows: Bangladesh, Cambodia, Hong Kong, India, Indonesia, Korea, Malaysia, Pakistan, the PRC; Philippines, Singapore, Sri Lanka, Taipei,China, Thailand, and Vietnam. Gross national investment for the PRC is calculated as a residual, based on current account and gross national savings data. This yields PRC investment slightly lower than the gross national investment data directly from the national income accounts.

PRC, this figure stays roughly constant in the rest of the 2000s, through 2007–08. The big surge in the region's excess savings clearly comes from the PRC as the aggregate current account balance including the PRC jumps to US$500 billion by 2007–08, driven by massive Chinese current account surpluses that hit US $440 billion in 2008.

National savings rates are quite high on average across all of the Asian economies. Even in this group, the PRC is clearly in a league of its own, with a national savings rate in excess of 50 percent of GDP. For most countries in the sample, savings rates have either increased or stayed roughly constant during this decade, with the exceptions of Korea, Cambodia, and Viet Nam, where the savings rate has declined by 2–3 percentage points. The PRC experiences the sharpest jump in the national savings rate, nearly 20 percentage points in an eight-year period. It is interesting to note that Viet Nam has a small decline in its savings rate but a spurt in its investment rate; these two factors together push its current account from a surplus in 2000 to a sizable deficit in 2008.

13.3.1 *Components of saving*

Since saving dynamics are a key component of the story driving shifts in current account balances in the region, I attempt to explore in more detail the different components of national savings—savings by households, firms, and the government.[3] Unfortunately, these data appear to be available only for a handful of countries. For these economies, Figure 13.2 shows the components of savings in the latest year for which data are available (upper panel) and for 2000 (lower panel). In the case of the PRC, corporate and government savings have both risen relative to GDP from 2000 to 2008. In the cases of Korea and the Philippines, household savings as a ratio to GDP drop significantly from 2000 to 2007–08. The increase in corporate savings in these two countries makes up for much of this decline, leading to a reasonably stable overall national savings rate. By contrast, in India there is a significant increase in the national savings rate from 2000 to 2008, with all three components contributing to this increase. Household and corporate savings have risen modestly and government savings, which had been negative in 2000, were positive in 2008.

In order to provide a broader regional perspective, Figure 13.3 shows the composition of aggregate savings (as a percent of aggregate GDP) for selected Asian economies for which data are available. Aggregate savings have risen from 31 percent of total GDP in 2000 to 45 percent in 2008. A striking development is that, by 2006–07, corporate savings have become the

[3] Household savings is generally defined as the difference between household disposable income and household consumption expenditures. Retained earnings (profits that are not paid out as dividends) are counted as corporate savings. These can of course be used to internally finance investment projects (if retained earnings of all firms in a country equaled domestic investment financed by those retained earnings, the effect on the current account would be nil). Government savings includes amounts that are used to finance public investment.

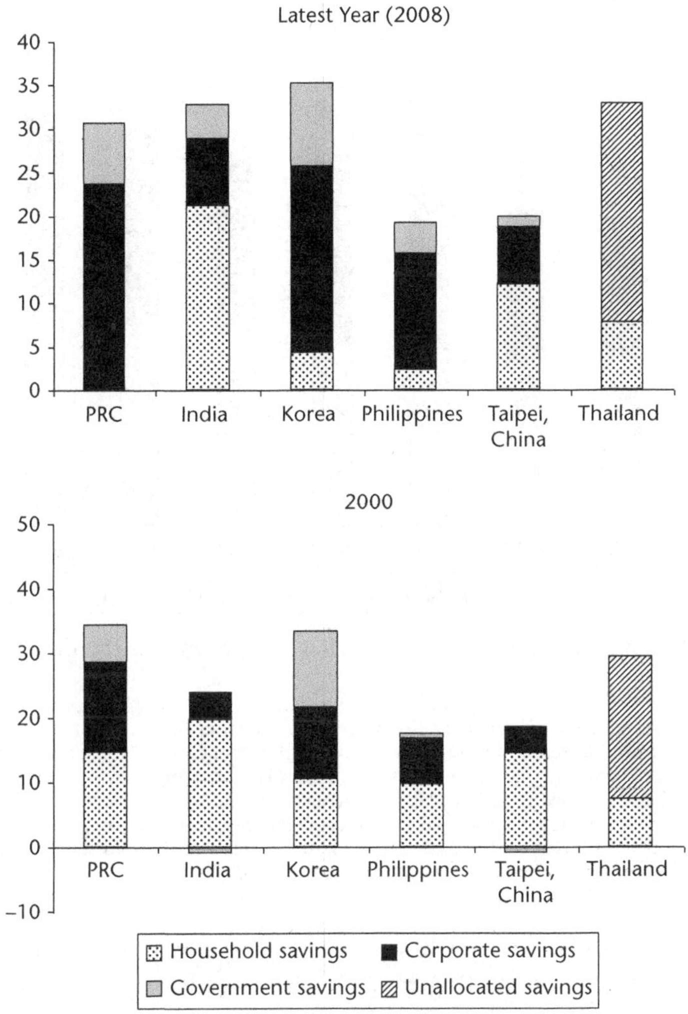

Figure 13.2 Components of national savings rates (% of GDP)[a]

Sources: CEIC, ADB, and author's calculations.

Notes: Korea's household savings rate is for 2007. The numbers for the PRC for 2008 are based on the author's estimates.

[a] Because of data availability: Figure 13.2 (latest year)—data for Korea; Taipei, China; and Thailand are for 2007.

dominant source of savings in the region, accounting for nearly half of aggregate savings.

The three economies—the PRC, India, and Korea—account for about three-quarters of GDP in Asia ex-Japan over the period 2000–08. In the PRC, the share of corporate saving has increased markedly in recent years, accounting for almost half of national savings in 2007 and a slightly lower share in 2008.

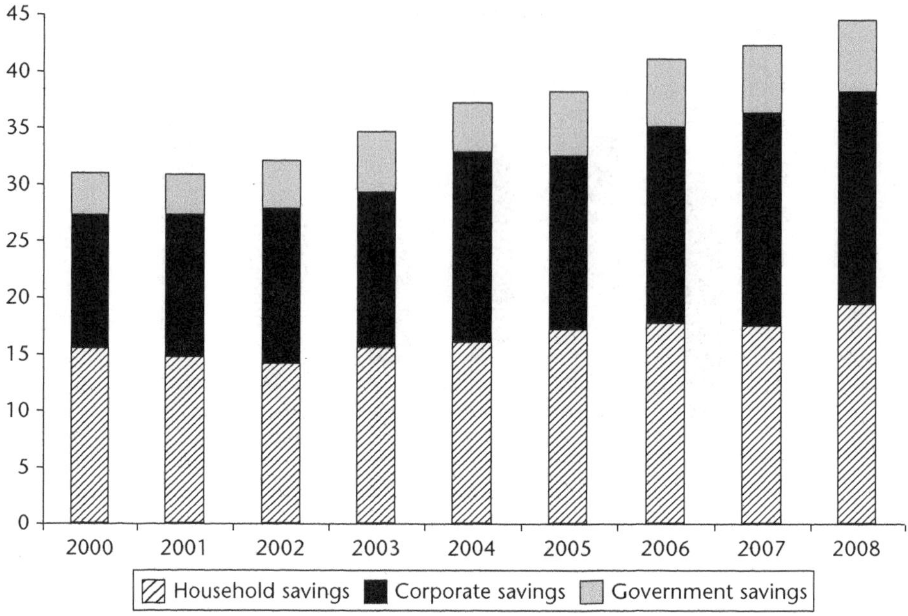

Figure 13.3 Composition of savings in selected Asian economies (% of GDP)

Sources: CEIC, ADB, and author's calculations.

Notes: This figure shows the composition of aggregate savings among a group of five Asian developing economies for which this breakdown was available on a consistent basis. The five economies are India, Korea, Philippines, the PRC, and Taipei,China. Savings in each category were expressed in a common currency (converted at market exchange rates), added up across the five economies, and then expressed as a ratio of aggregate nominal GDP in the five economies (also in the same common currency, converted at market exchange rates). The composition of the PRC's savings for 2006–08 is based on the author's estimates. Korea's household savings and Taiwan's savings in 2008 are kept at the same levels they were at in 2007.

Interestingly, in India, household savings have remained the dominant source of national savings, amounting to about 20 percent of GDP since the early 2000s. Corporate savings have become increasingly important in India over the last few years. In Korea, household savings as a ratio to GDP have fallen quite sharply since the late 1990s, driving down overall national savings slightly.

A different perspective on household savings is provided by looking at the savings rate relative to household disposable income rather than GDP. This is the relevant metric for understanding household saving behavior as it abstracts from changes in the distribution of national income between labor and capital (such changes would affect the share of household savings in GDP even if household saving as a share of disposable income remained constant). For the PRC, data came from the national accounts (which are incomplete and based on my estimates for 2006–08) and also from the household surveys, both for the aggregate economy as well as for urban and rural households separately. The survey-based measure shows that the household savings rate rose sharply during the second half of the 1990s and has continued to increase, although at a far slower pace, during the high-growth years of this decade. By 2008, it had climbed to about 28 percent of disposable income. The household saving rate in India has risen sharply over the last decade, from 20 percent of disposable income in 1998 to 3 percent in 2008. Indeed, India now seems to have the highest household saving rate among the Asian economies for which data are available. In contrast to the PRC and India, the household saving rate in Korea has fallen considerably, from nearly 30 percent in the late 1990s to 7 percent in 2007.

The cross-country comparison shows that there are substantial differences across countries in terms of the evolution of overall savings rates as well as the sources of national savings. The PRC accounts for about 62 percent of gross national savings in all of Asia ex-Japan in 2008. In terms of sheer magnitudes, the sharp increase in corporate savings and the evolution of Chinese savings clearly both play big roles in influencing overall savings patterns in Asia. Hence, I now look at the possible determinants of those two patterns in Asian savings. I start with a discussion of what could explain rising corporate savings in Asia. Since the PRC accounts for the bulk of overall corporate savings in Asia, it is useful to begin with a discussion of the reasons for the rise in Chinese corporate savings.

13.3.2 *Corporate savings*

Corporate savings largely reflect retained earnings, so understanding the profitability of firms is important for the story. Lin (2009) has argued that in the PRC the high level of corporate savings can partly be attributed to a financial structure dominated by state-owned banks and an equity market with restricted entry, both of which favor large firms. Similarly, Prasad (2009) notes that the repressed financial system in the PRC provides cheap capital (low real interest rates) to favored firms, most of which are large state-owned firms. In addition, subsidies on land and energy imply that there are massive state subsidies to these firms, which reduces input costs substantially. Combined with administrative monopolies in some sectors, this has led to high levels of profitability in some sectors, with the boom years until mid-2008 generating rising profits. In a fast-growing economy, retaining and reinvesting profits is clearly an attractive proposition when firms face an opportunity cost of funds that is very low.

The underdeveloped financial system also has a role to play in the high level of retained earnings among profitable Chinese firms. One of the aspects of financial repression involves a ceiling on deposit rates, which means that firms (like households) have faced very low or sometimes even slightly negative real rates of return on their bank deposits. This led some firms to use their profits to purchase shares on the equity market, which was booming and increased paper profits even more. Moreover, the lack of alternative financing mechanisms such as a deep corporate bond market has led firms to retain their earnings in order to finance future investment projects.

Another factor is that, until very recently, state-owned enterprises were not required to pay dividends to their shareholders or to the state, thereby creating an incentive for these firms to retain their profits rather than distribute them. Lin (2009) also notes that payouts from these large and profitable firms go disproportionately to the rich, who have higher saving propensities than the poor. This is another channel through which enterprise profits drive up national savings.

In short, the economic and financial structures in the PRC have not only played a role in the profitability of firms but also led to these firms retaining these profits rather than distributing them to households. There are similar phenomena at play in some of the other Asian countries, although in many of them the sheer pace of economic growth in recent years (until about mid-2008) has led to rising corporate profitability. While there are common threads, there are also country-specific institutional features that drive the dynamics of corporate savings in different countries. A more careful investigation of this issue is warranted in future work.

13.3.3 *Household savings*

I now turn to an analysis of the evolution and determinants of household savings in the Asian economies. Interestingly, even though the share of household savings in total savings has declined, household savings as a share of disposable income has continued to rise in the PRC and other countries. As the effects of the global slowdown permeate the Asian region and reduce corporate profitability, household savings could again regain their dominance. Since the PRC is clearly crucial for understanding developments in Asia, I will begin with a detailed analysis of household savings in the PRC and then discuss comparisons with a few other countries.

The rising household savings rate in the PRC is of considerable interest from two perspectives. First, this phenomenon obviously has a key role to play in explaining the rising current account surplus. Second, understanding what is driving the rising household savings rate is also crucial for devising policy measures to stoke private consumption growth. In the next section, I review a number of potential explanations for the level and trend in household savings.

13.4 Possible determinants of household saving patterns

In this section, I briefly review the main theoretical determinants of household saving rates.

- The life cycle permanent income (LCPI) hypothesis has implications for how savings should evolve over the life cycle for consumers who care about consumption smoothing (which is a natural implication of a concave utility function). The LCPI hypothesis implies that young workers should borrow against their future income, workers should have the highest saving rates when their incomes are highest in the latter stages of their careers, and retirees should start drawing down their savings upon retirement. This implies a hump-shaped age-savings profile. The life cycle model is also relevant for countries (in terms of stages of development)—in principle, less developed countries with relatively low capital–labor ratios should be running current account deficits and borrowing more. But this model doesnt seem to work well at either the household or national levels.
- Demographic factors, in conjunction with the life cycle permanent income hypothesis, can generate shifts in saving patterns. An aging population means that the dependency ratio—the ratio of the dependent population to the working-age population is expected to rise—which could drive up saving rates. This could be particularly important for a country like the PRC where the one-child policy is projected to generate a substantial demographic shift. There is limited evidence, however, that this factor is quantitatively important.
- Cultural factors. This is basically an explanation that people in some societies are just relatively more frugal and inclined to save more of their incomes (Zhou 2009). It is clearly not a theoretically well-grounded explanation but has been resorted to by many economists in the absence of other models that can convincingly explain the high levels of savings in East Asian economies. Formal evidence in support of this factor is, however, scant.[4] Moreover, it cannot explain *rising* saving rates in economies like the PRC.
- Habit persistence. This hypothesis implies that consumption reacts slowly to rising income because consumption may be influenced by previously established habits. This could explain why saving rates may increase during a period of rapid income growth. This hypothesis has

[4] It is obviously not easy to test this hypothesis. In an indirect test of the hypothesis, Carroll, Rhee, and Rhee (1994) compare the saving behavior of different immigrant groups in Canada and find no evidence of cultural effects on savings.

been used to explain why rapidly growing countries have relatively high saving rates (Carroll and Weil 1994) but the evidence in favor of this hypothesis is weaker in household data (Dynan 2000).

- Precautionary savings. Rising macroeconomic uncertainty and/or household-level risk can raise savings rates. High savings rates among households with young household heads may be driven by the need to build an adequate buffer stock of savings to smooth adverse shocks to their income, while households with older heads may be concerned about job loss and skill obsolescence. This could be particularly relevant for economies such as the PRC and Viet Nam that are becoming more market-oriented, and where the level of household-specific employment and income uncertainty has risen, even though average income growth has been high. There is considerable evidence that precautionary (or buffer-stock) savings is empirically very important in explaining the savings behavior of households.
- Savings related to financial underdevelopment. Recent research suggests that this is an important determinant of rising savings rates and it has also been identified by a number of authors (Caballero, Farhi, and Gourinchas 2008) as a driver of global macroeconomic imbalances. I now explore this factor in more detail.

13.4.1 *Role of financial system in high savings rate*

There are multiple reasons why an underdeveloped financial system could in fact lead to a high savings rate.

- In a fast-growing economy where the desired consumption bundle shifts towards big-ticket durable goods such as cars and houses, inability to borrow against future income streams could lead to households saving more in order to self-finance their purchases.[5]
- Lack of diversification opportunities for financial assets could in fact lead households to save more for precautionary purposes.
- Financial repression, which results in low or negative real interest rates, could lead to higher savings—the real interest rate elasticity of savings could be negative if the income effect dominates the substitution effect. This is sometimes referred to in the literature as the "target savings hypothesis".

[5] Jappelli and Pagano (1994) constructed a theoretical model and showed that this effect can be generated for plausible parameter values. They also document some descriptive empirical evidence consistent with this hypothesis.

All of these factors could be exacerbated in an environment where greater macroeconomic and household-level uncertainty—because of enterprise restructuring and other aspects of the transition to a market economy—increases precautionary savings.

13.5 Evidence from household survey data

I begin by discussing some results from an analysis of the determinants of the household savings rate in the PRC. I then briefly summarize results for other countries in the region. The Chinese case is particularly interesting to analyze in greater depth, both because the PRC is a very large economy and also due to its large current account surplus and dominant role in discussions of global imbalances.

13.5.1 *The PRC*

Chinese household savings, as a ratio to disposable income, has been on a gradual upward trend since 1990, rising to about 27 percent in 2008. This has been driven largely by the rise in the savings rate of urban households. The savings rate based on national income accounts data show a similar upward trend in recent years. The discrepancy between the household savings rates taken from the national accounts data and the survey data can be attributed to differences in data coverage (very rich households typically get left out of the survey data) and definitional issues (imputed rents on owner-occupied housing are treated differently in the two sources).[6]

The remaining figures in this section depicting household-level data are based just on the Urban Household Surveys, which are clearly more relevant for explaining the changing pattern of Chinese household savings, and are drawn from analysis done by Chamon and Prasad (2010). Household savings rates have increased almost across the board, except at the lowest part of the household income distribution.

In 1990, the age–saving profile exhibits a hump-shaped pattern, with the savings rate increasing with age, peaking at around age 50, and then declining with age. Such behavior is close to what life cycle theory would predict, given borrowing constraints that limit borrowing against future income and rising labor earnings over some range of the working life. However, the age–saving profile starts to shift to a U-shaped pattern in the mid-1990s, and this pattern becomes more pronounced in the 2000s. That is, young households save a lot

[6] Such differences between the survey-based and national accounts-based household saving rates are present in virtually all countries, including the US, where both sources are available.

more of their income than was the case a decade ago. Savings rates then decline with age with a trough around the 1940s, before rising as the household head approaches retirement age. This type of saving behavior—the relatively high savings rates at the early and late stages of the life cycle—is puzzling as it does not conform to the standard life cycle model, especially in the context of a fast-growing economy.

These simple age-saving plots of course mix together age, time, and cohort effects. For instance, different cohorts could have different saving propensities that affect these profiles. Chamon and Prasad (2010) use an econometric procedure to disentangle these effects, while explicitly controlling for demographic factors (or, more precisely, for the demographic composition of households in the sample). The results confirm that consumption tends to track income. The age effects show that income and consumption initially increase with age before steadily declining (after abstracting from the overall trend increase in these variables). The implied effect on the savings rate is similar to the savings rate profile as a function of age observed in the cross-section for the recent years (although the amplitude of the movements is smaller). It indicates that young households save substantially, but then savings rates gradually decline (by about 10 percentage points), reaching a trough around age 45. Savings rates increase rapidly after the age of the household head crosses the mid-40s and remain high even among much older households. The increase from age 45 to age 65 is about 6 percentage points. This U-shaped pattern of savings is highly unusual and is a striking departure from the traditional hump-shaped pattern found in most other economies. It is also inconsistent with the life cycle/permanent income hypothesis.

The cohort profiles of income, consumption, and savings suggest that younger and older cohorts had relatively higher income than those that were in their 20s and 30s in 1990. The resulting effect on savings suggests that the higher saving cohorts are those that were in their 40s and 50s in 1990 (saving about 7.5 percentage points more than later cohorts). This is an interesting result and may be capturing the fact that those cohorts may have been particularly hard hit by the reform process and bore the brunt of the increase in uncertainty associated with the move towards a market economy. The sharp increase in the savings rate in the later working years is also consistent with postponing retirement savings until retirement is near, which is the optimal response to rapid expected income growth.

Finally, consider the time profile of the savings rate. As expected, the (unrestricted) time effects point to upward trends in both income and consumption. Income grows more rapidly than consumption, resulting in a strong increasing trend in savings. Could this trend in savings be driven by the substantial demographic shifts that have taken place over the last two decades and that are likely to intensify over the next two decades. The estimated time effects explain a 9 percentage point increase in the savings rate from 1990 to 2005. This is a large figure, particularly considering the host of life cycle and demographic characteristics that are controlled for in the analysis, and accounts for most of the increase in average saving rates over this period. This suggests a limited role for demographic changes in explaining the rise in Chinese household savings over the last decade and a half.

Chamon and Prasad (2010) conclude that habit formation, demographics and the life cycle hypothesis cannot explain the rising household savings rate in the PRC in the face of rapid income growth. Instead, the increasing private burden of education and health expenditures seem to be among the strongest candidates for explaining the increase in savings rates, at least during a transition period. Health expenditure-related risks can largely explain the dramatic increase in savings rates among elderly households. The uncertainty related to those expenditures can also increase aggregate savings rates despite the higher consumption expenditures of the households suffering an adverse health shock. Their estimates suggest that the elimination of the risk of health expenditures exceeding 20 percent of income (through a catastrophic insurance scheme) would have lowered the median saving rate in 2005 by 3.5 percentage points, assuming no behavioral responses to such a scheme. Differences in saving behavior by households with children of different ages are consistent with expected future education expenditures increasing savings (or at least lowering consumption).

The effects of these shifts, together with precautionary motives stemming from state enterprise restructuring and market-oriented reforms, should eventually fade as households adjust their consumption plans and build up a level of assets appropriate for this post-transition environment. This buildup in savings could have been smaller if financial markets were more developed. Financial frictions also strengthen precautionary saving motives, and borrowing constraints can play an important role in driving up saving rates despite rapid income growth, especially among younger households. Finally, Chamon and Prasad also find some weak indirect evidence in support of the "target saving" hypothesis, whereby Chinese households have high saving rates because they are targeting a certain level of wealth and the real return on their savings, most of which goes into bank deposits, is small (and has recently become negative).

What are the implications of these findings for the debate about how to "rebalance" the PRC's growth by boosting domestic consumption? As financial markets develop, households should benefit from improvements in the ability to borrow against future income, better opportunities for portfolio diversification, and better rates of return on their savings. Another implication is related to government expenditures. The ratios of total and nondefense expenditures have risen relative to GDP in recent years. However, the share of social expenditure in total government expenditure remains low, which is not conducive to encouraging private consumption.

Improvements in the social safety net would pool the risks associated with idiosyncratic income shocks and health expenditures, reducing the need for households to save in order to self-insure against these risks. Increasing public provision of education could also lower household savings by reducing the need to accumulate assets to finance future education expenditure. Thus, policies that foster financial sector development and increased social expenditure could play an important role in helping to smooth consumption over the life cycle (Blanchard and Giavazzi 2006). This would moderate household savings rates and help to rebalance growth towards consumption.

13.5.2 *Other Asian economies*

In this section, I discuss the work done by other authors on selected Asian economies, including some preliminary analysis done by the ADB using household-level data from the Philippines.

In India, the household savings rate has increased over the last decade, as documented by authors such as Athukorala and Sen (2004). Households tend to hold about half of their savings in physical savings (including livestock, land holdings, and jewelry), with various forms of financial savings accounting for the other half.[7] Mohan (2008) notes that while gross financial savings of the household sector have risen in recent years, households' financial liabilities have also been increasing rapidly, albeit from a low base. He points to data showing that households' gross financial savings rose from 13.8 percent of GDP in 2004–05 to 18.3 percent in 2006–07, while their financial liabilities rose from 3.8 percent of GDP during 2004–05 to 6.8 percent during 2006–07. He attributes both phenomena to financial development as well as the broadening of access to the financial system. Lanot and Lawrence (2005) test the proposition that greater availability of credit due to financial development should increase consumption expenditures in areas where such credit is required, including durables consumption, education, and health. They do find a positive association of financial development variables with expenditures on durable goods, but the economic size of this relationship is small. Nair (2006), on the other hand, finds a statistically and economically significant effect of financial liberalization on household consumption.

Park and Rhee (2005) analyze data for Korea from the Family Income and Expenditure Surveys. They, too, find that there is a positive relationship between age of household head and the household saving rate, once the household head's age crosses the mid-40s. There is a decline in savings rates

[7] Moulick (2008) provides some qualitative evidence on how lack of access to the formal financial system affects saving patterns among poor people in the North East region of India, including the level of household savings and the forms in which savings are held.

post-retirement relative to the peak savings rates that are attained in the late 50s, but the average post-retirement savings rate is still quite high. These authors also conclude that increases in housing prices and increases in down-payment requirements can explain the rise in savings rates among households with relatively young household heads, a result that echoes the one reported by Chamon and Prasad (2010) for the PRC.

Analysis of the Family Income and Expenditure Surveys for the Philippines shows that the household savings rate has declined over time, consistent with the national-level flow of funds data shown in Figure 13.2. The age–saving profile shows an interesting pattern, with almost a monotonic increase in savings rates in tandem with the age of the household head, even though age–income and age–consumption profiles tend to be hump-shaped just as in most other economies. Remarkably, savings rates are highest among households whose heads are past the normal retirement age. Controlling for time and cohort effects using the same procedure used on the Chinese household data discussed in the previous section confirms that there is an almost linear relationship between the average household saving rate and age of the household head beyond age 46. From the age range in the mid-1940s to the mid-60s, there is a 4 percentage point increase in the household savings rate (from 12 percent to 16 percent).

Bersales and Mapa (2006) report similar results based on their analysis of the same dataset.

Deaton and Paxson (2000) show that the age–saving profile does have the traditional hump shape in Taipei,China. Data from Taipei,China also provide a nice natural experiment to test the impact of the provision of comprehensive national health insurance on savings rates. Chou, Liu, and Hammitt (2003) find that the 1995 introduction of the National Health Insurance scheme reduced household savings rates significantly (with declines of 9–14 percent in the average level of savings). In a subsequent study, these authors provide further evidence that precautionary saving is an important determinant of saving by Taipei,China's households and that the provision of social health insurance substantially weakens the precautionary motive for saving (Chou, Liu, and Hammitt 2006). Athukorala and Tsai (2003) conclude that the increased availability of social security provisions and enhanced credit availability tend to reduce household saving in Taipei,China.

Two common themes come out of the results from these studies based on household data. One is that a reliable social safety net, particularly the availability of health insurance, can reduce precautionary savings. This effect is particularly important for the elderly, who face rising life expectancy rates and rising health care costs. Besides, health care is a superior good and the demand for it is likely to rise as per capita income levels rise in the Asian region. Hence, the provision of comprehensive social health care can play an important role in influencing household saving behavior. The second theme is that financial development—as reflected in the availability of instruments to insure against idiosyncratic income risk and smooth consumption and also the ability borrow against future income to finance current purchases of durables, including houses—can reduce household saving and stimulate private consumption.

The effects of a rising old-age dependency ratio on average household savings are, however, not entirely obvious. Based on the traditional version of the life cycle permanent income hypothesis, one would expect older individuals and households with older heads to be drawing down on their savings to finance post-retirement consumption. This would generate a negative relationship between the elderly dependency ratio and average household saving rates. For instance, Kim and Lee (2007) apply panel vector autoregression techniques to macroeconomic data from East Asian economies and provide some time series evidence that higher old-age dependency ratios lead to lower saving rates. Can this be squared with rising savings rates across all age groups and the high savings rates of the elderly that have been documented using the household-level data? One difference between microeconomic and macroeconomic data is that the concept of savings tends to be different because of measurement as well as conceptual issues.[8] One also has to be careful in taking into account the factors driving family composition in different countries. In countries where it is the norm for elderly persons to live with their adult-age children, high household savings rates of households headed by older persons could reflect family composition rather than high individual savings rates of the elderly (this point is made by such authors as Deaton and Paxson (2000) and Szekely and Attanasio (2001)). Clearly, the aging of the population has complex effects on household savings.

13.6 A cross-country perspective on factors driving savings behavior

I now expand the discussion based on the analysis in the previous two sections to a broader set of countries. Figure 13.4 shows demographic projections for the countries in our sample. In virtually every country, the share of the elderly in the population is projected to increase, with particularly sharp increases in store by 2040 for the PRC; Hong Kong, China; and Korea. This could increase household savings rates in these countries in anticipation of rising dependency ratios and greater strains on public pension systems, although the evidence on the PRC in the previous section did not indicate

[8] For instance, the flow of services from owner-occupied housing is treated differently in the national income accounts than in household surveys. Household surveys also tend to undersample households near the top of the income distribution, who tend to have high saving rates.

that demographic factors have been a major determinant of trends in saving rates, at least in the recent past. Interestingly, the share of the working-age population is actually projected to *increase* slightly over the next three decades in Bangladesh, Cambodia, India, Pakistan, and the Philippines. This could have the opposite effects on savings behavior, other things being equal.

The household-data based analysis in the previous section suggested that financial underdevelopment can lead to a rising savings rate in a fast-growing economy. It is difficult to obtain a comprehensive measure of financial market development, so I resort to a rather crude measure—the sum of bank deposits, stock market capitalization, and bond market capitalization, expressed as a

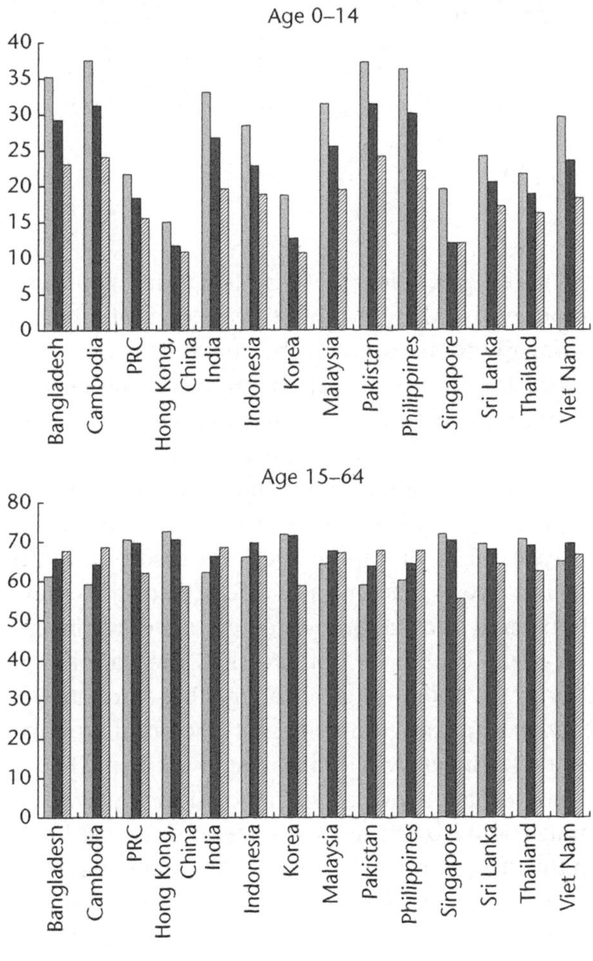

Figure 13.4 Demographic projections (shares of dependent and working-age populations in total population, %)

Source: World Population Prospects, The 2006 Revision, United Nations Population Division.

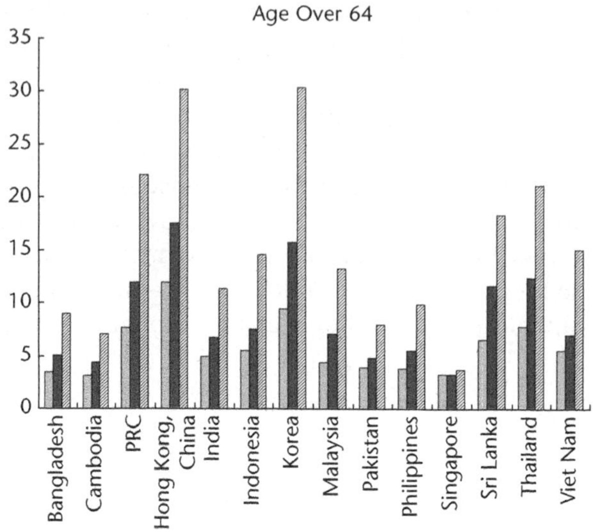

Figure 13.4 Continued

ratio to GDP (Figure 13.5). Clearly, there is a huge gap between the most advanced economies in this group—Singapore; Taipei,China; and Hong Kong, China—and all others based on this measure of financial development.

There is a more important aspect to financial market efficiency that is relevant for many of the features of balanced growth and savings–investment balances discussed earlier. Consider the case of the PRC, where capital is relatively cheap because financial repression and the government's policies have kept real interest rates low. Of course, this is not an entirely accurate picture of the availability of capital, because credit from the state-owned banking system has been preferentially directed towards state-owned enterprises rather than small and medium-sized private enterprises.

In addition to cheap capital, as noted earlier, the national government has subsidized energy prices and local governments have provided subsidized land. Given that energy and land are complementary factors of production for physical capital, this has created incentives for massive investment. This helps to explain the declining share of labor income in national income, which has fallen by almost 8 percentage points over the last decade, and also the low level of employment growth in the PRC. Also, as discussed earlier, state-owned enterprises in the PRC face the same low deposit rates as households and, until recently, were not required to pay dividends to the state or other shareholders. These firms therefore had an incentive to recycle their retained earnings into further investments.

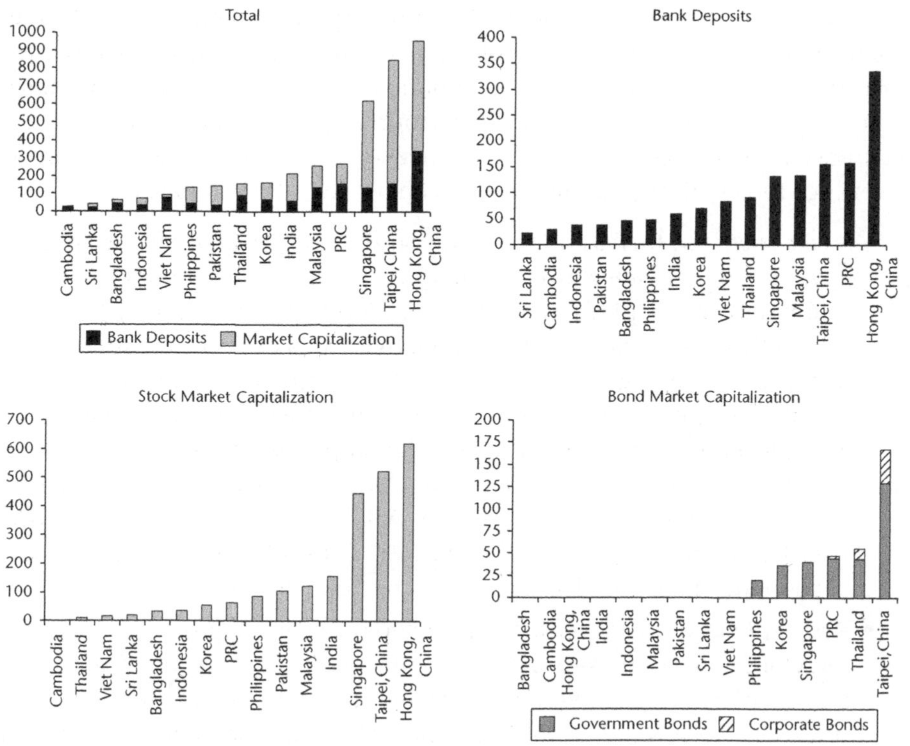

Figure 13.5 Bank deposits, stock, and bond market capitalization (% of GDP, latest year)[a]

Sources: CEIC and author's calculations.

Note: Limited bond market capitalization data are available, and here government bonds include Treasury bills and other public bonds. Singapore's corporate bond data are from 2007.

[a] Because of data availability: Figure 13.5 (total)—data for Cambodia and Bangladesh are for 2007, and data for Viet Nam are for 2006; Figure 13.5 (Bank Deposit)—data for Cambodia and Bangladesh, and Viet Nam are for 2007; Figure 13.5 (Stock market Capitalization)—data for Viet Nam are for 2007; Figure 13.5 (Bond market Capitalization)—data for PRC are for 2007.

Indeed, given the subsidies mentioned above, it made sense for firms to self-finance even marginally productive projects.

Thus, an inefficient financial system can create a variety of imbalances that discourage consumption growth and hold down employment growth.

13.7 Policy implications

The analysis in this chapter suggests a few avenues that could be pursued to rebalance growth in various dimensions that include promoting domestic demand growth (especially private consumption growth), reducing the dependence on external demand, and raising employment growth. I list below some preliminary suggestions for policymakers in Asian countries to rebalance growth as well as promote overall economic welfare. The relative importance of each of these recommendations of course depends on country-specific circumstances and constraints. Nevertheless, the points below have broad relevance for a majority of the countries analyzed in this chapter.

- *Social safety net.* Increasing spending on the social safety net and other government insurance mechanisms could help reduce precautionary motives for saving. This would help boost private consumption, especially in countries that have a relatively weak safety net and that are undergoing a change from a command economy to a more market-oriented one, which invariably involves an increase in employment risks at the level of the individual worker. Better provision and delivery of health care for older citizens is important to reduce the need for them to save more in order to self-insure. This will become increasingly relevant with lengthening life spans, the increasing cost of health care and rising dependency ratios of older persons to working-age persons.
- *Financial market development.* This includes the development of a broader array of financial markets including insurance, corporate bond markets, and a variety of "plain vanilla" derivates markets (such as currency futures). The objective would be to provide a larger set of instruments for saving and borrowing, which would allow for more efficient risk sharing and intertemporal smoothing of consumption. It would also allow for more diversification opportunities across different types of income (labor vs. financial income) and also across different types of assets. Firms would also need to rely less on retained earnings for financing their investment if a broader set of financing opportunities were available.
- *Improving financial system efficiency.* A better-functioning and well-regulated financial system could increase productive efficiency of capital by channeling funds into more productive uses, providing credit to corporations and entrepreneurs, and enabling more efficient risk sharing which would promote entrepreneurial activity. This would also help promote employment growth.
- *Financial inclusion.* An important aspect of financial development for many emerging markets, including the PRC and India, is that of financial inclusion since a large segment of the population, particularly in rural areas, does not have access to the formal financial system. This has implications not just for consumption and saving patterns, but also for economic welfare more broadly. Access to a formal financial system would generate better returns on savings and reduce the incentives for

households to save more in order to self-insure against health and other risks.[9] It would also give small-scale entrepreneurs the opportunity to raise funds without having to create and use their own savings.

- *Exchange rate policies.* In some countries that have tightly managed exchange rates, a more flexible exchange rate regime that allows the exchange rate to respond to productivity growth differentials relative to trading partner countries could generate positive wealth effects through favorable terms of trade changes. This would encourage private consumption and also reduce the reliance on foreign demand. A more flexible exchange rate, by creating space for more independent monetary policy, could also generate more macroeconomic stability, which in turn would have a more favorable effect on both output and employment growth.

There is no magic bullet for countries trying to rebalance growth away from an excessive dependence on exports and/or investment. A number of complementary policy measures, as laid out above, will be required to start and maintain momentum towards the objective of more balanced growth driven by domestic demand, which will not just prove beneficial for the concerned countries that take these steps but also help in promoting the stability of the international financial system.

References

Athukorala, P.-C. and K. Sen (2004). The Determinants of Private Saving in India, *World Development* 32(3): 491–503.

Athukorala, P.-C. and P.-L. Tsai (2003). Determinants of Household Saving in Taiwan: Growth, Demography and Public Policy, *Journal of Development Studies* 39(5): 65–88.

Bersales, L. G. S. and D. S. Mapa (2006). Patterns and Determinants of Household Saving in the Philippines, USAID/Philippines OEDG Paper. Available: http://www.stat.upd.edu.ph/papersmapa/TECHNICAL_PAPER2_BSP%20Saving%20Study%20Report%20New.pdf.

Blanchard, O. J. and F. Giavazzi (2006). Rebalancing Growth in China: A Three-Handed Approach, *China and the World Economy* 14(4): 1–20.

Bosworth, B. and S. M. Collins (2008). Accounting for Growth: Comparing China and India, *Journal of Economic Perspectives* 22(1): 45–66.

[9] Doorslaer et al. (2006) note that in most developing countries out-of-pocket payments continue to be the most important means of financing health care expenses. They argue that out-of-pocket payments on health care expose households to substantial financial risk and, sometimes, can result in impoverishment. The implication is that the absence of adequate government-financed health care can be a powerful incentive to increase private saving, especially with a greater need for health care in aging populations with lengthening life spans.

Caballero, R. J., E. Farhi, and P. Gourinchas (2008). Financial Crash, Commodity Prices, and Global Imbalances, *Brookings Papers on Economic Activity* Fall: 1–55.

Carroll, C. and D. Weil (1994). Saving and Growth: A Reinterpretation, *Carnegie-Rochester Conference Series on Public Policy* 40: 133–92.

Carroll, C., B.-K. Rhee, and C. Rhee (1994). Are There Cultural Effects on Saving? Some Cross-Sectional Evidence, *Quarterly Journal of Economics* 109(3): 685–99.

Chamon, M. and E. Prasad (2010). "Why Are Saving Rates of Urban Households in China Rising?" *American Economic Journal: Macroeconomics*, 2(1): 93–130.

Chou, S.-Y., J.-T. Liu, and J. K. Hammitt (2003). National Health Insurance and Precautionary Saving: Evidence from Taiwan, *Journal of Public Economics* 87: 1873–94.

—— (2006). Households Precautionary Behaviors—the Effects of the Introduction of National Health Insurance in Taiwan, *Review of Economics of the Household* 4: 395–421.

Deaton, A. and C. Paxson (2000). Growth and Savings among Individuals and Households, *The Review of Economics and Statistics* 82(2): 212–25.

Doorslaer Van, E., O. O'Donnell, R. Rannan-Eliya et al. (20 authors) (2006). Effects of Payments for Health Care on Poverty Estimates in 11 Countries in Asia: An Analysis of Household Survey Sata, *The Lancet* 368(9544): 1357–64.

Dynan, K. (2000). Habit Formation and Consumer Preferences: Evidence from Panel Data, *American Economic Review* 90(3): 391–406.

Jappelli, T. and M. Pagano (1994). Saving, Growth, and Liquidity Constraints, *The Quarterly Journal of Economics* 109(1): 83–109.

Kim, S. and J.-W. Lee (2007). Demographic Changes, Saving, and Current Account in East Asia, *Asian Economic Papers* 6(2): 22–53.

Lanot, G. and P. Lawrence (2005). Financial Liberalization and Household Financial Behaviour in India, Keele Economics Research Papers from Centre for Economic Research, No. KERP 2005/15, Keele University.

Lin, J. (2009). Paradigm Shift on Both Sides of the Global Imbalance, Presentation at the Brookings-Caijing Conference in Washington, DC, January 2009.

Mohan, R. (2008). The Growth Record of the Indian Economy, 1950–2008: A Story of Sustained Savings and Investment, Keynote Address at Reserve Bank of India at the Conference Growth and Macroeconomic Issues and Challenges in India organized by the Institute of Economic Growth, New Delhi. Available: http://www.bis.org/review/r080218c.pdf.

Moulick, M. (2008). Understanding and Responding to the Savings Behavior of Poor People in the North East of India, USAid, microREPORT, No. 103. Available: http://www.microlinks.org/ev_en.php?ID%20=%2024906_201&ID2%20=%20DO_TOPIC.

Nair, L. R. (2006). Financial Sector Liberalization and Household Savings in India, Indian Institute of Capital Markets 9th Capital Markets Conference Paper. Available: http://ssrn.com/abstract%20=%20876879.

Park, D. and C. Rhee (2005). Saving, Growth, and Demographic Change in Korea, *Journal of Japanese International Economies* 19: 394–413.

Prasad, E. (2009). Is the Chinese Growth Miracle Built to Last? *China Economic Review* 20(3): 103–23.

Szekely, M. and O. Attanasio (2001). Household Saving in Developing Countries: Inequality, Demographics and All That: How Different are Latin America and South East Asia? IADB Research Working Paper No. 427.

Zhou, X. (2009). On Savings Ratio, Note posted on the website of the People's Bank of China, March 24.

14

International Reserves and Swap Lines in Times of Financial Distress

Joshua Aizenman

14.1 Introduction

In this chapter, I discuss the implications of the ongoing global liquidity crisis on developing countries' use of precautionary measures aimed at mitigating their exposure to financial crises. The global liquidity crisis raises questions about the degree to which a large hoarding of international reserves (IR) suffices to deal with the financial exposure of emerging markets (EMs) in an efficient way. The crisis also renews the debate about the desirability of unfettered financial integration of developing countries. I provide an overview of this debate, and assess possible future options.

Over the last two decades, emerging countries have opted for increasing financial integration. Mundell-Fleming's "trilemma" implies that they must either forgo exchange-rate stability (if they wish to preserve a degree of monetary independence) or forgo monetary independence (if they wish to preserve exchange rate stability). Aizenman, Chinn, and Ito (2008) found that emerging countries have moved towards greater exchange-rate flexibility and deeper financial integration buffered with sizable reserve holdings. Both trends are more pronounced for the EMs than for the non-emerging developing countries. The data also point to differential trends among emerging Asia and emerging Latin America (LATAM). Figure 14.1 applies "Diamond charts" for emerging Asia and emerging LATAM, tracing the changing patterns of the trilemma configurations. Each of the charts shows the levels of the three trilemma policy goals and IR (as a ratio to GDP). The origin in the charts is normalized so as to represent zero monetary independence, pure float, zero international reserves, and financial autarky. The trilemma variables are normalized to a range of zero to one, where one corresponds to achieving the desired policy goal. A comparison of the regions reveals that emerging LATAM

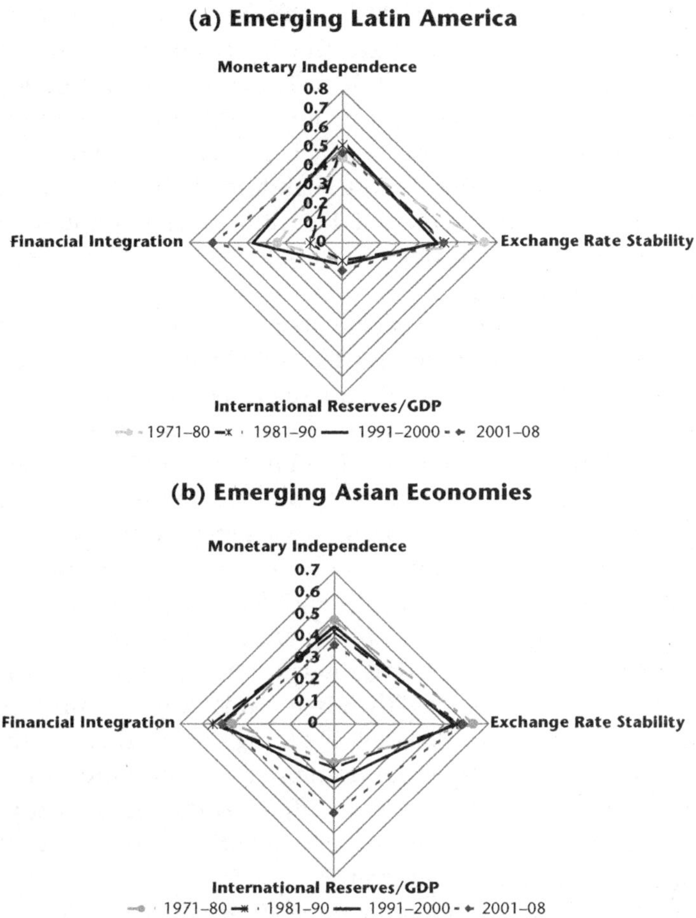

Figure 14.1 Regional patterns of the trilemma and IR configurations in EMs[a]

Source: Aizenman, Chinn, and Ito (2008).

Notes: "Emerging Latin America" includes Argentina; Brazil; Chile; Colombia; Ecuador; Jamaica; Mexico; Peru; Trinidad and Tobago; and Venezuela.
"Emerging Asian Economies" include the PRC; Hong Kong; China; Indonesia; Korea; Malaysia; Philippines; Singapore; and Thailand.

[a] Monetary Independence is defined as: $MI = 0.5[1 - corr(i_j, i_j)]$, where i refers to home countries and j to the base country. Exchange Rate Stability (ERS) is defined as $ERS = 0.01/[0.01 + stdev(\Delta \log(exch_rate))]$. II also apply a threshold to the exchange rate movement as has been done in the literature. Financial Openness/Integration is the Chinn and Ito index, which is based on information regarding restrictions in the IMF's Annual Report on Exchange Arrangements and Exchange Restrictions (AREAER). For further details see Aizenman, Chinn, and Ito (2008).

moved much more rapidly towards financial integration than emerging Asia. Emerging Asia opted to hoard more IR than emerging LATAM. Both blocks moved toward greater exchange rate flexibility. These trends have enabled them to retain a fair degree of monetary autonomy without hampering financial integration—a sort of "middle-ground Trilemma's configuration".

Indeed, the response of many EMs to the current crisis fits the "middle ground" trend—allowing real exchange rate depreciation mitigated by selling IR to take the first brunt of the adjustment. The absence of deeper adjustment in EMs (so far) as compared to the severe impact of the crisis in industrialized economies, testifies to the degree to which proper management of the trilemma's middle ground enables a softer landing in the aftermath of major external events. The combination of hoarding large stockpiles of IR and the growing exchange rate flexibility facilitated adjustment to deleveraging pressure induced by the crisis.

In Section 14.2, I outline the debate about desirable adjustment of EMs during the first phase of the ongoing crisis. I start by discussing the experience of the Republic of Korea (hereafter Korea)—a prime example of a country that opted for deeper financial integration in the aftermath of the 1997–98 crisis, buffered with a large hoarding of IR. The limited ability of the large initial stockpile of Korean IR (about US$250 billion) to stabilize domestic financial markets in the aftermath of the current crisis, renewed discussion about the desirability of financial integration. The provision of self-insurance to deal with growing exposure to sudden stop and deleveraging crises may require large and perhaps inefficient levels of IR hoarding. Looking at the experience of all EMs, their adjustments during the current crisis reveal a switch from "fear of floating" during the 1970s–80s toward "fear of losing IR." Intriguingly, only half of the EMs used their IR during the first phase of the current crisis as a shock absorber, depleting no more than one-third of their initial IR. The other half of the EMs opted to adjust to the crisis mostly through exchange rate depreciations. I end the section with an overview of the use of provisional swap lines during the crisis.

In Section 14.3, I reflect upon and assess future policy options. A way to alleviate sudden stops and deleveraging pressure may be a Pigovian tax-cum-subsidy scheme. Specifically, I consider an economy where domestic entrepreneurs borrow externally to fund long-term projects, exposing the economy to balance sheet fragility. Premature liquidation of long-term investment is associated with deadweight losses due to fire-sale congestion externalities. Under such circumstances, competitive laissez-faire equilibrium is inefficient. Each entrepreneur ignores the marginal impact of his borrowing on increasing the expected costs of a deleveraging crisis, and the impact of higher hoarding of IR on reducing the expected cost of a crisis. The fire-sale externality reduces the marginal social benefit of borrowing below the private benefit, and increases the marginal social benefit of hoarding IR above the private one. The optimal policy calls for taxing external borrowing, and subsidizing hoarding reserves. If such a tax-cum-subsidy policy is implemented before foreign capital flows in, then the policy would limit the exposure of the recipient country to possible deleveraging. The scheme induces domestic agents to internalize the externality associated with external borrowing and deleveraging crisis. A virtue of the tax-cum-subsidy scheme is that the optimal borrowing tax funds the optimal subsidy on hoarding IR. This scheme may mitigate concerns about costly hoarding of large stockpiles of IR needed to self-insure against a deleveraging crisis.

In Section 14.4, I discuss the case for deepening regional pooling arrangements, and the possibility of the emergence of a yuan (CNY) anchored currency block in the future.

14.2 IR as self-insurance during a crisis: the crisis experience of EMs

The experience of Korea during the last fifteen years outlines the contours of the debate about self-insurance by means of hoarding reserves. To recall, following the 1997–98 East Asian crisis, Korea embraced financial integration, buffered with large hoardings of IR. The significant stockpiles of IR provided the Korean authorities with precautionary savings to cushion against sudden stops and deleveraging. Figure 14.2 overviews these trends (1992–2008), tracing the short- and long-run external debt to gross domestic product (GDP) ratio, share of foreign ownership of the stock market, and IR to GDP ratio in Korea. The financial integration led to a rapid increase in the foreign ownership share of the Korean stock market, from less than 5 percent in 1992 to more than 40 percent in 2004. This was also a time when the ratio of the valuation of Korean stocks held by foreigners to Korean GDP reached about 30 percent. While IR:GDP hovered around 5 percent before the 1997–98 crisis, the financial upheaval triggered by the crisis induced major changes in the hoarding of IR. IR accounted for more than 25 percent of the GDP by 2004. By that time, Korea's IR exceeded the short-term external debt by more than 2.5 times, and in 2004 Korean's IR exceeded its total external debt.[1]

Less than ten years after the 1997–98 East Asian crisis, by conventional yardsticks Korea's IR:GDP ratio seemed more than adequate, with IR that exceeded short-term external debt and allowed the financing of several quarters of imports. Indeed, observers raised questions about the growing costs of stockpiling these reserves, asserting that their level in EMs, including Korea, potentially exceeded the social optimum (Jeanne and Ranciere 2006). Yet,

[1] I am grateful to Yeonho Lee for sharing the data. See Aizenman, Lee, and Rhee (2007), where I show that the 1997–98 crisis led to structural changes in the hoarding of Korea's international reserves—the Korean monetary authority gives much greater attention to a broader notion of "hot money", inclusive of short-term debt and foreigners' shareholding.

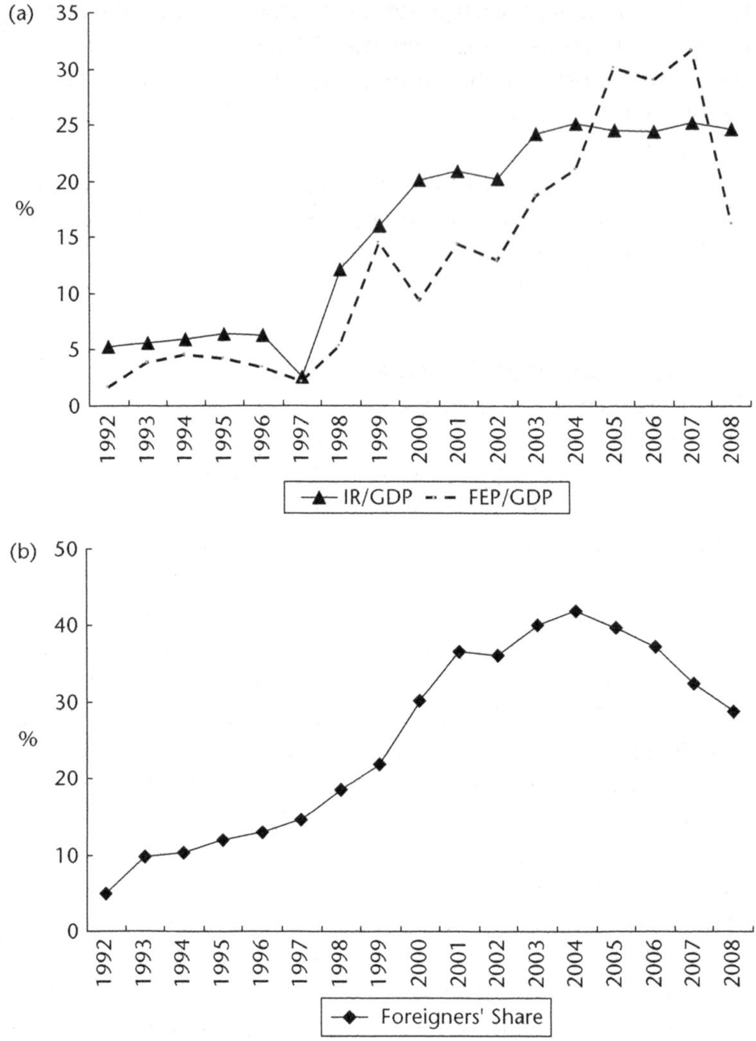

Figure 14.2 Korea 1992–2008 Korean experience, IR:GDP, external debt:GDP, and foreigners' equity:GDP

Source: Aizenman (2011).

Notes: FEP = foreigners' equity position based on market value of foreigners' shareholdings. SED = short-term external debt, TED = total external debt.

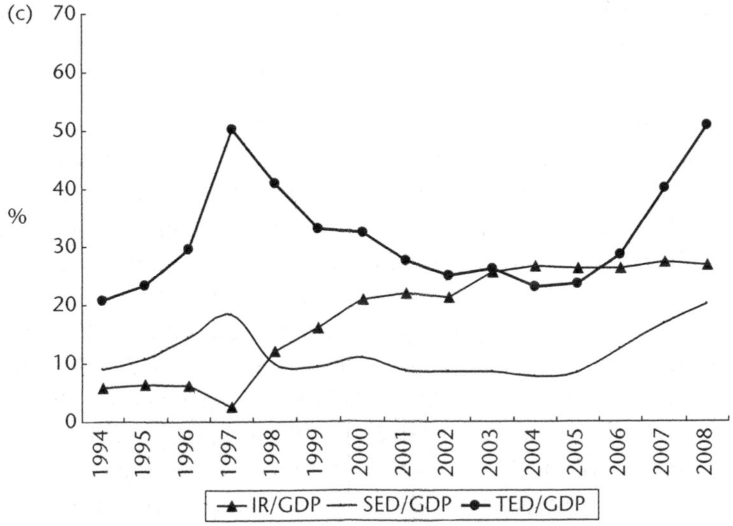

Figure 14.2 Continued

the onset of the current global liquidity crisis and the ensuing deleveraging changed the above-mentioned perception. During the first stage of the 2008–09 global liquidity crisis, Korea's reserves dropped by roughly US$60 billion in half a year, a decline of about 25 percent. Indeed, reserves were key to the bailout package the Korean government unveiled in the second half of 2008. The principal element of the package was a US$100 billion, three-year government guarantee for banks' debt raised abroad before July 2009. This sum was more than sufficient to cover Korean banks' foreign debt maturing by June 2009. The latter has been estimated by the Korean Ministry of Strategy and Finance to be about US$80 billion. Yet, observers noted that, despite the large hoarding of IR used to finance the bailout package, market concerns were not abated.

> Similar guarantees had failed to allay fears of financial meltdown at the beginning of the Asian crisis in 1997 and they failed again. As in 1997, the market reactions were indifferent. Only when Korea secured a swap line amounting to $30 billion from the Fed on October 30 the foreign exchange market settled down somewhat, but not very long. The foreign exchange rate shot up to 1,509 won per dollar three weeks after the swap had been announced, which was apparently not enough to remove uncertainties surrounding Korea's ability to service its foreign debt. Korea also managed to arrange won-local currency swaps with the central banks of both China and Japan, each amounting to an equivalent of $30 billion on December 13. Only when it

> was made clear that the Fed would renew the swap agreement, foreign investors' confidence in the Korean economy improved and stability in the foreign exchange market returned toward the end of the first quarter of 2009. Park (2009 p. 16)

Looking beyond Korea, other EMs cushioned their adjustment to the global financial crisis by a combination of exchange rate depreciation and partial depletion of their IR.[2] Yet, after the first phase of adjustment, central banks have been reluctant to further draw down their reserves. This reluctance possibly reflected the fear that further depletion of IR may signal growing vulnerability—a potential adverse externality arising from "keeping up with the Joneses' IR". Figure 14.3 portrays the IR dynamics during the first year of crisis in Korea, India, Russia, Poland, and Malaysia, July 2008–March 2009, reporting the ratio of IR (US dollar) relative to their level in July 2008. The inverted S-curve is consistent with the "fear of losing IR". Central banks used a share of their IR in the first quarters of the crisis to finance deleveraging pressures, thereby mitigating currency depreciation. Yet, after losing not more than one-third of their initial reserves, countries became more averse to further drawing down their stocks of IR. The choice of the optimum speed for drawing-down accumulated IR is a delicate one. It hinges on the anticipated future course of the global economy, the domestic adjustment capacity and the degree of financial integration of the country in question. The trade-offs for a country like India differs from those of, say, Chile. India is less integrated with the global financial system and the Indian government has less room for fiscal adjustment due to its significant and growing fiscal deficits. Brazil, Chile, and other EMs have preferred to adjust to the current crisis mostly through exchange rate depreciation. It is possible that the latter group of EMs have been saving their IRs for leaner years to self-insure against a potential prolonged period of weakness in their terms of trade.

Further insight about the "fear of losing IR" can be gained by looking at the differential patterns of using IR during the crisis across all EMs. To recall, investigating the patterns of exchange rates, interest rates, and IR during 1970–99, Calvo and Reinhart (2002) inferred the prevalence of the "fear of floating". Countries that claim they allow their exchange rate to float, mostly do not. Instead, the authorities frequently attempt to stabilize the exchange rate through direct intervention in foreign exchange market and through open market operations. The fear of floating may also provide an interpretation for the massive hoarding of IR during the last ten years by EMs and other

[2] The Bank of Russia adopted a bailout package similar to the Korean one, dealing with domestic banks' exposure. The Russian package was implemented in the context of intense involvement of the Russian state in managing its vast natural resources, including a willingness to impose what amounted to de facto capital controls. Russia's large stock of reserves before the crisis (exceeding US $600 billion) had prevented a complete collapse of its banking system.

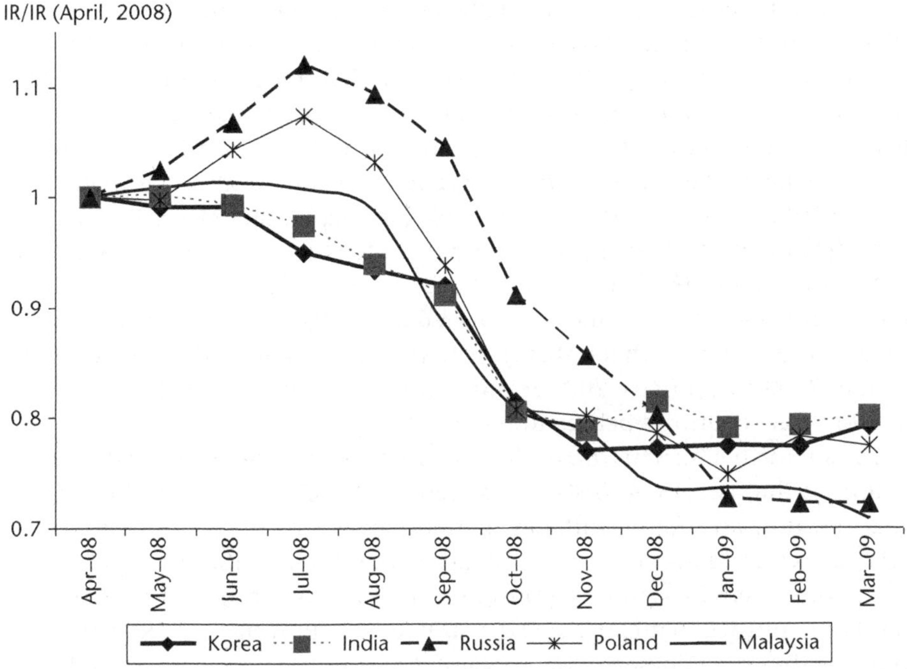

Figure 14.3 IR dynamics during the crisis window: India, Korea, Poland, Malaysia, and Russia

Source: Aizenman (2011).

developing countries. Alternative explanations of IR hoarding, however, include the precautionary and/or mercantilist motives (Aizenman and Lee 2007; Aizenman and Lee 2008), as well as the reincarnation of the Bretton Woods system (Dooley, Folkerts-Landau, and Garber 2009). The present crisis imposes daunting challenges to EMs. The "flight to quality", deleveraging, and the rapid reduction of international trade affected EMs from mid-2008, thereby testing their adjustment capabilities. While in several earlier crisis episodes, EMs were forced to adjust mostly through a rapid exchange rate depreciation, the sizable hoarding of IR during the late 1990s and early 2000s provided the same countries with a richer menu of choices.

Aizenman and Sun (2009) looked at the degree to which the large hoarding of IR "paid-off", during the current crisis in terms of allowing EMs to adjust by drawing down their IR. Their study follows the adjustment of 21 EMs during the window of the crisis, from January 2008 until February 2009, and reveals a mixed and complex picture.[3] Regression analysis shows that EMs with large

[3] The EMs' sample is composed of the countries listed in the FTSE (The Financial Times and Stock Exchange) and MSCI (Morgan Stanley Capital International) emerging market indexes. It did

primary commodity exports, especially oil exports, tended to experience large IR losses in the current global crisis. Countries with a medium level of financial openness and a large short-term external debt ratio also on average lost more of their initial IR holdings. Most of the countries that suffered large IR losses began depleting their IR during the second half of 2008, and many of them still have not recovered their pre-crisis level of IR holdings. Intriguingly, only about half of the EMs relied on significant depletion of their IR as part of the adjustment mechanism. The study proceeded by dividing the sample of EMs into two groups: countries that have sizable IR losses and countries that have either not lost IR or quickly recovered from their IR losses. The first group is defined as countries that lost at least 10 percent of their IR during the period of July 2008 to February 2009 relative to their highest IR level. Among the 21 EMs, nine countries belong to the first group.[4]

To gain further insight, the study compared pre-crisis demand for IR:GDP of countries that experienced sizable depletion of their IR, to that of countries that did not, and found different patterns between the two groups. Trade related factors (trade openness, primary goods export ratio, especially large oil exports) seem to be more significant in accounting for the pre-crisis IR:GDP level of countries that experienced a sizable depletion of their IR in the first phase of the crisis. These findings suggest that countries that internalized their large exposure to trade shocks before the crisis used their IR as a buffer stock in the first phase of the crisis. Their reserve losses followed an inverted logistical curve. After a rapid initial depletion of reverses, within seven months these countries reached a markedly declining rate of IR depletion, losing no more than one-third of their pre-crisis IR. In contrast, for countries that refrained from a sizable depletion of their IR during the first crisis phase, financial factors account more than trade factors in explaining their initial level of IR:GDP. The patterns of using reserves by the first group, and refraining from using reserves by the second group, are consistent with the "fear of losing reserves", Such a fear may reflect a country's concern that dwindling IR may signal greater vulnerability, triggering a run on its remaining reserves. This fear is probably related to a country's apprehension that, as the duration of the crisis is unknown, depleting IR too fast may be suboptimal. Rapid depletion exposes the country to the risk of abrupt adjustment in the

not include Singapore and Hong Kong, China because of their special economic structure, specializing in entrepôt services. In addition, due to the dramatic effect of the IMF's aid on Hungary's reserves changes, it was excluded from the sample (Hungary's IR had increased by nearly half in the two months after the IMF's stabilization package). The study also excluded Morocco and Pakistan due to unavailability of the relevant data.

[4] Countries facing large losses in stocks of IR include Brazil, India, Indonesia, Malaysia, Korea, Peru, Poland, Russia, and Turkey.

event that the crisis turns out to be deeper and more enduring than its initial intensity.

These findings suggest that there exists a clear structural difference in the pre-crisis demand for IR between EMs that were willing vs. those that were unwilling to spend a sizable share of their IR during the first phase of the 2008–09 crisis. Trade related factors are more significant in accounting for the pre-crisis IR level of the countries that experienced a sizable depletion of their IR in the first phase of the crisis, in line with the buffer stock interpretation of the demand for IR. Countries that depleted their reserves in the first phase of the crisis, refrained from drawing their IR below one-third of the pre-crisis level. The majority of these EMs used less than a one-quarter of their pre-crisis IR. Countries whose pre-crisis demand for IR was more sensitive to financial factors, refrained from using IR altogether, preferring to adjust through larger depreciations. My results suggest that the adjustment of EMs during the ongoing global liquidity crisis has been constrained more by their fear of losing IR than by their fear of floating.

These observations raise new questions. More work is needed to understand why countries differ in the weight assigned to financial vs. commercial factors, in accounting for their demand for IR. Intriguingly, the average exchange rate depreciation rate for the period from August 2008 to February 2009 was about 30 percent in both EMs that depleted and those that refrained from depleting their IR. A possible explanation could be that the shocks affecting EMs that opted to deplete their IR were larger than the shocks impacting EMs that refrained from using their IR. Testing this hypothesis requires more data, not presently available, including information on the deleveraging pressures and balance sheet positions during the crisis. Moreover, this hypothesis, if valid, implies that countries prefer to adjust to bad shocks first through exchange rate depreciation, and then supplementing it with partial depletion of their IR when the shocks are deemed to be too large to be dealt only with exchange rate adjustments.

The fear of using IR also suggests that some countries opt to revisit the gains from financial globalization. Earlier research suggests that EMs that increased their financial integration during the 1990s to the mid-2000s, hoarded IR due to precautionary motives, as self-insurance against sudden stops and deleveraging crises. Yet, the crisis suggests that for this self-insurance to work, it may require levels of IR comparable to a country's external financial gross exposure (see Park 2009 for the analysis of Korea's challenges during the crisis). In these circumstances, countries may benefit by supplementing hoarding with Pigovian tax-cum-subsidy policies (Aizenman 2011). A possible interpretation for the fear of losing IR is the "keeping with the Joneses' IR" motive—the apprehension of a country that a reduction of its IR:GDP ratio below the average of its reference group might increase its vulnerability to deleveraging and sudden stops. See Cheung and Qian (2009) for evidence of "keeping up with the Joneses' IR" in East Asia. These factors suggest a greater demand for regional pooling arrangements and swap lines (Rajan, Siregar, and Bird 2005), as well as possible new roles for international financial institutions (IFI), such as the World Bank and the International Monetary Fund (IMF). A better understanding of these issues is left for future research.

14.2.1 *The crisis and the provision of swap lines*

An example of alternative means of adjustment is the use of swap lines. A most intriguing development took place at the end of October 2008, when the US Federal Reserve (hereafter Fed), the central banks of Brazil, Mexico, Korea, and the Monetary Authority of Singapore announced the establishment of temporary reciprocal currency arrangements or swap-lines, worth US$30 billion each. These facilities were designed to help improve liquidity conditions in global financial markets and to mitigate the spread of difficulties in obtaining US dollar funding in fundamentally sound and well-managed economies. The practical meaning of it was the unprecedented provision of US$120 billion in swap lines to four EMs by the US Fed. It provided welcome relief and also sent an important signal. In the case of Korea, observers including Park (2009) credited this development with stopping the run on Korean reserves. While the Fed extended such swaps lines to numerous Organisation for Economic Co-operation and Development (OECD) countries, these arrangements were extended by the Fed to only four emerging markets.[5] This raises questions regarding the selection criteria behind the "chosen four EMs," and the degree to which these selective swap lines accomplished the goals spelled out in the Fed's press release.

While final evaluation of the impact of these swap lines requires much more data and a longer time horizon, Aizenman and Pasricha (2010) found that the exposure of US banks to EMs is the most important selection criterion. Inclusion of US trade exposure, capital account openness, and credit history of countries, along with the US banks' exposure in the estimations, provides a statistically accurate interpretation of the selected four swap lines. Their result is consistent with a Diamond and Dybvig (1983) model of an open economy. In circumstances of unanticipated deleveraging, emergency swap

[5] The ECB was a minor player in the provision of credit lines during the first quarters of the crisis. It provided Hungary and Poland with repo lines (euro in exchange for eligible collateral), of €5 and €10 billion, respectively. In contrast, the Bank of China provided significant CNY swap lines to its trading partners—CNY70, 200, 100, 180, 80 billion to Argentina; Hong Kong, China; Indonesia; Korea; and Malaysia, respectively (I am grateful to Shahin Vallee for providing this information). While useful, it is not clear that the CNY swap lines sufficed to deal with the US dollar shortages of some of these countries in the peak of the crisis.

lines prevent or mitigate costly liquidation today, thereby allowing investment projects to reach maturity. Emergency swap lines may provide valuable services in circumstances where the realized liquidity shock turns out to be much larger than the one expected *ex ante*. The impetus for "a larger than anticipated" liquidity shock may come from "financial contagion", or from an adverse real shock reducing the expected productivity of the investment. The first scenario is exemplified by deleveraging shocks due to a credit crunch and "flight to quality", affecting creditors that co-financed investment in EMs. The second scenario may correspond to news about an unfolding deep global recession—a recession that may cause further deterioration of EMs' terms of trade. The recent challenges facing various EMs reflect a mixture of both scenarios. Swap lines may also provide valuable positive option value. By averting massive liquidation today, if things improve by the end of the investment gestation period, the higher surplus would support higher profits and will reduce the ultimate cost of the capital flight. This in turn would possibly enhance the welfare of both the source and the recipient countries (i.e. the US and the four EMs).

The analysis of Aizenman and Pasricha (2010) suggests that swap lines had a relatively large short-run impact on the exchange rates of the selected EMs, but a much smaller effect on the spreads (measured relative to that of other EMs that were not the recipients of swap lines). Specifically, non-swap countries experiences an average depreciation of 0.15 percent on the day after the swap announcement, whereas swap countries witnessed their exchange rate appreciate, on average, by about 4 percent. Yet, all the swap countries faced a subsequent depreciation of their exchange rate to a level lower than the pre-swap rate, thereby calling into question the long-run impact of the arrangements. A note of caution is in order here—as the selective swap lines targeted countries with large US exposure, it potentially prevented an even deeper exchange rate depreciation of the four, as apparently was the case in Korea. Furthermore, only with the benefit of time would one be able to appreciate the fuller welfare implications of these arrangements.

The limited efficacy of the large stockpile of IR in preventing a run on reserves of countries such as Korea during a crisis calls into question the desirability of unfettered capital mobility. While hoarding IR prevented a replay of the 1997–98 crisis dynamics in Korea, the large depreciation of the Korean won renewed concerns about the residual exposure to balance sheet effects associated with depreciation. At the limit, eliminating the balance sheet exposure may require hoarding dollar liquidity per dollar external liability, practically nullifying the gains from financial integration (Park 2009). I turn now to evaluate possible future developments of policies and financial mechanisms to deal with the concerns discussed above.

14.3 IR at times of global financial distress: reflections and assessment of future options

A constructive way to evaluate the role of IR during the crisis is to apply the perspective of insurance mitigating exposure to risky activities. The self-insurance benefits associated with IR can be understood using two benchmarks: no self-insurance, and full self-insurance. To illustrate, Korea in the early 1990s refrained from hoarding IR for self-insurance against sudden stops. Korea's IR: GDP ratio was at a low level, about 5 percent, comparable of the level of OECD countries at that time. This reflected the presumption that Korea was not exposed to sudden stop events, both by virtue of its limited financial integration, and its history of high growth and an impressive record of adjustments to adverse shocks. The 1997–98 crisis however vividly illustrated that Korea and all emerging markets embarking on financial integration were exposed to sudden stop events. The Asian crisis induced a regime switch wherein the IR: GDP ratio in Korea more than quadrupled in less that ten years, thereby reducing the expected costs of possible sudden stops.

With most insurance schemes, agents rarely get full insurance against the relevant hazard because a typical insurance is associated with loading factors, deductibles, moral hazard, and other such constraining features. Thus full insurance is frequently too costly to attain, and rarely observed. This applies to personal hazards like health and car insurance, as well as to the macro self-insurance services provided by hoarding IR. Thus with partial insurance one should expect that the insurance would mitigate but would not eliminate the adverse effects of the hazardous event. In the context of financial integration, fully insuring against deleveraging may entail excessively costly hoarding. At the limit, the portfolio investment of foreign agents and the external borrowing of domestic agents should be matched by an equivalent level of international reserves. Such a scheme implies that the country is fully insured at too high a cost, as pointed out by Park (2009). Yet, this argument does not negate the beneficial effects of self-insurance, as the alternative of no self-insurance would be too costly. Thus, the question facing the central bank is to find the optimal level of self insurance.

The theory of optimal insurance suggests that with hazards impacted by agents' behavior, optimality calls for a mixture of partial insurance and preventive methods reducing the frequency and intensity of the calamity (installing a fire alarm and external lights to a house, driving a car at a lower speed, equipping a car with air-bags, etc.). This logic applies equally well to emerging markets' exposure to sudden stops and deleveraging shocks wherein a country may supplement hoarding IR with policies that would reduce its exposure to sudden stop events. As was pointed out by Rodrik (2006), such policies may include proactive steps to reduce exposure to external debt. Similarly, deleveraging a foreign equity position in an emerging market tends to induce real depreciation, thereby increasing the country's vulnerability to a crisis due to worsening balance sheet exposure.

Aizenman (2011) outlines the case of supplementing hoarding IR with a Pigovian tax-cum-subsidy scheme. The logic of the scheme follows from the negative fire-sale externalities associated with large inflows of capital. Specifically, Eichengreen, Hausmann, and Panizza (2003), and the related balance sheet literature showed that external debt associated with maturity and currency mismatches increases the downside risk of costly sudden stops crises. Greater balance sheet exposure frequently entails higher real depreciation triggered by deleveraging, inducing greater distress of the domestic banking system, and ultimately higher expected forgone output costs of a sudden stop and deleveraging crisis. If most foreign and domestic agents are price takers, each ignores its marginal impact on increasing the expected cost of such a crisis. This in turn entails an externality akin to "congestion", calling for a Pigovian tax-cum-subsidy scheme.

I construct a minimal model to explain the optimal self-insurance offered by international reserves in mitigating the output effects of liquidity shocks. The structure of the model is akin to Diamond and Dybvig (1983)—investment in a long-term project should be undertaken prior to the realization of liquidity shocks.[6] Hence, the liquidity shock may force costly liquidation of the earlier investment, reducing second period output. As our focus is on developing countries, I assume that all financial intermediation is done by banks, relying on a debt contract. I simplify further by assuming that there is no separation between the bank and the entrepreneur—the entrepreneur is the bank owner, using it to finance the investment. At the beginning of period 1 entrepreneurs fund investment by external borrowing D to finance planned second period capital, $K_{2,p}$, and banks' reserves, R; $K_{2,p} = D - R$. At the end of period one, after the commitment of investment capital, a deleveraging liquidity shock Z materializes. A fraction z of foreign lenders demands their deposits back, $Z = zD$. Assuming away sovereign risk and bankruptcy constraints, the deleveraging shock is first met by selling reserves. Any excess of the liquidity shock zD above reserves R is met by pre-mature costly liquidation of $MAX\{0, Z - R\}$. The liquidation reduces the actual second period capital from $K_{2,p}$to K_2, at a rate

[6] Our model follows the tradition of Bryant (1980) or Diamond and Dybvig (1983) in that the source of liquidity shock lies with the lender, rather than the borrower (Holmstrom and Tirole 1998). However, our model assumes away the market equilibrium among lenders (be it the risk of runs or the difficulty of the decentralized provision of liquidity). Abstracting from the question whether market-based liquidity insurance is available, I focus on the implication of large adjustment cost—including but not restricted to the liquidation cost—on the demand for reserves as self-insurance. In a similar vein, no distinction is made between the private sector and the monetary authorities which maintain the stock of international reserves.

that depends on the adjustment cost, θ: $K_2 = K_{2,p} - (1+\theta)MAX\{Z-R,0\}$. Premature liquidation implies that the impatient depositors get their money back without any interest payment. Only patient depositors are paid interest rate ρ upon realization of the investment. Final output is produced at period 2. The second period output finances the repayment of outstanding debt left to maturity, $D(1-z)(1+\rho)$. Unused reserves hoarded in period 1, $MAX\{R-Z,0\}$, provide the bank with a risk free return in the second period, $(1+r_f)MAX\{R-Z,0\}$.

In this economy, bank intermediation exposes the economy to the risk of sudden stop and a deleveraging crisis that may induce costly premature liquidation of tangible investment. Hoarding IR mitigates this risk. I show that the optimal allocation involves a tax on external borrowing, and a subsidy on hoarding IR. The logic of this Pigovian tax-cum-subsidy scheme follows from the negative externalities associated with large inflows of capital. If reserves are not plentiful, a deleveraging crisis induces a large number of banks to liquidate investments at the same time. This would depress the selling price of tangible capital, increasing the cost of deleveraging—the fire-sale effect. Large deleveraging in emerging markets increases the demand for foreign currency, needed in order to meet the deleveraging. If foreign currency reserves are limited, the deleveraging pressure would bid up the price of foreign currency, requiring each bank to liquidate more of its investment to fund a given deleveraging pressure. While each bank takes potential fire sale prices as given, as a group, they induce the fire sale prices. This leads to a fire sale externality, akin to congestion (Krugman 2000) on the experience of Korea in the 1997–98 crisis.[7] I show that the fire sale externality reduces the marginal social benefit of borrowing below the private benefit, and increases the marginal social benefit of hoarding IR above the private one. The optimal tax-cum-subsidy scheme reduces the distorted activity (external borrowing), inducing the borrowers to co-finance the precautionary hoarding of IR by means of the borrowing tax. Such a scheme may mitigate some of the recent concerns dealing with the costs of hoarding and using IR for self-insurance purposes.

Figure 14.4 summarizes this discussion. It plots the expected marginal productivity of investment funded by external borrowing, drawn for a given level of international reserves. Curve EMP_D^{PR} corresponds to the conditions facing the atomistic entrepreneur, in the absence of borrowing taxes. The debt threshold level $\sim D$ is the lowest external debt that induces liquidation [defined by $\sim D = IR/\tau$]. A further increase in external debt increases the expected cost of liquidation. In the absence of tax-subsidy policies, external borrowing is given by D_0. Curve EMP_D^{SO} is the expected social marginal benefit of borrowed funds. It coincides with EMP_D^{PR} as long as the probability of costly

[7] Bhattacharya and Gale (1987) investigated this externality in banking, as did Caballero and Krishnamurthy (2004) in international finance.

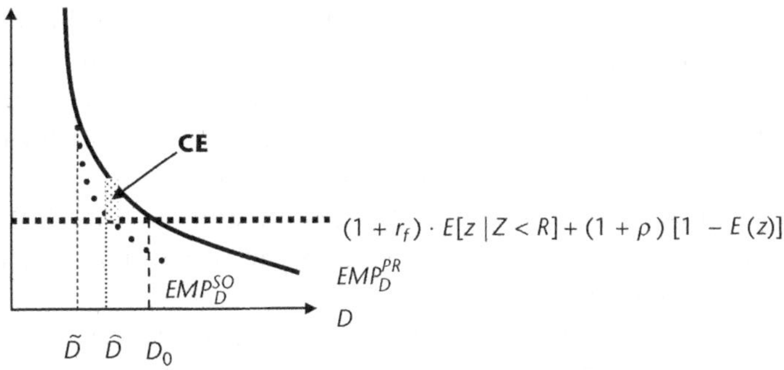

Figure 14.4 Sudden stop and external borrowing: the case of fire-sale congestion externality and optimal external borrowing tax
Source: Aizenman (2011).

liquidation is zero (for $D \sim D$). For $\sim D$<;D, the planner's curve EMP_D^{SO} is below the entrepreneur's curve ($EMP_D^{PR} > EMP_D^{SO}$), because it takes into account the negative fire sale externality associated with marginal borrowing. For the given initial IR, the optimal external borrowing is $\sim D$, well below D_0. The fire sale externality is given by the dotted line, *CE*. The optimal borrowing tax is defined by that externality, shifting curve EMP_D^{PR} downwards. Note that Figure 14.4 is a partial equilibrium treatment, drawn for a given level of international reserves. A similar figure can be drawn for the bank's and the planner's demands for IR. In comparison to the initial, no borrowing tax equilibrium, the impact of policies is to reduce the distorted activity [external borrowing], co-financing the precautionary hoarding of international reserves by means of the borrowing tax.[8,9]

14.4 The potential gains from regional pooling arrangements: the emergence of a CNY anchored block?

A frequent concern has been the growing costs of investing reserves in low yielding assets, thereby exposing the countries to possible losses (Park 2009).[10] A less benign interpretation of these trends has been that the growing current

[8] See Levy Yeyati (2008) for the moral hazard challenge facing the central bank in a dollarized economy.

[9] The design of the Federal Deposit Insurance Corporation (FDIC) deposit insurance scheme in the US may be viewed as generating similar outcomes as the tax-cum-subsidy scheme outlined in this paper. The FDIC charges insurance premiums on bank deposits at a rate that ideally should reflect the riskiness of banks' investments. The insurance premium is akin to a tax on banks' borrowing. The provision of insurance by the FDIC acts in ways similar to subsidizing hoarding liquid resources to provide self-insurance.

[10] This section overviews the discussion in Aizenman, Jinjarak, and Park (2009).

account surpluses in East Asia, and current account deficits in the US may lead to instability, requiring adjustment down the road. The adjustment took the form of a hard landing, more specifically a global financial and economic crisis rooted in the US subprime crisis. The onset of the crisis led to various unanticipated consequences such as the initial appreciation of the dollar due to the apparent flight to quality, and the massive proliferation of swap lines between the US Fed and other central banks as well as innovative regional swaps and sharing IR arrangements in East Asia.

Some observers view the crisis as a transitory shock that would not bring about the end of the "dollar standard" or the Bretton Woods II system. However, others view the crisis as caused by the failure of the informal "dollar-standard" to deliver the purported benefit of greater global stability.[11] Accordingly, tensions in the global system imply the fragility of the "dollar-standard". The stability of the dollar standard ultimately rests on the willingness of the US to refrain from abusing its "privileged position". Attaining this stability requires low inflation in the US, a stable US real exchange rate, as well as stability of financial intermediation in the US. Macroeconomic and regulatory policy in the US over the last ten years has raised serious questions about the ability of the US to deliver these outcomes. In addition, the continued rapid growth of Asian emerging markets has reduced the world GDP share of the US with a matching increase in the Asian world GDP share. This has raised questions about the sustainability and desirability of the "dollar standard" over time. The crisis also illustrated that the "superior intermediation services provided by the US" has been overstated. All these factors are reflected in the weakening trend of the dollar against the euro and other "hard currencies" during the last ten years.

The emergence of deeper economic cooperation within the Asian region, and the solid growth performance of the People's Republic of China (PRC) and India may weaken the precautionary motive for hoarding dollar reserves in Asia. Hoarding dollar reserves may be partially substituted by deeper regional swap lines, innovative IR pooling arrangements, diversification of the currency composition of precautionary savings away from US dollar to other currencies, and redirection of more hard currency surpluses towards sovereign wealth funds.

While the "dollar-standard" is attractive under ideal circumstances, the inability of the US to adopt domestic policies required to secure the attractiveness of the US dollar contributes to the gradual weakening of Bretton Woods II. Specifically, as long as the US tends to overplay its privileged position, the

[11] See McKinnon (2007) for an upbeat view of the "dollar standard", and Dooley et al. (2009) for Bretton Woods II.

"dollar-standard" creates the risk of more persistent and bigger US current account deficits. In the absence of more profound financial restructuring in the US, a return to a "dollar-standard" upon the onset of global recovery exposes Asia to the hazard of another global crisis down the road. The decline of the relative economic importance of the US has been a gradual process that started with the global recovery after World War II. The takeoff of the PRC and India has intensified the relative decline of the US. Many observers expect these trends to continue, with emerging Asia deepening its regional integration and gradually moving towards greater convertibility. All these factors suggest that attempts to return to the pre-crisis "dollar-standard" are suboptimal, and possibly infeasible.

The wish to return to the "dollar-standard" reflects a backward looking mindset of the last 60 years rather than a realistic assessment of probable future trends. A plausible scenario is that the international monetary system would converge into a tri-polar one, based on the euro, the US dollar, and new monetary arrangements in Asia, possibly a region-wide currency. Such a tri-polar configuration may be associated with significant volatility. The challenge facing Asia is to find, during the transition from the dollar standard to a multi-polar system, a path facilitating the gradual financial maturing of the region, and adopt steps to reduce its exposure to future volatility. Deepening regional pooling and swap arrangements may be the logical conclusion of such efforts.[12]

To a degree, the Chiang Mai Initiative (CMI) may be viewed as a first step, which can be extended to support the emerging needs triggered by the current crisis. An issue that deserves further attention is the optimal duration and size of these swap lines, balancing the interests of the parties involved, subject to possible moral hazard constraints and the structural factors explaining the linkages between various countries. The impact of the introduction of swap lines on the patterns of using and hoarding IR is complex. Several forces may be at work. Swap lines may act to stabilize market concerns about the risk of losing control due to deleveraging pressures, thereby preventing downward pressure on IR and the exchange rate and substituting the need to hoard reserves. This was possibly the case for Korea, where the introduction of the Fed swap line prevented a replay of the crisis dynamics of 1997. In these circumstances, access to swap lines would mitigate the need for Korea to hoard reserves to replace the US$60 billion of reserves it used during the first phase of the crisis. Yet, uncertainty regarding the duration of these swap lines,

[12] On the historical account of the early nineteenth century, Flandreau and Jobst (2009) find evidence in line with the prediction of Charles Kindleberger that currencies become international due to the importance of size (and thus the share in international trade), distance and inventory cost, consistent with the search-theoretic models of international currencies.

and lingering concerns that in the absence of the swap lines, the initial level of reserves is insufficient to prevent crisis dynamics, may induce Korea to further accumulate reserves in the future. Therefore, perceptions about the duration of swap lines play a key role in determining the future path of reserves. To the degree that regional arrangements like the CMI offer pooling schemes of indefinite duration, they may mitigate the urge to hoard reserves. Greater use of regional swap lines may also reduce excessive hoarding precipitated by the wish to signal that a country's reserves are above the average of its neighbors (the "keeping up with the Joneses' IR" motive).

A related issue that may be explored is the currency composition of swap lines. There is no reason why swap lines have to be denominated solely in US dollars. Just as countries typically hold reserves in different currencies, they could agree to help each other by providing a basket of currencies rather than a single currency. The denomination of swap lines in non-dollar hard currencies will speed up the diversification of reserves away from dollars into other currencies. For example, euro-denominated swap lines will raise the demand for euro reserves given that swap lines are ultimately a mutual promise to provide liquidity support in case of emergencies and the promise will not be credible in the absence of reserves. For Asian countries, a more realistic scenario is the denomination of swap lines in the currency of a dominant regional economy such as the PRC or even a real or notional Asian currency. Such a development would further hasten the shift away from dollar reserves and the emergence of an Asia-specific hard currency, like the Europe-specific euro. There is also an intriguing possibility that the broadening and deepening of the CMI could be transformed into a more permanent and institutionalized form of regional precautionary insurance against financial crisis.

Recent events call for a re-evaluation of the desirability and feasibility of pegging Asian currencies to the dollar as the keystone for the regional stability and future growth. The alleged gains from pegging to the dollar are debatable, and there is a scarcity of studies that have tested the idea carefully against alternative hypotheses. First, the instability of the dollar against the euro and other key currencies implies that pegging to the dollar would increase the domestic currency volatility against the euro, pound, and other currencies. This effect may be suboptimal for countries that experience an increase in the share of trade with the euro block over time. One way to deal with this issue is to evaluate what would have been the optimal weight of achieving real exchange rate stability against a basket of currencies that reflects the actual trading patterns of the region.

Recent studies dealing with the Trilemma (Aizenman, Chinn, and Ito 2008) are consistent with the notion that EMs have moved towards the Trilemma middle ground, associated with greater exchange-rate flexibility and limited but growing financial integration, buffered with sizable reserve holdings.[13] This has enabled them to retain a fair degree of monetary autonomy, even as financial integration continued (consider India and the PRC before the crisis, a time that both countries exhibited a rapid growth rate, while maintaining controlled financial openness and limited exchange rate flexibility). During that time, the PRC yuan appreciated significantly, without obvious downside effects. The onset of the crisis led to the renewed pegging of the yuan to the US dollar. However, it is not self-evident that returning to the yuan's rigid peg to the US dollar is desirable and sustainable once the world economy recovers. Applying data predating the crisis, Aizenman, Chinn, and Ito (2008) failed to find evidence that countries which pegged their currency to the dollar performed on average better than those that allowed controlled flexibility. During crises, many developing countries found that allowing the real exchange rate and monetary policy to take the initial brunt facilitated adjustment to the crises. Going forward, costs associated with investing IR in US dollar assets at times when the US dollar declines in value against the euro and other hard currencies, are projected to keep increasing.[14] These costs, and the favorable growth prospects of emerging Asia, should provide further impetus to the emergence of new regional schemes.

14.5 Concluding remarks

The unfolding of the crisis of 2008–09 may be a watershed of financial globalization. Emerging markets that embraced rapid financial integration before the crisis found that they were overly exposed to deleveraging propagated from the US. The crisis vividly illustrated that even a very large IR war chest did not seem to provide efficient self-insurance against contagion, and that the fear of losing IR constrained the adjustment of EMs more than the fear of floating. The risk is that some EMs would opt out of financial globalization. In this chapter, I outline a menu of options that deserves further exploration. Focusing on the challenges of each country in isolation, a tax-cum-subsidy policy is a plausible option. Such a scheme deals with the fire sale congestion externalities induced by foreign borrowing financing longer-term investment in the presence of deleveraging risks. Looking at the regional challenges, deepening trade networks and deeper trade dependency implies possible gains from IR pooling arrangements, and the formation of swap lines among

[13] Both trends are more pronounced for the emerging markets than for the non-emerging developing countries.

[14] See Obstfeld and Rogoff (2005), regarding the links between the growing external debt-to-GDP ratio of the US and the future real depreciation of the US dollar as well as recent estimates of the deteriorating US external net liability position.

countries in Asia. The hope is that such schemes would alleviate concerns about the cost and the inefficiency of hoarding IR and would also reduce the susceptibility of Asia to deleveraging shocks, thereby preventing even more drastic policies that may curtail future financial integration.

References

Aizenman, J. (2011). Hoarding International Reserves versus a Pigovian Tax-cum-Subsidy Scheme: Reflections on the deleveraging crisis of 2008–9, and a cost benefit analysis. *Journal of Economic Dynamics and Control*, 35(9): 1502–13.

Aizenman, J., and J. Lee (2007). International Reserves: Precautionary versus Mercantilist Views, Theory and Evidence. *Open Economies Review* 18(2): 191–214.

——(2008). Financial versus Monetary Mercantilism–Long-run View of Large International Reserves Hoarding. *The World Economy* 31(5): 593–611.

Aizenman, J., Y. Lee, and Y. Rhee (2007). International Reserves Management and Capital Mobility in a Volatile World: Policy considerations and a case study of Korea. *Journal of the Japanese and International Economies* 21(1): 1–15.

Aizenman, J., and G. K. Pasricha (2010). Selective Swap Arrangements and the Global Financial Crisis: Analysis and Interpretation. *International Review of Economics & Finance* 19(2010): 353–65.

Aizenman, J., M. D. Chinn, and H. Ito (2008). Assessing the Emerging Global Financial Architecture: Measuring the Trilemma's Configurations over Time. NBER Working Paper No. 14533. Cambridge, MA: NBER.

Aizenman, J., Y. Jinjarak, and D. Park (2009). On the future of the "dollar standard": International reserves and swap lines—substitutes or complements? manuscript, ADB.

Aizenman, J., and Y. Sun (2009). The Financial Crisis and Sizable International Reserves Depletion: From "fear of floating" to the "fear of losing international reserves"? National Bureau of Economic Research (NBER) Working Paper No. 15308. Cambridge, MA: NBER.

Bhattacharya, S. and D. Gale (1987). Preference Shocks, Liquidity and Central Bank Policy, in *New Approaches to Monetary Economics*, edited by W. A. Barnett and K. J. Singleton. Cambridge, UK: Cambridge University Press.

Bryant, J. (1980). A Model of Reserves, Bank Runs, and Deposit Insurance, *Journal of Banking and Finance* 4(4): 335–44.

Caballero, R. and A. Krishnamurthy (2004). Smoothing Sudden Stops. *Journal of Economic Theory* 119(1): 104–27.

Calvo, G. A. and C. M. Reinhart (2002). Fear of Floating. *Quarterly Journal of Economics* 107(2): 379–408.

Cheung Y. W. and X. Qian (2009). Hoarding of International Reserves: Mrs Machlup's Wardrobe and the Joneses. *Review of International Economics* 17(4): 777–801.

Diamond, D. and P. Dybvig (1983). Bank Runs, Liquidity and Deposit Insurance. *Journal of Political Economy* 91(3): 401–19.

Dooley, M. P., D. Folkerts-Landau, and P. Garber (2009). Bretton Woods II Still Defines the International Monetary System. NBER Working Paper No. 14731. Cambridge, MA: NBER.

Eichengreen, B., R. Hausmann, and U. Panizza (2003). Currency Mismatches, Debt Intolerance and Original Sin: Why They are not the Same and Why it Matters. NBER Working Paper 10036. Cambridge, MA: NBER.

Flandreau, M. and C. Jobst (2009). The Empirics of International Currencies: Network Externalities, History and Persistence. *The Economic Journal* 119(537): 643–64.

Holmstrom, B. and J. Tirole (1998). Private and Public Supply of Liquidity. *Journal of Political Economy* 106: 1–40.

Jeanne, O. and R. Rànciere (2006). The Optimal Level of International Reserves for Emerging Market Economies: Formulas and Applications. IMF Working Paper 06/229. Washington, DC: IMF.

Krugman, P. (2000). Fire-Sale FDI. In *Flows and the Emerging Economies: Theory, Evidence, and Controversies*, edited by S. Edwards. Chicago, IL: University of Chicago Press.

Levy Yeyati, E. (2008). Liquidity Insurance in a Financially Dollarized Economy. In *Financial Markets Volatility and Performance in Emerging Markets*, edited by S. Edwards and M. G. P. Garcia. Cambridge, MA: NBER.

McKinnon, R. (2007). U.S. Current Account Deficits and the Dollar Standard's Sustainability: A Monetary Approach. *CESifo Forum* 8(4): 12–23.

Obstfeld, M. and K. Rogoff (2005). The Unsustainable US Current Account Position Revisited., manuscript, UC Berkeley. Available: http://elsa.berkeley.edu/~obstfeld/NBER_final.pdf.

Park, Y. C. (2009). Reform of the Global Regulatory System: Perspectives of East Asia's Emerging Economies. Presented at the ABCDE World Bank conference, Seoul, June.

Rajan, R. S., R. Siregar, and G. Bird (2005). The Precautionary Demand for Reserve Holdings in Asia: Examining the Case for a Regional Reserve Pool. *Asia-Pacific Journal of Economics and Business* 5(12): 21–39.

Rodrik, D. (2006). The Social Cost of Foreign Exchange Reserves. *International Economic Journal* 20(3): 253–66.

Index

H

I

J

£65.00